Teaching Literature and Language Online

Modern Language Association of America
Options for Teaching

For a complete listing of titles,
see the last pages of this book.

Teaching Literature and Language Online

Edited by

Ian Lancashire

The Modern Language Association of America
New York   2009

MLA and the MODERN LANGUAGE ASSOCIATION are trademarks owned
by the Modern Language Association of America. For information about
obtaining permission to reprint material from MLA book publications, send
your request by mail (see address below), e-mail (permissions@mla.org), or fax
(646 458-0030).

Library of Congress Cataloging-in-Publication Data

Teaching literature and language online / edited by Ian Lancashire.
    p. cm.—(Options for teaching ; 26)
  Includes bibliographical references and index.
  ISBN 978-1-60329-056-2 (alk. paper)—
  ISBN 978-1-60329-057-9 (pbk. : alk. paper)
  1. Educational technology.   2. Language and languages—Study and teaching—
Technological innovations.   3. Literature—Study and teaching—Technological
innovations.   4. Web-based instruction.   I. Lancashire, Ian.
  LB1028.3.T386 2009
  418.0078'54678—dc22   2009029562

Options for Teaching 26
ISSN 1079-2562

Cover illustration of the paperback edition: *Infinity Nets*, by Yayoi Kusama. 2001.
Acrylic on canvas. Max Lang Gallery, New York. © 2001 Yayoi Kusama Studio

Published by The Modern Language Association of America
26 Broadway, New York, NY 10004-1789
www.mla.org

Contents

Ian Lancashire

Introduction:
Perspectives on Online Pedagogy

Instructors today teach in a range of formats, from traditional face-to-face courses to Web-assisted courses in physical classrooms to entirely online courses in which, outside occasional office hours and end-of-term examinations, the teacher and students never meet in person. Most courses are Web-facilitated. Martha Nell Smith observes, "Today, I cannot imagine offering a successful course—whether a small graduate seminar or a large lecture course—bereft of thoughtful application of technology." Teachers and students use course management systems such as *Blackboard* and open-source *Moodle* as convenient virtual common rooms for class schedules, reading lists, student grades, and links to recommended sites on the Web and in online library holdings. Occasionally these virtual spaces also allow students to discuss topics in a bulletin or discussion board or to work collaboratively with other students in a wiki or blog. Traditional courses that employ online resources in a supplemental way are called blended.

There are three key perspectives on online teaching: the institution's, the teacher's, and the student's. Institutional administrators favor blended or fully online courses in part because they respond to society's escalating demand for high technology in all walks of life and to the enthusiam of

students. Fully online courses enable an institution to offer complete programs and degrees to those students who cannot attend classes on campus because of work, child care, geographic isolation, or illness. Both the
Alfred P. Sloan Foundation and Pew Internet show that fully online courses
have a rapidly growing share of postsecondary education. Yet most faculty
members enjoy teaching blended courses, and many are mistrustful of
fully online courses and distance education.

In 2003 the Sloan Foundation, a strong advocate of distance education, reported that 1,970,000 American students enrolled in at least one
online course in fall 2003, and it predicted that 2,600,000 would enroll
in fall 2004 (Allen and Seaman, *Entering* 20).[1] In October 2007, the
Sloan Consortium reported that almost 3.5 million students and 20% of
all higher-education students took at least one online course during the
fall 2006 term (Allen and Seaman, *Online Nation* 1). The growth rate
for enrollments in online courses, 9.7%, exceeds the student population
growth, 1.5%. As of this writing, 977 online educational programs are in
the "Sloan-C Catalog," which lists "regionally accredited universities, colleges, and community colleges" that are members in its consortium. The
Pew Internet's "Latest Trends" reports that, of the 71% of American adults
online in February to March 2007, 12% "[t]ake a class online for credit
toward a degree of some kind," 13% "[t]ake a class online just for personal
enjoyment or enrichment," and 57% do "[r]esearch for school or training." The Sloan Foundation's *Online Nation* reports that 59.1% of over
1,000 colleges and universities see online education as a "critical" long-
term strategy (Allen and Seaman 8).

Despite rapid adoption by many educational institutions, distance
education remains controversial in private institutions. In 2002, over
18% of all faculty members did not accept "the value and legitimacy of
online education" (Allen and Seaman, *Sizing* 14). Five years later, this
statistic dropped to 11% (Allen and Seaman, *Online Nation* 19). A third
of the faculty members of most departments are sympathetic to digital
pedagogy. Fully online teachers are a small percentage even of those faculty members who use computing resources heavily, who have their own
Web pages, or who collaborate with others in online research. Moreover, distance education requires institutions to make a large investment
in computing infrastructure in a sometimes uncertain marketplace and
often relies on a nomadic teaching community.[2] Accordingly, some large
research-intensive institutions, including mine, are reluctant to offer
online courses. I thought that this neglect arose primarily from a mis-

trust of courses in which students are not evaluated face-to-face. The Sloan Consortium, however, reports that 80% of all academic leaders surveyed recognize one critical obstacle, and it is not faculty indifference or disapproval—a fear that the working conditions and professional status of teachers would suffer—but a conviction that "[s]tudents need more discipline to succeed in online courses" (Allen and Seaman, *Online Nation* 21). Online courses are thought to attract more-motivated students. Blended courses, in contrast, are widely accepted in postsecondary education.

The perspectives of students and teachers overlap. Both see the benefits in blending and are eager to experiment with new resources and software. A fully online course, however, is a risk-reward opportunity. It gives flexibility in scheduling and relief from physical traveling and can offer a close-knit sense of community, but it exacts a heavier workload than a course in a physical classroom.[3] Learning, reading, writing, researching, e-mailing, and Web exploring can take place on one device, the personal workstation. Students may work on their courses at their own pace. Those fearful about speaking in class may express themselves more easily online. Online courses may increase a teacher's mastery of a subject and improve a student's grades, but they also exhaust and unduly isolate some dedicated teachers and cause some lagging students to drop out. Yet the extensive attendant online course materials—teacher commentaries, discussion-board entries, and chat room logs—ensure that students pay full attention to what a teacher says and can review every word uttered during a course up to the final examination.

This volume has three parts. The essays in part 1 present overviews of online education for MLA disciplines. Parts 2 and 3 offer case studies in online language and online literature courses and software. In all essays contributors discuss important issues in the context of their personal experience in online teaching. They voice different perspectives on how they have taught online and why they did so. Most are pioneers, finding new uses for emerging technologies. When agreeing and overlapping, they point to a consensus on the best practices in many disciplines across a geographically and educationally diverse cross-section of universities and colleges. Literary course content extends from Old English and ancient world literature to Shakespeare and modern poetry, prose fiction, and theory. Languages include Aymara, Chinese, English (composition and English as a second language), French, German, Italian, Japanese, and Spanish. Technologies encompass multimedia Web sites, cyberplay and gaming, bulletin boards, chat rooms, e-mail, blogs, wiki, natural language processing, podcasting, and course management systems.

The MLA Committee on Information Technology invited me to discuss editing a volume about online teaching in 2003. This volume was developed between 2004 and 2008. Technology in teaching moves on relentlessly since then.

This collection illuminates the realities of a mainly post-Web phenomenon, not from an institutional or student viewpoint, but from the perspective of the MLA teacher. Most contributors are not resource professionals, those who teach teachers how to use technology, but instructors who hold standard academic appointments in departments. Contributors share experiences with and thoughts about online pedagogies, realizing that these approaches too will change, since they are grounded in and constrained by the technological infrastructure that makes them possible. As today's technology writes over last year's, so in five years the teaching tools we use now will be obscured by future computing innovations. Contributors to this book, for that reason, describe the online teaching tools with which they work. Not to do so would prevent future teachers from recognizing the constraints under which today's online teachers work as well as the ingenuity with which they apply the technologies so far available to them.

In summarizing the essays in this volume, I focus on what I take their collective advice would be to a novice, an adjunct faculty member, or a graduate assistant on how to teach a fully online course. Blended-course and open-source teachers (who place teaching materials freely online) may also gain some insight into online educating. Neither group faces the daunting challenge that a novice online teacher, especially if untenured, does. Teachers in a physical classroom transfer and nurture knowledge in students through oral conversation, but online teachers have to construct their classroom, fashion their cyborg self, and imaginatively re-create their students from traces of what Jerome McGann has called their "radiant textuality." William Kuskin, once a novice who learned to lecture to a huge class in streaming video, describes his experience vividly:

> I have come to see Hybrid English 203 as a concentration of postmodern space. In this space, our identities as teachers and students were not merely represented but represented as information *in motion*— literally as ones and zeroes streaming from server to user and back.

Others communicate this excitement, which relates to an astonished recognition that online work has in effect refashioned one's self.

Before the Online Course Begins

An instructor should think twice before accepting an offer to teach online. A student debates whether to take an online course, and a teacher should do likewise before agreeing to give one. Can I work for long hours at a workstation and welcome showers of e-mail requests from worried students at all hours? Can I go for weeks without seeing colleagues in the corridor? How am I going to replace the blackboard? If I have a history of blowing off steam in e-mail, will I refrain from doing so online with my students? Am I willing to commit the time—three months at least—to assemble online e-texts; to convert mental, penned, or typed notes to electronic form; and to learn what new skills I will need during the term? Does my department or my institution have the necessary online infrastructure for online courses—hardware, software, technical staff—so that I do not need training as a technologist? Do I need to have students in a physical classroom with me before I can teach?

Some case studies address these personal questions. Laura L. Bush chose to undertake online teaching of courses in English literature at Arizona State University, knowing that it required training in "instructional design, document design, and technology-related skills." She acquired that expertise but, having no physical classroom, experienced a "solitary confinement." Her essay draws attention to her sense of "profound loss" at "teaching literature in a disembodied space," the online discussion board, of being what Kuskin calls "information in motion." Although Bush teaches a mixture of classroom, blended, and online courses today, she candidly says, "Many days I have wondered why in the world I ever chose to teach online."

Noriko Nagata teaches Japanese language online at the University of San Francisco. Since 1999, trained in computational linguistics and natural language processing, she has developed *Robo-Sensei: Personal Japanese Tutor* to replace imperfect human teachers with perfect software both inside and outside the physical classroom. *Robo-Sensei* responds to the teacher's inability to give personal, immediate feedback to students who are doing exercises on their own or in the classroom. Nagata's natural-language-processing system "includes a lexicon, a morphological generator,

a word segmentor, a morphological parser, a syntactic parser, an error detector, and a feedback generator." These functions replace and, trials show,
do a better job at what they do than human teachers. *Robo-Sensei* needs
no classroom.

Both Bush and Nagata test the efficacy of a posthuman teacher-
function against our professional norm, a human being talking, in the
flesh, in a classroom with students. Their case studies suggest that literature, theory, and practice cannot be taught online as successfully as Japanese language rules. The litmus test of all teaching is effectiveness. Any
teaching method fails or succeeds on the merits of its performance. A
method that incapacitates the teacher, whether online or classroom-based,
fails. So does one that produces comparatively weaker students. As Mary
Ann Lyman-Hager says, we should not be debating the merits of face-to-
face and online teaching but trying to solve pedagogical problems. Gillian Lord's rationale for experimenting is also "affordances-based" (a term
in studies of usability and human-computer interface research and practice): she asks, Can online teaching enhance anything? Novices in online
teaching should believe that it can.

Novice instructors who do decide to teach fully online courses need
to begin with a good course management system. This includes basic
teaching tools: a way to publish auditory, written, and videotaped files that
students can read, listen to, or watch; a student name–database and grades
manager; Web access; technology to create and give tests or quizzes; asynchronous interaction devices like a discussion board, a blog (Web log), and
a wiki (communal writing and editing space for encyclopedic content);
podcasting ("anywhere-anytime listening and speaking practice in a variety of ways made simple by the use of computer, Internet, iPod, or even
cell phone" [see Hanson-Smith's essay in this volume]); and synchronous
tools like a MOO (multi-user-domain, object oriented) and a chat room.
Asynchronous devices enable everyone on a list to post comments under
specified themes or topics at any time, day or night. In a synchronous
space, teacher and students log into one site at the same time so that they
can type and publish comments to a common screen in a live conversation
that scrolls up off the display but whose dialogue is logged for later reading. Sometimes chat rooms and MOOs allow visual and oral interaction.
Literary researchers have developed digital tools for close reading (especially the concordancer), role-playing in computer gaming to enhance
critical discussion, and online critical editions offering multiple perspectives on studied texts. Any institution should be able to supply a novice

online teacher with a course management system because blended-course instructors frequently use one.

Second-language teachers and literary researchers in the digital humanities have for decades innovated methods in online teaching. Language teachers have shown that the most important feature of successful teaching is painstaking, close interaction among teacher and students. Toward this end, instructors should use a wide selection of online tools, including a closely monitored discussion board. Teaching materials are very important, but they pale in importance to the making of an online learning community. Scientific case studies by English-as-a-foreign-language and English-as-a-second-languages teachers also show that online courses, especially if they increase teacher-student interaction, require students to work harder than they would in classroom courses and produce academic results of equal or (in a few student groups) higher quality (see the essays by Blake, Blair, and Nagata). Some literature teachers confirm these findings anecdotally.

Institutional responsibility to teachers does not end with sufficient instructional software and hardware so that students and teachers do not need to buy or upgrade equipment to access course materials. The novice should make sure that, when students register for an online course, they know that it is online and that the system automatically gives them a user name, a password, and instructions on how to access the course Web site. (Chasing down lost students and getting them logged on can take several weeks' hard work by the instructor or the department office if the registration process does not already handle these tasks.) It makes sense to ask in advance how one's online course will be assessed. Is there an online site where students can anonymously fill out a course and instructor evaluation? (Paper evaluation forms, obviously, cannot be distributed online.) No online teacher should have to supply or set up his or her own workstation to access the course site and to run its software. It is always in the best interest of an institution to standardize as far as possible the equipment of staff members, faculty members, and students.

Within a department or faculty, novices training to teach fully online may well think of themselves as Lone Rangers, pioneering new applications in technology and pedagogy. A few teachers, like Gerald Lucas, have trained themselves both technologically and pedagogically and created powerful online courses alone. However, in our global community, many teachers, over several decades, have published about, practiced, and studied online teaching in peer-reviewed journals (see the closing

"Resources" section). Professional organizations also exercise steward-ship over distance education. The former counsel of the American Asso-ciation of University Professors (AAUP), Donna R. Euben, has published legal advice on faculty rights and responsibilities in online teaching, which the MLA has seconded (Committee). MERLOT, NINCH, EDUCAUSE, the Conference on College Composition and Communication, *Literary and Linguistic Computing*, *Kairos*, and other professional groups and jour-nals publish instructional resources, model courses, and best practices. There also springs from the Web an inexhaustible flow of online resources by open-source teachers—software by such as Jerome McGann, Geoffrey Rockwell, and Stéfan Sinclair and annotated editions by such as Michael Best and Martha Nell Smith—and by institutions such as the Library of Congress, the National Endowment for the Humanities, *Project Guten-berg*, and academic libraries everywhere. There is good reason to take pride in learning how to teach in the classroom by yourself, but a novice would be wise to take advantage of this help.

Teachers who give online courses, even on the same subject, will sel-dom know one another, but novices should make an effort to find col-leagues who have faced similar online courses before. The *World Lecture Hall* at the University of Texas, Austin, offers an archive for online cours-es.[4] Academics and information technologists who are novices in each other's area often collaborate successfully in designing learning products. Douglas Morgenstern's model "virtual university"—a massive telecollab-orative language and culture tool called the *MITUPV Exchange*—got up and running rapidly through "joint teacher-student conceptualization and design," open-source applications (from computer science), help from faculty members in various disciplines, and multimedia content that in-course students created as part of their requirements. Haun Saussy worked with programmers and colleagues from other disciplines to develop an innovative hypermedia component in classical Chinese literature for gen-eral liberal arts undergraduates. My ventures, *Representative Poetry On-line* and *Lexicons of Early Modern English*, would have been impossible without collaboration with librarians and information technologists.

During intellectual immersion in online teaching, novices will quickly see the issues that energize it. These include the role of Web-based com-munities of practice in pedagogy-driven (as against institution- or software-driven) course design, best practices in online literacy, and significant differences between classroom and online courses. Other matters invite

controversy and concern: emotional behavior online (Halio), the dispro-
portionate burden that adjunct faculty members shoulder in online teaching, a heavy faculty workload (Tomei), a teacher's intellectual copyright of
academic materials (Seadle), a student's right to privacy (United States;
Office, "Privacy Legislation"), and "unbundling." Euben explains this last
phenomenon:

> The fundamental difficulty with institutions that rely heavily, or ex-
> clusively, on distance education is that they are characterized by a
> practice called "unbundling." In that practice, course materials are
> prepared by a "content expert" and delivered by a "faculty facilitator,"
> in a uniform manner, producing predictable and measurable "out-
> comes" that fit uniform assessment tools. Such a process of turning
> education into modular units represents a basic change in an essential
> characteristic of higher education.

Issues inevitably arise in technology-mediated pedagogic methods. It
is impossible to separate tools from what they shape: information technology tends to be a procrustean bed for everything it holds. Most of us do
not understand, in advance of giving or taking online courses, how best
to manage learning in an environment of Web sites, discussion boards,
chat rooms, and newfound scheduling freedom. One person worries about
translating what the course teaches, its knowledge content, from oral lectures to a digital medium. Another frets about making a welcoming, self-
regulating online community in the course where students can interact
with teachers and one another (Conrad 31) and about protecting students
from succumbing to temptation in the mixed Internet of today, a world (as
Michael Best says) of "the good, the bad, and the inevitable." Best recom-
mends that "we should be constructing more assignments that benefit
from collaboration" and the use of online research materials so as to forestall the many commercial services that profit from plagiarism. Formerly,
teaching and research lived in different print worlds, but now a research
archive like the Early English Books Online Text Creation Partnership
differs qualitatively from its ancestors, the Early English Text Society and
the STC Microfilm Project, by rewarding teaching applications and student projects. Research that goes online directly enters the bloodstream of
education. New pedagogies that bear the signature of Web life will continue to emerge as more and more teachers experiment with online courses.
Essays in this collection and those listed in "Resources" treat these issues.

During the Online Course

What is the signature pedagogy of online teaching? It is a strength of its practitioners that there are several. Kristine Blair, Dawn M. Formo, and Kimberly Robinson Neary show how the process-based workshop model translates into an online course exceptionally well. Martha Westcott Driver and William Kuskin describe how multimedia lectures succeed in knowledge- and reading-based courses. Knowledge-based courses use tools to monitor closely the student's practice of writing skills, and reading-based courses transmute communications technology and computer-mediated communication into course subject matter. Online pedagogies do not replicate a traditional classroom model but bring new paradigms and new best practices to the fore, as Elizabeth Hanson-Smith says. Online teaching has the power to surprise. Who would have thought something as superficially alienating as information technology could make someone's Web-based environment into a social community just as personal as a seminar room? or that this intimate community could span both institutions (Driver) and oceans (Nike Arnold and Douglas Morgenstern)? And online teaching can help save endangered languages (Lord). It can do what human teachers cannot do (Nagata).

During an online course, then, a novice should consciously shape a signature pedagogy. This personal method cannot be taken off a shelf but must emerge from a teacher's own mind and sensibility. Those excited by exploration of ideas with others, whether in seminars, letters, or informal gatherings, can channel that energy into blogging, as Kathleen Fitzpatrick and Gerald Lucas do. Theorist-editors like McGann and Smith use online spaces to discuss texts in ways that books and classroom sessions cannot. Bush introduces role-playing ingeniously into the threaded discussion board. Language and literary historians link their courses to open-source databases: Murray McGillivray's students come from as far away as Yugoslavia, Turkey, and China; the *Internet Shakespeare Editions* and *Representative Poetry Online* dissolve the distinction between students, ordinary readers, and faculty members. Saussy shows how Stanford University marshaled substantial resources to produce a technological showcase that subjected a single chapter in the *Shang shu*, the Chinese book of documents, to editorial, historical, and comparative literary analyses for a general liberal arts course.

As in physical classroom courses, online teachers divide between those who want students to discover a subject, through discussion, and those who deliver knowledge or interpretation directly to students and challenge them to assess it. The self-discovery method prefers an asynchronous discussion board in which the teacher sets down questions and allots roles to students in answering them. Although articulating these roles and maintaining a structured discussion require the teacher's constant attention, this method models critical analysis and gives students a logical and rhetorical framework for undertaking independent study later. Formo and Neary create a novel digital learning environment, asynchronous "online response groups (ORGs)," that can be used to foster self-teaching writing communities in any college with e-mail. Kathryn M. Grossman employs threaded discussion boards in teaching French literature. Stephen L. Tschudi, David V. Hiple, and Dorothy M. Chun painstakingly derive four "pedagogical touchstones" that should govern discussion groups: "Tasks must be clearly defined and include an identifiable outcome or conclusion," topics should be "connected to students' daily lives," teachers should foster "the emergence of a student leader," and students must be taught cohesion (that is, consciously relating their work to the work of others in the class). McGillivray places himself among the students as one of the immersed, a facilitator and guide rather than an authority.

The delivery method places a premium on carefully prepared multimedia materials and examines a student's grasp of them through conventional essays and quizzes. Here the interactive component may include unstructured bulletin-board student questions and teacher responses, e-mail, and synchronous chat rooms in which the teacher leads a directed discussion. Self-discovery asks both the teacher and the students to craft discussion-board contributions carefully. Students strive for clarity of thought and expression, and the teacher for a neutral and nondirective but encouraging style that tolerates and suggests rather than critiques student ideas (as James Fitzmaurice illustrates). The delivery method, which gives well-formed commentaries to students, balances them often with a relaxed communal space for discussion, such as a game place or a chat room. To tame the potential for crossed threads and ill-distributed turn taking, a teacher must have good moderating skills, a facility at typing, and a quick mind. Chat room moderation, even with just half a dozen participants, can be mentally exhausting, but it enables students to join in a "collaborative construction of knowledge" and yet is still "an unexploited tool for language learning and teacher development" (Gonzalez; see Cawsey and Lancashire in this volume). But Bush believes that chat rooms have a "potential for mass confusion, frustration, and lawlessness" and may not readily promote "deep critical thinking." A survey of school choices in distance-education technology in 2002–03 showed that 35% of school districts employed asynchronous technology (discussion boards) but only 9% employed synchronous technology (chat rooms) (Setzer and Lewis).

Online teachers sometimes require advanced students to write their own blogs or to build a wiki. In blogging, a student initiates discussion on a topic and lays out ideas in a way that tempts other students to add their comments or rejoinders: in effect, the blogger imitates the teacher. Any wiki is a delivery mechanism. If we entrust students to create a wiki, we ask them to collaborate and imitate us in delivering knowledge explicitly. The more kinds of student-teacher, student-student interactions an online course implements, the better the needs of different kinds of learners will be met.

Student privacy is an important issue in online education. The fair-use doctrine exists in the United States, but not in other countries, like Canada. Teachers should not publish significant passages by others without permission, especially commentary by students in as long-lasting a medium as the Web. For that reason, teachers should take care to password-protect any course-management site, to disguise the names of student bloggers with pseudonyms (as Fitzpatrick does), to avoid the use of student webcams, and to be very clear in explaining when students' work will be done collaboratively or be shared with the rest of the class. Sharing student work with other students, teachers, and the public without the student's permission can have serious legal consequences. The United States' Family Education Rights and Privacy Act requires that "schools must have written permission from the parent or eligible student [aged 18 or above] in order to release any information from a student's education record" (see *Epic.org*). Canada's federal Personal Information Protection and Electronic Documents Act (PIPEDA) likewise applies to colleges and universities. As ethics review boards govern researchers' use of human subjects, so increasingly are institutions of higher education acting to protect students' writings, grades, and even identity in a course. Contributors to this volume, for that reason, have obtained permission from any student whose words are quoted in their essays.

After the Online Course: Issues and Future Directions

Nothing is waste until someone wastes it. *MITOpenCourseWare* "shares free lecture notes, exams, and other resources from more than 1800 courses spanning MIT's entire curriculum." These initiatives are welcome endorsements of how significantly online teachers can contribute to society. However, faculty members cannot rely on the Internet Archive's superb *Wayback Machine* to store password-protected course materials at educational institutions but must ensure that online institutional memory does so. Until recently, the intellectual adventures of faculty members in languages and literatures have survived only in the research record of scholarly and critical journals and books. By the early twenty-first century, online courses and their teaching materials, notably blogs, have begun to supplement that record. The knowledge base of our profession is changing, for the Web is a great corpus of pedagogical conservation and experimentation. Even the novice online teacher should plan to save as much as possible of the course experience. After grades for the online course are in, it can remain a living influence, unlike most traditional classroom courses. Archived online courses and open-source teaching materials help teach the novice teacher how to teach. They can assert the importance of pedagogy in the profession and help balance the research-intensive, socially isolating side of academe.

The Internet is unsettlingly transformative. People now have new ways of buying groceries, making travel plans, finding partners, sending letters, organizing reading groups, lobbying, publishing books, and building libraries. Governments interact with their citizens by means of Web forms. Online teaching in languages and literatures now permits the same interaction. The pressure to integrate teaching with information technology today is strong. Sharing our knowledge electronically with others everywhere promotes intellectual inquiry worldwide.[5] Open-source exchange of information and ideas in online teaching is a powerful tool for global understanding. Teachers and students use computers to prepare for classes, to write and grade papers, to publish course descriptions and enroll in courses, and to search and read in electronic libraries at home and abroad with equal ease. Students more and more use online texts and critical works rather than seek out books on library shelves now that huge digitalization projects convert entire libraries. Online courses are thus attractive options, especially for students who are physically disabled or prevented from taking courses because they are primary caregivers, must work full-time, or reside in isolated communities.

The MLA Publications Committee asked me why instructors would go through more effort in teaching online to get the same results as teaching in a physical classroom. The contributors to this volume would agree that they work harder than classroom teachers do but would disagree that they get the same results. Different teachers, naturally, have different methods, and the academy looks carefully at student evaluations before intervening in a teacher's choices. One way to answer the question Why online teaching?, then, is to listen to students, for whose benefit our profession exists.

Most students are enthusiastic about virtual interaction. Anyone born since 1992, when the Web came into being, is literally born digital. In Marc Prensky's term, they are "digital natives" in contrast to their teachers, who are, up to the present time, "digital immigrants" (see Blair and Lyman-Hager in this volume). Grossman observes that "students love to form highly collaborative communities of interest through such Web sites as *Facebook* and *MySpace*" and are already well acculturated to online courses. Assuming that most students obtain their bachelor of arts when they are twenty-one or twenty-two years old and that graduate students take a further six years to obtain their doctorate and start teaching, the first teaching assistants born digital will reach the classroom in 2015, and the first generation of assistant professors born digital will begin full-time teaching in 2019. Even now, "university faculty members lose the respect of their students when they do not attempt to use even the most modest of technologies" (see Hanson-Smith in this volume). How will information technology have transformed academe by 2019?

If we extrapolate from the past fifteen years, the wireless cell phone, the iPod, the iPhone, and the computer will be a personal pocket device by which students and teachers will be able to access most books, manuscripts, and images and attend lectures, seminars, cultural events, and exams virtually. Publishers will simultaneously bring out books and journals in print and digital forms. Every college, globally, will aspire to be a library of Alexandria. If each keystroke of a digital file can be tagged with a fingerprint or other identifier and if files can be seamlessly authenticated by rerunning their making, keystroke by keystroke, students will be able to take tests and examinations anywhere. If artificial intelligence research can harness chat bot technology, we all may have personal robot assistants. Professionals will no longer just word process; they will check and, if necessary, annotate the works they teach and their own work automatically from semantically encoded online resources. Discussion boards and chat rooms will be replaced by computer conferencing with natural image and sound.

Speculation is always beguiling, but today's generation of teachers, students, and institutions must still decide the role that online teaching should play in the profession and must revisit that decision annually. The best way to make those decisions is to attend to how languages and literatures are taught online.

One of the unstated rules in any profession is do no harm. It would be harmful to urge teachers and students who work well in traditional classrooms to transplant themselves online. Is there further evidence that online courses of any kind, however, are harmful? Thomas L. Russell's analysis of 355 research reports, summaries, and papers finds no significant differences in student outcomes between in-person and online "modes of education delivery." Although statistics do not lie, they level individual differences that are important for the teaching profession. Robert Blake's recent statistical survey of a very large number of students in Spanish without Walls finds these missing differences, as do others. Although both hybrid and distance-learning technologies enable students to develop "comparable levels of oral proficiency during their first year of study," distance learning "is not the appropriate learning environment for everyone": it favors the person who works full-time and thrives on independent study. James Koch states that his study of over 75,000 students at Old Dominion University shows that

> gender, age, ethnic background, distance learning experience, experience with the institution providing the instruction, and measures of academic aptitude and previous academic success are statistically significant determinants of student success. (2)

Women and older students fared better, gradewise, than men and younger students. The Sloan Foundation surveys show that institutional worry about general student outcomes is the most significant factor in slowing the adoption of online curricula.

Case studies tell various stories of teachers and students who have been energized by online courses. Arthur W. Chickering and Zelda F. Gamson's "Seven Principles for Good Practice in Undergraduate Education," Blair reminds us, begins, "Good practice . . . [e]ncourages contact between students and faculty" (1). Lord cites the five Cs in the National Standards in Foreign Language Education: communication, cultures, comparisons, connections, communities. Repeatedly, teachers describe how they have engineered effective online course communities in which people can talk to people they know; and yet Bush's sense of "profound loss" shows that unanimous agreement does not exist on that point. An annotated log of a chat room session shows to what lengths a teacher and students will go to talk together (see Cawsey and Lancashire in this volume). Any one pedagogical method, however, benefits individuals differently. For this reason, MLA disciplines should offer faculty members and students a well-informed choice among traditional, blended, and online courses. In Blake's term, everyone must "self-select" in giving and taking online courses.

What affordances do online courses offer well-informed institutions, teachers, and students that are free to choose? Will there be harmful consequences if our profession neglects fully online courses? Teachers will have to judge for themselves how heavily student preferences and outcomes should be allowed to affect curriculum, but a good case is being made now that, without online courses, capable students are deprived of an education. Many persons cannot readily attend an institutional place at a given time and need computer-mediated courses. Society justifiably recognizes "Hurricane Katrina and the resulting Sloan Semester for displaced Louisiana college students" (see Blair in this volume).[6] Without prior online-teaching initiatives by several colleges and universities, this cohort would have been stopped in its tracks. Online courses can rescue entire communities and individuals who have no other educational lifeline and are isolated by personal circumstances.

Online teaching also appears to do more than meet the needs of circumstantially disadvantaged students. Best, in "Teaching Shakespeare to Judith," concludes, "The ideal for online teaching is to provide additional choices for students," and observes that, in his discussion groups, he found "a more equal contribution from women than is the norm in face-to-face classroom" (see Cawsey and Lancashire in this volume).[7] If online teaching helps free up one part of humanity to participate on equal terms with the other, it deserves serious attention as a student option.

More ambitious use of online courses, however, will happen only when the tasks in which teachers and students routinely engage are being done uniformly better online.[8] McGann says that "if we want to develop strong online educational resources, we should begin by putting the study of books at the center of our attention." After all, book analysis is our stock in trade. To that end, he has developed, at the Institute for Advanced Technology in the Humanities, *IVANHOE* (a "collaborative online game space" in which readers can do "imaginative thought experiments"),

Juxta (a tool for comparing scholarly texts), and "social software," *Collex* within *NINES*, which will "search and collect online materials and then repurpose them as instructional materials." As early as 1997, Saussy's hypertext scholarly edition of the *Shang shu* 尚書, or *Book of Documents*, anticipated these visionary ideas. Smith's *Virtual Lightbox* packages texts with text-analysis tools that enable undergraduates to "simulate the work of advanced researchers" in understanding how Emily Dickinson wrote a poem. Smith uses technology to recover one woman's right to publish differently, among friends, in letters, in multiple varying texts, and in forty unexpected bundles of papers left to her estate. Nondigital publication of Dickinson's works actually falsifies them. It is hard to believe that, after reading Smith's essay, any teacher would reject blended courses. By allowing students the right to practice all the professional skills that the teacher-researcher has honed over years of effort, Smith creates a distinctly online learning community.

The essays and case studies in this book take snapshots of online teaching, in its variety, as teachers—many of whom grew up with Bob Dylan's "The Times They Are A-Changin'" rather than Dylan Thomas's "Fern Hill"—have struggled to meet student needs in the grip of the same information-technology juggernaut that, every few years or so, hammers everyone on its anvil of change. (The "old road is / Rapidly agin'.") The "digital natives" that fill our courses, like the sons and daughters of Bob Dylan's new road, are stirring, not least in playing 250 million computer games sold in the United States alone (Van Eck 17). Yes, "the times, they are a-changin'."

Whether you agree or disagree with the contributors, consider what a healthy catalyst online teaching is to rethink pedagogy in our disciplines. Now that literature teachers are joining their language colleagues in offering blended courses, pedagogy is shifting. Language teachers affirm that interaction, not content, is basic to successful online courses, but literature teachers offer them another perspective. McGann and Smith urge that it is precisely content, the research we do digitally, the computer-based games that students play, and the prospect of copyright-free "interchangeable course modules" (which Best hopes will reduce the infrastructural costs of online teaching) that will energize course communities both online and classroom-based. Content-focused multimedia courses on literature, described by Driver, Kuskin, and others, also show that online courses can have large enrollments and be marked successes.

Notes

I would like to thank Joseph Gibaldi, David G. Nicholls, James C. Hatch, and the MLA Publications Committee and its anonymous assessors for their contributions to making this volume and of course the essayists themselves, who have been, in equal measure, patient with me and demanding of themselves.

1. Four major for-profit online schools either closed or fused with their institutions' regular programs from 2001 to 2003: Fathom (Columbia University), NYUonline (New York University), Virtual Temple (Temple University), and UMUOnline (University of Murcia).

2. The National Center for Education Statistics reported in 2003 that 3.08 million American undergraduates in about 1,600 two-year and four-year institutions took distance-education courses in 2000–01 (Waits and Lewis).

3. Tomei estimates that online teaching requires at least 14% more time than classroom teaching, and he estimates the ideal online class size to be a dozen students.

4. It archives 146 courses in the following 13 (of 83) categories: African and African American (2); American studies (1); comparative literature (6); cultural studies (7); English, writing, and rhetoric (78); French (12); Germanic studies (4); humanities (12); language and languages (7); linguistics (9); Spanish and Portuguese (3); theater and dance (1); and women's studies (4). Most date from the late 1990s.

5. The State University of New York, Illinois, North Carolina, and Maryland, for example, have prospering online programs. The University of Phoenix is a well-known virtual institution.

6. A total of 1,587 students requested and took an average of 2.6 courses each in over 150 institutions in 38 states through this program ("Sloan Semester Archives").

7. Best adds that "men make up 21% of the two classes, and thus far have made up 23% of all postings."

8. Smart and Cappel report that students in two unidentified undergraduate courses who lacked experience in online modules in a blended course were lukewarm to them.

Works Cited

Allen, I. Elaine, and Jeff Seaman. *Entering the Mainstream: The Quality and Extent of Online Education in the United States, 2003 and 2004. Sloan*-C. Sloan-C, 2004. Web. 15 Oct. 2006.

———. *Online Nation: Five Years of Growth in Online Learning. Sloan*-C. Sloan-C, 2007. Web. 24 Jan. 2008.

———. *Sizing the Opportunity: The Quality and Extent of Online Education in the United States, 2002 and 2003. Sloan*-C. Sloan-C, 2003. Web. 15 Oct. 2006.

Best, Michael. "Teaching Shakespeare to Judith: Gender Politics in Distance/Online Teaching." *Working Papers on the Web* 4 (2002): n. pag. Web. 10 Oct. 2008.

Chickering, Arthur W., and Zelda F. Gamson. "Seven Principles for Good Practice in Undergraduate Education." *Honolulu Community College.* U of Hawai'i, 18 Oct. 2007. Web. 10 Oct. 2008.

Committee on Information Technology. "The AAUP *Statement on Distance Education*: Special Considerations for Language and Literature." *Modern Language Association.* MLA, 2002. Web. 8 Oct. 2008.

Conrad, Dianne. "University Instructors' Reflections on Their First Online Teaching Experiences." *Journal of Asynchronous Learning Networks* 8.2 (2004): 31–44. Web. 15 Oct. 2006.

Euben, Donna R. "Faculty Rights and Responsibilities in Distance Learning." *American Association of University Professors.* AAUP, 2000. Web. 8 Oct. 2008.

Gonzalez, Dafne. "Teaching and Learning through Chat: A Taxonomy of Educational Chat for EFL/ESL." *Teaching English with Technology* 3.4 (2003): n. pag. Web. 15 Oct. 2003.

Halio, Marcia Peoples. "Teaching in Our Pajamas: Negotiating with Adult Learners in Online Distance Writing Courses." *College Teaching* 52.2 (2004): 58–63. Print.

Koch, James. "Does Distance Learning Work? A Large Sample, Control Group Study of Student Success in Distance Learning." *E-Journal of Instructional Science and Technology* 8.1 (2005): 1–21. Web. 15 Oct. 2006.

"Latest Trends." *Pew/Internet: Pew Internet and American Life Project.* Pew Internet and Amer. Life Project, 2008. Web. 25 Jan. 2008.

McGann, Jerome. *Radiant Textuality: Literature after the World Wide Web.* New York: Palgrave, 2001. Print.

MITOpenCourseWare. MIT, 2008. Web. 10 Oct. 2008.

Office of the Privacy Commissioner of Canada. "Personal Information Protection and Electronic Documents Act." *Government of Canada.* Gov. of Can., 2006. Web. 10 Oct. 2008.

———. "Privacy Legislation in Canada." *Government of Canada.* Gov. of Can., 2004. Web. 5 Sept. 2006.

Prensky, Marc. "Digital Natives, Digital Immigrants." *On the Horizon* 9.5 (2001): 1–6. Web. 16 Oct. 2008.

Russell, Thomas. *The No Significant Difference Phenomenon.* 5th ed. Distance Educ. Certification Center, North Carolina State U, 2001. Web. 16 Oct. 2008.

Seadle, Michael. "Copyright in the Networked World: Copies in Courses." *Library Hi Tech* 24.2 (2006): 305–10. Print.

Setzer, J. Carl, and Laurie Lewis. "Distance Education Courses for Public Elementary and Secondary School Students: 2002–03." *Education Statistics Quarterly* 7.1-2 (2006): n. pag. Web. 15 Oct. 2006.

"Sloan-C Catalog." *Sloan-C.* Sloan-C, 2007. Web. 24 Jan. 2007.

"Sloan Semester Archives." *Sloan-C.* Sloan-C, 2008. Web. 15 Oct. 2006.

Smart, Karl L., and James J. Cappel. "Students' Perceptions of Online Learning: A Comparative Study." *Journal of Information Technology Education* 5 (2006): 201–19. Web. Oct. 2006.

Tomei, Lawrence A. "The Impact of Online Teaching on Faculty Load: Comput-
ing the Ideal Class Size for Online Courses." *Journal of Technology and Teacher
Education* 14.3 (2006): 531–41. Print.
United States. Dept. of Educ. "Family Education Rights and Privacy Act." *Ed.gov.*
GPO, 2007. Web. 15 Oct. 2008.
Van Eck, Richard. "Digital Game-Based Learning: It's Not Just the Digital Na-
tives Who Are Restless." *EDUCAUSE Review* 41.2 (2006): 16–30. Web. 15
Oct. 2006.
Waits, Tiffany, and Laurie Lewis. *Distance Education at Degree-Granting Postsec-
ondary Institutions: 2000–2001. National Center for Education Statistics.* Natl.
Center for Educ. Statistics, 2003. Web. NCES 2003-017. 15 Oct. 2006.

Part I

Overview

Robert Blake

From Web Pages to Distance Learning: Technology in the Foreign Language Curriculum

Although the foreign language profession routinely concedes the importance of technology for the curriculum, many teachers still harbor deep-seated doubts about whether a hybrid course, much less a completely distance-learning class, can provide second-language learners with a way to reach linguistic proficiency, especially in oral language skills. In this study, I examine Spanish without Walls, a first-year language course offered at the University of California, Davis, in both hybrid and distance-learning formats. The Spanish without Walls curriculum includes materials delivered through DVD programs, online content-based Web pages, and synchronous bimodal chat (sound and text). I evaluate the contribution of each of these components in the context of a successful technologically assisted course. To address the issue of oral proficiency, I compare the results from both classroom and distance-learning students who took Ordinate's twenty-minute Versant for Spanish, delivered by phone and automatically graded. The data generated by this instrument show that both the hybrid and distance second-language learners reach comparable levels of oral proficiency during their first year of study as compared with students learning Spanish in a traditional classroom setting. I also refer to two other ongoing efforts to provide distance-learning courses, in Arabic and Punjabi, two languages whose special difficulties in their writing systems have an impact on the design of the distant-learning format. I examine the rationale for offering language courses in either a hybrid or distance-learning format more generally in the light of the current national goals of eventually bringing students up to level 3 proficiency.

Background

"Do you use technology in your foreign language classroom?" Few language teachers would dare to answer no to this question for fear of being classified as outdated or out of touch with best practices. Not surprisingly, most teachers routinely use Web pages to distribute syllabi assignments, cultural material, and even lecture notes (since *PowerPoint* presentations are now easy to convert into Web pages). But when foreign language faculty members are polled about accepting credit for language courses delivered in a hybrid or completely distance-learning format, their smiles evaporate and the positive attitudes toward technology start to fade. Foreign language teachers tend to doubt whether a hybrid course, much less a virtual one, could provide their students with an accepted way to gain linguistic proficiency, especially oral proficiency, and I suspect that many secretly worry about whether these new distance-learning classes will displace them.

No one would dispute that to reach advanced or superior proficiency (Interagency Linguistic Roundtable level 3) second-language students need to interact face-to-face with native speakers, preferably in the target country. Dan E. Davidson's longitudinal study of second-language learners of Russian conclusively shows that study abroad—and a year program as opposed to a semester program—is a sine qua non for reaching these more advanced levels.[1] The issue addressed here, however, focuses on the lower levels, specifically on beginning Spanish-language instruction: Can the hybrid or distance-learning format render results comparable with the traditional second-language classroom that meets five days a week? Do distance-learning classes have a role to play in the foreign language curriculum, perhaps as a way to start on the long road to advanced proficiency, a feat that requires from 700 to 1,320 hours of instruction (Bialystok and Hakuta 34)?

Robert Blake and Ann Marie Delforge have already provided data for Spanish learners based on discrete grammar exams. Their results show distance-learning students often perform significantly better than their traditional counterparts, but many research difficulties mitigate the strength of these findings. First, the profession is now concerned more with evaluating data on oral proficiency than with discrete grammar tests. Second, as with much research in second language acquisition, more data on distance learners would make findings like Blake and Delforge's more reassuring (Thompson and Hiple). Unfortunately, distance-learning students are particularly recalcitrant when responding to requests for cooperation outside the boundaries of class assignments. After all, with virtual students there is no physical presence in the first place. Researchers tend to have had more luck getting classroom students to cooperate, maybe because of the ready access to a present audience. Finally, the burden of isolating the experimental treatment to focus on the medium (distance-learning versus classroom) to the exclusion of all other factors presents a daunting challenge.

Not all these factors can be solved at once, but the need to provide more data on oral proficiency looms first and foremost. Here I look at oral proficiency data from two first-year Spanish courses, one hybrid course (two days instruction a week plus six hours of study through technology) and one completely virtual course. I then compare the results with a large data bank from classroom students (n=248). The oral-proficiency instrument is a Spanish phone test developed by Ordinate, the Versant for Spanish. The test is based on W. Levelt's construct of oral proficiency that requires students to listen, repeat, and respond. The scoring is done automatically using voice-recognition software, a parser, and a probabilistically constructed grammar (Bernstein, Barbier, Rosenfeld, and De Jong). My findings support the notion that hybrid and distance-learning instruction allow students to develop comparable levels of oral proficiency during the first year of study. The results also suggest that the available proficiency testing measures—the American Council on the Teaching of Foreign Languages's Oral Proficiency Interview (OPI), the Interagency Linguistic Roundtable Oral Proficiency Interview (ILR/OPI), and the Common European Framework exam (CEF)—are less successful in distinguishing among the first four quarters of classroom instruction (i.e., the first two hundred hours). After that, second-language students experience a demonstrable jump in abilities. The distance-learning formats, whether partial or complete, produce similar results as those found in the classroom environment in those first two hundred hours. No one would suggest that advanced proficiency (i.e., 3 is 700 to 1,320 hours) could be achieved entirely through a distance-learning mode of instruction delivery, but this format should be included as a valuable component of the foreign language curriculum.

Methodology: Students, Proficiency Testing, and Baseline Data

Why would anyone want to take a language course that did not involve five days of class each week? In fact, the distance-learning format is not the appropriate learning environment for everyone; it self-selects. A completely virtual course appeals, in particular, to people who work full-time and therefore need special access to instruction, as well as to those who prefer to work independently. The popularity of a hybrid course also responds to these factors, but more disjunctively: those who want fewer days of class (and some who think less class time means less work) or those who like to work independently. Many students belatedly find out that the distance-learning format requires a high degree of self-motivation and independent work skills, which accounts for the high dropout rate for the distance-learning environment for all disciplines (Carr). Ironically, students with strong motivation to learn a less commonly taught language such as Arabic, Punjabi, or Farsi may find to their dismay that there are no language offerings available locally, making the distance-learning format the only way to get started. For Spanish there is an overdemand for instruction that ends up being satisfied by both classroom and distance-learning courses. Such was the motivation for Spanish without Walls, with the understanding that the lesson learned might be applicable to delivering less commonly taught languages, too.[2]

Spanish without Walls and Its Hybrid Cousin

Spanish without Walls is a yearlong course divided into three quarters that combines multimedia language materials from three sources: *Tesoros*, a multimedia course that follows a detective story (Blake, Blasco, and Hernández); content-based Web readings and *Adobe Flash* activities;[3] and a collaborative computer-mediated communication tool running on the *Adobe Flash* communications server that allows for both asynchronous and synchronous textual communication (both controlled character-by-character and by carriage return) in addition to half-duplex sound exchange.

The DVD served as the course textbook. The remaining online materials were packaged into a course management system designed to teach first-year Spanish grammar and vocabulary, provide exercises, conduct testing, present authentic Spanish-language readings, and enable oral communication with teachers and peers. Students alternated between use of the DVD and the Spanish without Walls Web site to cover the scope and sequence of a normal university Spanish-language course. They were held accountable for the DVD material by online exams that covered the vocabulary, story line, and grammar presented by *Tesoros*. Students were also required to chat live with their instructor in groups of no more than three at least once a week for one hour and several more times with their assigned partners as time and schedules permitted to complete the collaborative content-based tasks. One student would research the capital cities of four Latin American countries, while his or her partner would investigate the same type of information for four other countries. During the chat, the students would share their results with each other in jigsaw fashion.

The hybrid courses (SPA 2V and 3V) are the equivalent of the last two-thirds of an introductory college-level Spanish course. The curriculum is derived from Spanish without Walls; students meet with their instructor two days a week and then perform Web activities and computer-mediated communication synchronous dialogues using *Adobe Acrobat Connect* (which provides text chat, Voice over Internet Protocol, and electronic whiteboard and character-by-character text exchange). The course materials and exercises focus on developing the same array of skills promoted in the traditional classroom sessions and provide students with exposure to a variety of Spanish accents from Spain and Latin America, extensive reading knowledge of authentic texts, guided writing practice, the second part of first-year grammar and vocabulary sequence, and cultural awareness of the Spanish-speaking world.

Measuring Proficiency: Versant for Spanish

Versant for Spanish from Ordinate is loosely based on Levelt's model of speech. In Levelt's model, both speaking and listening activate similar processing modules, although only one mode, speaking, specifically involves articulation. But in all other terms of processing, speaking and listening activate identical mechanisms. The Ordinate phone test asks participants to read aloud, listen and repeat, say the opposite, answer short questions, build sentences from jumbled-up word combinations, answer open questions, and retell stories. The responses from test takers for all but the last two categories are scored automatically by means of a speech recognition and parser program based on a probabilistic grammar built from 435 native speakers from a variety of Spanish-speaking countries as well as 579 second-language learners of Spanish (Bernstein, Barbier, Rosenfeld, and De Jong). The Ordinate algorithm divides the linguistic data into separate values for vocabulary, sentence mastery, pronunciation, and fluency and then combines these values to come up with an overall score on a scale from 20 to 80.

Most important, the results from the test have a correlation with the OPI, ILR/OPI, and CEF exams, 0.86, 0.90, and 0.92, respectively (Bernstein, Barbier, Rosenfeld, and De Jong 4). The twenty-minute phone sample provides sufficient data to the algorithm to identify the proficiency of the speaker, and human judges are able to evaluate the speaker using the protocols developed by the other proficiency exams. The purpose of my study, however, is not to argue for the merits or statistical validity of Versant for Spanish over the other human-scored proficiency tests. Rather, I accept Versant for Spanish as one legitimate way of assessing the oral proficiency of those learning Spanish as a second language that has proved its compatibility with other assessment tools for the field. For doing assessment research with distance-learning students, who are hard to track down, the test is particularly advantageous because the participants can take it anywhere in the world, at a time of their own choosing, using only a phone. That the exam takes approximately twenty minutes to complete further heightens its attractiveness as a research instrument in the distance-learning context. Consequently, my main interest was to administer the exam to as many classroom students as possible to establish a reliable basis of comparison for any data generated by distance-learning students.

Establishing a Baseline for Comparison

I first set out to establish an oral-proficiency baseline for traditional classroom students enrolled in lower-division language classes at the University of California, Davis, from 2005 to 2006 using the Versant for Spanish measure. This population consisted of the first seven quarters of Spanish-language instruction along with one class of heritage speakers enrolled in a special lower-division language series designed for native speakers. The language strengths of heritage learners vary considerably: while some have distinct oral advantages over nonheritage learners, they also tend to lack competence with academic Spanish or the more formal registers (see Blake and Zyzik). Nevertheless, I predicted that the heritage learners would strongly outperform the nonheritage learners on Versant for Spanish, an expectation that was confirmed by the results.

From fall 2005 to spring 2006, the test was administered to 248 classroom students from the eight levels mentioned above to produce a baseline for comparative purposes. With the classroom students in hand to serve as a norm, I then compared their scores against those of the additional 32 distance learners. In comparing the scores of the classroom and distance learners, I demonstrated the relative efficacy of the distance-learning format without minimizing the problems of individual differences that plague most second-language-acquisition studies (Skehan).

Results and Discussion

Figure 1 displays the Versant for Spanish scores by level for 248 classroom learners as a function of their respective cumulative densities: each test value is matched to the proportional number of students from that group who have reached that score or below.[4] Given the range of language proficiency among these eight levels, any particular percentage value should correspond to radically different test values. The results from plotting the cumulative density function suggest that certain language levels as defined by quarters should be clustered together. This visual impression was statistically tested by means of a Tukey's Honestly Significant Difference Test, the most appropriate statistical measure to use when no a priori hypotheses exist with respect to groupings. The Tukey's test results are displayed in table 1. Three statistically distinct groups emerge: a first-year group that includes quarters 1–3 and, somewhat more weakly, quarter 4; a second-year group that consists of quarters 5–7 (although note that quarter 7 is the beginning of the third year); and the heritage speakers group.

The Tukey's test values for the quarter 4 group deserve further comment. While the quarter 4 students were statistically different from quarter 1 students, there were no differences among the performance of the

Table 1
Tukey's Test for Versant for Spanish Scores by Quarter

Quarters	1	2	3	4	5	6	7	Heritage Learners
1	–	.97	1.0	.43	.00	.00	.00	.00
2		–	1.0	.97	.00	.00	.00	.00
3			–	.71	.00	.00	.00	.00
4				–	.09	.00	.00	.00
5					–	.77	.36	.00
6						–	1.0	.00
7							–	.00

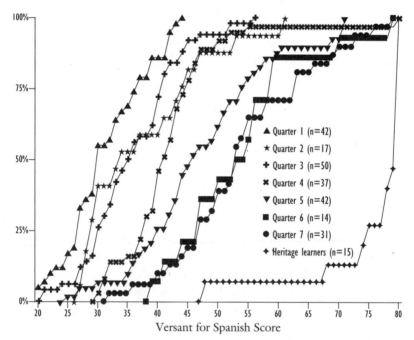

Figure 1. Cumulative density functions for each quarter

second-, third-, and fourth-quarter students. Clearly, the fourth-quarter group represents a transition class after which these second-language students experience a demonstrable jump in linguistic capabilities to the next plateau (levels 5–7). The score ranges, eliminating the tenth and ninetieth percentiles, can be summarized as follows:

Quarter	Versant for Spanish Score
1, 2, and 3	25–43
4	31–49
5, 6, and 7	37–68

These facts are captured graphically in figure 2, in which the cumulative density functions have been plotted after pooling the data into three groups to dramatize the differences in oral proficiency that occurs after the fourth quarter of language study. In terms of oral proficiency, the heritage students, not unexpectedly, outperformed all the nonheritage groups.

Figure 3 plots the cumulative density function for all distance learners in hybrid and virtual classes along with the scores from classroom learners in quarters 1–7 for comparative purposes (n=280). Notice in figure 3 that the distance-learning students clearly follow the trends set by the group of classroom learners in quarters 1–4. The hybrid learners at the higher percentages of cumulative density are performing slightly poorer than the classroom quarters 1–4 group, but remember that this

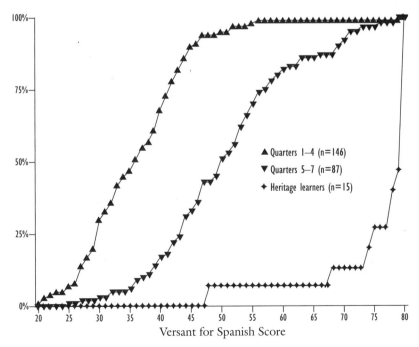

Figure 2. Cumulative density function for classroom student by quarter clusters

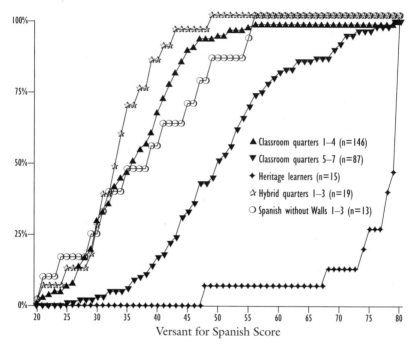

Figure 3. Cumulative density function for classroom and distance-learning students

group includes students from quarter 4. The totally virtual students (Spanish without Walls) are performing slightly better than those in the classroom quarters 1–4.

More important, the individual t-tests given in table 2 reveal no significant differences between partial or complete distance learners (those enrolled in hybrid levels 2 and 3 and Spanish without Walls 1 and 2) and their respective classroom counterparts. The number of distance-learning students who took Versant for Spanish is limited, and more data points are being collected for a future study. This obvious shortcoming, however, is mitigated by the strength of the baseline results: the large corpus establishes a placement norm against which each distance-learning score can be compared and situated into a curricular space. Looked at from this perspective, both types of distance-learning formats and curricula have allowed students to develop a level of oral proficiency that is commensurate with the expectation for the classroom learning environment. The distance-learning format is doing a sufficient, if not good, job.

Table 2
T-Test Results Comparing Distance-Learning and Classroom Formats

	Course Level					
Course	1 (n=42)		2 (n=17)		3 (n=50)	
Spanish without Walls 1 (n=8)	t(48)=1.03	p=0.35	–	–	–	–
Spanish without Walls 2 (n=4)	–	–	t(19)=0.96	p=0.35	–	–
Hybrid 2 (n=15)	–	–	t(30)=1.63	p=0.11	–	–
Hybrid 3 (n=4)	–	–	–	–	t(52)=1.00	p=0.32

t = t distribution
p = probability

Pinpointing which factors are responsible for putting the distance-learning students on an equal footing with their classroom counterparts is not an easy task. On the one hand, the Spanish without Walls students are older, more mature, and more self-motivated than their younger classroom counterparts—virtual courses self-select, as I mentioned earlier. Distance learners are undoubtedly more efficient and responsible second-language learners since they pay in advance for their courses. One might expect that hybrid students would follow suit, but many students have enrolled in the hybrid course expressly to take advantage of the reduced class time; that is, some are actively avoiding work. And classroom students sometimes project the attitude that they have already shown up for class five days a week and have no plans to work on their Spanish outside class. The required synchronous chat sessions in the two distance-learning formats, which tend to provide students with more individual attention from the instructor than is possible from an instructor in a fifty-minute class of twenty-five to thirty students, directly contribute to the similar performances on Versant for Spanish. The profession is just beginning to study how to use these computer-mediated communication tools most effectively (Blake; Thorne and Payne)

Finally, the foreign language profession should recognize that the available oral-proficiency testing instruments are less efficient at distinguishing among the different proficiency levels of first-year students. In part, this inefficiency is due to the plateaulike development pattern that the findings from this study have illustrated. Implicitly, many of the most prominent assessment instruments have taken these development trends into account. For instance, the ILR exam classifies speakers as 0± (what does 0+ mean, if the speaker is still a 0?), a label that sticks with the examinee for most of the first two hundred hours, or up to the first four quarters of college instruction. Likewise, the OPI rubrics—novice low, novice mid, novice high—although they provide a somewhat gentler nomenclature than 0, still point to the same insight: students do not appear to make much progress until they reach the two-hundred-hour threshold level, even when graded by human interviewers. Beginning students are making significant progress during the first two hundred hours, even if it is difficult to calibrate with the existing assessment tools.

Conclusions and Future Prospects for Distance-Learning Language Instruction

The foreign language profession should remember that getting to advanced proficiency (ILR level 3) is an arduous task that requires five or more years of college instruction and critically depends on the language involved. Languages like Arabic and Chinese require more hours of instruction than the Romance languages do. Yet advanced proficiency is precisely what the nation wants to attain, especially in this post–9/11 era and given the urgent need to develop a national language capacity in some of the more politically strategic less commonly taught languages.[5] To get to that point, no method should be privileged or eliminated, although a well-articulated and prolonged study-abroad component has a proven track record of success (Davidson).

The current interest in the distance-learning format must be situated in this context: second-language students need access, students need to work at it for a long time, and students need to study abroad. A distance-learning course is only one piece in this equation, but an important avenue to afford students access to introductory instruction of less commonly taught languages when local classroom options are lacking. Adding the distance-learning component to the possible curricular formats appears to be a responsible and reasonable option, with palpable benefits for oral proficiency. Those wedded to the OPI will, no doubt, quibble with Ordinate's construct of oral proficiency, and others will note that not enough distance-learning students have been tested to provide conclusive proof, but the findings presented here should, at the bare minimum, pique the interest of even the most cynical Luddites in the foreign language profession. No doubt, students will continue to select the type of language instruction they prefer whenever possible. The profession should concern itself with

providing legitimate options and increasing all avenues of access to language instruction, especially for less commonly taught languages.

The Spanish without Walls project and its hybrid derivatives represent
a successful experiment in perfecting the distance-learning option for Spanish. The ten campuses that make up the University of California system are
engaged in other projects for providing distance-learning language instruction: Arabic (Arabic without Walls), from the Irvine campus, and Punjabi,
from the Santa Barbara campus.[6] Both projects have received funding from
the Department of Education (the FIPSE and IRS programs, respectively).
Unlike Spanish, both Arabic and Punjabi present formidable writing problems: Arabic because of the alternative letters and linking, in addition to the
right-to-left processing; and Punjabi because of the dual scripts, Gurmukhi
(Sanskrit based) and Shahmukhi (Persian or Arabic based). Using software
and programming that respect the Unicode conventions simplifies most of
the potential problems for conducting a distance-learning course in languages like these.

The real challenge, however, lies in implementing distance-learning
language instruction in sound pedagogy, a conversational framework (Laurillard 86–89) that seeks "to persuade students to change the way they experience the world through an understanding of the insights of others,"
blending experiential and formal knowledge (23). This formidable task is
academic and should be the business of the foreign language profession.
The foreign language teacher, not the medium, will ultimately determine
whether any given instantiation of a distance-learning language course
makes a positive contribution to the second-language student's long march
to advanced proficiency.

Notes

I would like to acknowledge Jennifer Balogh's expert help with the statistical sections, Cristina Pardo Ballester and María Cetto's assistance in administering Versant
for Spanish, and Cristina Pardo Ballester's teaching expertise with the Spanish without Walls and hybrid students. Any errors herein are my responsibility alone.

1. For earlier work on this topic, see Brecht, Davidson, and Ginsberg.

2. Spanish without Walls was funded by a three-year grant, P116B000315,
from the Fund for the Improvement of Postsecondary Education (FIPSE). For a
brief description of the project, see Pol.

3. The Spanish without Walls Web pages were produced by María Victoria
González Pagani, co–Principal Investigator of the FIPSE grant.

4. Each data point graphed in a cumulative density function is associated
with a test score and a percentage. The percentage reveals how many students

reached that score or below. In this manner, the complete graph gives an idea of how the class did on the exam as a whole. More advanced groups will have a larger percentage of students associated with a higher score than less proficient groups. If 80% of the class is associated with a score of 44, this is about as high a score as one should expect from that group. The percentage score shows how and where the class bunched up on the test (i.e., cumulative density).

5. See, for instance, "National Flagship Language Initiative."

6. Other teleconference efforts are well along in Danish, Swedish, and Filipino (see *UCLA Center*). This study does not address the teleconference model for distance learning.

Works Cited

Bernstein, Jared, Isabella Barbier, Elizabeth Rosenfeld, and John De Jong. "Development and Validation of an Automatic Spoken Spanish Test." *InSTIL/ICALL 2004 Symposium on Computer Assisted Learning. ISCA Archive*. Intl. Speech Communication Assn., 2004. Web. 4 Sept. 2006.

Bialystok, Ellen, and Kenji Hakuta. *In Other Words: The Science and Psychology of Second-Language Acquisition*. New York: Basic, 1994. Print.

Blake, Robert. "Bimodal CMC: The Glue of Language Learning at a Distance." *CALICO Journal* 22.3 (2005): 497–511. Print.

Blake, Robert J., Javier Blasco, and Cesar Hernández. *Tesoros: A Multimedia-Based Course*. Boecillo Editoria Multimedia, n.d. Web. 16 July 2009.

Blake, Robert, and Ann Marie Delforge. "Language Learning at a Distance: Spanish without Walls." *Selected Papers from the 2004 NFLRC Symposium: Distance Education, Distributed Learning and Language Instruction*. Ed. Irene Thompson and David Hiple. *National Foreign Language Resource Center*. U of Hawai'i, 2005. Web. 4 Sept. 2006.

Blake, Robert J., and Eve C. Zyzik. "Who's Helping Whom? Learner/Heritage-Speakers' Networked Discussions in Spanish." *Applied Linguistics* 24.4 (2003): 519–44. Print.

Brecht, Richard D., Dan Davidson, and Ralph Ginsberg. "Predictors of Foreign Language Gain during Study Abroad." *Second Language Acquisition in a Study Abroad Context*. Ed. Barbara F. Freed. Amsterdam: Benjamins, 1995. 37–66. Print.

Carr, Sarah. "As Distance Education Comes of Age, the Challenge Is Keeping the Students." *Chronicle of Higher Education*. Chronicle of Higher Educ., 2 Nov. 2000. Web. 10 Dec. 2005.

Davidson, Dan E. "Capabilities and Outputs of the U.S. Education System: Proficiency Outputs." National Language Conference. Inn and Conference Center, Adelphi. 22–24 June 2004. *National Language Conference*. Web. 22 Oct. 2008.

Laurillard, Diana. *Rethinking University Teaching*. London: Routledge, 2002. Print.

Levelt, W. *Speaking: From Intention to Articulation*. Cambridge: MIT P, 1989. Print.

"National Flagship Language Initiative." *National Foreign Language Center.* U of Maryland, 2008. Web. 27 Oct. 2008.

Pol, Jeff van de. "Spanish without Walls: Using Technology to Teach Language Anywhere." *IT Times* Mar.-Apr. (2001): n. pag. Web. 4 Sept. 2006.

Skehan, Peter. *Individual Differences in Second-Language Learning.* London: Arnold, 1989. Print.

Thompson, Irene, and David Hiple. Preface. *Selected Papers from the 2004 NFLRC Symposium: Distance Education, Distributed Learning and Language Instruction.* Ed. Thompson and Hiple. *National Foreign Language Resource Center.* U of Hawai'i, 2005. Web. 6 Mar. 2006.

Thorne, Steven L., and J. Scott Payne. "Introduction to the Special Issue." *CALICO Journal* 22.3 (2005): 369–70. Print.

UCLA Center for World Languages. U of California, 2008. Web. 27 Oct. 2008.

Kristine Blair

Writing as Process and Online Education: Matching Pedagogy with Delivery

Although rhetoric and composition specialists have focused extensively on the role of computers in the writing classroom during the last twenty years, fewer treatments have focused on the impact of fully online delivery on the teaching of writing. As Patricia Webb Petersen queries, "When these kinds of courses are moved online, what is lost and what is gained? These questions are yet to be discussed fully by scholars within composition studies" (360). Admittedly, Webb Peterson is writing in 2001; however, the focus on fully online writing instruction is still a nascent enterprise for many composition programs, in which discussions are just beginning to address both the relative suitability of the undergraduate composition curriculum for completely virtual delivery and the academic labor involved in making this transition.

Not unlike other disciplines that possess "signature pedagogies" (Shulman), composition, in its reliance on a process-based workshop model, may be compatible with online education. Such compatibility has its basis in the use of online communication tools for inventing, drafting, and revising, as well as for fostering critical, cultural, and contextual approaches to the teaching of writing that move the curriculum beyond its perceived function as a service course by both students and administrators. Because of these potential connections, I stress the compatibility between writing instruction and distance education for both new and established composition instructors. I rely on research from computers and writing studies, as well as more global treatments, about the possibilities and constraints of establishing virtual community (Palloff and Pratt). Grounded in student-centered curricula, quality composition instruction is as possible online as it is face-to-face, particularly if we rely in part on guidelines for overall good practice in undergraduate education, such as Arthur W. Chickering and Zelda F. Gamson's "Seven Principles." We must also consider the ways in which newer multimodal writing and communication tools may address instructors' concerns about the potential loss of curriculum and community. But despite the presumed compatibility between pedagogy and technology, current and future online writing instructors must pay attention to the use of technology in the classroom (Selfe), making visible the labor of online writing instruction to colleagues and administrators.

Signature Pedagogy, Virtual Community, and Writing Instruction

In his *Liberal Education* article "Pedagogies of Uncertainty," Lee Shulman defines "signature pedagogies" as discipline-specific practices that attempt to keep students engaged and visible in the classroom:

> A persistent problem of most forms of education is that they permit student invisibility, which breeds disinterest and leads to zoning and to non-learning. . . . Signature pedagogies make it hard to disappear and become anonymous . . . [and] tend to be interactive, meaning students are not only accountable to the teacher but also to fellow students.

While Shulman relies on both law and medical schools as models of signature pedagogy in practice, many disciplines and subdisciplines, including composition studies, have their own standard classroom practices, be it the lecture or the workshop. The signature pedagogy of the writing classroom is connected to the move from product-based to process-based models of composing and, as a result, composition instruction. Relying on stage models of prewriting, drafting, and revising that have their roots in the early research of Janet Emig and the more recursive models of Linda Flower and John R. Hayes, typical composition pedagogies are highly interactive, employing a workshop model that emphasizes student composing processes that conform to Shulman's concept of signature pedagogies. Yet even Shulman contends that despite the general success of such pedagogies, they nonetheless can lead to "inertia" and are in need of repair. Although there exist numerous critiques of the potentially formulaic aspects of process-based pedagogies—leading to the postprocess movement—the "nature of the post-process writing course," as Webb Peterson notes, continues to be a "small, interactive group of students working together to investigate and write about current, key issues" (360). The similarity between Shulman's definition of signature pedagogies and Webb Peterson's description of composition instruction is striking.

Because signature pedagogies of writing instruction are highly collaborative, however, it is no surprise that despite the use of a wide range of asynchronous and synchronous electronic communication tools in the writing classroom during the 1980s and 1990s, there is suspicion among teachers that relying on a completely virtual curriculum would detract from rhetorical, audience-based frameworks that are at the core of most writing curricula. Part of this concern stems from the earliest manifestations of distance learning as exactly that, distant, a one-way correspondence model or television satellite model in which a teacher transmitted a lecture to a class of passive listeners, which was then reinscribed as the primary source of information transfer (Nasseh). If such models were employed in the teaching of writing, the result would represent a step backward rather than forward and ultimately be incompatible with the social, audience-based pedagogies of process-based instruction. In the field of computers and writing, however, the use of ListProcs, MOOs, and process-based software such as the *Daedalus Integrated Writing Environment* and its synchronous chat program *InterChange* helped pave the way for more interactive approaches to computer-mediated writing instruction.

Regardless of the growing role of technology in writing instruction, at the time Webb Peterson edited the special issue on distance learning for *Computers and Composition* in 2001, she was accurate in her claim that very little research contextualized distance learning in the teaching of writing, despite the growing influence of the subdiscipline of computers and writing in rhetoric and composition. Webb Peterson notes other factors that should make writing instructors pay more critical attention to distance learning, such as the emphasis on the written word in both composition instruction and distance education, not to mention the status of composition as a service course that is required for almost all students and is thus a likely choice among administrators for online delivery. Since the 2001 special issue, there has been a second *Computers and Composition* special issue and several newer books and edited collections on the topic, including Beth L. Hewett and Christa Ehmann's *Preparing Educators for Online Writing Instruction: Principles and Processes*, Lee-Ann Kastman Breuch's *Virtual Peer Review: Teaching and Learning about Writing in Virtual Environments*, and Jonathan Alexander and Marcia Dickson's *Role Play: Distance Learning and the Teaching of Writing*.

Matching Distance Delivery with Pedagogy

As distance education has become more prevalent, in part because of the student populations returning for a college degree who can benefit from the flexibility and convenience of online scheduling, recognition of the varying learning styles of these diverse populations has also led to the use of digital tools better able to foster multimodal learning across disciplines, and composition is no exception. Particularly common are public discussion forums in which students engage in invention and prewriting activities about course content and possible writing projects, as well as share and review drafts. These tools have been the subject of much pedagogical scholarship, notably in the relative contribution of online dialogue to both classroom community and classroom conflict (Faigley). At the same time, there exist competing metaphors in distance learning that both enable and constrain pedagogical possibilities in composition. The first are metaphors of convenience. Student populations are becoming increasingly mobile and decreasingly residential because of work and family obligations among adult learners and the tendency of all students to hold part-time, and in some cases full-time, jobs. Universities targeting these populations use powerful marketing messages that appeal to the distance-learning demographic, notably working women with families (Kramarae). Indeed, at my institution, our distance learning unit is IDEAL, or Interactive Distance Education for All Learners, and both the acronym and full title stress accessibility and diversity. Part of the accessibility issue involves a gap between the administrative goal of increasing student numbers in online courses and the instructional goal of keeping class sizes low to better serve the needs of student writers. A digital dialogue has taken place on the Writing Program Administrators ListProc (WPA-L) about making arguments for reduced class size in online courses, suggesting a gap between higher administration and composition studies. While I have argued elsewhere that rhetorics of convenience must be interrogated in the light of faculty workload and curricular integrity (Blair and Monske), natural disasters such as Hurricane Katrina and the resulting Sloan Semester for displaced Louisiana college students emphasize accessibility and students' material conditions as significant concerns.

What better unites both composition instruction and online delivery are metaphors of community that shape virtual learning environments. Such models charge students to become engaged and accountable, as much as, if not more than, they would be in traditional face-to-face settings. In their *Building Learning Communities in Cyberspace*, Rena M. Palloff and Keith Pratt contend that "without the purposeful formation of an online learning community in distance learning, we are doing nothing new and different" (9). Such a statement suggests that community formation involves more than the mere use of discussion board or chat room; it requires significant planning and communication of learning outcomes to the students, as well as the documentation of faculty expectations of students to meet those outcomes. Equally important, faculty members must determine to what extent the use of technology enables and constrains the achievement of outcomes.

Moreover, the dependence of first-year writing courses on a portfolio model can be challenging in those courses that continue to rely on print portfolio paradigms despite the move to a fully online course format. Instructors can easily become compilers of their students' portfolio components and may have more control over the final product than the students. As Elizabeth A. Monske's research suggests, writing programs must rethink their logistics as they shift composition courses online to increase the ease of delivery, access, and assessment. Instructors often express concern at the ways in which online course delivery not only increases their workload, requiring of teachers excessive amounts of printing and responding to volumes of e-mails, but also turns instructors into technical troubleshooters. Instructor participants in Monske's study, for instance, expressed concern about technology obscuring the visibility of students' actual writing process; as one instructor concluded:

> It was much more a matter of "I've got all of your papers, so you fill out the self assessment and we'll get this done." In my face-to-face classes there is much more review of their writing and analysis of what they've learned so far and how far they've come over the semester. (98)

A presumed emphasis on technology at the expense of pedagogy can lead to faculty skepticism about maintaining curricular integrity, particularly in communication- or writing-intensive courses where both student-to-student and teacher-to-student dialogue is crucial to success. Faculty members express concern that they must spend more time monitoring the number of postings to ensure appropriate participation but that the quality of student interaction is less. They also worry about how to transmit content and about what will be lost through presentation tools such as *Microsoft PowerPoint* or the limits of communication tools available through course management systems such as *WebCT* or *Blackboard*. As computers and writing specialists such as Darin Payne suggest, these systems are often hierarchical spaces that limit student expression of difference and foreground capitalist rather than liberatory ideals (505). Payne also argues that *Blackboard*, as a course management system,

> undermines many of the professed goals of English studies . . . [and] pedagogical practices in *Blackboard* become homogenizing spatial practices that contribute to (re)inscriptions of normalized identities and ways of knowing privileged and maintained through dominant cultural modes of production and reception. (485)

In this space, metaphors of convenience fuel the tension between pedagogy and technology. *Blackboard* and other systems are generic courses in a box that offer limited opportunities for customization and need supplemental integration of a range of digital tools that most writing instructors have little time to explore.

Part of this problem is inherently tied to the inconsistent progress of technologies and pedagogies. Technologies change so quickly that many instructors can barely keep up. Just when we master one system, the technology du jour switches to another. While such tools as the blog, the wiki, and the podcast stress a level of interactivity that aligns with Shulman's concept of signature pedagogies in general and our own sense of composition's student-centered, process-based pedagogical practice in particular, consider that even new software associated with podcasting can conform to traditional hierarchies, a recent example being the open-source software *Profcast*, whose name alone suggests a distance-learning power dynamic in which teachers talk and students listen. Such examples also indicate a need for teachers using any digital tool to consider again what it enables and what it constrains, "paying attention" to the technological spaces in which teaching and learning occur: "In scholarship and research efforts, teachers need to recognize that developing an increasingly critical perspective on technological literacy and technology issues is a responsibility of our profession" (Selfe 151).

Despite Cynthia Selfe's call, distance-learning research in composition continues to be limited, since much of what we know in terms of theory and application is interdisciplinary. Of the many interdisciplinary heuristics and quality-control rubrics for assessing the effectiveness of online learning at the course, program, and institutional levels, I foreground here Chickering and Gamson's "Seven Principles for Undergraduate Education." Initially published in 1987, the principles have since been widely adopted by state and national organizations and adapted to applications in digital learning spaces, most notably by Chickering and Stephen C. Ehrmann in their 1996 "Implementing the Seven Principles: Technology as Lever":

1. Good Practice Encourages Contacts Between Students and Faculty
2. Good Practice Develops Reciprocity and Cooperation Among Students
3. Good Practice Uses Active Learning Techniques
4. Good Practice Gives Prompt Feedback
5. Good Practice Emphasizes Time on Task
6. Good Practice Communicates High Expectations
7. Good Practice Respects Diverse Talents and Ways of Learning

Much of Chickering and Ehrmann's application of the principles to technology emphasizes increased student interaction and collaboration through online communication tools in ways that successfully coordinate across the curriculum, including composition's emphasis on social aspects of invention and revision despite acknowledged shifts in technological tools and delivery. As Ehrmann notes in a 2002 addendum to his work with Chickering:

> Since 1996 . . . much has changed but much has remained the same. For example, offerings in distance education have exploded. However, these same seven principles, and these seven kinds of technology use, seem equally important for all kinds of learners (and faculty) in all kinds of situations. Whether students come to campus every day or not at all, for example, student interaction can be increased and improved by some of the same online approaches.

Writing instruction and distance learning are closely aligned with the seven principles. Distance-learning programs as diverse as the Ohio

Learning Network; the Teaching, Learning, and Technology Round-tables; and the Michigan Virtual University use these guidelines. Writing instructors and program administrators, however, do not necessarily articulate and assess the ways in which digital delivery is more than just adding a course management system with a discussion forum and a digital drop box and presuming that the same curricular goals will take place or, conversely, presuming that the tools themselves may somehow inhibit learning. Indeed, in writing classrooms, it is important to remember the role of composition in the university, specifically general education programs, where outcomes assessment is vital to reaccreditation for the institution in general and writing programs in particular. Although writing program administration and assessment are major subdisciplines in rhetoric and composition, the research and scholarship on distance learning in these contexts have again been limited. The Council of Writing Program Administrators (WPA) is attempting to address this limitation through the addition of a technology section to its outcomes document (Peckham). As Chickering and Gamson originally contend, while "teachers and students hold the main responsibility for improving undergraduate education," they also require the support of administrators who are equally committed to sustaining learning. This support includes "shared purposes, adequate funding, consistent policies and procedures, and, perhaps most importantly, continuing examination of how well the purposes are being achieved." Because of the importance of assessment, organizations such as the Teaching, Learning, and Technology Group and the Ohio Learning Network have developed rubrics and checklists for faculty members and programs to test the curricular alignment of online or technology-intensive courses to the principles, often with strategies for strengthening the match between the two.

Faculty Members as Digital Immigrants?

Part of the problem of unifying technology with curricular outcomes is having access to the tools; many English instructors have developed a strong sense of resistance to digital writing and research, in part because they want to teach writing, not technology, and because Internet resources are considered less reliable and credible than the print resources in the brick-and-mortar library. Many of our colleagues experience difficulty envisioning fully online writing curricula when there has been limited opportunity for face-to-face computer-mediated writing instruction in networked lab spaces. Some programs can boast that all sections of first-year writing are taught in networked environments, but they are certainly a logistical exception rather than a rule, because of the gap between numbers of sections and students and the actual number of available labs in a department or on campus. Equally common is the generational gap between faculty members who have had training in graduate programs that include computer-mediated pedagogies and their colleagues across the English curriculum whose pedagogies, signature or not, remain rooted in the delivery of content from teacher to student rather than those that place learning in the hands of the students. Regardless, numerous researchers inside and outside the discipline note the impact of digital tools on learning processes, including video games, text messaging, or MP3 players. As the literacy theorist James Gee argues, "The theory of learning in good video games fits better with the modern, high-tech global world today's children and teenagers live in than do the theories and practices of learning they see in school" (7). For gaming and e-learning experts such as Marc Prensky, this gap, most notably between adolescents and teachers, is a gap between digital natives and digital immigrants. Defining these groups, Prensky contends:

> Today's students—K through college—represent the first generations to grow up with this new technology. They have spent their entire lives surrounded by and using computers, videogames, digital music players, video cams, cell phones, and all the other toys and tools of the digital age. . . . But the most useful designation I have found for them is *Digital Natives.* Our students today are all "native speakers" of the digital language of computers, video games and the Internet. So what does that make the rest of us? Those of us who were not born into the digital world but have, at some later point in our lives, become fascinated by and adopted many or most aspects of the new technology are, and always will be compared to them, *Digital Immigrants.*" (1–2)

Prensky's binary between natives and immigrants is admittedly extreme; he does acknowledge, however, that helping educators "go native" is not as difficult as it seems and that the gaps may be as much ideological as they are technological. Still, there exists a range of constraints, the most notable being the increasing numbers of digital tools available to the online educator. A great deal of computers-and-writing research has focused on specific digital tools for blended and in some cases fully online course delivery: asynchronous and synchronous communication forums such as Daedalus; Multiple Object Oriented spaces (MOOS) such as Lingua Moo

(Haynes); Web-authoring and digital imaging applications such as *Adobe Dreamweaver* and *Adobe Photoshop*, which allow both teachers and students to have an online presence or digital portfolio; and immensely popular and utilitarian course management systems such as *Blackboard* and *WebCT*. Yet the tools change quickly; already we have moved toward technological options that are more multimodal—visual, aural, animated, yet verbal as well—whether it be the podcast, the blog, the wiki, or numerous other open-source tools that are meant to give educators alternatives for those tools that may be limiting to curricula or financially inaccessible at host institutions.

What constrains the implementation of these newer tools is what constrains the implementation of any technology and curriculum initiative: time and workload. Many instructors, particularly those employed at teaching-intensive institutions or the non-tenure-track faculty members (including graduate students) who make up a large portion of the composition workforce, are limited by what may often be a standardized curriculum or by necessity a well-established signature pedagogy that allows the instructor with the heavy teaching load to cope. While Webb Peterson has made a strong connection between writing instruction and distance learning, others, including Kevin DePew, contend:

> [As] composition studies continues to design social-epistemic pedagogies that challenge and resist the efficacy of efficiency, many writing programs are repurposing these courses for the Distance Education environment, an environment in which efficiency is valued.
> (DePew, Fishman, Romberger, and Ruetenik 53)

DePew and his coauthors continue to note a material and metaphoric tension between curriculum and convenience, for although they acknowledge research that suggests students may have more access to the instructor, supportive infrastructures that compensate faculty members in terms of class size and course load are often lacking. This concern affects English studies in general and composition studies in particular given that the academic job-market glut continues to reinscribe a two-tiered system of non-tenure-track faculty members with heavier teaching loads in first-year writing in both universities and community colleges. Often these non-tenure-track faculty members hold master's degrees in English and thus have few teaching opportunities outside the part-time labor market of first-year writing or other similar scenarios.

Appropriately, the Association of Departments of English has raised concerns about the placement of graduates of master's programs in English, questioning the ethics of English departments who recruit bodies for underenrolled graduate seminars with little emphasis on the professional development and success of graduates (Steward). Mix in the admitted labor of distance teaching, without appropriate incentive and reward structures, and the result, as Robert Samuels has suggested, is that there is little protection for the largest population of those teaching composition: nontenured faculty members. For that reason, Samuels argues:

> It is essential that we concern ourselves with the status and working conditions of the composition community, particularly non-tenured faculty and graduate students who are often not represented or are under-represented in faculty senates and administrative debates. (68)

Paying Attention to Online Learning

Of course, in advocating online pedagogies in the writing and English curriculum, early adopters of such pedagogies should acknowledge the successful face-to-face teaching methods of their colleagues. The newer tools, along with some of the old standbys, are sufficiently multimodal to allow for the types of student-centered and student-accountable curricula, both old and new, endorsed by Shulman, along with Chickering and Gamson. A related constraint, however, is that a radical shift in pedagogy can disrupt student expectations. Shulman asserts:

> One persistent error teachers make is to get a bright idea for a different way of teaching and then to spring it on students without preparation. Suddenly, a teacher unleashes a combination of group collaborative learning with portfolios and technology and expects students to respond positively to this new game.

These concerns invite the question, How do we better match writing as process with online delivery? Because faculty members express concern about what is lost pedagogically when transitioning to a fully online environment, a response to this question should certainly include a discussion of the ways in which successful signature pedagogies manifest themselves digitally, from invention to drafting, teacher-student conferencing, peer review, and other forms of assessment. For Breuch, what makes activities such as virtual peer review successful is less dependent on the technology than on well-defined goals that are clearly communicated to students

(109); as a result, she advocates a "technological flexibility," or the ability to let the "goals we have for writing tasks drive our choices and uses of technology" (110). In this way, writing pedagogy aligns not only with Chickering and Gamson's original seven principles but also with Shulman's concept of signature pedagogies.

Although Webb Peterson's early discussion of distance learning and writing pedagogy in part stressed compatibility on the basis of the writing process and the largely text-based environments of distance learning (be they MOOs, course management systems, or others), there are future concerns for our discipline in that our field's emphasis on textual responses to writing tasks is in transition. Similarly, the text-heavy tools for use in online learning are being supplemented and replaced by those that are more multimodal. The transition to such multimodal tools may indeed help address concerns about the loss of both classroom curricula and classroom community, as teachers struggle to determine how to best deliver content while reinventing their own roles as coaches and facilitators. These roles are already very common to the writing curriculum and beneficial to online learning environments in which students should be held accountable for contributing to their own successes as learners through participation, collaboration, and self-assessment. At the same time, much of the technology training for the adjunct and graduate student writing instructors is limited to the two-hour faculty development workshop or the one course in the graduate curriculum that addresses computer-mediated writing theory and practice, where distance learning is just one topic among many.

To provide a more sustained technological training initiative in my department, I developed a fully online course, Online Learning for English Educators, typically offered during summer sessions as a second rhetoric and technology course in our graduate program. While such a course allows students to review some of the distance-learning research that takes place outside English studies, the primary goal is for future online teachers to assume roles as students in such settings, navigating course management and other digital interfaces that they may actually have to use at both their current and future institutions. This view is consistent with leading online education scholars such as Greg Kearsley, who contends:

> The effectiveness of online instructors is a function of their experience with online teaching, mastery of the online environment, and overall teaching skills. . . . One clear answer is that teachers must acquire some experience as online learners in order to properly teach online. (91)

In addition to course projects that included a fully online unit plan for a writing or literature course and a review of at least one digital teaching tool not used in the course itself, the course included a range of virtual guest speakers, including the director of Distance Learning, an associate dean, as well as current online-writing instructors, some of whom were teaching in this environment for the first time. Several students completing this course served as educational technology consultants in the department, assigned to faculty across programs teaching online courses for this first time. Instead of simply doing the work for the faculty members, graduate student consultants conducted curricular needs assessments and helped faculty members match various technological tools with their goals for presentation, communication, and assessment. In this way, faculty development for online course delivery was discipline specific and moved beyond the workshop model to work in a more sustained, individual consultation model.

These and other efforts can help us heed Payne's call that English teachers "become more involved in distance-education planning and policy making, constructing, for instance, guidelines that will ensure fidelity to the evolution of disciplinary theory and practice" (504). Yet as we embrace online learning in the English curriculum and assume both evaluative and advocacy roles in our home institutions, we must continue to argue for making the labor of such teaching, research, and service efforts in online learning initiatives visible to our colleagues, just as the MLA and the Conference on College Composition and Communication have called for in their publications promoting the awareness of the impact of technology on academic labor and scholarly publishing (Committee; Conference). Even as we write about the benefits of technology-based teaching in volumes such as this one, to what extent does our existing professional preparation of future faculty members in rhetoric and composition reinscribe the presumed binary between digital natives and digital immigrants? To what extent are we talking only to ourselves as a community of teachers and scholars? How can we educate administrators about the benefits of online curricula as we argue for incentive and reward for the increased labor of developing and delivering online pedagogies? How can we better talk to and ultimately train current and future colleagues for the promises and potential perils of online learning?

To even begin to address these and other questions raised in this essay, we need to work with instructors at their current level of technological expertise, moving progressively toward use of a range of multimodal tools that will support curricular goals in online learning environments as well as enhance the range of learning styles possible—visual, verbal, and aural—modes that can become part not only of the curriculum but also of the writing process. Ultimately, we must help our colleagues see that Webb Peterson's early call to pay attention to the connections between writing instruction and online learning is still viable, particularly if we reconsider the impact of today's digital tools on our signature pedagogies and on the academic labor that it takes to design, develop, and deliver them.

Works Cited

Alexander, Jonathan, and Marcia Dickson. *Role Play: Distance Learning and the Teaching of Writing.* Cresskill: Hampton, 2006. Print.

Blair, Kristine, and Elizabeth Monske. "*Cui bono?* Revisiting the Promises and Perils of Online Learning." *Computers and Composition* 20.4 (2003): 441–53. Print.

Breuch, Lee-Ann Kastman. *Virtual Peer Review: Teaching and Learning about Writing in Online Environments.* Albany: State U of New York P, 2004. Print.

Chickering, Arthur W., and Stephen C. Ehrmann. "Implementing the Seven Principles: Technology as Lever." *TLT Group.* TLT Group, Jan. 2008. Web. 27 Oct. 2008.

Chickering, Arthur W., and Zelda F. Gamson. "Seven Principles for Good Practice in Undergraduate Education." *Honolulu Community College.* U of Hawai'i, 18 Oct. 2007. Web. 27 Oct. 2008.

Committee on Information Technology. "Guidelines for Evaluating Work with Digital Media in the Modern Languages." *Modern Language Association.* MLA, Nov. 2002. Web. 27 Oct. 2008.

Conference on College Composition and Communication Committee on Computers and Composition. "Promotion and Tenure Guidelines for Work with Technology." *National Council of Teachers of English.* NCTE, Nov. 1998. Web. 18 June 2006.

DePew, Kevin, Teddi A. Fishman, Julia Romberger, and Bridget Fahey Ruetenik. "Designing Efficiences: The Parallel Narratives of Distance Education and Composition Studies." *Computers and Composition* 23.1 (2006): 49–67. Print.

Emig, Janet. *The Composing Processes of Twelfth Graders.* Urbana: NCTE, 1971. Print.

Faigley, Lester. *Fragments of Rationality: Postmodernity and the Subject of Composition.* Pittsburgh: U of Pittsburgh P, 1992. Print.

Flower, Linda, and John R. Hayes. "A Cognitive Process Theory of Writing." *College Composition and Communication* 32.4 (1981): 365–87. Print.

Gee, James. *What Video Games Have to Teach Us about Learning and Literacy.* New York: Palgrave, 2003. Print.

Haynes, Cynthia Ann. "HELP! There's a MOO in This Class." *High Wired: On the Design, Use, and Theory of Educational MOOs.* Ed. Haynes and Jan Rune Holmevik. Ann Arbor: U of Michigan P, 1998. 161–76. Print.

Hewett, Beth L., and Christa Ehmann. *Preparing Educators for Online Writing Instruction: Principles and Processes.* Urbana: NCTE, 2004. Print.

Kearsley, Greg. *Online Education: Learning and Teaching in Cyberspace.* Belmont: Wadsworth, 2000. Print.

Kramarae, Cheris. *The Third Shift: Women Learning Online.* Washington: Amer. Assn. of U Women, 2001. Print.

Monske, Elizabeth A. *Transitioning into the Fully Online Writing Course: A Pilot Study.* Diss. Bowling Green State U, 2004. Ann Arbor: UMI, 2004. Print.

Nasseh, Bizhan. "A Brief History of Distance Education." *Adult Education in the News.* SeniorNet.org, 1997. Web. 18 June 2006.

Palloff, Rena M., and Keith Pratt. *Building Learning Communities in Cyberspace.* San Francisco: Jossey-Bass, 1999. Print.

Payne, Darin. "English Studies in Levittown: Rhetorics of Space and Technology in Course-Management Software." *College English* 67.5 (2005): 483–507. Print.

Peckham, Irvin. "Suggest Section." Online posting. *WPA Outcomes: Technology Sections.* Blogger, 22 June 2006. Web. 27 Oct. 2008.

Prensky, Marc. "Digital Natives, Digital Immigrants." *On the Horizon* 9.5 (2001): 1–6. Print.

Samuels, Robert. "The Future Threat to Computers and Composition: Nontenured Instructors, Intellectual Property, and Distance Education." *Computers and Composition* 21.1 (2004): 63–71. Print.

Selfe, Cynthia L. *Technology and Literacy in the Twenty-First Century: The Importance of Paying Attention.* Carbondale: Southern Illinois UP, 1999. Print.

Shulman, Lee. "Pedagogies of Uncertainty." *Liberal Education* 91.2 (2005): n. pag. Web. 18 June 2006.

Sloan-C. "The Sloan Semester." *Sloan-C.* Sloan-C, 2008. Web. 27 Oct. 2008.

Steward, Doug. "The Master's Degree in Modern Languages since 1966." *ADE Bulletin* 136 (2004): 50–68. Print.

Webb Petersen, Patricia. "The Debate about Online Learning: Key Issues for Writing Teachers." *Computers and Composition* 18.4 (2001): 359–70. Print.

Elizabeth Hanson-Smith

Tools for Teaching
Language and Literature Online

Literature for Language Study

In the field of English for speakers of other languages (ESOL), an umbrella term for English as a second language (ESL) for programs in native-English-speaking countries and for English as a foreign language (EFL) for programs outside native-English-speaking countries, the study of literature has several purposes:

Assisting the study of language and stylistics, including composition, rhetoric and the genres of various academic subjects;

Preparing nonnative-speaking English majors (who often become EFL teachers) for advanced work in the formal study of English literature;

Helping students understand the adopted culture they live in or in preparation for study in an English-speaking country;

Providing a means to self-exploration and personal growth in the liberal arts tradition. (Lazar 22–47; see Carter and Long 1–3 for related but slightly different paradigms)

The best texts for teaching ESOL composition through reading, such as Ruth Spack's *Guidelines*, incorporate all these aspects by providing

53

authentic texts (that is, fiction and nonfiction written for native-speaking audiences), accompanied by grammar and vocabulary exercises specific to ESOL needs and by suggestions for ways to explore in depth the texts' structure, meanings, and potential personal significance for the student. Spack also offers suggestions for best practices in ESOL pedagogy: group work in brainstorming, peer review and editing of papers, and development of composition topics (including an extensive research-based essay), as well as approaches to reading that include finding topic sentences, exploring structures, and appreciating the emotional weight of simile and metaphor. (For more on the significance of literature for language study, see Carter and McRae; Duff and Maley; Kramsch; Widdowson). My approach to teaching ESOL and educating graduate students preparing to teach in the field has been to emphasize the importance of literature while seeking the best technologies for language learning.

Most teachers are familiar with one of the simplest, most readily available technologies, the word processor, which admirably suits the process-based approach to writing: multiple drafts are required, and, in ESOL classes in particular, the focus in initial drafts is to locate the desired meanings or develop the rhetorical structure of the paper. Only in successive drafts are students alerted to grammatical errors and vocabulary difficulties, and usually these are worked on in descending order of importance (see Zamel; Ferris and Hedgecock). Only with an electronic text can students make the necessary global revisions and detailed corrections that are required by the process approach. Courses throughout the university, however, are increasingly moving beyond the word-processor comfort zone toward blended (face-to-face meetings with a variety of online support) or wholly online situations, and teachers may well wonder how to translate the activities of the typical humanistic curriculum into the new, totally electronic environment. Additionally, for ESOL or foreign language courses, teachers must consider grammar and vocabulary development, the potential need for remediation in fundamentals, the importance of commanding oral aspects of language, and cultural differences that may mean a fear or distrust of technology (especially in adult learners), as well as culture shock or cultural misunderstandings. Often courses in intensive programs preparatory to university admission and first-year English classes for entering freshmen are organized by skill—listening, speaking, reading, writing—and so teachers must also bring together these skills in such a way that they support and enrich one another: reading to write, listening combined with oral production, grammar embedded in composition, and so on. How well can an electronic environment support a comprehensive approach, particularly when a focus on literature seemingly implies silent, private communication with an author?

Further problems arise with the question of the digital divide, which extends not only to who has access to computers and the Internet but also to how comfortable instructors are using appropriate technologies. Often teachers who are not "digital natives" will have some apprehension about using technology (Prensky). Experienced teachers may fear the loss of authority they hold in a face-to-face class, or they may perceive the online experience as depersonalizing. Yet reports from the field indicate that more student interaction, both with the instructor and with peers, can take place online than in class and that most instructors who make the effort to teach online find it exceptionally satisfying, as several of the classes described in this essay testify. My focus here is on free or nearly free tools, most of which are available for easy download or are used entirely online.

This essay looks at the three major types of online tools that make language learning online not only possible but in some ways superior to activities in a physical classroom. The first type of tool allows access to a virtual classroom environment. The second offers ways to access content that are especially helpful in the online environment. The third involves tools for oral and written production and interactive communication. In examining the technology, I draw on examples from a variety of content and skill-oriented courses for ESOL learners, referring to their projects and tasks as examples of best practices. I indicate how these tools are applied in teaching language, literature, and culture and then suggest their future potential. I also suggest some of the pitfalls of using electronic technologies to teach language and literature.

Tools for Access to the Online Classroom

Most teachers enter the world of online learning by instinctively attempting to replicate typical forms and modes of classroom presentation and assessment: the delivery of lectures (whether the primary focus is language or literature), whole class discussion, small-group discussion, peer review of paper drafts or other student work, the writing and delivery of compositions, oral tests or essay examinations, and research-based writing. Most university-sponsored online courses are run through a course management system, such as *Blackboard* or the free, open-source *Moodle*

Suite. A course management system typically allows the delivery of content, that is, a place where students can find the syllabus and related course assignments, read the instructor's lecture notes, and drop off papers. For those without university support for such a system, *Yahoo! Groups* provides many of the same facilities and is totally free of charge, though heavily loaded with advertisements. Student profiles, with accompanying photos, stored at the course management system are one of several ways in which online learning is personalized: How many university lecturers know that a student's hobby is ant farming or would have thought to ask about hobbies at all? Instead of a seating chart (with or without photos), the teacher sees a little snapshot of the students' lives.

Another personalizing feature of a course management system is the opportunity for live chat using text, voice, and—in the more powerful systems—webcams, so that students and professor may hear and see one another. The instructor may deliver a lecture live to a global audience or hold virtual office hours with individual students, who in turn may form small study groups of their own to chat about paper topics or research assignments, regardless of where they are located in the world. In reviewing online and blended courses, I have found that experienced online teachers usually set up a general bulletin board reserved for class announcements and then organize students into groups, by particular task, by level, or by discussion topics—or combinations of all these—each group with its own separate forum or bulletin boards. Students may read the board online or receive its messages by e-mail. Students can choose to receive e-mails in a daily digest or individually. Table 1 summarizes ways that a course management system is generally used to create an online classroom. (See Schramm for more details on the ethnography of classroom interactions.) It is important to keep in mind the differences between *synchronous*, or real-time communication, and *asynchronous*, or time-independent communications, which may be very rapid, almost real-time exchanges. Synchronous communications on the Web, however, may be readily archived as voice, video, and text files for future reference.

The record-keeping functions of online classrooms are generally far superior to those of physical classrooms. In a physical classroom, the instructor may arrange groups but will hear only a small segment of what each group says. Often the pull to stay too long with one group is irresistible, thus shorting attention to the other groups. In an online setting, the teacher can listen to or read all the interactions and make notes at leisure about who needs help, how the discussion should be redirected or ex-

Table I
Classroom Functions in a Course Management System

Physical Classroom Course	Web Equivalents, Synchronous	Web Equivalents, Asynchronous
Lectures	Web presentations with whiteboard, slideshow, and Web tour (lecturer controls students' desktops, leading them to selected Web sites), accompanying voice, text, and video chat	Web pages that may be read or referred to at any time Slideshow and lecture that may also be archived on the Web and run like a video
Materials duplicated by the instructor (handouts)		Documents, media files, URLs, among other resources, stored in Web archives Web pages, wikis, or blogs used to store student-created materials
Whole-class discussion	Whole class chat with voice, text, and video	Class bulletin boards that may be organized by topic Archived chats
Small group meetings	Designated group chat rooms	Small group bulletin boards Archived group chats
Study groups	Students may create their own chat rooms for study groups or informal meetings	Students create their own bulletin board, blogs, or other online positings Archived chats
Office hours	Text, voice, or video chat Phone (Voice over Internet)	E-mail Archived chats
Assessment	Voice chat for oral-aural tests	Online quizzes, papers submitted electronically, electronic portfolios, self-evaluation using rubrics, and voice and video recordings

panded, and so on. Similarly, in a physical class or small-group discussion, one or two students may monopolize the conversation. With an online bulletin board, every student has a better chance to participate, and the written archive of discussion allows the instructor to pinpoint students' strengths and weaknesses. Students have a record to refer to for later study, and once they realize that group work can receive close perusal, they respond more fully and with more care. As one of Mike MacCarthy's students describes King Middle School's laptop experiment, "Nobody feels stupid around here anymore" (Curtis par. 13).

One challenge of online learning and teaching is keeping track of the volumes of messages and documents that are generated. In a six-week session of a free online course sponsored by the international association Teachers of English to Speakers of Other Languages and run through *Yahoo! Groups*, an average week brought over five hundred messages. These messages are threaded (i.e., organized by topic when read online, rather than placed in separate forums), but teachers must plan to help students organize the workload. This effort entails valuable study and technology skills: creating and labeling folders to sort and access information effectively, organizing the scholar's day to include periodic reading of accumulated materials and e-mail, staying on time and up-to-date with class and group work in progress, and so on. The great temptation of anywhere-anytime learning is procrastination to the point where information overload causes the student to give up the course. The greatest difficulty for teachers is the amount of time an online course or blended activities can take, especially the first time. And while teachers may be tempted to sit back and expect the syllabus to be followed and the course management system to run the course for them, in fact, online teaching demands a far higher degree of involvement with students' lives, both academic and personal.

Tools to Enhance Content

Beyond the course management system, which provides a framework for the online classroom, other types of resources on the Internet can vastly enrich access to literature and language learning. Students can reach the life of a writer in ways unimagined even a decade ago. They can listen to poets and authors being interviewed live; for example, a discussion with Donald Hall, the poet laureate of the United States in 2006, is archived on National Public Radio's Web site, along with the author's reading of his own work ("U.S. Poetry's New Chief"). Many communities around the country name their own local poet laureates, and their work may be found by a quick online search. If the class is international or national, students may share their findings and favorite authors. Another good source of listening and reading is *Poem Present*, which archives live readings and lectures for the University of Chicago Program in Poetry and Poetics (http://poempresent.uchicago.edu). Most contemporary authors have their own Web sites with their photos, snippets of new work, a bulletin board to write directly to them—most will answer rapidly—thoughts about books and writing, a schedule of appearances, and other links (see, e.g., *Judy Blume on the Web*, for young readers, or *StephenKing.com*, for adults; some sites organize regular online discussions, such as Barnes and Noble does for their authors). Such pages are a remarkable means to motivate reading and provide a way to interact with an authentic audience of other readers. An author's site may be of special importance when nonnative speakers are attempting to understand the cultural background of a work and can send questions directly to the author or to avid native-speaking fans.

While one would never recommend reading lengthy works online, the fact that literary texts appear in readily accessible electronic format presents many advantages to students. *Project Gutenberg* offers eighteen thousand copyright-free texts, about a third of which are available for download (www.gutenberg.org); they are mainly the classics but do include some lesser-known works such as W. E. B. DuBois's *Suppression of the African Slave Trade*. The *International Children's Digital Library* offers free electronic texts from many cultures and languages (and includes several age-appropriate search engines for its site [www.icdl.org]). The electronic version of works allows manipulation of the text in ways that are particularly instructive for the language learner. *VoyCabulary*, for example, uses online software that creates a new Web page with all the words in a given URL hyperlinked to an online dictionary or thesaurus selected by the user. Language learners can thus spare themselves the tedium (and interruption) of transferring the gloss from the back of a textbook or dictionary to the margins of the page. *Babel Fish Translation* lets the user paste in a chunk of text and then translates it into the designated language, thus providing a crude but usually effective bilingual version of the text.

Advanced students may also use the online concordancer, *The Compleat Lexical Tutor* (www.lextutor.com), to search for the meanings of words by comparing their occurrences in strings of text from large bodies of academic prose. For a rough-and-ready concordancer for online reading, students can use the Find function of their browser to locate all instances of a word in a Web page. They can thus obtain a more comprehensive idea of its usage than they can from random and isolated encounters with it in an extensive or relatively rapid reading on paper. (See Sökmen for a review of research-informed techniques for vocabulary study, including expanded opportunities for rehearsal, engagement with meanings on deep levels, and opportunities for meaningful practice.) This type of Internet-based language manipulation offers the additional advantage of providing students with autonomous and individualized study of precisely those words or grammatical structures that cause them the most difficulty. After reading a text on paper, students may reread using sophisticated electronic tools to explore language and style while reflecting on details and larger meanings. Such vocabulary and stylistics work would also be of value for non-ESOL students. Teachers should, however, explore these tools in advance and write directions for their own courses and particular student populations.

The possibilities of Internet searches about literature are immense. In addition to authors' Web sites and official pages, students may, for example, link online from a place name in a story to a regional map at *Google Maps*, from a date to a historical brief at *History.com*, from the author's name to a biography at *Biography.com*, from a title to a book review at *Amazon.com* or to a film review at the *Movie Review Query Engine* (www.mrqe.com). Children can read book reviews written by other kids at the *Spaghetti Book Club* (www.spaghettibookclub.org). For the more advanced student, scholarly articles are also becoming increasingly abundant on the Web; many journals are expanding their Web presence, and new, wholly online journals are springing into existence. In turn, many e-journals are taking on entirely new functions as resources for online tools and as communities of practice (see, e.g., the *Reading Matrix* [www.readingmatrix.com], which offers articles online, a community bulletin board for teachers, a quiz tool, and other options).

One of the most important online tools for students to master is the search engine. Whether finding a line in a poem or song or researching an author's life, students will have to learn the intricacies of advanced search techniques. The study of search engines is also an opportunity to understand the differences among advertising, personal opinions (as expressed in blogs), and scholarly works. When a student can simply copy and paste text from a Web page to a word-processed document, the dangers of plagiarism in the electronic era may at first seem to loom very large, but in fact, Web search engines can assist the teacher who suspects a student has committed illegal borrowing: by pasting a phrase or two into such an engine, the teacher may quickly find any Web page a student could readily access. Naturally, the best defense against plagiarism is to teach in advance the conventional forms of citation and techniques for incorporating references. Helpful online handouts and interactive worksheets are available at online writing labs such as Purdue University's *OWL* (http://owl .english.purdue.edu). Of particular difficulty for ESOL students may be that standards for plagiarism as defined in Anglo-American academic culture do not exist in their own or that the concept may not have been introduced in their own language or in prior educational experience. Many online resources, and some local libraries, offer handouts to evaluate Web findings (see "Web Page").

Tools for Oral and Written Production in ESOL

In the remainder of this essay, I focus on free online tools that enable the reader, particularly the ESOL reader, to respond to literature as well as to study the language, style, and culture of literary texts.

Project-Based Learning Online

I have already mentioned the significance of the word processor in process-based writing. Other familiar electronic tools, such as slideshow software, can be used to create multimedia presentations about literature combining text, graphics, and photos obtained through Internet searches. Project-based learning is an important aspect of language study, since it involves a significantly high level of cognitive activity and—particularly in group projects—practice in communication skills. Project-based learning is a model for classroom activity that shifts away from the classroom practices of short, isolated, teacher-centered lessons and instead emphasizes learning activities that are long-term, interdisciplinary, student-centered, and integrated with real-world issues and practices ("Why?" par. 1).

In working with middle and high school students during a Title VII program, I found that the technology became a motivating factor for young language learners working in groups to explore one anothers' cultures (Hanson-Smith). The students became caught up in the excitement of learning to manage Internet searches about their homelands; find audiovisual materials to include in their presentations; create original interviews, stories, poems, and artwork with electronic media; and master the presentation software we used, while working together in multilingual, multicultural, multiaged groups to complete the projects and rehearse their oral presentations for a huge audience of proud parents and friends. Many students incorporated their own poetry, as well as peer-to-peer interviews, artwork and cartoons, and photography and video, into their presentations. (See also Jewell, who describes high school students' community service projects, completed with word processors and *PowerPoint.*)

The Blogosphere and Wiki Worlds

Project-based learning online offers the additional benefits of giving students an international audience and an easy way to display products to friends and relatives overseas. In preparation for a project or as a ready means to interact with a text, students should be encouraged to use blogs (Web logs) and wikis (Web pages that can be easily edited online and contributed to collaboratively). While formerly Web pages had to be created by learning HTML or employing special editing software and then repeatedly uploading and downloading drafts, blogs and wikis can be written directly in the browser and published online with a click. Corrections and redraftings are quick and easy. Many instructors of blended and online courses supplement lectures and homework assignments by requiring students to keep personal or collective blogs. Teachers and students can use blogs for up-to-the-minute announcements, exam review, self-evaluation, online portfolios, and so forth. Language learners might benefit from viewing the blogs of others struggling to learn a language (see, e.g., *Virtual Mandarin* [http://pienews.blogs.com/mandarin]). For a lengthier explanation of blogs and their uses, with numerous links to examples, see Barbara Dieu's slideshow and the discussion by the sixth-grade teacher George Mayo.

Many teachers recognize the value of keeping a reading journal, in which students make notes of their impressions, observations, and responses as they read. These journals help students remember plot incidents, characters, and tropes and may form the basis for a paper or a study aid for class discussion and exams. If a reading journal is kept in a blog, teachers and classmates may also read students' notes, which can become the basis for class discussion. The teacher can quickly see where class members are having difficulty with the reading or where the sparks of connections are ignited. Instead of lugging home notebooks to read (often a task that is put aside for more immediate concerns), online teachers can use an aggregator that informs them through RSS (really simple syndication) when new information is added to their students' blogs. The *Bloglines* aggregator displays the titles of blog feeds (those with new matter in bold font), the current content, and a link to the actual site. A "Sub with Bloglines" button can be added to any browser menu bar to allow sites to be added automatically. Even more convenient for some instructors is a subscription service, such as *FeedBlitz*, that sends a daily digest of changes at selected blogs, wikis, or any Web page to an e-mail address.

Free blogs and wikis may be claimed all over the Internet. While blogs are most effective for individual work, wikis are extremely efficient for creating and archiving group or class projects. Both types of Web sites can readily incorporate media created by students. Among popular wikis are *PBwiki*, which can incorporate HTML, and *Wikispaces*. Blogs often used by ESOL learners include *Blogger*, which has an exceptionally friendly set of help pages, and *Elgg*, which can be incorporated into a *Moodle* course management system. Some blogs, such as *DiaryLand*, target younger students, but for maximum safety, a school should consider maintaining something like the user-installed *WordPress* on its own server so that it cannot be accessed from the Internet directly. *Dekita.org* offers links to ESOL classes seeking to exchange blogs and other Web activities and an aggregation of feeds (the "Orchard") from a selection of those classes (Ammann). Thus any teacher can easily have students join the international asynchronous conversation or an exchange of projects.

Podcasting

With the addition of audio and video to the blogosphere, the potential for more challenging kinds of projects and interactions has taken on new dimensions. In an average physical ESOL class, students can never get enough speaking practice. In a fifty-minute class with twenty-five students, if the teacher speaks half the time, and the remaining time is shared equally (which it never is), each student will have had only one minute of oral practice. Podcasting (iPod broadcasting) offers anywhere-anytime listening and speaking practice in a variety of ways made simple by the use of computer, Internet, iPod, or even mobile phone. Students can record whenever they feel the urge, and teachers can listen and comment at their leisure. Many universities now use podcasting to deliver lectures for review, practice for foreign languages, or videos that would take up too much class time.

While a number of language teachers have created interesting listening activities using podcasts, by far the most exciting uses of audio on the Internet involve student productions. Performing works of literature is a natural follow-up to reading, particularly after students have listened to authors read their works. Oral performance is especially appropriate for poetry and drama and through repetition and practice allows ESOL students to master the expressive details of rhythm, intonation, and pronunciation. The students in Aiden Yeh's speech class in Taiwan use *podOmatic* to deliver speeches, self-evaluate, and offer comments on one another's work. Yeh then comments directly on their offerings and invites international ESOL teachers to listen and comment. Student work may be heard at *Aiden Yeh's Speech Class Podcast*; comments may be made by joining and signing in to the podcast.

Students may record a podcast directly online, as at *podOmatic*, or use recording software on their computer, such as *GarageBand* or the free *Audacity*, which is multiplatform. Fee-based services, such as *Audblog*, allow users to deliver audio to a blog or voice mail. The audio quality is good enough that Uwe Klemm in southern Germany had his students use podcast technology to produce a radio play, *Kutikula*, that they wrote, directed, and read expressively—and that won a prestigious award from their state media board.

Video Online

A great deal of material for teaching on the Web is moving to video. For generations raised on television, "listening with the eye" seems natural (P. Riley, qtd. in Gruba 77), but, in fact, students process visual images in greater depth and with cognitive benefits when they are producing rather than merely viewing. When I taught the introduction to medieval literature I always incorporated student productions of the mystery cycle plays. Because of the expense and fragility of the videotaping system at the time, I usually had to tape the productions for them. With the new digital technologies, short skits can be made with a webcam, a digital still camera (most of which at the higher levels will take movies with sound), or a higher-end mobile phone. Students can write, act in, film, and edit their work, using free software like *iMovie* or *Windows Movie Maker*, both of which have extensive tutorials online. End products might consist of skits based on dramas, short stories, and poetry; interviews with local personnages; travelogues showing visitors around a hometown; fictional works created by the students; or contributions to an online magazine. (For more ideas, see *Examples of Digital Stories*.)

Video chat is possible with many course management systems; free video chat is widely available in such venues as *Yahoo! Messenger*; numerous sites offer video-based ESOL learning materials like *Real English* (www .real-english.com) and *The Daily English Show* (www.thedailyenglishshow .com); and "vlogs" (video blogs) offer an exciting medium to enhance the types of projects described earlier, such as online magazines. Video can be created directly online with a webcam or cell phone (e.g., at *BlogCheese .com*) or off-line with digital hardware, and results can be stored free at sites like the *Internet Archive* (www.archive.org). Productions can then be linked to a Web page or blog for online presentation. Social software, such as that found at *YouTube*, allows tagging to identify and find content, storage of favorites, creation of friends' lists, and other ways to involve learners in further interactions about their production. Instead of producing a single video or CD, students can easily access their work and view it together, even if separated by continents. Conceiving, storyboarding, filming, and editing a video project involves a considerable investment of student (and teacher) time and energy but is well worth the effort in terms of deeper emotional and cognitive involvement. As with other creative group projects, students should be engaged in the development of standards or rubrics by which their products will be judged. Projects should always include the opportunity for self-evaluation.

Students are very much aware of the need both to learn English and to use technology in the global village. As Maggie Sokolik found in a study of students rating their professors' use of technology, university faculty members lose the respect of their students when they do not attempt to use even the most modest of technologies. Conversely, students appreciate the opportunity to use technologies that are becoming increasingly familiar to the digital generation. Rita Zeinstejer's young adult ESOL students in Rosario, Argentina, talked about cultural differences and similarities with Spanish learners in the United States synchronously using *Skype*, a free Voice over Internet Protocol that allows the user to call anywhere in the world. Here is one student's summary of her experience:

> How to describe the experience we had last week is quite complex.
> The project we are doing is an amazing idea in order to learn the language in another way. To my mind, that's very important to know to how to communicate correctly in English with other people, especially if they are from abroad. This opportunity that we had was a perfect occasion to do it!

We were able to do something that, I think, not many students would ever do. Luckily, I and my classmates could do it! We talked with Spanish students from the USA. We exchanged opinions about many different and interesting topics.

In my personal case, I talked with Lucia, Maya and Daniel who were really talkative and knowledgeable. They were interested in very controversial and well-known topics, such as kidnappings, the policies of Hugo Chavez and what people all around the world think of him. Luckily, I knew something about these topics and I could help them a bit in their final projects.

That's not all; we also talked about our daily routines and customs. We were able to spot how different we are as regards social customs! But these won't prevent us to keep in touch and help each other when there's a need; and why not . . . making some new friends . . . ha!

It's highly important to realize that this opportunity is unique and that we must take profit from it!

To sum up, I reckon this was a spectacular experience. I was able to take advantage from it and to learn that the most important part of learning a language is to know how to communicate with it!

Thanks Rita for giving us this exceptional and superb chance!
(Denise)

The enthusiasm rings true. These digital natives enjoy the freedom and excitement that genuine communication affords. Their teachers are willing to take the risk of using new technologies, and they have discovered how the walls of the classroom may be torn down.

Works Cited

Ammann, Rudolf. "Welcome to the Dekita Orchard." Online posting. *Dekita. org: Open EFL/ESL*. Dekita, 29 May 2006. Web. 18 June 2006.

Carter, Ronald, and Michael N. Long. *Teaching Literature*. Harlow: Longman, 1991. Print.

Carter, Ronald A., and John McRae, eds. *Language, Literature, and the Learner: Creative Classroom Practice*. London: Longman, 1996. Print.

Curtis, Diane. "Laptops on Expedition: Embracing Expeditionary Learning." *Edutopia*. George Lucas Foundation, 19 Jan. 2004. Web. 17 June 2006.

Denise. "Denise." *CAE B's Podcast*. Zeinstejer, 2 May 2006. Web. 5 Nov. 2008. Podcast.

Dieu, Barbara. *Je blogue et vous, vous bloguer? Les blogues dans l'enseignement et apprentissages des langues*. 26 Aug. 2004. Web. 17 June 2006.

DuBois, W. E. B. *The Suppression of the African Slave Trade to the United States of America, 1638–1870*. 1897. *Project Gutenberg*. Project Gutenberg Literary Archive Foundation, 2008. Web. 31 Oct. 2008.

Duff, Alan, and Alan Maley. *Literature.* New York: Oxford UP, 1990. Print.

Examples of Digital Stories. Maricopa Center for Learning and Instruction. Maricopa Community Colls., 20 June 2006. Web. 31 Oct. 2008.

Ferris, Dana R., and John S. Hedgecock. *Teaching ESL Composition: Purpose, Process, and Practice.* 2nd ed. Mahwah: Erlbaum, 2004. Print.

Gruba, Paul. "Playing the Videotext: A Media Literacy Perspective on Video-Mediated L2 Listening." *Language Learning and Technology* 10.2 (2006): 77–92. Web. 18 June 2006.

Hanson-Smith, Elizabeth. "Multimedia Projects for EFL/ESL Students." *CAELL Journal* 7.4 (1997): 3–12. Print.

Hanson-Smith, Elizabeth, and Sarah Rilling, eds. *Learning Languages through Technology.* Alexandria: Teachers of Eng. to Speakers of Other Langs., 2006. Print.

Jewell, Mary. "Real-World Contexts, Skills, and Services for Secondary School Language Learners." Hanson-Smith and Rilling 175–86.

Klemm, Uwe. "Second Show—Students' Radio Play." *Schoolmaster's Blog.* Klemm, 15 Jan. 2006. Web. 17 June 2006.

Kramsch, Claire. *Context and Culture in Language Teaching.* Oxford: Oxford UP, 1993. Print.

Lazar, Gillian. *Literature and Language Teaching: A Guide for Teachers and Trainers.* Cambridge: Cambridge UP, 1993. Print.

Mayo, George. "About This Project." *Mrmayo.org.* N.p., n.d. Web. 4 Nov. 2008.

Prensky, Marc. "Digital Natives, Digital Immigrants." *On the Horizon* 9.5 (2001): 1–6. Web. 31 Oct. 2008.

Schramm, Andreas. "Making Online Students Connect: Ethnographic Strategies for Developing Online Learning Experiences." *Distance Education and Languages: Evolution and Change.* Ed. Borje Holmberg, Monica Shelley, and Cynthia White. Clevedon: Multilingual Matters, 2005. 230–41. Print.

Sökmen, Anita J. "Current Trends in Teaching Second Language Vocabulary." *Vocabulary: Description, Acquisition and Pedagogy.* Ed. Norbert Schmitt and Michael McCarthy. Cambridge: Cambridge UP, 1997. 237–57. Print.

Sokolik, Maggie. "Mismatch or Missed Opportunity? Addressing Student Expectations about Technology." Hanson-Smith and Rilling 137–49.

Spack, Ruth. *Guidelines: A Cross-Cultural Reading/Writing Text.* 2nd ed. New York: St. Martin's, 1996. Print.

"U.S. Poetry's New Chief: Donald Hall." *National Public Radio.* Natl. Public Radio, 14 June 2006. Web. 17 June 2006.

"Web Page Evaluation Checklist." *Evaluating Web Pages: Techniques to Apply and Questions to Ask. UC Berkeley Library.* U of California, 13 July 2008. Web. 31 Oct. 2008.

"Why Do Project-Based Learning?" *The Multimedia Project: Project-Based Learning with Multimedia.* San Mateo County Office of Education, 2001. Web. 17 June 2006.

Widdowson, Henry G. *Stylistics and the Teaching of Literature.* London: Longman, 1975. Print.

Yeh, Aiden. *Aiden Yeh's Speech Class Podcast.* Yeh, 2006. Web. 17 June 2006.

Zamel, Vivian. "Teaching Composition in the ESL Classroom: What We Can Learn from Research in the Teaching of English." *Landmark Essays on ESL Writing*. Ed. Tony Silva and Paul Kei Matsuda. Mahwah: Erlbaum, 2001. 27–36. Print. Landmark Essays 17.

Zeinstejer, Rita. *CAE B's Podcast*. Zeinstejer, 1 Apr. 2006. Web. 17 June 2006.

Mary Ann Lyman-Hager

Teaching World Languages Online

In the 1980s, the comedian Don Novello appeared regularly on *Saturday Night Live* as Father Guido Sarducci and, in one particularly memorable spoof on higher education, as a spokesperson for the Five Minute University. In this skit, Father Sarducci proposes a simplified university degree, based on what graduates actually remember from their college experiences after five years. He suggests, for example, that for Spanish, all graduates would learn is *¿Cómo está usted?*—and the usual appropriate response—*Muy bien, gracias.* These phrases would suffice, he reasons, since students remember nothing else from the two years of required Spanish classes. Likewise, business schools would just teach the notion of buying something at a low price and selling it at a higher one, and economists would only discuss supply and demand. A twenty-second spring break and Polaroid graduation pictures are included in the graduation package, and the fees for the degree are quite reasonable, claims Father Sarducci.

Father Sarducci's description of the Five Minute University's Spanish curriculum is perhaps painfully humorous to the generation of language learners trained in the audiolingual classrooms of the twentieth century, which emphasized discrete structures, memorized dialogues, and drills.

It may even strike a familiar note with those language learners who, some time later, fulfilled their two-year requirement at the university level in the "communicative competence" or "proficiency-based" classrooms of the late twentieth century.

With new emphases on learner-centered and sociocultural approaches to language learning (Warschauer and Kern), is there renewed hope that relevant and meaningful language learning might occur in both second-language classrooms and in online learning environments? Could new theories of language acquisition, new approaches to language teaching—whether in face-to-face, online, or hybrid (i.e., blended) language courses—and their methodologies, assist educators in revitalizing and individu-alizing language learning? What unique roles will students, teachers, and technology play in transforming language learning in the twenty-first century?

The task before language educators is to determine not whether on-line education (e-learning) functions less well, as well, or better than face-to-face learning but how to create face-to-face educational settings, blended online environments, and distance courses that, unlike Sarducci's offerings, make participation in language communities memorable for students and relevant to their needs. What have we learned about theory and method-ology that can aid us in realizing this goal?

The last half of the twentieth century was punctuated by shifts in theories, methodologies, and technologies of language learning.[1] Which of those might have inspired Father Sarducci's *SNL* skit, and why does his Five Minute University Spanish curriculum, in particular, still resonate with its audience? Reviewing recent historical and theoretical approaches that underpin language-learning practices can inform us as we reevaluate these theories and practices and the roles they might play in online lan-guage learning today. What new theoretical approaches to e-learning and intercultural communication are flexible enough to incorporate the best and most appropriate methodologies from these eras?

Beyond Behaviorism and Communicative Competence: Pedagogical Perspectives

As a reaction to grammar-translation methodologies of the early twenti-eth century, the so-called Army method, also referred to as the audio-lingual method, was launched, inspired by behaviorist psychology and fol-lowers of B. F. Skinner and John B. Watson. The audiolingual methods and the technologies that supported them (the language laboratory and the textbook's audiotaped drills) were standard fare for several generations of language learners.

Language learners trained in this era are possibly those who, like graduates of the Five Minute University, remember little from their foreign language training. Fortunately, language practitioners have largely distanced themselves from rote memorization and methodologies stressing pattern and substitution drills derived from the behaviorist schools of thought. The linguist Noam Chomsky's historic challenge to Skinner ("Review")—occurring shortly after the Sputnik launch and the revalorization of language learning—paved the way for a new conceptualization of the processes and cognitive strategies underlying language learning. Chomsky and his followers exercised enormous influence on the field of second language acquisition in the latter half of the twentieth century, and the accompanying theories, tests, methodologies, and language classroom practices reflected the construct of the homogeneous idealized native speaker. Generative grammar exercises and native speech from a specified standard target population provided grist for speakers and listeners in language labs and classrooms.

Chomsky and his followers reconceived language learning as language acquisition and posited new theoretical approaches that emphasized humankind's innate, cognitively encoded capacity to communicate and create verbal meaning. Second-language acquirers process data or input and store relevant material for production after the internalization of the data. Grammar mistakes were viewed as indications of "interlanguage" (Selinker), not as quasi-fatal flaws in structural knowledge that needed immediate correction lest they be internalized.

The notion of the idealized native speaker-listener has excited heated controversy (Valdés). This concept derives from Chomsky's theories presented in *Aspects of the Theory of Syntax* and has served as a unit of analysis, not only for language teaching, but also for oral testing practices of the government (the Interagency Language Roundtable scales) and of K–16 educational settings (ACTFL, *Proficiency Guidelines*). Chomsky's ideal (i.e., native) speaker has subsequently become the object of linguistic theory and of teaching approaches and methodologies:

> Linguistic theory is concerned with an ideal speaker-listener, in a completely homogenous speech-community, who knows its language perfectly and is unaffected by such grammatically irrelevant conditions as

memory limitations, distractions, shifts of attention and interest, and errors (random or characteristic) in applying his knowledge of the language in actual performance. (*Aspects* 3)

The communicative competence and proficiency movements begun in the 1970s and 1980s dominated the theory and practice of language learning through the late 1990s, and, arguably, still do today. Stephen D. Krashen and Tracy D. Terrell and others reinforced the trend toward communicative language teaching in educational settings through textbooks. Among the theories underpinning communicative language teaching, Krashen's five hypotheses (*Principles*), especially, resonated with classroom language teachers. Despite detractors who bemoaned the absence of research to confirm Krashen's theories, the "comprehensible input hypothesis," in particular, remains extremely influential in determining the practices of second-language classrooms and of asynchronous out-of-class activities (6–7). The comprehensible-input hypothesis argues that students most efficiently acquire (as opposed to learn) language by processing input targeted at a level just beyond their current functioning level, posited as "input + 1". This input is necessary and, as Krashen argues, sufficient, for language to be acquired.

As Margot Steinhart suggests, in many communicative language teaching classrooms, reading and writing, as well as in-depth cultural analysis, took a back seat to listening and speaking as small peer groups engaged in communicative tasks (such as simulations and role-playing) involving primarily oral skills and in-class cohorts. The communicatively oriented topics and tasks of the small groups, because of the low proficiency level of these first- and second-year students, were interpersonal. Content about culture—or, rather, the pluralistic cultures of native speakers—went missing from syllabi, since communication among peers was the time-consuming, all-important task of classroom learning. The interesting part of learning a language—its underlying cultures and learners' responses to these cultures—was systematically reserved for upper-division courses where, suddenly, reading and writing became key to success. By then, Sarducci's putative language student had finished the language requirement and was on to more relevant learning in the so-called content areas outside language studies.

The excesses of "communicative competence" have since been challenged by Renate A. Schulz and by Claire Kramsch, among others. Kramsch, in particular, laments the single-minded emphasis on oral communication, which she feels has perverted or "resignified" the original construct of "communicative competence" as outlined by Michael P. Breen and Christopher N. Candlin and others so that it means "the ability to exchange information speedily and effectively and to solve problems, complete assigned tasks, and produce measurable results" (250; see Hymes). She advocates a more appropriate stance for language learning and uses the term "symbolic competence" to foreground the new set of skills that have been ignored in the latter-day erosion of the original concept of "communicative competence" (250). By "symbolic competence," Kramsch appears to mean an understanding of the array of possible contexts surrounding communicative exchanges, uttered or written by speakers and authors from other cultural backgrounds. Perhaps taking a jab at Krashen's notion of "comprehensible input," Kramsch seems to imply that understanding the input alone is not sufficient for learners to comprehend these arrays of possible values, contexts, situations, and meanings that are at the heart of communication, particularly in a world where native monolingual speakers are not likely the norm:

> In order to understand others, we have to understand what they remember from the past, what they imagine and project onto the future, and how they position themselves in the present. And we have to understand the same things of ourselves. This understanding cannot come from merely being exposed to authentic and comprehensible input. In the real world, the input has become inordinately complex: Marketing techniques, newspeak, and political propaganda have commodified meanings and blurred the genres; the Internet has diversified the modalities of meaning making. Today it is not sufficient for learners to know how to communicate meanings; they have to understand the practice of meaning making itself. (251)

Kramsch underscores the importance of "subtle semiotic practices" in revealing to nonnatives how others "position themselves in the world" and how they "find a place for themselves on the global market of symbolic exchanges" (250). Linguistic and semiotic evidence for learners can come from inputs such as texts, recorded speeches, and even RSS (really simple syndication) feeds or audio or video podcasts. Yet Kramsch asks much more of learners than that they comprehend the input. The input, much richer than merely comprehensible language, has a wealth of underlying background cultural knowledge essential for intercultural global exchanges in the twenty-first century.[2]

Technology's Role in Language Teaching

Mark Warschauer and Richard Kern invite renewed explorations of the role of technology (network- or Internet-based dialogic frameworks) as a catalyst for researching and uncovering new language-learning paradigms. In their introduction to *Network-Based Language Teaching*, Kern and Warschauer describe three major perspectives of modern language education: structural, cognitive-constructivist, and sociocognitive (4–7). These categories appear to be chronologically ordered and to imply progressively greater expectations of student performance and autonomous activity as language learners. Increasingly complex primary units of analysis mark this performance, moving from isolated sentences (structural) to sentences and connected discourse (cognitive) to stretches of connected discourse (sociocognitive). Kern and Warschauer reflect on how technology has accompanied each of the three pedagogic perspectives:

> Interestingly, shifts in perspectives on language learning and teaching have paralleled developments in technology from the mainframe to the personal to the networked computer. As will be seen, they also correspond roughly to three metaphors of computer-based education posited by Charles Crook (1994): namely, a tutorial metaphor (computer-as-tutor), a construction metaphor (computer-as-pupil), and a toolbox metaphor (computer-as-tool). (7)

Effective e-learning programs have been shown to appropriate a variety of these metaphorical computer functions, depending on the needs and position of students on the skills-getting and skills-using continuum. In the period of the computer-as-tool metaphor, drill and practice on specific language forms supplemented class instruction. Terminal feedback provided learners with correct answers and the opportunity to correct their responses (see descriptions of the early *PLATO* system at the University of Illinois, Urbana [Wooley]). The goal of this type of online education appeared to "focus on forms" rather than on meaningful contacts for language communication (Doughty and Long 63).

The period of the computer-as pupil featured online communicatively based or task-based exercises that often focused on listening and reading skills in hypertextual environments, providing the print or media links to contextualize the cultural meaning of texts. The Internet, as it appeared early on in labs and classrooms in the 1990s, gave learners access to a new world of native-language texts. In those days, techno-logical constraints limited interactivity among learners and focused feedback.

In contrast, task-based learning methodological principles relate well to the possibility of creating "optimal psycholinguistic environments" for e-learning (Doughty and Long 52). Catherine J. Doughty and Michael H. Long elaborate elements of well-conceived task-based distance-education programs that effectively address the learner's need for communicative practice while emphasizing a form. In ten methodological principles that they contrast with pedagogical procedures, Doughty and Long stress that the student completes a specific task or set of related tasks, accessing "elaborate" input to shape language use, employing inductive reasoning in learning, receiving "negative feedback" on performance,[3] negotiating meaning through interaction or simulated interactions, and engaging in collaborative learning (66–76). In their examples, the task itself functions as the "unit of analysis in place of the text" (52). Texts used in support of the task should be "elaborated" and authentic, not simplified (58).

Doughty and Long conceive of the use of technology as a "pedagogic procedure" that in and of itself has no inherent "necessary or sufficient" psycholinguistic attributes that contribute to learning (54). They also unfortunately find that no existing distance-learning program that fo-cuses on task-based instruction in the teaching of less commonly taught languages (LCTLs) fully demonstrates in practice the principles they es-pouse. Yet they do illustrate how to implement their principles in three situ-ations that lend themselves as informants to future distance-education of-ferings in LCTLs. These situations illustrate how an instructor's precourse analysis of the specific language tasks for putative learner cohorts can deter-mine the content and direction of the online learning environment. Finally, they advocate that instructors using rich input (audio, video, and text-based corpora, dictionaries, and concordancing tools) construct task-specific cor-pora for use by students (52).

The need for learners to use rich input appears to link Doughty and Long's task-based language teaching approach to Krashen and Terrell (input at the i + 1 level) and to the communicative competency movement. Several elements of their "focus on form" concept (53), however, contrast sharply with "focus on meaning" communicative language-teaching prin-ciples. Without returning to discrete-point grammar-driven syllabus, Doughty and Long draw the learner's attention to producing language that is accurate and appropriate to the needs of a particular situation. While they promote cooperative and collaborative learning as important to tasked-based language learning, they also cite research findings of network-based language teaching environments where failure to articulate clear goals for collaborative tasks at the beginning caused students to disengage with the technology and, hence, with one another (66). The tasks appear fairly predictable and immutable, with few variations in the script, particularly in the distance-education iteration, where the instructor or other native speaker is not present to mediate or negotiate meanings across a broad range of possible responses.

Warschauer suggests that sociocultural theory might provide an appropriate "lens" to view the array of new online approaches to language learning ("Sociocultural Perspectives" 48). Scholars as varied as L. S. Vygotsky, J. V. Wertsch, and Jean Lave and Etienne Wenger, as cited in Warschauer (41–44), urge readers to reflect on practices of second-language practitioners and theorists of the twentieth century and to consider investigations of intercultural communications privileged and enabled by the advent of global networks.

Thus researchers associated with sociocognitive perspectives (Warschauer and Kern; Thorne, "Artifacts"; Belz; Warschauer, "Sociocultural Perspectives"), unlike Doughty and Long, do not assign a neutral role to computer technology. Rather, technological tools mediate all human activity (Warschauer "Sociocultural Perspectives"; see also Vygotsky, "Genesis," and Wertsch). To understand computer-assisted language learning, in the sociocultural or sociocognitive framework, one must place it in "its broader historical, social, and cultural contexts" (Warschauer, "Sociocultural Perspectives" 43).

Learners and Teachers: Digital Natives, Digital Immigrants

Several contributing factors have converged to create an arguably privileged, pivotal role for effective intercultural e-learning environments, particularly those situated within a sociocognitive learning paradigm. First, a new conceptualization of e-learners as globally connected "communities of learners" has valorized the use of many contexts and reference points that reflect learners' diversity (Warschauer, *Electronic Literacies*; Kern and Warschauer). Second, sociocultural (sociocognitive) theoretical frameworks of collaborative learning have effectively assigned a role for these communicative technologies in situated language learning (Vygotsky,

Thought; Lantolf; Thorne, "Artifacts," *Second Language Acquisition*), applications for which Warshauer and Kern illustrate in their seminal work *Network-Based Language Teaching*. Meaning making in sociocultural contexts is expressed in a deeply personal manner, and students are thus engaged in collaborative tasks that have relevance and importance to them as learners.

Finally, present-day language learners exhibit distinctly different profiles from those of the previous generation: though at times older, they are more comfortable with technology than their instructors. Globally connected through the Internet and other communication technologies, the younger generation of college-bound students, in particular, have been "born digital" (Prensky). Marc Prensky characterizes their instructors, on the other hand, as "digital immigrants."[4] They are just learning to use computers as tools of instruction and are experimenting with their possible functions as intercultural communication devices.[5]

Thorne summarizes three case studies that poignantly illustrate the generation gap between digital immigrant teachers and their digital native students, as well as clashes in intercultural understanding occurring between French and American peers ("Artifacts" 34–56). In each case study, researchers' expectations that technology would enhance intercultural communicative practices among peers from the two countries were dashed or at least partially disappointed. In two cases, the peer-to-peer intercultural communication difficulties were actually resolved by the students themselves when they chose another more peer-friendly technology (instant messaging, or IM) over the one required by the researcher (e-mail).[6] These three case studies underscore the meditative effect of the computer-as-tool and the transformative function that technology played in the outcomes of the research. When e-mail proved to be dysfunctional, one party broke the ice and suggested using IM in what might be categorized as "illicit" learning, that is, an activity that could not be tracked within the system for later analysis and was, therefore, not part of the learner's official grade. It was precisely in this nonsanctioned space where real intercultural communication and language learning occurred.

Learning Management Systems

Learning management systems, also referred to as course management systems, have hastened the technology-learning process for digital immigrants.

Learning management systems include the ubiquitous *Blackboard* and *WebCT* and also encompass newer developments, notably *ANGEL* and *Moodle*. The advantages of learning management systems are many: they are easy for instructors to learn; they allow course content, such as syllabi and course requirements, to be posted on the Internet instantly; instructors can create quizzes that are typically self-correcting, or, for open-ended questions, that allow instructors to manually enter scores. Media and print resources can be electronically appended and made available to students in the course at any time, and, since they are password-protected, faculty members can easily comply with legal provisions of fair use guidelines for copyrighted material (see *CONFU*).

Learning management systems as course-authoring systems assume no particular underlying pedagogical perspectives but allow instructors the flexibility of choosing and building their own methodologies into the system. (These systems, of course, are only as good as the instructor's teaching abilities and instructional design.) As Warschauer and Kern, Thorne ("Artifacts"), and Kramsch and Thorne say, learning management systems have interpersonal communicative functionality, that is, virtual classroom capabilities: interactive whiteboards, synchronous chat, and ancillary programs such as *Horizon Wimba*, which features audio capabilities and Voice over Internet Protocol. Many systems also enable text messaging or IM. The advantage to the second-language researcher is that all this communication is tracked electronically and stored for later analysis.

Finally, with group work, discussion boards, and forums, students can communicate with one another and with instructors in asynchronous mode, replicating features found in networked communication software such as *Daedalus Interchange* and described in some earlier research studies as supporting sociocultural and sociocognitive approaches (see Warschauer, *Electronic Literacies*; Beauvois; Chun). Configured as such, these learning management systems support sociocognitive theoretical, behaviorist, and cognitively inspired approaches. (True/false, multiple choice, and fill-in-the blank questions are options built into the system for assessment, allowing for drills and comprehension-based activities.)

Blackboard and *WebCT* automatically enter students enrolled in a class on a subscribing campus through the learning management system. In the latest iterations of these systems, student data, including e-mail addresses and other contact information, no longer need to be manually entered by the instructor before the class or by students after they have enrolled. Information comes directly from student enrollment services. As long as student data are up-to-date, they are seamlessly conveyed to the system and to the instructor. This data-transfer capability helps the instructor, who can instead focus on the architecture and content of the course and the task of securing supporting documents, authentic materials, and media contained in the courseware. All materials, once gathered, remain available 24-7 and are archived beyond the end of the course. Instructors can reorganize the course content and even migrate the course from a hybrid mode (partially face-to-face, partially online) to a purely distance-education offering.

The disadvantages of learning management systems, however, may outweigh their advantages in one important way. Engaging international peers in dialogic and collaborative learning, as mentioned by Thorne and by Warschauer and Kern, among others, is virtually precluded by the learning management system, particularly in the newest versions. The learning management systems supporting sociocognitive theoretical approaches with synchronous chat and discussion boards do not allow participation by international peers or groups of students in external systems. Students who are not officially enrolled in a particular class are shut out from the learning management system environment. Rich intercultural communication and dialogic exchange among members of various cultures, as envisioned by proponents of sociocultural language-learning perspectives, is thus precluded by system constraints. For some disciplines represented in subscribing higher-education institutions, this limitation is not problematic, but for intercultural e-learning in world-language classes, it is a fatal flaw.

Using *Moodle* or other open-source learning management systems bypasses institutional constraints imposed by the registration system and by the concept of institutional subscription to allow those outside the system to participate in intercultural communicative activities. Open-source systems are collaboratively and incrementally developed by a community of interdisciplinary scholars and computer scientists committed to sharing development costs, information, research, and maintenance of the system. Open-source learning management systems have the same features, including an archival and tracking system, that are attractive to institutions and to teachers. The possibility of open enrollment and of incorporating newly emerging tools makes these systems amenable to evolution.

Demographics of E-Learners: Who Are They, What Do They Want?

It is clear that the changing demographics of the population of higher-education learners affect how and what is learned. As Kramsch says, the exigencies of modern society require learners to shift from producing language without much consideration of underlying culture-bound meaning to skillfully attending to what is beneath the surface, embedded in authentic texts and discourse features of speech. Communications spanning a wide range of modalities that are used by a language community thus become legitimized and valued as objects of study and debate.

Significant changes in our society have occurred since the 1970s, when communicative competence and communicative language teaching started to prevail. Especially in urban, multicultural environments, college-age students come into frequent contact with those skilled and experienced in negotiating multicultural communicative exchanges (Kramsch). Compared with their past counterparts, today's students are more predisposed to demand relevance and meaning from these exchanges and are less inclined to engage in work they perceive to be nonessential or to use technologies they perceive as *vieux jeu*. From their familiarity with the Internet, today's students—much more than their predecessors—have come to expect 24-7 access to online resources. They are also rapidly going beyond the computer in exploring technology as tool. Handheld communication tools (personal digital assistants, or PDAs) and text messaging on cell phones in multilingual formats, genres of communication that occur outside the confines of the physical classroom, have become de rigueur. Can we keep up with these tools, inserting what our knowledge and experience have revealed to us as best practices in e–language learning?

Online communication has taken on an increasingly global perspective, and although English was at first dominant as the language of Internet-based communication, other languages (Chinese in particular) are positioned to challenge English as the default language of global communicative exchanges. Technologies that emphasize multilingual formats in textual displays, as in IM and text messaging, will be essential to cross-cultural communication among peers.

Examples from the Field: Convergences of Theory and Practice

Meaningful content- and task-based instruction coupled with appropriate goals and online activities that reflect learners' particular needs have proved effective in enhancing cultural learning. To be fair, Doughty and Long cite no working examples of online task-based learning in less commonly taught languages, and Thorne ("Artifacts"), Julie A. Belz, and Kramsch and Thorne relay several counterexamples from sociocultural research studies where the choice of tool or lack of access to technology thwarted the intercultural communicative potentials of participants. Numerous ongoing research studies, however, show that computer-assisted task-based learning or sociocultural learning (or learning motivated by other perspectives) occurs with satisfying and significant results (Kern, Ware, and Warschauer).

The *Cultura* intercultural communications project at the Massachusetts Institute of Technology and the Institut National de Télécommunications, developed by Gilberte Furstenberg, Sabine Levet, and Shoggy Waryn (see Furstenberg; Furstenberg, Levet, English, and Maillet), stands out as exemplary. This project has illustrated and documented growth in participants' cross-cultural understanding through the use of online dialogic exploration of topics occurring naturally in the performance of communicative tasks shared by two intact cohorts, one French, the other American. (See Kern, Ware, and Warschauer for an evaluation of the importance of this project.) *Cultura* enables peer participants from Paris, France, and Cambridge, Massachusetts, to view, post, and comment on media, film, photography, and other artifacts of culture. American students communicate in English and French students in French about what objects might signify. Unlike students in the telecollaborative research projects at Pennsylvania State University, neither side's communicative output is constrained by the need to produce nonnative target language. French inquiries about what Americans really mean when they use the word *love* in seemingly trivial communications with a French speaker require each cohort to use the native language because of their relative lack of proficiency in the second language. International cohorts communicate over the Internet and see a nonnative language naturally produced in the exchange. The coconstructed Web site is archived and allows participants to reference past exchanges. The exchange of ideas about culture engages in semiotic analysis of the sort outlined by Kramsch as essential to understanding the complexity of living in an increasingly global economy. Kern, Ware, and Warschauer note the change in the role of the student, as well as the teacher:

> Through the interactive exchange of viewpoints and perspectives, students using Cultura are not "receiving culture" but are involved in a reciprocal construction of one another's cultures . . . created and *problematized* through juxtapositions of materials, interpretations, and responses to interpretations. . . . The teacher shifts out of the "omniscient informant" role and focuses on structuring, juxtaposition, interpreting on intercultural experiences. (249)

Cultura was designed to initiate intermediate-level language learners into the fascinating world of cross-cultural exchange, looking at cultural content not from a monolithic viewpoint but in ways that reflect the multiplicity of speakers' backgrounds. The question remains: What happens next in the foreign language curriculum? The level of intensity and interest generated by intermediate-level learners on both shores appears remarkable, but how can this enthusiasm be transformed later in the course sequence into the French-French (or English-English) language usage required in advanced-level coursework and beyond?

Cultura is not a fully fledged distance-education course but rather a supportive ancillary intercultural communicative activity, arranged through collaboration by professors at each institution. As such, it is fragile, dependent on the good will of each supporting institution and the professors who arrange to continue the exchange. Institutionalization of the approach, involving long-range curricular planning at both sites, will decrease the program's fragility. Each site must also plan for and fund evolving technological platforms to support e-learning for the long-term viability of the program. In addition, both sites should anticipate how to bring learners more profoundly transformative and memorable learning experiences that will lead them not only to the next level of proficiency but also toward the intercultural competency needed in today's increasingly globalized societies.

Appearances notwithstanding, this essay is not a sweeping, all-inclusive overview of e-learning projects in world languages, from the early correspondence study models to the distance-education movement and the recent distributed learning (hybrid or blended) approaches. Such an overview is an ambitious undertaking best reserved for a book-length work that also involves international researchers and distance educators.

Several topics worthy of mention are missing here, such as the pros and cons of distance or on-line versus face-to-face language learning and teaching. Research summarized by Thomas L. Russell inexorably points to the "no significant difference" phenomenon, partially because the assumptions of many of these studies are inherently flawed (see also *No Significant Difference Phenomenon*). It does not feature programs that illustrate best practices and serve as models for new online language-learning programs. Many researchers have detailed these programs extensively (Godwin-Jones; United States). Others have underscored the importance of linking local institutional contexts to a well-defined population of online learners and their unique needs. Best practices models may fail to perform as described in the literature with different target populations and institutional settings or constraints. Finally, the reader must check elsewhere for endorsements of model applications. The technologies to support distance education are now widely available, and what is problematized are pedagogies and their accompanying assumptions, including the technologies of practice used naturally by today's digital natives (Kramsch).

To return to our original question—how to create environments where language learners might find relevance and meaning—we again ask, Where do we go from here? Why is Father Guido Sarducci as humorous today as he was in the 1980s?

The world has changed immensely since the Sputnik era, the cold war, and the audiolingual method of language learning, and especially since the 1980s, when communicative language teaching emerged as the dominant perspective in language classrooms. Since that time, through reflective practice and refinement of learners' interactive role in acquiring language competence using their own online tools, new paradigms of language learning have emerged that merit serious consideration.

The challenge for world language educators today, as it was then, is to create, or to facilitate the creation of, learning environments that are memorable, relevant, meaningful, and affordable for all participants enrolled in either on-line or face-to-face classes. Both learning environments must give high-quality educational experiences: both must reduce the escalating costs associated with higher education and make educational opportunities available to students from many backgrounds, using broadly available technologies.

Theoretical models deriving from inquiries as disparate as constructivism (Jonassen, Beissner, and Yacci; Duffy and Jonassen), social interactionism (Lantolf), and interactionism (Moore, "Editorial," "Independent Study," "Learner Autonomy") can assist in imagining the backbones of the system. Language acquisition theories, particularly related to the importance of input and methodologies that highlight "noticing" (Schmidt) or "focusing on form" (Doughty and Long) also contribute to shaping what is on the surface.

Adopting task-based learning principles, with an in-depth analysis of learner needs before online-course implementation, will suggest a pragmatic list of tasks, corresponding to what learners want and need in the here and now. In an uncertain future, however, where graduates change jobs and even professions more frequently than in the past, today's pressing tasks cannot entirely predict future ones. Any task analysis that projects present or future needs should, however, envisage e-learners in dialogic communication with other cultures, using tools that attain the status of "agency" where the tools themselves act as significant players in affecting outcomes (Thorne, "Artifacts"). Keeping up with the Bob Godwin-Joneses will tell us what technologies are on the horizon and which ones today's youth are likely to use in cross-cultural communications. Awareness of new paradigms in online education, as suggested by sociocultural and sociocognitive frameworks, will ensure the success of programs in which students may well be set to engage native speakers from another language culture in intercultural dialogue.

Notes

1. See Hadley; Savignon; Larsen-Freeman; Kern and Warschauer 3–7; Kern, Ware, and Warschauer; and Kramsch. The United States Department of Defense report ties these approaches to accompanying technologies (5–11). See also Liu, Moore, Graham, and Lee.

2. Steinhart laments the overemphasis on oral skills in proficiency-based or communicative competence-based classrooms and the exclusion of content in basic language acquisition classes. As a consequence, she argues, reading and writing abilities have declined, and both students and their teachers thus lose the possibility of teaming up with international peers on collaborative projects, such as those advocated by the American Council on the Teaching of Foreign Languages (*Standards*).

3. "Negative feedback" as used in task-based language teaching refers to a variety of error-correction strategies that cause learners to modify their output (Doughty and Long 54).

4. Prensky coined the terms "digital natives" and "digital immigrants" to differentiate between those who were "born digital" and those who have learned or are still learning to adapt to the digital era.

5. Two studies that have found evidence of this generational conflict are the Pennsylvania State University's Telecollaboration Project, funded by the United States Department of Education International Research and Studies Program grant (CDFA 84.017A; Thorne, "Artifacts"; Belz), and Kramsch and Thorne's study at the University of California, Berkeley ("Foreign Languages"). Thorne was a coprincipal investigator for the Telecollaboration Project.

6. IM appears to be the preferred means of communication among digital natives. It is closer to synchronous communication than e-mail, which Thorne's research subject uses only to communicate with teachers and parents ("Artifacts" 56).

Works Cited

American Council on the Teaching of Foreign Languages. *Proficiency Guidelines: Speaking. American Council on the Teaching of Foreign Languages.* Amer. Council on the Teaching of For. Langs., 1999. Web. 27 June 2006.

———. *Standards for Foreign Language Learning: Preparing for the Twenty-First Century. American Council on the Teaching of Foreign Languages.* Amer. Council on the Teaching of For. Langs., 1996. Web. 27 June 2006.

Beauvois, Margaret Healy. "E-Talk: Computer-Assisted Classroom Discussion—Attitudes and Motivation." Swaffar, Romano, Markley, and Arens 99–120.

Belz, Julie A. "Linguistic Perspectives on the Development of Intercultural Competence in Telecollaboration." *Language Learning and Technology* 7.2 (2003): 68–117. Web. 6 Nov. 2008.

Breen, Michael P., and Christopher N. Candlin. "The Essentials of a Communicative Curriculum in Language Teaching." *Applied Linguistics* 1.2 (1980): 89–112. Print.

Chomsky, Noam. *Aspects of the Theory of Syntax.* Cambridge: MIT P, 1965. Print.

———. "A Review of B. F. Skinner's *Verbal Behavior.*" *Language* 35.1 (1959): 26–58. Print.

Chun, Dorothy M. "Using Computer-Assisted Class Discussion to Facilitate the Acquisition of Interactive Competence." Swaffar, Romano, Markley, and Arens 57–80.

CONFU: The Conference on Fair Use. Crash Course in Copyright. U of Texas, 2001. Web. 16 July 2006.

Doughty, Catherine J., and Michael H. Long. "Optimal Psycholinguistic Environments for Distance Foreign Language Learning." *Language Learning and Technology* 7.3 (2003): 50–80. Web. 16 July 2006.

Duffy, Thomas M., and David H. Jonassen, eds. *Constructivism and the Technology of Instruction: A Conversation.* Hillsdale: Erlbaum, 1992. Print.

Furstenberg, Gilberte. "Reading between the Cultural Lines." *Reading between the Lines: Perspectives on Foreign Language Literacy.* Ed. Peter C. Patrikis. New Haven: Yale UP, 2003. 74–98. Print.

Furstenberg, Gilberte, Sabine Levet, Kathryn English, and Katherine Maillet. "Giving a Virtual Voice to the Silent Language of Culture: The Cultura Project." *Language Learning and Technology* 5.1 (2001): 55–102. Web. 6 Nov. 2008.

Godwin-Jones, Bob. "Emerging Technologies: Tools for Distance Education: Towards Convergence and Integration." *Language Learning and Technology* 7.3 (2003): 18–22. Web. 16 July 2006.

Hadley, Alice Omaggio. *Teaching Language in Context: Proficiency-Oriented Instruction*. 2nd ed. Boston: Heinle, 1993. Print.

Hymes, Dell. "On Communicative Competence." *Sociolinguistics: Selected Readings*. Ed. J. B. Pride and Janet Holmes. Harmondsworth: Penguin, 1972. 269–83. Print.

Jonassen, David H., Katherine Beissner, and Michael Yacci. *Structural Knowledge: Techniques for Representing, Conveying, and Acquiring Structural Knowledge*. Hillsdale: Erlbaum, 1993. Print.

Kern, Richard, and Mark Warschauer. "Introduction: Theory and Practice of Network-Based Language Teaching." Warschauer and Kern 1–19.

Kern, Richard, Paige Ware, and Mark Warschauer. "Crossing Frontiers: New Directions in Online Pedagogy and Research." *Annual Review of Applied Linguistics* 24 (2004): 243–60. Print.

Kramsch, Claire. "From Communicative Competence to Symbolic Competence." *Modern Language Journal* 90.2 (2006): 249–52. Print.

Kramsch, Claire, and Steven L. Thorne. "Foreign Language Learning as Global Communicative Practice." *Globalization and Language Teaching*. Ed. Deborah Cameron and David Block. New York: Routledge, 2002. 83–100. Print.

Krashen, Stephen D. *Principles and Practice in Second Language Acquisition*. London: Prentice, 1982. Print. English Language Teaching Series.

Krashen, Stephen D., and Tracy D. Terrell. *The Natural Approach: Language Acquisition in the Classroom*. Hayward: Alemany, 1983. Print.

Lantolf, James P. "Second Culture Acquisition: Cognitive Considerations." *Culture in Second Language Teaching and Learning*. Ed. Eli Hinkel. Cambridge: Cambridge UP, 1998. 28–46. Print.

Larsen-Freeman, D. "Second Language Acquisition Research: Staking Out the Territory." *TESOL Quarterly* 25.2 (1991): 315–42. Print.

Lave, Jean, and Etienne Wenger. *Situated Learning: Legitimate Peripheral Participation*. Cambridge: Cambridge UP, 1991. Print.

Liu, Min, Zena Moore, Leah Graham, and Shinwoong Lee. "A Look at the Research on Computer-Based Technology Use in Second Language Learning: A Review of the Literature from 1990–2000." *Journal of Research on Technology in Education* 34.3 (2002): 250+. *Questia*. Web. 15 July 2006.

Moore, Michael G. "Editorial: Distance Education Theory." *American Journal of Distance Education* 5.3 (1991): n. pag. Web. 30 Sept. 2006.

———. "Independent Study." *Redefining the Discipline of Adult Education*. Ed. Robert D. Boyd, Jerold W. Apps, et al. San Francisco: Jossey-Bass, 1980. 16–31. *American Center for the Study of Distance Learning*. Web. 2 Sept. 2006.

———. "Learner Autonomy: The Second Dimension of Independent Learning." *Convergence* 5.2 (1972): 76–87. *American Center for the Study of Distance Learning*. Web. 2 Sept. 2006.

The No Significant Difference Phenomenon. Western Cooperature for Educ. Tele-communications, 2008. Web. 6 Nov. 2008.

Novello, Don. "Father Guido Sarducci's Five-Minute University Video." *Carteret County Public School System.* Carteret County Public School System, n.d. Web. 10 Nov. 2008.

Prensky, Marc. "Digital Natives, Digital Immigrants." *On the Horizon* 9.5 (2001): 1–6. Web. 8 July 2006.

Russell, Thomas L. *The No Significant Difference Phenomenon.* 5th ed. Raleigh: Intl. Distance Educ. Certification Center, North Carolina State U, 2001. Print.

Savignon, Sandra J. *Communicative Competence: Theory and Classroom Practice: Texts and Contexts in Second Language Learning.* 2nd ed. New York: McGraw, 1997. Print.

Schmidt, Richard. "Attention." *Cognition and Second Language Instruction.* Ed. Peter Robinson. Cambridge: Cambridge UP, 2001. 3–32. Print.

Schulz, Renate A. "Reevaluating Communicative Competence as a Major Goal in Postsecondary Language Requirement Courses." *Modern Language Journal* 90.2 (2006): 252–55. Print.

Selinker, Larry. "Interlanguage." *International Review of Applied Linguistics in Language Teaching* 10.3 (1972): 209–31. Print.

Skinner, B. F. *Verbal Behavior.* New York: Appleton, 1957. Print.

Steinhart, Margot. "Breaching the Artificial Barrier between Communicative Competence and Content." *Modern Language Journal* 90.2 (2006): 258–62. Print.

Swaffer, Janet K., Susan Romano, Phillip Markley, and Katherine Arens, eds. *Language Learning Online: Theory and Practice in the ESL and L2 Computer Classroom.* Austin: Daedulus, 1998. Print.

Thorne, Steven L. "Artifacts and Cultures-of-Use in Intercultural Communication." *Language Learning and Technology* 7.2 (2003): 38–67. Web. 7 July 2006.

———. *Second Language Acquisition and the Truth(s) about Relativity. Center for Language Acquisition.* Pennsylvania State U, 2007. Web. 6 Nov. 2008.

United States. Dept. of Defense. *Second Language Acquisition: Analysis of Innovation.* Navy Human Capital Development. Comp. George Coffin for Ken Wagar. 30 Apr. 2006. Print. Unclassified document.

Valdés, Guadalupe. "Nonnative English Speakers: Language Bigotry in English Mainstream Classrooms." *ADE Bulletin* 124 (2000): 12–17. *Modern Language Association.* Web. 10 July 2006.

Vygotsky, L. S. "The Genesis of Higher Mental Functions." *The Concept of Activity in Soviet Psychology.* Ed. J. V. Wertsch. Armonk: Sharpe, 1981. 141–88. Print.

———. *Thought and Language.* Ed. and trans. Eugenia Hanfmann and Gertrude Vakar. Cambridge: MIT P, 1962. Print.

Warschauer, Mark. *Electronic Literacies: Language, Culture, and Power in Online Education.* Mahwah: Erlbaum, 1999. Print.

———. "Sociocultural Perspectives on CALL." *CALL Research Perspectives.* Ed. Joy L. Egbert and Gina Mikel Petrie. Mahwah: Erlbaum, 2005. 41–51. *University of California, Irvine, Department of Education.* Web. 10 July 2006.

Warschauer, Mark, and Richard Kern, eds. *Networked-Based Language Teaching: Concepts and Practice*. New York: Cambridge UP, 2000. Print.

Watson, John B. "Is Thinking Merely the Action of Language Mechanisms?" *British Journal of Psychology* 11 (1920): 87–104. Print.

Wertsch, J. V. *Voices of the Mind: A Sociocultural Approach to Mediated Action*. Cambridge: Harvard UP, 1991. Print.

Wooley, David R. *PLATO: The Emergence of Online Community. Thinkofit*. Thinkofit, 2008. Web. 6 Nov. 2008.

Jerome McGann

Humane Studies in Digital Space

Central Questions for Humanities Education and Digital Technologies

With respect to the use of digital technology among humanities scholars in colleges and universities today (2006), the widespread reality is that the greater the institution's primary mission is conceived in research terms, the less will the faculty be involved with digital technology. Educators now regularly use e-mail and word processing, and casual, non-authoritative online reference work is also increasingly common. Beyond that, however, few humanities educators in the so-called major research institutions have ventured. At my institution, the University of Virginia, which is well-known for its commitment to digital scholarship, the situation has scarcely changed since 1992, when I first began my serious involvement with digital resources. At that time, four faculty members in an English department of some four dozen were actively engaged with digital work. Today we have five.

This state of affairs is particularly arresting because of the changes that have come in the intervening years. On the one hand, we witness remarkable advances in technology—the World Wide Web, *Google* and

Google Scholar, vast online repositories of important cultural materials. On the other hand, we observe, with marked apprehension, the rapidly growing crisis in paper-based scholarly publishing. No one today can doubt that scholarly research exchanges—communication and authorized publication—will be, will have to be, digitally organized and executed in a regular way very soon. We have few institutional mechanisms for such activities. It seems that because the faculties at major research institutions can still, for the most part, use existing paper-based entities for scholarly exchange, a shift to online research and publication has not been felt as urgent.

Reflecting on this situation several years ago, I wrote:

> [T]he general field of humanities education and scholarship will not take the use of digital technology seriously until one demonstrates how its tools improve the ways we explore and explain aesthetic works—until, that is, they expand our interpretational procedures.
> (*Radiant Textuality* xii)

This assessment still seems true to me, though now it also seems not true enough. To make the transition to digital resources, educators and scholars need professionally sanctioned online-publishing mechanisms. More than that, we need to have such mechanisms completely integrated with our research work and the "interpretational procedures" in which it is invested.[1]

Varieties of Online Educational Experience

Online teaching usually means three kinds of activities. First, it applies to courses offered online either by traditional colleges and universities or by the recently founded online colleges and universities: online distance learning.

Second, it applies to a variety of learning activities that can be enabled by digital technology. Software has been designed that allows students to interact with one another and with their course instructor—communicating and collaborating in various ways—outside the classroom and at any convenient time. The interaction can be chat-informal, or it can be organized in whatever more formal ways might seem useful for the particular circumstances. Students can share work and turn in their assignments electronically, instructors can respond the same way, special work groups can be arranged, textual, audial, and visual course materials can be put online or made URL-accessible. For the instructor, additional benefits offered by this kind of digital technology involve automated book orders, course enrollments, and grading.[2]

Third, online teaching can mean that students use and investigate various online materials—Web sites, databases, games, wikis, and so on—and (perhaps) create their own digital materials for their course assignments.

For the humanities educator in particular, some of these digital resources can be quite useful. The seminar classroom has been perhaps the optimal space and time for traditional humanities education because it promotes the conversation and exchange that puts a student's individual studies and investigations into a scene of critical reflection so that students can work together and interact at every stage of their learning.

In our work at the University of Virginia at the Institute for Advanced Technology in the Humanities (IATH) and the Applied Research in Patacriticism group (ARP), our focus has been elsewhere. We have been primarily concerned with books and our vast legacy of paper-based knowledge and information. As our conversations and exchanges get increasingly invested in digital environments and as we produce increasing amounts of born-digital objects of various kinds, questions have come up: What is the importance of our paper-based inheritance? How might we engage with it? And what contribution—beyond its raw content—does it make to a learning scene that is getting digitally transformed?

These questions are pertinent because, contrary to the view of many, what we call the book is both an index and a metonym for a machinery that functions very like digital technologies. *The book* locates a highly articulated set of simulation mechanisms for storing, accessing, distributing, and remediating knowledge and information. *Hypertext* and *remediation* are new words for very ancient processes and devices. Thus the study of bibliographic machineries in all their networked complexity is never more urgent than at this moment, when we are trying to learn how to think about and use our new digital resources (see Chartier; Johns).

Briefly, and perhaps provocatively, then, I will say this at the outset: if we want to develop strong online educational resources, we should begin by putting the study of books at the center of our attention. That view, at any rate, has guided all the work that we have been doing over the past twelve years at the University of Virginia.

The Rossetti Archive as a Scene of Critical Reflection

Our development work has been focused on three pieces of software: *IVANHOE*, *Juxta*, and finally *Collex*.[3] *IVANHOE* is a collaborative on-line game space for investigating cultural materials, particularly imaginative materials like stories and poems (though it can be and has been used for any kind of material, digital or paper-based, imaginative or informational). *Juxta* is a device for comparing and collating the differences between equivalent textual works (like different editions of *Bleak House* or versions of "The Lake Isle of Innisfree") and outputting schedules of differences by line or paragraph or any defined textual unit. *Collex*—a mechanism for collecting and exhibiting online-accessible materials—is a set of functionalities that facilitate the creation and publication of critical studies of cultural work. *Collex* is the decisive mechanism for promoting online peer-reviewed scholarship and its publication.

Each of these software development projects grew out of our work on *The Rossetti Archive*, which we began to design and build in 1992 (McGann). We came to see the educational usefulness for humanists of certain types of software—in fact, the need and pertinence of it for college and university scholars—in the course of our work on the *Archive*. What we learned was not entirely fortuitous, though in many respects it was surprising.

The Rossetti Archive began with an initial design premise: it should be structured on the assumption that the *Archive* would function in a totally digital knowledge environment, as if all the world's libraries and museums were already online and connected. Absurd in obvious ways, the premise created (or rather, exposed) numerous and often insurmountable difficulties. But in one key respect it was the correct one to assume. It forced us to think about the structure of *The Rossetti Archive* not as a stand-alone scholarly project—a kind of object—but as a social space and system.

Of course, the *Archive* was also being built from ideas about knowledge representation based on the technology of the book, so different in so many ways from digital technology. The tension, or collision, between these two technologies, proved fruitful and enlightening.[4]

From the outset, the *Archive* was conceived less as an edition or body of textual and graphical content than as a laboratory for reflecting critically on the design and creation of the *Archive* itself. Taking the development process as our primary subject, we hoped to learn more about how the scholarly and educational interests of traditional humanists (like me) might use and benefit from digital tools. As it turned out, these investigations kept pushing us to rethink our primary data, in particular books and their machineries, for in trying to build digital simulations of Dante Gabriel Rossetti's works, we kept discovering that our most basic ideas about these familiar objects were riven with various kinds of illusions and incompetencies (for instance, that a book and any part of it are self-identical entities).

This misconception is technical, perhaps even philosophical, and as such would prove important for the way we approached design and development issues. Ultimately, however, that kind of rethinking proved less catastrophic to our educational and scholarly ideas than the social scene in which our work took place. Developing *The Rossetti Archive* necessarily involved collaboration of a kind that cut across and undermined most of the in-place academic hierarchies of authority, which are based on a ranking of expertise and persons presumed to know. Professors, students (undergraduate as well as graduate), and technicians worked together in ways that shifted the authority structure so that teacher and learner roles were in a perpetually volatile state.

In addition, the interdisciplinarity of the work was substantially altered from what humanists commonly engage with. We were not "English lang and lit" scholars mixing with, say, philosophers or art historians, though that certainly happened. We were those kinds of groups mixing and conversing with computer scientists, mathematicians, librarians, and specialist technicians (systems analysts, programmers of various kinds). Though focused on a single project, we all spoke different languages and approached the work with often radically different attitudes and frames of reference or attention.

In such a research and development scene, traditional ideas about the relation of teacher to student, and hence about the character of an instructional environment, necessarily undergo a critical reevaluation.

Another important feature shaped our work with the *Archive*. It was developed in an institutional framework—IATH—that operated under an assumption common to all research-oriented higher educational entities: that a scholar's research drives the most advanced and interesting pedagogy. To the degree to which this assumption is true, online teaching would have to be closely tied to the research and publishing work that scholars are regularly involved with.

IVANHOE: The First Foray

Named after Walter Scott's famous romance fiction, the software called
IVANHOE is a collaborative online play space for readers interested in
exploring how acts of interpretation get made and reflecting on what
those acts mean or might mean.

The connection to Scott is not incidental. Probably the single most
influential work on later nineteenth-century European fiction, *Ivanhoe*
developed a complex and vastly articulated publication and reception history. That history—a kind of cultural double helix—locates the numerous
changes, modifications, and transformed adaptations that Scott's original
work underwent over time (and continues to undergo). Indeed, the seeds
of those transformations were clearly sown in Scott's original work, as we
can see from its initial reception by readers, many of whom found fault
with the work because its hero, Ivanhoe, in the end marries Rowena and
not Rebecca, who is plainly the book's central female presence—indeed,
she is the book's moral touchstone *tout court*. In other words, *Ivanhoe* had
built into itself certain unresolved tensions and possibilities, of which this
choice was the most apparent, but by no means the only one.

The interpretive situation of Scott's *Ivanhoe* is interesting and important. First, it exemplifies how a work's production and reception histories
comprise schedules of interpretive (transformational) moves made on the
work. Second, in making that situation so apparent (in explicit historical
ways), the work illustrates some key truths about what is involved in interpreting cultural materials: they are not objects but events; furthermore,
they are always collaborative events, building on the work of others; and
finally, they are always transformational, selecting and changing received
materials in a concerted process of understanding what the study of these
materials means or might mean. As such, Scott's work helped shape our
ideas about how to design a piece of software that might "improve the
ways we explore and explain aesthetic works [and thus] expand our interpretational procedures."

The explorations come as active interventions in the textual field that
is the target of the readers' interests. The game space is initially organized
around a work to be interpreted. This might be a single poem or story, a
historical event (say, the Salem witch trials), or some literary or cultural
issue or problem. Players can introduce documents into the field (textual,
audial, visual), they can edit documents in the field (adding or deleting

material from them), and they can link documents together. In making these moves the player is also required to annotate the action with an explanation of its significance. The software stores the documents and actions in a database that preserves the specific character of each, its date, and the specific relationships that players have specified for the moves they make and the materials they have engaged.

These interventions are then returned to the players in various kinds of visual transformations useful for critical reflection on the interpretative process. The reflections appear as computerized transformations of the discourse field—visualizations that expose interpretive relationships and possibilities. The visualizations are mapped to three interrelated coordinates: the players acting in the field; the moves executed by the players (comprising sets of multiple actions); and the documents that are acted on. *IVANHOE* creates a formalized digital space where these three coordinates dynamically interact. Such interactions generate a complex interpretive space whose possibilities of meaning are returned to the interpretive agents in visualizations designed to provoke critical reflection and reexploration.

Because a key object of *IVANHOE* is to promote critical self-awareness in the interpreting agents, the game space requires them to interact not only with the documentary materials but also with the other interpreting agents. Robert Burns's famous observation at the climax of "To a Louse" makes the point of this constraint clear: "O wad some Power the giftie gie us / To see oursels as ithers see us!" (91–92). A second constraint functions in a similar way: the requirement that the players act *en masque*, choosing a role and then operating from the player's understanding of the way that person would be thinking under the given circumstances. The role can be a real or an imaginary person, and players can create and operate in multiple roles. As with any critical move in the game space, players must annotate and explain the roles they adopt.

Designed to promote imaginative acts of critical thinking, *IVANHOE*'s game space is modeled on a seminar or discussion group. It is an educational design that emerged from a certain way of thinking about a course-study setting. The software allows the game initiator—typically, an instructor in a particular course—to modify the game play in various ways, adding further constraints of different kinds. Instructors might assign specific roles rather than leave the choice up to the players; the length of the game play can be set; the type of moves (and the sequence of moves) might be prescribed, and so forth. These added determinations would reflect an instructor's or discussion leader's specific pedagogical or intellectual goals.

Two final comments: *IVANHOE* is perhaps most useful as a tool for promoting imaginative thought experiments and for gaining an initial sense of the possibilities and the limits these entail. Of course, a game play can be organized so that players are constrained toward moves that involve scholarly research. Indeed, the object of study and the role constraint move players to undertake a certain amount of archival research if their game play is to have any real bite or purchase. Thus one game play, initiated in a graduate course on textual theory and method, focused on the problem of William Blake's *The Four Zoas* and how it might be edited. Each student was required to assume the role of a specific critical or editorial scholar and construct an editorial rationale and practical methodology for dealing with Blake's famously intractable text.

Perhaps most important of all, however, *IVANHOE* is a game and as such encourages a freewheeling and ludic attitude in the players. Because this ludic element is a key feature—playing with ideas and materials, coveting the pleasures of surprise, and (so to say) moving about in worlds not realized—*IVANHOE* resists the goal orientation that is built into most research work. The Blake project was undertaken exactly because its intractability exposes the hypothetical character of all editorial ventures and perhaps of all humanistic investigations. *IVANHOE*'s main function is not to answer questions but to expose and explore what questions are interesting in the first place and why. In this pursuit the study of the students—of the scholars—is essential.

Juxta and the Ground of Scholarship

Here is an interesting question: when we play in the *IVANHOE* game space, how do we choose our materials and what do we know about them even before we make any further interpretive moves? Whether we work online or not, that is a fundamental and unevadable question. *Juxta* is a piece of software designed to meet the question and deal with it in an online environment.

> Juxta is a cross-platform tool for collating, comparing, and analyzing any kind or number of textual objects. The tool can set any textual witness as the base text and can filter white space and/or punctuation.

It has several kinds of visualizations, including a heat map of textual differences and a histogram that can expose the filtering results. When collations are being executed, Juxta keys textual transcriptions to the digital images that may stand behind the transcriptions as their documentary base.

Juxta also allows the collations and analyses to be annotated and saved for further use. ("Juxta")

The need for a device that collates and compares equivalent documentary materials is basic to humane studies. Acts of interpretation must distinguish the objects to be investigated. In the case of our cultural inheritance, those objects should be framed with the greatest care so that we know what it is—or what we think it is—that we are trying to study.

In the *Juxta* (as opposed to the *IVANHOE*) frame of reference, then, the primary act of cultural interpretation is the editorial (or curatorial) act. So far as textual works are concerned, critical editing is the fundamental scholarly move, and the critical edition is without question the supreme invention and pursuit of the scholar's work as well as one of the greatest inventions of the human mind. While every interpretive study depends on—indeed, assumes—a reliability in the materials being investigated, few make the status of those materials an issue of critical reflection. We regularly set aside such matters in our interpretive work precisely because the reliability of our materials can be assumed as having been critically established by others.

While this assumption is often necessary, it is also dangerous. Scholars are expected to understand the danger and to set their research programs accordingly, making sure that if they do not make a close study of the status of their materials, at least they are clear about how the materials have been authorized. In short, we regularly assume that others have established the character of the documents we use.

Some of the strongest resistance to online research and scholarship comes from humanists who are well aware of the unreliability of online materials. The problem is especially acute for humanists, whose work requires reliable corpora of data and, above all, documents. It is a truth universally acknowledged, however, that very little of the online archive most important for humanists has been critically examined, authorized, and produced. It is also a truth universally acknowledged, at least in the smaller universe of interested parties, that the establishment of reliable online materials—digital versions of our paper-based archive—is both a difficult and costly task. Shameful to say, this work, like all editorial work, tends to be professionally and institutionally undervalued.

To the degree that online teaching is a function of the reliability of what we read and study (the *Juxta* frame of reference), as opposed to how and why we do this (the *IVANHOE* frame), *Juxta* is another digital tool of first importance. The remediation of our paper-based archive as a trusted online corpus has been slow to develop because we have lacked fundamental text-analysis tools that can be used with a wide variety of materials. Recent projects to put the holdings of great libraries online involve, at best, what scholars call facsimile editions. If done with care these projects can be immensely useful. Nonetheless, their limitations are significant so far as the working teacher and scholar is concerned. The materials come with a minimum of scholarly commentary and they are produced in digital forms that do not lend themselves to critical analysis. *Juxta* was developed to introduce a traditional scholarly perspective to the process of remediating our cultural archive for online study and publication.

Collex and the Project of *NINES*

The need to develop the *Collex* software was created by the decision to establish *NINES*, the *Networked Infrastructure for Nineteenth-Century Electronic Scholarship*. And the establishment of *NINES* came about because a group of nineteenth-century scholars decided to try to develop an online body of peer-reviewed, open-source content for scholars and students working in the long nineteenth century (British and American). This project required two things: a professional or institutional mechanism for vetting and publishing online scholarly work and a set of digital tools that would facilitate born-digital humanities scholarship.

An entity like *NINES*, we can now see, is the implicit demand shaping the history of the development of *The Rossetti Archive*, of *IVANHOE*, of *Juxta*, and, finally, of *Collex*. These individual projects all forecast a situation where the teaching and scholarly work of the humanities scholar are being carried out in an integrated online environment. *IVANHOE* and *Juxta* address two basic critical and research needs of every humanities scholar. *Collex* responds to a third, a need reflecting the scholar's place in the large community of other scholars.

> **Collex** . . . is an open-source collections- and exhibits-builder de-
> signed to aid humanities scholars working in digital collections or
> within federated research environments like NINES. Collex operates
> under the assumption that the best paths through a complex digital
> resource are those forged by use and interpretation.
>
> A Collex approach works to assist scholars in recording, sharing,
> and building on the interpretive purposes to which they put their on-
> line teaching and research environments. ("Collex")

Collex within *NINES* is a model for how humanists can do their regular work in research, teaching, and publishing in an online environment.
The enabling software exploits recent developments in semantic-Web technology so that one can search and collect online materials and then repurpose them as instructional materials for class, as ongoing research projects
to be shared with others, and as online scholarly publications.

Collex is generally based on data-mining software that tracks and organizes the histories of online activities. It is fundamentally the same kind
of technology that became infamous in the recent illegal spying work conducted by the United States government, since it is structurally the same
as the software powering (for example) *Google*'s ability to organize its
searches or *Amazon*'s to propose, when you visit that site, a list of books
that *Amazon* says might interest one. More particularly, it takes inspiration from wiki-type environments and the social software that they promote and thrive on.

Collex refashions that technology for uses pertinent to the day-by-day
activities of scholars and teachers. Most important, *Collex* functions in
the controlled content environment of *NINES*-authorized materials. The
NINES scholar thus always accesses peer-reviewed materials and always
observes the research work of others who are also working only with
peer-reviewed materials. This constraint is fundamental to the reliability
of research and teaching, particularly in the context of an online network
where the available content, especially content of interest to humanists,
has been produced with no scholarly or critical oversight.

In the highly sophisticated social space of paper-based research materials, scholars know immediately how to weigh the authority of their materials and where to engage in serious and interesting scholarly exchanges
(i.e., where to read and publish). Functioning within *NINES*, *Collex* re-
defines the environment to the research needs of scholars and educators.
NINES enables us to search relevant and reliable materials, locate other

scholars who are working in related areas and projects, and publish new content for this population.

In practical terms, *Collex* works within *NINES* to let one

collect, tag, analyze, and annotate trusted objects (digital texts and images vetted for scholarly integrity);

without any special technical training, produce interlinked online exhibits using a set of professional design templates;

share collections and exhibits with students and colleagues, in a variety of output formats for fresh critical perspectives.

Some Final Reflections

It is conceivable that we will not carry on our normal research and scholarly interactions in a paper-based environment for very much longer. Accessing, investigating, and sharing work on our cultural legacy has been supported for more than five centuries by a social software machinery tied to the microtechnology of the book. Today we are not witnessing the disappearance of the book or of book technology, however. Rather, we are watching the demise of book technology as our normal means of scholarly intercourse and communication.

The digital remediation of our cultural inheritance continues to accelerate. To what extent is this process of reediting the materials in our libraries and museums being done with a view to society's interest in scholarship and education? The answer to that question is dismayingly unclear. Certainly one can see that the process to date has been driven primarily by commercial entities, by libraries and museums, and perhaps most of all by individuals operating as independent online agents. The involvement of the broad educational and scholarly community, however, has remained marginal.

Thus the work comes with only a minimal amount of critical reflection on the materials, means, and modes of production that go into this process of remediation. Librarians want to preserve and protect, commerce wants to buy and sell, and individuals want to satisfy very particular desires. These are basic storage, access, and use functions, but they are not in themselves critical functions. Scholars and educators approach the cultural inheritance from a somewhat different perspective. Our vocation is to promote the critical study of these materials across and throughout society at large.

Inherent in that mission is the self-conscious understanding that culture and critical reflection are shared activities and social acts. Reflection outside a social network is not critical reflection; it is either (at best) meditation or (at worst) rumination. So a book is a piece of social software. "Objects (as objects) are fixed and dead," Samuel Taylor Coleridge rightly observed (1: 304), and when digerati—as they commonly do—imagine that digital systems are dynamic whereas the book is inert, they merely exhibit an ignorance one wants to clear away. A book moans round with many voices, all of them by no means linguistic. It is a kind of radio wave from many pasts to any present, a message in a bottle of the possibility of an ongoing social event that requires our participation to continue. We study books to reflect on those social events in a continuing social present where the events get rethought and hence transformed again. If this function did not exist—if we did not need to do this as human beings—one copy of Plato or Aeschylus would suffice, for Plato, Aeschylus, and their works would be self-identical things.

The intercourse of scholars is simply a specialized version of a larger critical conversation we call education. Enabling that conversation to persist and flourish in a communicative system that is digitally based has been the mission of the tools development work described here, and ultimately of *NINES*, the supervening social software mechanism that gives those tools a local habitation and a name.

Since I have been invoking the idea of social software in both general and particular ways, I think one final remark is called for. Wikipedia defines *social software* in this way:

> Common to most definitions of social software, is the observation that some types of software seem to facilitate a more egalitarian and meritocratic "bottom-up" community development, in which membership is voluntary, reputations are earned by winning the trust of other members, and the community's mission and governance are defined by the communities' members themselves.
>
> Communities formed by "bottom-up" processes are often contrasted to the less vibrant collectivities formed by "top-down" software, in which users' roles are determined by an external authority and circumscribed by rigidly conceived software mechanisms (such as access rights). ("Social software")

This comment about software might easily be extended—indeed, frequently has been extended—to describe the difference between a hidebound, arthritic community of pedants obsessed with standards and a "bottom-up" world of "free culture" where work is identified and valued by democratic assent rather than by "top-down" authority. But here a proverb of Blake comes to mind: "These two classes of men are always upon earth and they should be enemies. Whoever seeks to reconcile them seeks to destroy existence" (40). Contradictory imperatives are in play here, each of them representing important values. *NINES* was imagined and founded in the belief that there are communities, not least of all the educational community, that pledge allegiance to both.

The great nineteenth-century German philologist August Boeckh once described his discipline as "Die Erkenntnis der Erkannten" ("the knowledge of what is known"; 11; my trans.). This brilliant formulation captures in the most succinct way the codependent relation that organizes the work of all humane studies and the intimacies that bind the living present to the living past, the noble living—what we would like to be—to the noble dead.

Notes

1. For essential discussions of this matter, see Bolter; Burnard, O'Keefe, and Unsworth; Lessig, *Free Culture* and *Future*; McCarty; Nowviskie; Shreibman, Siemens, and Unsworth.

2. The University of Virginia uses a flexible suite of software tools called *The Instructional Toolkit* for all these purposes (Howard).

3. This software was developed by the ARP group.

4. For a more detailed discussion of the theoretical and methodological relation of the book and the computer, see McGann, "Textonics" and "Culture and Technology."

Works Cited

Applied Research in Patacriticism. U of Virginia, n.d. Web. 21 Aug. 2006.

Blake, William. "The Marriage of Heaven and Hell." *The Complete Poetry and Prose.* Ed. David V. Erdman. Commentary by Harold Bloom. New and rev. ed. Berkeley: U of California P, 1982. 33–45. Print.

Boeckh, August. *Enzyklopädie und Methodologie der gesamten philologischen Wissenschafton.* Ed. Ernst Bratuschek. Leipzig: Teubner, 1877. Print.

Bolter, Jay David. *Remediation: Understanding New Media.* Cambridge: MIT P, 1999. Print.

Burnard, Lou, Katherine O'Brien O'Keefe, and John Unsworth, eds. *Electronic Textual Editing.* New York: MLA, 2006. Print.

Burns, Robert. "To a Louse." *Poems, Chiefly in the Scottish Dialect.* Kilmarnock, 1786. Facsim. ed. Glasgow: Smith, 1927. 194. Print.

Chartier, Roger. *The Order of Books: Readers, Authors, and Libraries in Europe between the Fourteenth and Eighteenth Centuries.* Trans. Lydia G. Cochrane. Stanford: Stanford UP, 1994. Print.

Coleridge, Samuel Taylor. *Biographia Literaria; or, Biographical Sketches of My Literary Life and Opinions.* Ed. James Engell and Walter Jackson Bate. 2 vols. Princeton: Princeton UP, 1983. Print. Bollingen Series 75.

"Collex." *NINES.* NINES, n.d. Web. 11 Nov. 2008.

Howard, Alice G. "The University of Virginia Instructional Toolkit—Class Home Pages without Angst or HTML." *EDUCAUSE.* EDUCAUSE, 1999. Web. 21 Aug. 2006.

Institute for Advanced Technology in the Humanities. U of Virginia, 2006. Web. 21 Aug. 2006.

Johns, Adrian. *The Nature of the Book: Print and Knowledge in the Making.* Chicago: U of Chicago P, 1998. Print.

"Juxta." *NINES.* NINES, n.d. Web. 11 Nov. 2008.

Lessig, Lawrence. *Free Culture: How Big Media Uses Technology and the Law to Lock Down Culture and Control Creativity.* New York: Penguin, 2004. Print.

———. *The Future of Ideas: The Fate of the Commons in a Connected World.* New York: Random, 2001. Print.

McCarty, Willard. *Humanities Computing.* New York: Palgrave, 2005. Print.

McGann, Jerome. "Culture and Technology: The Way We Live Now, What Is to Be Done?" *Institute for Advanced Technology in the Humanities.* U of Virginia, 2006. Web. 21 Aug. 2006.

———. *Radiant Textuality: Literature after the World Wide Web.* New York: Palgrave, 2001. Print.

———, ed. *The Rossetti Archive: The Complete Writings and Pictures of Dante Gabriel Rossetti. Institute for Advanced Technology in the Humanities.* U of Virginia, 2000. Web. 21 Aug. 2006.

———. "Textonics." *Institute for Advanced Technology in the Humanities.* U of Virginia, 2006. Web. 21 Aug. 2006.

NINES: A Networked Interface for Nineteenth-Century Electronic Scholarship. NINES, n.d. Web. 21 Aug. 2006.

Nowviskie, Bethany. *Collex: Semantic Collections and Exhibits for the Remixable Web. NINES.* NINES, Nov. 2005. Web. 21 Aug. 2006.

Schreibman, Susan, Ray Siemens, and John Unsworth, eds. *A Companion to Digital Humanities.* Oxford: Blackwell, 2004. Print.

"Social Software." *Wikipedia.* Wikipedia, 3 Nov. 2008. Web. 11 Nov. 2008.

Stéfan Sinclair and Geoffrey Rockwell

Between Language and Literature: Digital Text Exploration

We need to rethink the creation and use of computing resources for teaching at the interstices of language and literature. The computing resources developed for language learning rarely intersect with the literature resources, even though at an advanced level language learners are typically learning about literature in the target language. Much of the teaching in undergraduate language departments is a blend of linguistic and literary content: the goal is often for students to achieve a better grasp of the mechanics of language to better understand and express ideas about texts (though the emphasis on linguistic proficiency may vary according to the level of the course and the native language of the students). Alas, very few electronic resources attempt to integrate both linguistic and literary sensibilities.

Computer-assisted language learning has, in over three decades, experimented with a variety of techniques for enhancing the teaching and learning of languages (particularly second languages). Many of its most compelling exemplars are interactive and adaptable learning modules that address a specific linguistic area (for instance, mastering nominative and object pronouns). Although texts are sometimes used in computer-assisted-language-learning programs, they are most often hard-coded (determined) and secondary in importance to the linguistic objectives.[1]

Computer-assisted text analysis has also matured in the past twenty years, from a time when computers were primarily used as a means of producing concordances for print more efficiently to now, when sophisticated packages exist for performing a variety of statistical and quantitative functions. Nevertheless, rarely do text-analysis tools blend text and linguistic data views, and more rarely still are tools designed for enhancing the understanding of both language and literature.

Our objectives here are twofold: to describe design principles of digital texts and tools that better correspond to the context of teaching in undergraduate language program (elements from tools that we have developed will be offered as examples) and to provide instructors with some practical suggestions for using digital text exploration in the classroom as a means to both linguistic and literary ends. We begin by providing a brief introduction to computer-assisted text analysis, particularly as it pertains to possible uses in language instruction.

What Is Text Analysis and Why Is It Important to Learning Online?

Text analysis is a way of asking questions of a text that has its roots in concording.[2] When we encounter a text we ask questions like: What is this article about? What happens to Hamlet in the end? Where is that passage about the war of 1812? What does the author have to say about "friendship"? Reading the text is one way to answer the questions, but most of us learn to skim ahead, to use an index, or to use a tool like a concordance to answer certain questions. Computer-assisted text analysis leverages the searching and counting capabilities of the computer to help readers answer questions. Text analysis is really not one thing but a class of interpretative methods that can be used appropriately or inappropriately in the careful study of a text.[3]

The task of creating concordances of verbose authors was so time-consuming, prone to error, and selective in its vocabulary (focusing especially on content words such as nouns and verbs) that starting in the 1940s people like Roberto Busa began to imagine how to use information technology to automate the creation of concordances (Raben). In the 1960s researchers developed software like *COCOA* for mainframes for

```
sceptic (11)

[1,47]      abstractions. In vain would the sceptic make a distinction
[1,48]       to science, even no speculative sceptic, pretends to entertain
[1,49]     and philosophy, that Atheist and Sceptic are almost synonymous.
[1,49]          by which the most determined sceptic must allow himself to
[2,60] of my faculties? You might cry out sceptic and railer, as much as
[3,65]       profession of every reasonable sceptic is only to reject
[8,97] prepare a compleat triumph for the Sceptic; who tells them, that
[11,121] to judge on such a subject. I am Sceptic enough to allow, that
[12,130]         absolutely insolvable. No Sceptic denies that we lie
[12,130]     merit that name, is, that the Sceptic, from habit, caprice,
[12,139]            To be a philosophical Sceptic is, in a man of
```

Figure I. *TACTWeb* keyword in context (KWIC)

batch concording, and this software evolved into microcomputer concording tools like *MicroOCP* (*Oxford Concordance Program*). Electronic
concording became more than a tool for the preparation of print concordances with the advent of interactive tools like *TACT* (*Text-Analysis Computing Tools*), which was released by the University of Toronto in 1989.
TACT and its online successor *TACTWeb* made it easy to iteratively ask
questions, search for words, view passages concorded, and look at the
distribution of words (see fig. 1).

Interactive concording tools are study aids that replace the print concordances and indexes we use to help understand a text. As such their
primary use in learning is to help students think through a text, whether
literary, linguistic, or cultural. Text-analysis tools give students the ability
to do research quickly and across large collections of information, but the
tools and appropriate learning materials are not always accessible. Books
like Ian Lancashire's *Using* TACT *with Electronic Texts* provided manuals
to help students understand the applications of text analysis. As tools like
TACTWeb and *HyperPo* became available on the Web, access became
easier since users did not have to pay or install software. *TACTWeb* also
provided a workbook that integrated tutorial material with working pan-
els where students could experiment with text analysis on prepared texts
(see fig. 2).[4]

Generally speaking, there are three uses of computer-based text analysis for learning:

> *Search large texts quickly.* Text-analysis environments that combine
> large text collections with easy-to-use search tools let students find
> information otherwise only available to experts. In the teaching of

6.1 Searching for a List of Words

Often if you are following a theme through a text there is no single word that covers the theme, but a set of words. It is useful then to search for and display the results from a search for a list of words that you have prepared.

In the TACTweb query language you separate the words you are looking for with commas (","). So the query you would enter might look like this if you were looking for words that have to do with seasons:

`spring, summer, fall, winter`

Try It -- Searching for a List of Words

1. Type in your list of words (separated with commas!)

> [   ]

2. Click on this button (Submit Query) to see a KWIC display of the list of words you specified.

3. Remember to click the **Back** button to return here.
- **Question:** Does "fall" fit in the "season words". Can you think of other words that belong there?

Figure 2. *TACTWeb* workbook

history, for example, students can use text analysis to survey electronic archives for evidence. Even *Google* can be thought of as a large index to the Web and can be used to find patterns of linguistic use.

Conduct complex searches. Increasingly, text-analysis environments provide the ability to conduct complex searches that look for the co-occurrence of words (specified words that appear in close proximity) or for patterns rather than words (using wildcards and special characters that represent a class of characters). Language and linguistics students can use text analysis to study the use of language in collections of authentic materials, including Web pages in the target language. Further, text-analysis environments become the site for reflection on textuality and patterns in language. Having to use a tool forces students to ask what the tool can do with text, how to use it, and ultimately what computers can find about a text.

Present results in informative ways. Text-analysis environments can present information in ways that provoke reflection rather than simply answer questions. Concordances are designed to juxtapose passages that agree in some fashion, such as passages that contain the same word. The juxtaposition of passages can provoke insight into the coherence or lack thereof in a text. This educational use of text analysis encourages students to make connections between passages. The danger, however, is that students will assume naively that there has to be a connection between passages in a text where there might not be one. Naive concording can lead to awkward attempts to span different texts as if they had to agree, as if everything an author writes is coherent. Naive concording can also lead students away from reading original texts to depending on computer-generated perspectives. Visualization tools take us even further from the linguistic text by providing interactive graphic representations that can be interpretatively suggestive (Rockwell; Rockwell and Bradley).

Text-analysis tools are particularly useful for students dealing with evidence online. As the wealth of evidence becomes available in digital form, computer-assisted research methods are becoming important. With an estimated two exabytes of new information being produced each year, we are all experiencing information overload (Lyman and Varian). Much of this excess information is textual, and most of it is born digital on computers and thus is accessible to computer methodologies. Being able to use search-and-analysis tools is an important way of dealing with the excess— a way that has its roots in traditions of humanistic thought. It is also useful for the study of contemporary culture, whether foreign or native, for students of cultural studies and languages. The Web is a unique source of evidence of contemporary culture that text-analysis tools can help students think through.

To teach students how to use text analysis, one needs to create an environment, or build on an existing one, where the appropriate electronic texts and tools are brought together. For many pedagogical uses, existing environments suffice, but where an instructor can control the environment, there are three ways it can be prepared for student learning with text analysis:

> *Text enrichment.* The electronic text itself can be enriched with annotations, associative links, or linguistic information.
> *Powerful tools.* Tools can be provided that are optimized for answering certain types of questions.
> *Rich interfaces.* The electronic texts can be displayed in conjunction with other resources to create a conducive study environment.

The Web of Evidence

A consideration of the evolution of technology-assisted language and literature instruction reveals an intriguing paradox. On the one hand, pioneers in the discipline are consistently among the first implementers—and sometimes innovators—of new technologies. When online virtual worlds in the form of multiuser dungeons were first developing in the early 1980s, educators were already finding ways of integrating them into the classroom. Likewise, when CD-ROMs were being disseminated as data media for games and other interactive activities in the early 1990s, instructional applications were among the first to appear (though this time often with a more commercial impetus). On the other hand, the broad adoption of specific technologies in the classroom is usually much more gradual, often slower than that technology's general penetration into society. Readily recognizable factors are at play, of course, including the economic realities of acquiring and maintaining technologies within scholastic budgets and the usually bureaucratic pace of change of curricula and instructional techniques. We may lament the relatively slow pace of change in some ways, but it may also be argued that the delay provides an opportunity to fully determine the viability and promise of certain technologies.

If any technology since the personal computer has proved its potential for a range of instructional purposes, it is certainly the Web. And though the Web may seem as prevalent and ubiquitous as any technology currently available, on closer inspection its use in instruction has followed the same trajectory as other classroom technologies: educational pioneers made intense, creative use of the Web as far back as the first half of the 1990s, but high-speed Internet, properly equipped computer labs, and integration of Web-based activities into the curriculum were not commonplace in schools until the first part of the 2000s (colleges and universities have had a faster rate of adoption, but in all cases the hardware and software almost always precede effectively framed uses).[5]

We take the discrepancy between the broad, public use of the Web and its much more limited use in the language and literature classroom to be a reflection of two realities in particular: an unfamiliarity with many of the Web-based resources and with effective techniques for exploiting them and a paucity of easy-to-use, flexible, interactive, and instructionally sound online resources for language and literature learning (particularly ones that go beyond relatively simple grammar exercises).

We aim here to contribute, however modestly, to the first point, that of familiarity with resources and their use. We refer to several resources that may be of use to some readers, but our primary objective is to encourage a rethinking of Web-based resources, not as neatly packaged and ready-to-use activities or exercises, but as endlessly observable and reconfigurable digital texts, ones that have unfathomable potential for the learner (and teacher) of a language and its literature. As a primarily text-based medium (almost all Web searches, even for images, are text-based), the Web is a trove of useful content for language learning, representing the entire spectrum of authentic production (authentic in the sense of not contrived for the purposes of a pedagogical exercise), from the struggling nonnative speaker to the most eloquent writer.

The second point, regarding a lack of worthy resources, has a natural link with the first: developers of Web-based language resources have operated largely within the same paradigm as the pre-Web world, for the most part replicating functionality that has long been possible with electronic gadgets and personal computers (and even the printed page). Relatively little effort, it seems, has been devoted to exploiting the Web as a rich and enormous corpus of authentic digital texts. We wish to emphasize the digital nature of these texts, that is, the fact that they are essentially composed of many discrete units of information that can be broken down, analyzed, reconfigured, and reassembled in innumerable ways. Such operations are the strength of text analysis.

Recipes for Text Analysis in the Instruction of Language and Literature

In this section we provide a set of recipes—or scenarios—that suggest some practical ways for teachers to use online text-analysis tools in the instruction of language and literature.[6] For some readers, these recipes may provide the outline for concrete activities to use in a course; for others, they may spark ideas for different recipes. Our primary intent is to demonstrate how text analysis can be used in conjunction with the Web to study language and literature in ways that were not previously possible.

Following a Theme through a Work

We often ask literature students to discuss how a theme is handled in a literary or intellectual work. Students have traditionally used indexes, where available, to follow a theme through a work. With access to an electronic version of a text, a student can now use the search function in a word processor to search for words that would be indicative of the theme. With more advanced search tools or text-analysis environments students can build their own study concordance of passages around a theme by taking the following steps:

Accessing an appropriate edition of the text under study. The instructor who wants to encourage text analysis for learning should guide the students to appropriate editions.

Identifying the theme for study. This step can be difficult since most interesting themes are not found simply by searching for a single word. Students should be encouraged to develop a list of words that might be indicative of theme. These words could be synonyms (an online thesaurus, such as *Thesaurus.com* or *WordNet*, can help here).

Using a search-and-concordance tool (like *TAPoRware Find Text—Concordance*). Such a tool lets users submit the URL for an HTML version of a work and provides a list of words to search for. It then generates a concordance of passages for reflection. *HyperPo* is an online interactive concordance that lets users explore by clicking on words.

The challenge of using searches to follow a theme provides an opportunity to engage students on the issue of words and meaning. Some strategies to enhance this recipe use other *TAPoRware* tools.[7] Collocation tools like the *TAPoRware Find Text—Collocation* show what words are located near the word one searches for. Students can search for a word clearly related to the theme to find other words that might help follow the theme. The words frequently in the neighborhood of a keyword can also provide a sense of the semantic field of an idea. This information can be useful for brainstorming around a theme to develop original essay ideas. Students should be encouraged to ask what terms are anomalies—what words did they not expect? What stands out?

TAPoRware List Words helps identify interesting themes by providing a list of words sorted by frequency. The words that appear often in a text, aside from function words like *the* and *a*, can indicate themes. Students should be encouraged to ask why an author would use a particular content word frequently. An alternative approach is to compare the text with another in order to identify words that appear more often in the target text than in a control sample.

TAPoRware Googlizer uses *Google* to build a corpus of pages associated with a keyword or phrase that can be used where there is no text. For language and culture students, tools like the *Googlizer* automate what they often do manually—gather a collection of Web pages on a subject to study how that subject or linguistic pattern is handled.

Grammar Verification

Another common exercise for a language student is the written composition (where the practice of correct written expression is more important than the topic). With the decline of handwritten submissions (even in primary schools), word processors have become a key location of language production and learning. Yet surprisingly the multilingual orthographic and grammatical capabilities of common word processors (like *MS Word* or *WordPerfect*) are seldom used, particularly for languages other than English (open-source and online editors, such as *OpenOffice* or *Google Docs*, usually lack grammar-checking capabilities). Rarer still is the use of stand-alone grammar checkers (such as *Le Correcteur 101* or *Antidote* for French). This situation may be explained in part by the additional cost of some language modules and in part by the additional steps needed to install those modules, assuming the user is aware that they exist. But mostly, word processors are underused because the relevant technologies are almost never integrated directly into the instructional context. This is a shame, since the moment of production is pivotal in effective language acquisition (catching mistakes as they happen rather than expecting students to thoroughly examine a teacher-corrected text).

BonPatron is a free, online tool designed specifically for learners of French as a second language. Its initial objectives were twofold: to provide students with friendly, accessible explanations of common linguistic pitfalls (feedback from grammar checkers is usually aimed at native speakers and can be linguistically complex and difficult to comprehend) and to help the instructor avoid repetitive corrections for common mistakes—in other words, a first line of defense for both instructor and student.

Codeveloped by Terry Nadasdi and Stéfan Sinclair, *BonPatron* differs from most grammar tools in its pedagogical design: potential errors are flagged and explained but not automatically or even easily corrected. The student must become an active participant in learning by manually correcting the text rather than, say, right-clicking on a suggested edit, thereby circumventing the need to actually write the correct form (see Lyster). Feedback is intended to explain a grammatical point clearly; it is left to the student to apply the principle (see Lightbown and Spada). When the explanation is insufficient, an additional built-in page of explanation can be invoked, including some interactive exercises, or external resources are suggested (in particular, Martin Beaudoin's *Pomme* [www.pomme.ualberta

.ca/pomme]). These linked resources are an exemplary way of making the most of the Web-based learning context.

As is, *BonPatron* can be a useful tool for the French-language learner and instructor (as of January 2009, the site receives on average more than 20,000 visitors a day from all over the world and processes more than 100,000 texts), which are examined to help improve the correction engine. One activity that can be done with students is to examine closely some of the strengths and weaknesses of the tool and to speculate, linguistically, on the reasons for each. This evaluation emphasizes for students a fundamental reality: no grammar checker on the market today is perfect (far from it), for a variety of reasons, including the potential for syntactic complexity and semantic ambiguity. For instance, one of *BonPatron*'s greatest weaknesses is its inability to deal intelligently with proper nouns; almost all capitalized words are ignored (as potential proper nouns), even at the beginning of a sentence. Though this is a weakness of the tool, it can also lead to classroom discussion about some characteristics of the French language.

A common drill in the toolbox of the language instructor is the fill-in-the-blank exercise (see fig. 3). This type of exercise has easily made the transition from paper to the screen, often to great benefit. Creators of electronic fill-in-the-blank exercises are able to anticipate a variety of mistakes and have the computer provide immediate and meaningful feedback to

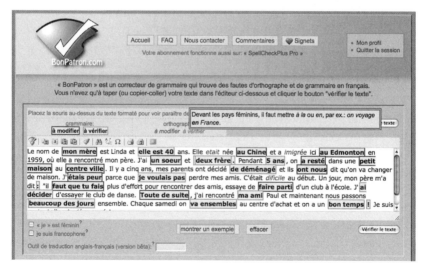

Figure 3. Fill-in-the-blanks for dynamic texts

the student—an obvious improvement over the print counterpart. Yet despite excellent tools for creating electronic exercises (such as *Hot Potatoes* [http://hotpot.uvic.ca/]), electronic exercises take considerable time to develop and involve hard-coded content (the same way that hypertextual links are almost always hard-coded in a document).

Since tools exist to perform syntactic and morphological analysis of texts (identifying parts of speech and canonical forms like the singular of a plural word), it should be possible to automatically generate fill-in-the-blank exercises, using any text on the Web (in the appropriate language). *HyperPoet: Linguistic Fill-in-the-Blanks*, also developed by Sinclair, functions this way (see fig. 4). Users can point to a Web address, upload a file, or paste content into a box, and the tool uses the specified options to create a fill-in-the-blank exercise (in English, French, Italian, German, or Spanish). For instance, one page could be returned where the infinitive of all verbs is provided and the student must fill in the box with the correctly conjugated form. Alternatively, all prepositions could be replaced by blanks, and the student would need to provide the appropriate word.

One remarkable feature of such tools is that students are able to generate useful exercises for themselves; they are not dependent solely on the instructor. Students can decide which type of text corresponds best to their level (e.g., newspaper articles, forum discussions, or poetry) and generate as many exercises as they wish from authentic texts. Of course, such automatically generated exercises can also have disadvantages, such as misleading errors in the morphological-analysis engine or the inability for instructors to provide contextual feedback (based on a specific incorrect answer). Still, much is gained in the use of text analysis on the rich corpus of authentic texts on the Web.

Several techniques have been developed by text-analysis scholars for algorithmically quantifying the level of language of a text. Each technique has its particular strengths and weaknesses, and some may be more applicable to certain genres than to others. Potentially more revealing than the results of any of these techniques, however, is an examination of the techniques themselves and the linguistic principles underlying them.

One readily accessible text-analysis tool that can provide a variety of data on a text is *Textalyser* (many other tools exist online, including those found at *TAPoR*). Each step in the use of *Textalyser* is a pedagogical opportunity to better understand language analysis and methodologies. The interface on the first screen, as relatively simple as it is, contains terms such as "stoplist" and "polyword phrases." Similarly, the results screen

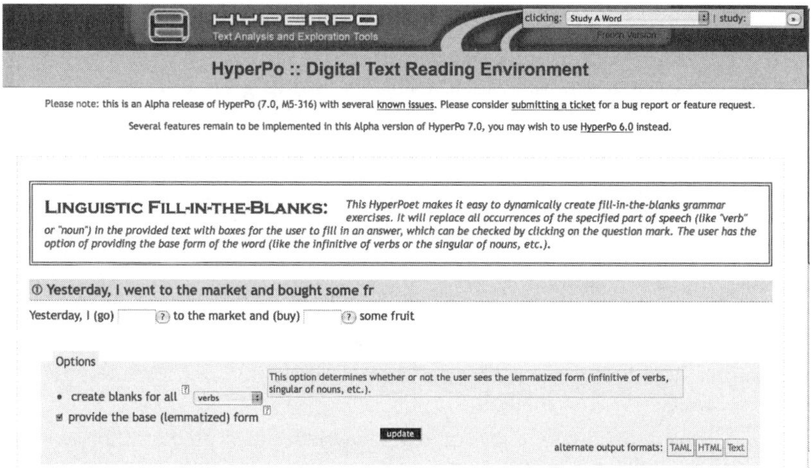

Figure 4. *HyperPoet*'s fill-in-the-blanks exercise

contains several terms that are worth examining closely, such as "lexical density" and the "Gunning-Fox Index"; a valuable exercise might be to have students research these terms on the Web and compare their definitions. This essay is not the appropriate venue to consider each one of the concepts and merits underlying the results of the *Textalyser*, but suffice it to say that there is plenty of fodder for discussion of issues of language and its analysis.

We have found that students enjoy submitting their own texts to these types of analysis tools, where they discover aspects of their writing of which they were not aware (like a propensity for repeating a given phrase). An engaging activity can be to have students try to find texts on the Web that most closely resemble the data profile of their own texts. Doing so can provoke interesting results and awaken students' curiosity about the relationship between text analysis and linguistic proficiency.

The use of the Web for the instruction of language and literature has two noteworthy characteristics: first, most tools (such as interactive grammar exercises) are modest reformulations of what was possible before the Web (and in some cases even more modest reformulations of what was possible before computers), and, second, links to helpful resources on the Web are often compiled, but the actual textual content—a corpus of authentic texts—is seldom fully exploited. Computer-assisted text analysis can play a transformative role in the teaching of language and literature,

especially when explored in the context of the Web. The recipes that we
have provided might serve as a starting point for further exploration of
the interstices of computer-assisted literary and linguistic study.

Notes

1. Typical courseware for language learning is often drill software for grammar. Drill software uses fill-in-the-blank and multiple-choice questions to reinforce knowledge. *Hot Potatoes* is an example of a suite of tools for creating drill courseware (see Winke and MacGregor).

2. Concording is the process of creating a concordance, which is a collection of passages that agree in some way, usually because they contain the same word. Concording was first practiced in the thirteenth-century concordances to the Bible (see McCarty; Howard-Hill).

3. A good collection of essays on text analysis are presented in Ramsay.

4. The *TACTWeb* workbook, developed by Geoffrey Rockwell and John Bradley, is at http://tactweb.mcmaster.ca/tactweb/doc/twwbmenu.htm. See Rockwell, Bradley, and Passmore for a study on the use of *TACTWeb* in undergraduate instruction.

5. Though students have obviously taken the initiative in exploiting the rich resources of the Web (see Miall), it is far less certain that teachers have been able to effectively harness the Web's language and literature instruction capabilities. An informal survey by the authors of almost two dozen colleagues in both K–12 and university settings reveals that the Web is hardly used in a deliberate and conscious manner by instructors. Beyond token Web pages of useful links and resources or the reliance on relatively superficial features of course management systems, the onus for benefiting from the Web is left to students. (This is not to say that there are not many outstanding uses of the Web by language and literature instructors, but what we know of these tend to be isolated cases reported anecdotally in conferences and journals—by no mean a reflection of the norm.)

6. Shawn Day has written an extensive set of text-analysis recipes for the *TAPoR* portal (http://tada.mcmaster.ca/Main/TaporRecipes).

7. Visit the *TAPoR* tools prototype site (http://taporware.mcmaster.ca) for a full description of all *TAPoRware* tools. Rockwell is a project leader of *TAPoR*.

Works Cited

Day, Shawn. "TAPoR Portal Recipes." *Text Analysis Developers Alliances.* Text Analysis Developers Alliance, 14 Apr. 2007. Web. 31 Mar. 2009.
Howard-Hill, T. H. *Literary Concordances.* Oxford: Pergamon, 1979. Print.
Lancashire, Ian, et al. *Using* TACT *with Electronic Texts. Modern Languages Association.* MLA, 1996. Web. Oct. 2006.
Lightbown, Patsy M., and Nina Spada. "Focus-on-Form and Corrective Feedback in Communicative Language Teaching: Effects on Second Language Learning." *Studies in Second Language Acquisition* 12.4 (1990): 429–48. Print.

Lyman, Peter, and Hal R. Varian. "How Much Information? 2003." *School of Information Management Systems.* U of California, Berkeley, 2003. Web. 29 May 2006.

Lyster, Roy. "Negotiation of Form, Recasts, and Explicit Correction in Relation to Error Type and Learner Repair in Immersion Classrooms." *Language Learning* 51 (2001): 265–301. Print.

McCarty, Willard. "Handmade, Computer-Assisted, and Electronic Concordances of Chaucer." *Computer-Based Chaucer Studies.* Ed. Ian Lancashire. Toronto: CCH Working Papers, 1993. 49–65. Print.

Miall, David. "The Library versus the Internet: Literary Studies under Siege?" *PMLA* 116.5 (2001): 1405–14. Print.

Raben, Joseph. "Humanities Computing Twenty-Five Years Later." *Computers and the Humanities* 25.6 (1991): 341–50. Print.

Ramsay, Stephen. "Special Section: Reconceiving Text Analysis: Toward an Algorithmic Criticism." *Literary and Linguistic Computing* 18.2 (2003): 167–74. Print.

Rockwell, Geoffrey. "The Visual Concordance: The Design of Eye-ConTact." *Text Technology* 10.1 (2001): 73–86. Print.

Rockwell, Geoffrey, and John Bradley. "Printing in Sand; Scientific Visualization and the Analysis of Texts." *GeoffreyRockwell.com.* StevensRockwell, 2004. Web. Oct. 2006. Trans. of "Empreintes dans le sable: Visualisation scientifique et analyse de texte." *Litterature, informatique, lecture.* Ed. Alain Vuillemin and Michel LeNoble. Paris: Pulim, 1999. 130–60.

Rockwell, Geoffrey, John Bradley, and Graham Passmore. "TACTweb: The Intersection of Text-Analysis and Hypertext." *Educational Computing Research* 17.3 (1997): 217–30. Print.

Sinclair, Stéfan. "Computer-Assisted Reading: Reconceiving Text Analysis." *Literary and Linguistic Computing* 18 (2003): 175–84. Print.

Winke, Paula, and David MacGregor. "Review of *Hot Potatoes.*" *Language Learning and Technology* 5.2 (2001): 28–33. Web. Oct. 2006.

Part II

Case Studies in Languages

Stephen L. Tschudi, David V. Hiple, and Dorothy M. Chun

Fostering Cohesion and Community in Asynchronous Online Courses

As online teaching has gained acceptance as a mode of instruction, in both pure distance-education formats and hybrid or distributed formats (e.g., conventional face-to-face meetings combined with online interactions), computer-mediated technologies present compelling opportunities to language educators, both longtime practitioners and preservice professionals. Some instructors in the field have embraced these opportunities enthusiastically, and others have kept them at arm's length. Teachers have been called the "gate-keepers" of technology (Zhao and Tella 1), since it is largely they who determine how and to what extent it figures in instruction. Technology has always played a role in instruction, of course, but computer-mediated technologies have proved to have an especially profound potential, and thus the challenge for language educators is "not only how to use the technology, but how to use it to teach" (Zhao and Tella 2).

At first, teachers used technology often more for its own sake than to teach, and so early efforts with computer-mediated technologies were unimaginative and did not exploit the full potential for language learning (Strambi and Bouvet 87). Instead, they focused on mechanical manipulation of forms and neglected the possibilities of using technology as a tool

121

for enhancing communicative tasks among learners. In recognition of this shortcoming, some advocated that computer-based materials should provide opportunities for negotiation of meaning similar to those seen in human interaction, such as in the classroom (Blake, "Computer Mediated Communication" 120; Chapelle 24).

The advent of the Internet presented an opportunity for educators to move beyond computer-mediated exercises that tended to isolate learners from one another. Thus considerations about software design could include more compelling issues now that instruction could be facilitated through online learning communities. Computer-mediated communication provided online environments for learners to use and to experiment with the target language (Beauvois; Pennington), and as technology surrounding learning communities evolved, pedagogy was seen to drive technology rather than the other way around (Felix). A distinction can be made between "virtual communities," which are simply groups that use networked technologies to communicate and collaborate, and "communities of practice," which are cultural entities that emerge from the establishment of a virtual organization (Wenger, McDermott, and Snyder). Designing a virtual community does not guarantee that a community of practice will arise because an underlying task-based learning need must exist (Johnson 56).

Pedagogy and Learning Environments

Technology is not a methodology; it constitutes a set of tools. How these tools are used depends on the approaches and pedagogical principles that an educator applies (Blake, "What"; Doughty and Long). In other words, technology can be used to create an optimal psycholinguistic environment for foreign language distance learning and can implement principles of second language acquisition and task-based language instruction. Antonella Strambi and Eric Bouvet observe that, just as in traditional face-to-face instruction, pedagogically sound principles for language teaching should be applied to online language-learning environments (97). Our objective must be not to construct different pedagogies that distinguish online teaching from conventional face-to-face classroom teaching but to integrate best practices from classroom-based pedagogy in our instruction online. As tremendous resources are allocated throughout the public and private sector for Web-based course development, what are the pedagogical touchstones that should be kept in focus as technology is applied in online language teaching?

There is general consensus in the field that language instruction should provide learners with opportunities to engage in task-based interactions involving negotiation of meaning, that is, activities where one learner has information that another learner needs to accomplish a task (Doughty and Pica; Lightbown and Spada). Such linguistic tasks should also be authentic—they should model real-life activities a student might perform in the target language (Breen) because authentic tasks are motivators that facilitate personalized interaction among learners and lead to comprehensible output (Nunan). One goal of task-based instruction is to assist in the development of higher-level thinking skills. Ramon Ribé and Nuria Vidal suggest that task-based instruction develops students' communicative competence in context in the target language, taps individual awareness and motivation, and enhances personal involvement.

How does the teacher enhance students' personal involvement in an online learning environment? It is clear that motivational aspects associated with language learning, especially at a distance, play a critical role. In addition to the features of the learning environment, students' positive perceptions about their interactions in it have been deemed especially relevant (Deci and Ryan; Schmidt, Boraie, and Kassabgy). Thus because learners' interaction with one another and their teacher will partly determine students' perception about the learning environment, virtual or conventional, it is incumbent on the teacher to ensure that

> learners come to perceive the learning environment as a place where assistance can be obtained whenever needed and where everyone's opinions are respected and valued as contributions to the group's culture. This is especially true of distance learning environments, where face-to-face contact is limited or non-existent. (Strambi and Bouvet 85)

Initially, computer-mediated communication appeared to be a nonthreatening learning environment and an ideal medium (Lamy and Goodfellow; Pennington; Warschauer). In an online-class forum, students can participate without the anxiety of being caught by surprise or put on the spot. They might be more inclined to take risks; they all have the same and equal opportunity to post messages. Students can rehearse and refer to resources, potentially fostering a more positive attitude toward participation in the learning community.

Cohesion and Community

While online computer-mediated communication may create a nonthreat-ening learning environment, physical distance and separation can reduce a sense of community among learners in an online environment. This lack of a sense of community may lead to learner disconnection, dissatisfac-tion, and dropout (Johnson 54; Rovai, "Building" 2). David W. McMillan and David M. Chavis define community as "a feeling that members have of belonging, a feeling that members matter to one another and to the group, and a shared faith that members' needs will be met through their commitment to be together" (9). Is an online learning community an en-tity different from a conventional face-to-face learning community to such an extent that a corollary definition is required? Barry Wellman says that community can be separated from place when it is viewed as what people do together. If so, a group of online learners is indeed a community, albeit a disparate one. Rena M. Palloff and Keith Pratt characterize community as a sense of togetherness and group membership, of "sharing who we are as people," and stress the importance of fostering this sense in online courses (78). As in real life, "not all communities are effective in carrying out their tasks; some communities work together effectively while others splinter and struggle to accomplish their goals" (Rogers 384).

How, then, do members of an online learning community (both teach-ers and learners) overcome time and space to foster a sense of community online? Computer-mediated communication provides a means and a space for them to share their personal opinions and feelings as they complete online tasks. Such engagement is seen in online forums (the primary means enabling asynchronous communication) when participants call one another by name, refer to one another's postings, and participate substantially in discussions. Community is also apparent in online forums when discussion in the forums exhibits cohesion.

By *cohesion* we mean the sustained advancement of relevant topics by participants in a conversation—in essence, their creation of a single text (Halliday and Hasan). Cohesion is characterized by sequential coherence—for example, by participants' anaphoric references to one another's post-ings (Herring). In our study, we found that another indicator of cohesion was low redundancy in the content of postings by different members of a group, suggesting that members were attending to the topic and develop-ing it with due attention to previous contributions.

In the community of practice constituted by students in an online course, community knowledge is coconstructed by the individuals of the community and is larger than the knowledge of each individual (Johnson 49). This group knowledge is developed through discussion and collaboration (Bielaczyc and Collins; Smith, Ferguson, and Caris). The community generates and expands its group knowledge through the negotiation of meaning (Wenger, McDermott, and Snyder), a necessary condition for language acquisition (Long) that typically occurs in a language instructional setting as learners complete communicative tasks (Pica, Kanagy, and Falodun). In the asynchronous online course examined in this study and in others like it, traces of the process of negotiating meaning remain in the archive of contributions to the course—the postings that students and teacher make online as they engage in teaching and learning activities—and can be made available for subsequent analysis. When compared with the ephemeral real-time environment of the traditional classroom, which can only be captured for analysis through note-taking or some means of electronic recording, asynchronous Web-based distance education provides an important advantage to the researcher wishing to observe the process of the development of knowledge in a community.

The College of Languages, Linguistics, and Literature at the University of Hawai'i, Mānoa, has been offering language courses online since 1996. More than twenty-five offerings, mostly in the less commonly taught languages of Asia, are taught partly or entirely online. This study examines archived data from the spring 2003 iteration of Chinese 332, Advanced Web-Based Reading and Writing, a one-semester online course in standard Chinese. Our aim is to identify key factors contributing to cohesion and community in the Web-based environment. Examining task, performance, and behavior in specific online discussions, we tabulate indicators of cohesion and community and then, after analysis of these indicators, discuss how educators may nurture a successful learning community in an online environment.

The Course

The course examined in this study is a third-year course for learners wishing to focus on reading and writing in standard written Chinese (*baihua*), which is essentially a written register of Mandarin Chinese (Norman). The course attracts a mixture of students, but heritage students—students who have some family background in Chinese or who immigrated to the United States at an early age—predominate. Typically, such heritage students come from a non-Mandarin-speaking family background and, as a precondition of admission to the course, are assessed with deficiencies in their standard written Chinese arising from lack of adequate training (usually due to emigration at an early age) and differences between Mandarin and their home dialect. Students are sufficiently proficient in standard written Chinese to be able to handle, at least half of the time, typical advanced-level functions such as narration, description, and comparison and to sustain discussions that feature these functions, using Chinese characters exclusively as a means of communication. The curricular goal of the course is to strengthen these advanced-level functions in reading and writing while building greater accuracy.

Interaction

Chinese 332 is conducted wholly on the Web using *BRIX*, a course management system developed in-house for asynchronous Web-based language teaching and learning (Fleming and Hiple). As with many Web-based courses in the humanities, teaching and learning in the course happen largely by means of interaction among teacher and students in the course's Web-based forums, which are similar to those available in the popular commercial course management systems *WebCT* and *Blackboard*.

In a wholly Web-based asynchronous course such as Chinese 332, students never meet in a classroom. Instead, each student participates in the course individually by logging in and completing tasks by specified deadlines. With a window of time in which to complete each task, rather than a specific time to log in, the students and teacher engage in a series of "conversations in slow motion," or, a "hybrid phenomenon that falls somewhere between writing and speaking" (Beauvois 198), consisting of forum postings appearing in chronological order but at varying intervals in the timeframe of the specific task.

The communicative tasks carried out in the forums in Chinese 332 are designed to approximate tasks typically performed by small groups in the traditional brick-and-mortar classroom. Alfred P. Rovai has noted that "augmenting individual learning activities with small group activities promotes a sense of community by helping students make connections with each other" ("Building" 9). In the traditional classroom setting, social cohesion is supported by face-to-face communication, while in the asynchronous Web-based forum, students separated in space and time depend on their text-based interactions to establish a feeling of community that will support their participation (Rovai, "Building"). These text-based interactions are important in determining the degree of cohesion and community in a course, and analysis of these interactions can yield insights for online educators wishing to foster cohesion and community in their own courses.

Data

Chinese 332 is a sixteen-week course covering eight instructional units, each lasting two weeks. The CD-ROM used as the basic text in the course was originally designed as a tool for independent computer-assisted language learning in advanced Chinese reading. The course was designed for a community of users of the CD-ROM who communicate with one another in writing about these advanced-level texts—hence the course title, Advanced . . . Reading and Writing. In each unit, members of the cohort first engage in preparatory activities together. Then they use the CD-ROM independently outside the course environment. After using the CD-ROM, they return to the course site to participate online in text-based communicative group activities that are related to the content of the CD-ROM. The activity focused on in this research is the Small Group Forum, the first activity that learners perform after returning from individual study of the CD-ROM. The Small Group Forum, designed as a midpoint exercise in each unit, has tasks aimed at building toward an endpoint essay-writing assignment at the advanced level. Small Group Forum tasks themselves may blend intermediate-level and advanced-level functions.

For the Small Group Forum in each unit, students are divided by the teacher into groups of four, five, or six to converse through written postings. In this study, two Small Group Forum discussions from spring 2003 became the focus of analysis. One forum was chosen from unit 2 (weeks 3 and 4), early in the course, and one from unit 6 (weeks 11 and 12), relatively late in the course. In this semester, the teacher reshuffled membership in the small groups in every unit. In unit 2, students in six groups carried out a task involving negotiation, while in unit 6 students in four groups worked on narration. In each unit, each group had its own forum, in which only members of that group were able to make postings.

In the *BRIX* course management system, interaction in each small group's forum takes place within one or more topic threads, each of which is essentially one Web page that accepts student postings and displays them in chronological order, so that as postings accumulate, a discussion emerges within the thread. A display of accumulated postings is seen in figure 1. A group converses by adding responses at the bottom of a page of accumulated postings. Below the display, a box is available for typing and submitting one's response.

We examined the groups' discussions in units 2 and 6 for patterns of cohesion and community and analyzed certain features of the forums from which the data were obtained. Analysis combined quantitative methods, such as calculating mean length of utterance and counting references to other postings in each thread, with qualitative methods, such as observation of online student behaviors and strategies. Analysis of the data was performed within threads, so that results from one thread could be compared with results from another.

To obtain quantitative data, we employed structured query language to extract data from the course database and passed that data through

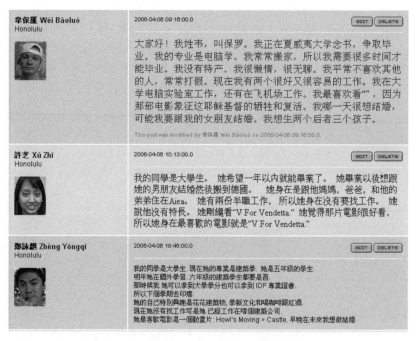

Figure I. Several postings in one thread in a forum

additional special scripts to obtain reliable character and utterance counts. For purposes of this study, a word was defined as either one non-Chinese word (string of characters bounded by white space) or one Chinese character, with punctuation excluded. An utterance was defined as a string of text bounded by full commas (Western comma or Chinese *douhao*—but not *dunhao*) or full stops (Western or Chinese periods). After these automated counts were performed, postings from the forums were closely read and scored by one of us for references to other people and to other postings in the forum.

Analysis and Discussion

We observed three striking patterns in the analyzed data. Two supported cohesion and community in the Small Group Forum, and the other disrupted cohesion and community. These patterns illuminate important principles for online educators wishing to foster cohesion and community in their own courses.

The first pattern was an increase of participation, direct interaction, and personal involvement when the topic of a discussion drifted away from the assigned role-play toward a topic closely related to students' daily lives in their local environment. This pattern points to two important principles: instructor flexibility regarding students' focus on the assigned task and the fostering of connections to students' daily lives and real-world interests. The second pattern was the emergence of a student leader who consistently made conversational moves that effectively shepherded other students in the forum toward task closure. This pattern points to the importance of promoting leadership in the group and providing guidelines for interaction. The third pattern was a sharp decrease in interaction and cohesion in a case where students failed to participate in a single common thread, despite delayed prompting from the instructor. This pattern points to the importance of clear instructions and sustained leadership from the instructor during each task as well as clear definitions of task completion.

Pattern 1: Topic Drifts toward the Personal, Sparks Interest

The topic of unit 2 of Chinese 332 is Chinese regional cuisine. The lesson on the CD-ROM for unit 2, based on a pamphlet published by the Hong Kong Tourist Association for Chinese-speaking visitors to Hong Kong, details four different regional cuisines of China that can be sampled in Hong Kong and describes the distinctive characteristics of each. After independently completing lesson activities on the CD-ROM, students returned to the online course to participate in the Small Group Forum, where the following instructions were given for a role-play:

> You and your friends are on a trip and are transiting through Hong Kong for just one night. Tonight you would like to eat a particular kind of Chinese cuisine you read about in the pamphlet (Cantonese, Sichuanese, Taiwanese, or Hakka). Please discuss with your fellow group members what you would like to eat. You should post at least two replies.[1]

The course designers intended the Small Group Forum task in unit 2 as a midpoint task in the unit to elicit negotiation on a topic related to this reading. While the overall course goal targeted advanced functions such as narration, description, and comparison, midpoint tasks often targeted intermediate functions such as negotiation, leaving advanced functions for later in each unit's instructional sequence. The midpoint task facilitates a transition from receptive skills (the reading the students had just finished) to productive skills (writing), paving the way for the final essay-writing task at the advanced level.

Of six groups completing the unit 2 Small Group Forum task, group 4 showed a distinctive pattern of strong participation, direct interaction, and high personal involvement with the topic. As shown in table 1, group 4 had the highest number of postings, the highest number of postings per participant, the highest total word count, the second-highest rate of references to other group members (by name or by pronoun), and the highest rate of anaphoric references to previous postings. The mean length of utterance in group 4—the total word count divided by the total number of utterances—was similar to that in the other small groups.

By examining the discussion in group 4 (for a full translation, see app. 1), we can see that the higher level of participation appears to be connected with personal interest in the topic—after the point where the discussion drifted away from the assigned role-play toward a related topic that was closely connected with students' daily lives in their local environment. The instructor, evidently valuing the students' enthusiastic participation in discussion of the new topic, decided to go with the flow rather than attempt to drag the discussion back to the assigned topic.

Table I
Quantitative Data, Small Group Forum, Unit 2

Small Group Number	I	2	3	4	5	6
Number of postings	12	7	7	*17*	11	6
Mean postings per active participant (excludes teacher postings)	2.40	1.75	1.75	*4.00*	3.33	2.50
Total word count (excluding teacher postings)	550 (550)	331 (331)	238 (238)	*800 (730)*	735 (682)	221 (197)
Mean length of utterance	11.22	10.68	10.82	10.13	10.07	12.28
Reference to other participants per number of postings	.17	.43	.14	1.12	1.45	.67
Reference to other postings per number of postings	.75	.57	.86	*1.06*	.91	.67

The discussion in group 4 consists of seventeen postings by four group members: Hannah, Wendy, Flora, and Robert. (The names of all participants have been changed.) Since the students had read a pamphlet describing Chinese regional cuisines available in Hong Kong, the assigned role-play was set in Hong Kong. Although all students lived in Honolulu, in other small groups, students familiar with Hong Kong suggested names of actual restaurants in that city.

Hannah, Wendy, Flora, and Robert started the discussion in group 4 by each making one posting. All these postings reflected the students' personal experience and opinion of Chinese cuisine, and all were high in cohesion and community. They pointed toward a group consensus that they should have Taiwanese cuisine. In the fifth posting in the forum, Wendy's second posting, she referred to a Taiwanese restaurant not in Hong Kong but in Honolulu, shifting the frame of reference from a completely fictional role-play to a scenario in which the group members might actually get together to eat in Honolulu. At this point the instructor jumped into the discussion to ask the location of the restaurant Wendy had mentioned, to mention another Taiwanese restaurant in Honolulu, and to query other restaurants that the students might choose from. The instructor's posting exemplified a flexible attitude: she followed Wendy's lead while inviting further negotiation into which the students entered with gusto. If the instructor had rigidly insisted on a return to the assigned role-play, students would not have been able to use their real-world knowledge of Honolulu, nor would their enthusiasm about the real possibility of eating out together have been brought into play.

The high level of participation in group 4 and the strong cohesion and community shown in participants' postings suggest that the instructor's flexibility regarding students' refocus of the assigned task was a pedagogically effective strategy. Furthermore, the instructor's fostering of connections to students' daily lives and real-world interests facilitated increased participation and personal involvement.

Pattern 2: Student Leader Emerges, Spurs Interaction

The discussion in group 4 reveals a second important pattern relating to cohesion and community in online courses: the emergence of a student leader who effectively directed other students in the group toward completing the task. Students' personalities and communication styles play an important role in the formation of their online relationships. Sometimes students take on leadership roles, supplying conversational moves that encourage other participants to move toward the conversational goal. Such students' communication style has been characterized as emerging from an active participation paradigm of persuasive communication (Burgoon and Miller). Active participation by one such student may mean the difference between success and failure for a group. This is not to say that these students are categorically the best performers or that students who do not supply such moves contribute less; rather, these leaders focus and energize the discussion in a way unlike other students.

The moves made in group 4 by Hannah, the first in the group to make a posting, exemplify the active participation paradigm. She started with a concrete proposal ("Let's have Taiwan cuisine today!"), made two statements relating to her personal experience and knowledge ("I have never had authentic Taiwanese cuisine before. I've heard that Taiwan cuisine is very distinctive"), and closed by soliciting others' opinions ("What do you all think?"). Her posting provided a firm anchor for further discussion because she both made a decisive recommendation and solicited others' opinions.

Hannah made her next move after everyone else in the group had posted at least once and the teacher had responded favorably to the shift from a fictional role-playing in Hong Kong to an actual group dinner in Honolulu. First she summarized her perception of the group's agreement on the decision they had been assigned to make ("O.K., so we'll go have Taiwan cuisine"), and then she moved on to the next decision they had to make: which restaurant to eat at ("I think K.C.'s beef noodles are good. I heard that there was another Taiwan-style diner in the Cultural Plaza called 'Elegant Orchid' that also serves Taiwan snacks"). She closed her posting with a question ("Have you all ever been there?"), inviting further contributions from fellow group members—another leadership move.

Other group members failed to decide on a single restaurant and continued to defer to one another. Robert alone raised a question that could determine the choice of restaurant: which place had the best beef noodles? Hannah exercised subtle leadership in her next posting when she offered a judgment ("I think K.C. Kitchen and the 'Elegant Orchid' both have good beef noodles. So it does not really matter which one we go to"), while holding back from flatly recommending a single restaurant. Instead, she again invited participation from the group ("Which one do you all want to eat at? You decide"). After one more turn in which Flora failed to offer any direction, Hannah asserted leadership more directly, while acknowledging Robert's contribution ("Since Robert said he likes to eat beef noodles, let's go to K.C. Kitchen to try their Taiwan snacks"). However, she continued to seek agreement ("How about it, you all?"). Flora immediately affirmed Hannah's choice and then made her only leadership move in the whole forum by raising the new question of when to go. The forum ended after two more inconclusive moves as the class went on to other activities. Hannah's final posting answered a question from Robert and offered further support ("K.C. Kitchen is in the Cultural Plaza in Chinatown. Do you know where that is?"). Overall, her postings exhibited a strong, but not overbearing, leadership that furthered the decision-making goals of the group.

Hannah's strategy of active participation contrasts with Flora's strategy, despite similarities between the two students in other respects. They were both high achievers in the course, and their total number of postings in the course was exactly the same. In group 4, the women made five postings each; Hannah's total word count was 226, and Flora's was 228. Despite the statistical similarities between the two women, Flora's conversational style and strategies are more typical of what Michael Burgoon and Gerald R. Miller term the "passive message reception paradigm" (201). Flora's turns provided little guidance and she was content to leave decision making to others. In four of her five postings, she exhibited a passive, deferential attitude:

> [I]t doesn't really matter. I can eat anything, whatever you like. . . . [W]herever you all decide to go, I will go with you. . . . When you all decide, just tell me what time to go. . . . It doesn't really matter to me either; I can go to whichever. . . . [W]e'll go to whichever one that you think is best, OK?

Only in her final posting did Flora help make a decision ("Good! I have no problem with that! I have been wanting to try Taiwan cuisine for a long time now!") and actively solicit feedback ("So when are we going?").

One wonders what would happen if a forum consisted solely of students like Flora. Clearly Hannah's leadership was critical to the success of the group 4 discussion. The pattern revealed in Hannah's and Flora's contrasting communicative styles shows the importance of promoting leadership in the group and providing guidelines for interaction. Rather than depend on chance to supply a Hannah in each group, instructors can foster Hannah-like behavior in others. Students who seem to be working from the active participation paradigm can be distributed among small groups to leaven the discussion. Instructors can also give all students guidelines on the communicative behavior expected of a group leader and then assign one student in each group to serve as leader. This is not to imply that all participants need to be leaders all the time; indeed, students like Flora also play a role in discussions.

If the instructor assigns responsibilities in this way, students will assume that the instructor is responsible for facilitating discussion. It is up to the instructor to change this perception and stress that designating group leadership actually decentralizes authority in the class; in essence, it is a way to "*share the responsibility* for facilitation with the participants" (Palloff and Pratt 120; emphasis added). To designate student leaders is to foster behavior characteristic of skilled and experienced online teachers, so that not only the teacher but everyone in the learning community acquires skill in facilitating discussions by raising his or her consciousness of what comes naturally in face-to-face speech but that is less salient in online discussion—although computer-mediated communication has been shown to increase interactive competence of language learners (Chun

17). Issuing guidelines for effective facilitation of discussion early in the course, perhaps as a special topic in a forum in the introductory unit in the course, can also help. Guidelines may include the following types of information:

> How many times and for how long each student will be expected to serve as a group leader during the semester and how the instructor will let each student know
>
> Why having group leaders is important (For example, it helps compensate for deficiencies of online asynchronous communication and ensure that discussions move toward their objectives.)
>
> What good group leadership looks like (For example, students might be encouraged to discuss the transcript of group 4 from this study.)
>
> What behavior helps a good group leader manage interaction in the group

The instructor should encourage discussion of the guidelines and seek more examples of effective behavior from the students. The instructor may wish to suggest the following:

> "Priming the pump," that is, leading with one's own contribution as a spur to others
>
> Asking individuals to participate ("I'd like to hear what Gina thinks about . . .")
>
> Requesting additional detail and clarification ("I'd like to hear some reasons why John feels that . . .")
>
> Making clear references to previous postings ("I see what Rolf means about the differences between the city and the countryside, but . . .")
>
> Summarizing old topics and nominating new ones ("So it looks like everyone is in agreement on place and time. How about budget?")
>
> Mediating conflicting opinions and attempting to break stalemates in discussion

Group leadership like Hannah's is clearly desirable. Instructors who can successfully distribute responsibility for facilitating interaction across the whole class are likely to see an increase in such leadership. The discussions occasioned by such leadership are likely to show strong cohesion and community as students' participation is encouraged.

Pattern 3: Group Splits into Multiple Threads, Loses Cohesion

In group 3 in the Small Group Forum in unit 6, cohesion suffered when students failed to participate in a single thread—a single conversational page—in the Web-based forum. The group splintered into multiple threads, and the highly redundant content of their postings indicated that students were not paying attention to what others had already posted—a hallmark of low group cohesion. A look at what happened in this group provides clues about how to prevent such breakdowns and foster group cohesion.

The topic of unit 6 in Chinese 332 was crime; its CD-ROM lesson was based on a newspaper article about the hijacking of a plane in China. Instructions were as follows:

> Each small group will be responsible for one criminal case. Search the Internet for information about the crime, such as the background to the crime, the time and place, what happened, and a description of the perpetrator(s). Each person should contribute three or four sentences. Here are the crimes each small group is assigned:
>
> > Group 1: Matthew Shepard Murder
> > Group 2: Columbine High School Massacre
> > Group 3: Amadou Diallo Case
> > Group 4: Martin Luther King Jr. Assassination

Following these instructions was a sample description of the case of Bonnie and Clyde to serve as a model for students' postings. It was broken down into background, description, and narration, as follows:

> *Background.* Bonnie and Clyde, both from Louisiana, were lovers. In the early 1930s they committed several dozen armed robberies and murders in the western United States and also helped five fellow criminals escape from prison. Both were from poor families. After stealing money, they would usually flee to another state and spend the money on clothes.
> *Description.* Bonnie was fond of wearing flower-print dresses with a leather belt, into which she would stick two or three handguns. Clyde preferred wearing striped suits in bold colors. Both carried themselves fearlessly and became heroes of a sort in the people's imagination.
> *Narration.* Bonnie and Clyde killed an officer of the law. The FBI pursued them, expending two years in the effort. Finally the law staged

a successful ambush and shoot-out in Louisiana, riddling [the criminals'] bodies with bullets and bringing their lives to an end.

The objective was that each person in the group contribute new information about the crime: one person would describe the background, another the sequence of events, another the perpetrators, and so forth. The instructions did not make these goals clear enough: students had to intuit this division of labor from the model postings for background, description, and narration. This lack of clarity may have contributed to the breakdown.

Typically, for an online conversation to cohere, it must take place within a single topic thread, which is established either by the teacher or by the first student to make a posting. On entering the forum, others have only to click on the single thread to enter it and participate in the conversation (see fig. 2).

Group 3 was assigned to discuss the case of the shooting of Amadou Diallo in New York. A breakdown occurred, and the participants posted multiple times alone in the threads each had created. As a result, group 3 was the only group in which the minimum objective of the task—a full description of the crime—was not met. The multiple threads in this small group forum can be seen in figure 3; note that in three of the five student threads there are zero replies.

As shown in table 2, a comparison of all groups in unit 6, the total number of postings and the average number of postings per participant were similar across all groups, but group 3 had the lowest total word count

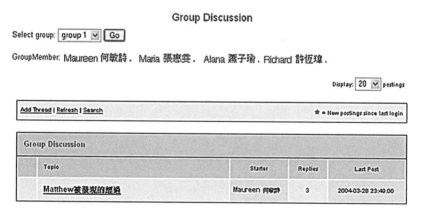

Figure 2. Forum with a single topic thread

Group Discussion

Select group: group 3 ▾ Go

GroupMember: Leanna, Linlin, Katherine, Robert, Jolene,

Display: 20 ▾ postings

Add Thread | Refresh | Search   ★ = New postings since last login

Group Discussion

Topic	Starter	Replies	Last Post
Amadou Diallo	Katherine	1	2003-04-01 20:18:00.0
阿媽度 Case	Leanna	0	2003-03-31 00:28:00.0
諸同一小組的人在同一Thread下張貼！	Qin_laoshi	0	2003-03-26 17:50:00.0
Amadou Diallo	Robert	0	2003-03-24 15:26:00.0
Amadou Diallo Case	Linlin	0	2003-03-22 03:14:00.0
Matthew Shepard Murder	Robert	2	2003-03-24 15:05:00.0

Figure 3. Group 3 forum with multiple topic threads, most showing no replies to the head posting in each thread

and the lowest mean length of utterance. Students in this group had the least to say and used short sentences for the little they did say.

In unit 6, rates of reference to other participants and to other postings were very low overall and are not shown here. Yet the quantitative data tell only part of the story. It is important also to examine what happened and to read the postings from group 3. (See app. 2 for a complete translation of group 3 postings. Students' names have been changed.)

The first posting in group 3 was from Robert, who opened a thread on the wrong topic, not realizing that his group was assigned to describe the Amadou Diallo case. Linlin responded with a correction, and Robert acknowledged his error. In the meantime, Linlin established a new thread with her own contribution—the most elaborate in the whole group—about the Amadou Diallo case. Robert could have followed up in Linlin's thread but instead established yet another thread. This began the splintering process, which snowballed. The reasons for Robert's decision are unclear; having been the first in the group to establish a thread (albeit on the wrong topic), he may have felt that he should repost a thread rather than respond to someone else's. At this point, the instructor should have

Table 2
Quantitative Data, Small Group Forum, Unit 6

Small Group Number	1	2	3	4
Number of postings	7	10	9	9
Mean postings per active participant (excludes teacher postings)	1.50	2.00	1.60	1.80
Total word count	910	538	*465*	535
Mean length of utterance	19.78	13.79	*10.29*	14.86

intervened with clear instructions to the group, for example, by replying to Robert's new posting in the same thread, telling him to copy his posting to Linlin's thread, and advising the other students to follow him. Instead, the instructor started yet another thread and placed the message that she wished to convey—"Everyone in each small group should post inside one thread!"—in the subject line of her additional thread, leaving the head posting in the thread empty. The students may have been aware that she was unhappy about the proliferation of threads but unsure of how they should remedy the situation. Her failure to provide clear guidance allowed further splintering of the group. After her notice, Leanna started yet another thread on the Amadou Diallo case. No one responded. Finally, Katherine established a thread and made a very short posting, to which Jolene responded.

The exact reasons for these multiple sterile threads (i.e., threads to which no one responded) are unknown, but some possibilities suggest themselves:

The case assigned to this group, the shooting of Amadou Diallo, was not as well-known as the other assigned cases. Students may not have been able to obtain much information.

If students lacked information, they may have posted redundant information, repeating what was already posted by others.

A norm of group cohesion is to discourage redundant posting in the same thread, as in a spoken conversation one does not repeat what another person has just said. Postings in the other groups in unit 6 obeyed this norm: they posted in one thread but showed much less redundancy of content than those in group 3. Students in group 3 also avoided overtly violating this norm, but only by establishing new threads, in which they did repeat information.

The teacher offered mixed signals. She told students to post within a single thread but undercut her own advice by not offering specific instructions about which thread they should enter and which thread they should avoid. She also set a bad example by adding another new thread.

Perhaps the most interesting posting in this entire group is Jolene's last posting. She alone observed the norm of group cohesion that discouraged redundant posting. While Katherine's first posting in the thread was too short to meet the full requirements of the assignment, it provided an anchor to which Jolene responded effectively. Without repeating either of Katherine's propositions (i.e., that the police were acquitted or that people were shocked by the verdict), Jolene added facts that fleshed out Katherine's topic—namely, the acquittal of the shooters—by clarifying that the case was handled internally by police administration and that the police officers involved subsequently switched careers. It is clear that Jolene read Katherine's posting and tried to avoid saying exactly the same thing; the lack of redundancy between these two postings shows that Jolene was taking up a conversational thread that Katherine had established and was responding skillfully to it in accordance with the norm of cohesion. Jolene's posting contrasts with postings by her fellow students, who repeat the facts of the case: the victim's name and nationality, the date, the number of shots, and the number of police. No one commented on the several discrepancies in the postings regarding the facts of the case. There was no group attempt to create a single, accurate group narrative.

Groups 1, 2, and 4 in the unit 6 Small Group Forum successfully completed the task of providing sufficiently detailed accounts of their criminal cases. In those groups, students posted in a single thread and clearly paid attention to one another's postings, avoiding redundancy, much as Jolene did in response to Katherine. As a result, each thread in the other groups cohered as a conversation. The splintering of group 3 was an isolated incident in the spring 2003 offering of Chinese 332 and points to the importance of clear instructions and sustained leadership from the instructor during each task as well as clear definitions of task completion. The instructor's contribution to the group's failure in this case is undeniable and is consonant with Rovai's finding:

> [F]eelings of disconnectedness and isolation that have been reported
> in many post-secondary e-learning courses tend to be related to indi-
> vidual course design and/or pedagogy. . . . The data also suggests that
> experienced online instructors can build and sustain levels of commu-
> nity that are at least equal to those experienced in traditional class-
> rooms. ("Preliminary Look" 52)

To conclude, we return to the original questions in our opening, namely,
What pedagogical touchstones should be kept in focus in online language
teaching? What key factors contribute to cohesion and community in the
Web-based environment? On the basis of our analyses of two sets of Small
Group Forum data from an advanced Web-based reading and writing
course in Chinese, we offer the following pedagogical principles, all of which
are important in traditional language teaching, as essential in asynchronous, distance learning environments:

> Tasks must be clearly defined and include an identifiable outcome
> or conclusion; students must know what they are to do and when
> they have done it. Detailed instructions for online forum discus-
> sions might include a minimum number of times a student is ex-
> pected to participate in an activity.
>
> Tasks, when possible, should be realistic, connected to students' daily
> lives, and have some relation to students' knowledge and experi-
> ence. Schemata that are unfamiliar to students need to be intro-
> duced before the instructor assigns the task.
>
> Instructors should prime the pump in the initial stages of the task to
> launch students in the right direction. They should maintain a pres-
> ence and attempt to keep students focused on the task, but they
> should also be flexible and adapt to alternative interpretations of the
> task by the students or to unanticipated directions that students
> might choose to explore.
>
> Instructors should be ready and willing to share the responsibility of
> discourse management and, when necessary, should designate stu-
> dent leaders to keep the pump primed and keep classmates on task
> (Chun; Palloff and Pratt). Leader roles should be rotated among
> class members, but natural leaders could be identified and distrib-
> uted among small groups.

The above four principles are in line with those presented in the
community-of-practice framework for fostering coherence in virtual learning
communities (Wenger, McDermott, and Snyder; expanded on by Rogers

390), whose goal is to create "learning communities in which students are willing, even enthusiastic, to share the responsibility of learning" (Rogers 390).

Note

1. All instructions have been translated from the Chinese by Stephen L. Tschudi.

Works Cited

Beauvois, Margaret Healy. "Conversations in Slow Motion: Computer-Mediated Communication in the Foreign Language Classroom." *Canadian Modern Language Review* 54.2 (1998): 198–217. Print.

Bielaczyc, Katerine, and Allan Collins. "Learning Communities in Classrooms: Advancing Knowledge for a Lifetime." *NASSP Bulletin* 83.604 (1999): 4–10. Print.

Blake, Robert. "Computer Mediated Communication: A Window on L2 Spanish Interlanguage." *Language Learning and Technology* 4.1 (2000): 120–36. Web. 26 June 2006.

———. "What Language Professionals Need to Know about Technology." *ADFL Bulletin* 32.3 (2001): 93–99. Print.

Breen, Michael P. "Learner Contributions to Task Design." *Language Learning Tasks*. Ed. Christopher N. Candlin and Dermot Murphy. Vol. 7. Englewood Cliffs: Prentice, 1987. 23–46. Print. Lancaster Practical Papers in English Language Education.

Burgoon, Michael, and Gerald R. Miller. "An Expectancy Interpretation of Language and Persuasion." *Recent Advances in Language, Communication, and Social Psychology*. Ed. Howard Giles and Robert N. St. Clair. Mahwah: Erlbaum, 1985. 199–229. Print.

Chapelle, Carol A. "Multimedia CALL: Lessons to Be Learned from Research on Instructed SLA." *Language Learning and Technology* 2.1 (1998): 22–34. Web. 26 June 2006.

Chun, Dorothy M. "Using Computer Networking to Facilitate the Acquisition of Interactive Competence." *System* 22.1 (1994): 17–31. Print.

Crookes, Graham, and Susan Gass, eds. *Tasks in a Pedagogical Context: Integrating Theory and Practice*. Clevedon: Multilingual Matters, 1993. Print.

Deci, Edward L., and Richard M. Ryan. *Intrinsic Motivation and Self-Determination in Human Behavior*. New York: Plenum, 1985. Print.

Doughty, Catherine, and Michael H. Long. "Optimal Psycholinguistic Environments for Distance Foreign Language Learning." *Language Learning and Technology* 7.3 (2003): 50–80. Web. 26 June 2006.

Doughty, Catherine, and Teresa Pica. " 'Information Gap' Tasks: Do They Facilitate Second Language Acquisition?" *TESOL Quarterly* 20.2 (1986): 305–25. Print.

Felix, Uschi. *Language Learning Online: Towards Best Practice*. Lisse: Swets, 2003. Print.

Fleming, Stephen, and David V. Hiple. "Distance Education to Distributed Learning: Multiple Formats and Technologies in Language Instruction." *CALICO Journal* 22.1 (2004): 63–82. Print.

Halliday, Michael Alexander Kirkwood, and Ruqaiya Hasan. *Cohesion in English.* New York: Longman, 1976. Print.

Herring, Susan C. "Interactional Coherence in CMC." *Proceedings of the Thirty-Second Hawai'i International Conference on System Sciences.* 5–8 Jan. 1999, Maui. Los Alamitos: Inst. of Electrical and Electronics Engineers, 1999. *IEEE Xplore.* Web. 23 June 2006.

Johnson, Christopher M. "A Survey of Current Research on Online Communities of Practice." *Internet and Higher Education* 4.1 (2001): 45–60. Print.

Lamy, Marie-Noëlle, and Robin Goodfellow. "'Reflective Conversation' in the Virtual Language Classroom." *Language Learning and Technology* 2.2 (1999): 43–61. Web. 26 June 2006.

Lightbown, Patsy M., and Nina Spada. *How Languages Are Learned.* 2nd ed. Oxford: Oxford UP, 1999. Print.

Long, Michael H. "Input and Second Language Acquisition Theory." *Input in Second Language Acquisition.* Ed. Susan M. Gass and Carolyn G. Madden. Rowley: Newbury, 1985. 377–93. Print.

McMillan, David W., and David M. Chavis. "Sense of Community: A Definition and Theory." *American Journal of Community Psychology* 14.1 (1986): 6–23. Print.

Norman, Jerry. *Chinese.* Cambridge: Cambridge UP, 1988. Print.

Nunan, David. "Task-Based Syllabus Design: Selecting, Grading, and Sequencing Tasks." Crookes and Gass 55–68.

Palloff, Rena M., and Keith Pratt. *Building Learning Communities in Cyberspace: Effective Strategies for the Online Classroom.* San Francisco: Jossey-Bass, 1999. Print.

Pennington, Martha C. "The Power of the Computer in Language Education." *The Power of CALL.* Ed. Pennington. Houston: Athelstan, 1996. 1–14. Print.

Pica, Teresa, Ruth Kanagy, and Joseph Falodun. "Choosing and Using Communication Tasks for Second Language Instruction and Research." Crookes and Gass 9–34.

Ribé, Ramon, and Nuria Vidal. *Project Work: Step by Step.* Oxford: Heinemann, 1993. Print.

Rogers, Jim. "Communities of Practice: A Framework for Fostering Coherence in Virtual Learning Communities." *Educational Technology and Society* 3.3 (2000): 384–92. Print.

Rovai, Alfred P. "Building Sense of Community at a Distance." *International Review of Research in Open and Distance Learning* 3.1 (2002): 1–16. Web. 23 June 2006.

———. "A Preliminary Look at the Structural Differences of Higher Education Classroom Communities in Traditional and ALN Courses." *Journal for Asynchronous Learning Networks* 6.1 (2002): 41–56. Web. 23 June 2006.

Schmidt, Richard, Deena Boraie, and Omneya Kassabgy. "Foreign Language Motivation: Internal Structure and External Connections." *Language Learning*

Motivation: Pathways to the New Century. Ed. Rebecca Oxford. Honolulu: U of Hawai'i Second Lang. Teaching and Curriculum Center, 1996. 9–70. Print. Technical Report 11.

Smith, Glenn Gordon, David Ferguson, and Mieke Caris. "Teaching over the Web versus in the Classroom: Differences in the Instructor Experience." *International Journal of Instructional Media* 29.1 (2002): 61–67. Print.

Strambi, Antonella, and Eric Bouvet. "Flexibility and Interaction at a Distance: A Mixed-Mode Environment for Language Learning." *Language Learning and Technology* 7.3 (2003): 81–102. Web. 26 June 2006.

Warschauer, Mark. "Interaction, Negotiation, and Computer-Mediated Learning." *Educational Technology in Language Learning: Theoretical Reflection and Practical Applications*. Ed. Véronique Darleguy, Alex Ding, and Maria Svensson. Lyon: Natl. Inst. of Applied Sciences, 1998. 125–36. Print.

Wellman, Barry. "The Network Community: An Introduction to *Networks in the Global Village*." *Networks in the Global Village*. Ed. Wellman. Boulder: Westview, 1999. 1–48. Print.

Wenger, Etienne, Richard A. McDermott, and William M. Snyder. *Cultivating Communities of Practice: A Guide to Managing Knowledge*. Boston: Harvard Business School P, 2002. Print.

Zhao, Yong, and Seppo Tella. "From the Special Issue Editors." *Language Learning and Technology* 6.3 (2002): 1–4. Web. 26 June 2006.

Appendix I

Translation of unit 2 Small Group Forum, group 4. Items in *italics* appeared originally in English lettering.

HANNAH: Let's have Taiwan cuisine today! I have never had authentic Taiwanese cuisine before. I've heard that Taiwan cuisine is very distinctive. What do you all think?

WENDY: Okay! (rep) What restaurant do you want to go to? I have also never eaten authentic Taiwanese cuisine. Do you know what dishes from Taiwan are good?

FLORA: I have also never eaten Taiwanese cuisine. I've heard their snacks are very good. I have only ever had Cantonese cuisine. I would also like to try Sichuan cuisine because I like spicy food. But it doesn't really matter. I can eat anything, whatever you like.

ROBERT: I think Taiwan cuisine is delicious. Their beef noodles are the best. And their snacks are very popular too. So let's have Taiwan cuisine, OK?

WENDY: I know that many people are of the opinion that Taiwan's snacks are delicious. So I would like to eat with you guys. Doesn't the "Hometown Diner" specialize in Taiwan cuisine? We could go there to eat. How about it?

QIN_LAOSHI: Wendy, where is the "Hometown Diner"? Have you noticed that during the last lesson *Tsu-hou* said that the restaurant his parents run, the *K.C. Kitchen*, is a Taiwan-style diner and their food is delicious! Besides these two, what other places are there?

FLORA: I am not quite sure where there might be a Taiwan restaurant, because I have never eaten Taiwan cuisine. So wherever you all decide to go, I will go with you.

HANNAH: O.K., so we'll go have Taiwan cuisine. I think *K.C.*'s beef noodles are good. I heard that there was another Taiwan-style diner in the Cultural Plaza called "Elegant Orchid" that also serves Taiwan snacks. Have you all ever been there?

WENDY: The "Hometown Diner" is in Chinatown. I have not been to the *K.C. Kitchen*, but if you all want to go, then I will go with you. When do you all want to go?

ROBERT: Which of the three—the "Hometown Diner", the "Elegant Orchid", and *K.C. Kitchen*—have you all been to? Which one has the best beef noodles? I can go anytime.

FLORA: I have also heard that the Taiwanese restaurant inside the Cultural Plaza is very good. When you all decide, just tell me what time to go.

HANNAH: I think *K.C. Kitchen* and the "Elegant Orchid" both have good beef noodles. So it does not really matter which one we go to. Which one do you all want to eat at? You decide.

FLORA: It doesn't really matter to me either; I can go to whichever. So if you say that you have been to both restaurants, then we'll go to whichever one that you think is best, OK?

HANNAH: Since Robert said he likes to eat beef noodles, let's go to *K.C. Kitchen* to try their Taiwan snacks. How about it, you all?

FLORA: Good! I have no problem with that! I have been wanting to try Taiwan cuisine for a long time now! So when are we going?

ROBERT: Where is the *K.C. Kitchen*? Can anyone go with me?

HANNAH: *K.C. Kitchen* is in the Cultural Plaza in Chinatown. Do you know where that is?

Appendix 2

Translation of unit 6 Small Group Forum, group 3. Threads rearranged here to reflect chronological order. Items in *italics* appeared originally in English lettering.

Thread 1 - *Matthew Shepard Murder*

ROBERT: *Matthew Shepard* was a homosexual studying at *the University of Wyoming*. He died at *Poudre Valley Hospital* at the age of twenty-one.

LINLIN: *Robert*, in Group 3 we are supposed to discuss the *Amadou Diallo case*

ROBERT: *sorry i did the wrong case. please ignore this.*

Thread 2 - *Amadou Diallo Case*

LINLIN: February 4, 1999, in the middle of the night, an African-Haitian immigrant, *Amadou Diallo*, died as a result of 41 shots from guns fired by four New York police officers. Diallo was returning home from work that night, preparing to enter the house, when he suddenly changed his mind and thought he would like to go out and have something to eat. When he turned around, four police officers suddenly opened fire, firing 41 rounds, 19 of which struck him. He died just outside his apartment building.

Thread 3 - *Amadou Diallo*

ROBERT: Amadou Diallo was an African-American who died as a result of being shot 41 times by New York police. This case caused great discontent among African-Americans, and some felt that racism was involved.

Thread 4 - Everyone in each small group should post inside one *thread!*
[Empty thread created by the teacher with no posted content, only the subject heading]

Thread 5 - Amadou *Case*

LEANNA: Amadou, a 22-year-old North African immigrant, died February 4, 1999 after the New York City police fired 41 shots at him, hitting him 19 times. Because the police thought that he looked like a suspected rapist, they wanted to question him. But because the police mistakenly thought that he was about to pull a gun and resist them, they opened fire first and shot him.

Thread 6 - *Amadou Diallo*

KATHERINE: After this incident occurred, the police were acquitted, and this verdict shocked many people!
JOLENE: The two officers in question were not subject to legal penalties. The case was handed to internal police administration to be handled. The two police officers who fired their guns became firefighters.

Dawn M. Formo and Kimberly Robinson Neary

Constructing Community: Online Response Groups in Literature and Writing Classrooms

TIMOTHY: ... after finding these evidences you still need to prove ... homosexuals couples are going to feel happier and be more productive as workers.

JUSHENG: yeah

HA YOUNG: i c. good advice—

JUSHENG: yeah cos now ure just assuming they are unhappy now which equates to less productivity

KIMBERLY: you guys are going to put me out of a job[1]

We look forward to moments like this one in our classrooms: clear demonstrations that a collaborative digital writing community is emerging. As instructors with several years of experience, we have found peer response to be an integral part of the design of our literature, writing, and (even) film courses. Committed to facilitating classroom writing communities and to integrating technology into writers' processes, we created online response groups (ORGs)—small course-based groups of students who respond to one another's writing online. In our study of these groups, we concluded that ORG pedagogy engenders engaged writing communities dedicated to useful response.

147

Buttressed by writing center and writing studies research and our experience designing and facilitating an asynchronous online writing lab (OWL), we designed ORGs and a concomitant pedagogy for our classrooms. The ORG pedagogy we present here through a case study provides students with a productive language for response that minimizes students' frustration with specious comments. Even more, this type of focused digital response helps students recognize the value of revision and develop the skills required to provide and receive useful digital feedback.

Connections: In-Class Peer Response, OWLs, ORGs, and Writing Centers

In-class peer review, OWLs, and ORGs all have origins in writing centers— places on campuses for writers to engage in honest, collaborative conversations about their texts.[2] For classroom response theory and pedagogy, there is a clear heritage of the community-building values integral to brick-and-mortar writing centers.[3] The digital-response environment shares the same community-building values; as digital-response research suggests, however, fulfilling these values requires different strategies.[4] David Coogan captures the inherent challenge of the online environment by comparing the dynamic of the face-to-face and digital communities: "[I]n a face-to-face meeting, the student and tutor talk 'over' a paper. The paper connects them. . . . The underlying question soon becomes, what will be DONE to the paper?" Online, however, "[a]ll we have is text" (3). The shift from dialogue to text is the challenge instructors face when transitioning to online response.

To meet this challenge, digital scholars and practitioners encourage colleagues new to digital-response environments to keep face-to-face writing center theory and practice and in-class peer-review research fresh in their minds when moving to online spaces. On the one hand, as Eric Miraglia and Joel Norris underscore, OWL (and ORG) designers should "get technology out of the way of what [is] really important: the social, interactive spaces in which patrons and tutors . . . interact" (91). On the other hand, we must heed Lee-Ann Kastman Breuch and Sam J. Racine's reminder to consider the nature of digital technology and the ways it can influence the writing process and enrich the response experience for writers (Breuch and Racine; Breuch). Digital scholars acknowledge differences between the face-to-face and digital environments and call for both pedagogical and theoretical shifts in consulting online. Digital response does not just provide another mode for conferencing; having texts, not dialogue, at the center of response influences writers in intellectually distinct ways.

Moving to Course-Based ORGs

Even as the focus shifts from dialogue to text, the power of these environments as productive sites of response does not change. There is value in writing centers, in-class peer response, and OWLs.

Given these established response environments, why emphasize the value of ORGs in the writing classroom? ORGs are necessary, not because they abandon established response pedagogy, but because they combine and extend the best practices of writing-center, face-to-face-classroom, and OWL-response pedagogy. In addition to the comparative features noted in table 1, ORGs accomplish the following:[5]

> Help students develop technology literacy skills
> Engage students actively in the feedback process as egalitarian peers rather than as mentors or mentees
> Redistribute workload for faculty members because student-respondents are integral to the class's design
> Place responsibility for response on students

Of these features, the last is particularly significant. ORGs contribute to a collaborative pedagogy that requires instructors and students to share responsibility for the class dynamics. This shared responsibility allows for the community building that students in our case study demonstrate as a hallmark of ORGs.

An ORG in the Classroom: A Case Study

In the spring semester of 2006, Kimberly taught WRIT 140, a 100-level class at a private, Research I university that uses a workshop model to teach expository writing. There were fifteen students in the class: seven women and eight men. Eight of the students were nonnative English speakers, and their home languages included Korean, Chinese, Portuguese, and Malay. Students' majors ran the gamut from theater to electrical engineering. As

Table 1
Comparison of Peer-Response Environments

Environmental Features	Writing Center, Face-to-Face	Classroom, Face-to-Face	OWLs	ORGs
Focus of session	Honest dialogic conversation	Honest dialogic conversation	Submitted text	Submitted text
Feedback	Oral and impromptu; not traceable or recorded	Oral; may be impromptu or planned; not traceable or recorded	Written; recordable; may be impromptu (synchronous) or planned (asynchronous); may be traceable.	Written, planned, recordable, and traceable
Status of respondent	"Outsider" to the community of writers, since the course materials and discussions may not be familiar	"Insider" to the community of writers; shares an understanding of the course materials and discussions	"Outsider" to the community of writers, since the course materials and discussions may not be familiar	"Insider" to the community of writers; shares an understanding of the course materials and discussions
Body language	Nonverbal cues acknowledged	Nonverbal cues acknowledged	Nonverbal cues not available	Nonverbal cues not available
Instructor responsibility	Not applicable	At faculty discretion	Not applicable	Initial set-up required; periodic check-in suggested
Challenges	Feedback not always specifically recalled by writer after the session is over; limited by hours of operation	Feedback not always specifically recalled by writer after the session is over; limited to class time	Technology glitches can be intrusive; can feel like dehumanized interaction	Requires class period to introduce language of response

part of the curricular design, WRIT 140 students exchanged and responded to essays over *Blackboard*. Along with homework and in-class activities, ORG participation contributed to ten percent of students' overall grade.

At the end of the semester, the students anonymously completed a survey about their online experiences. When asked to describe the feedback they received, most of the students identified global-level issues, rather than surface-level issues, as helpful.[6] Three students noted that the "specificity" of the comments helped them target particular issues. As one student explained, "I was able to understand what specifics I needed to change." In addition, four students thought that the ORGs gave them the opportunity to gain multiple perspectives on their work.

Most students, however, felt that the ORGs helped them with the global-level issues named in the writing program's rubric (cogency, support, control, and addressing the issue). By the semester's end, they appropriated this language for their feedback to their peers. Their survey responses suggest that the quality of feedback and the response language they developed created an engaged community.

Creating Community through Response

To better understand their ORG experience and its implications for community building, we looked to the students' ORG comments to see if, in fact, they had generated the types of useful comments they acknowledged in their survey responses. In the response process, students provided two forms of feedback—marginal comments in the body of the texts and letters at the end. As the survey comments suggest, students praised the ORGs for the specific comments peers provided, which were evident most often in the marginal comments. For that reason, in this case study, we chose to focus on the marginal comments rather than the letters. Students generated 883 marginal comments over 90 essay responses for an average of 9.8 comments for each essay.

Their responses fell into six discrete categories, as identified in figure 1 and table 2. In our analysis, two of the response categories, void and word choice, were less productive than the others in facilitating a sense of community in the ORGs. Even the students recognized these comments as useless—only one student identified surface-level comments as useful on the survey. Yet many students could not escape the allure of these comments. With practice, however, students moved beyond these types of comments.

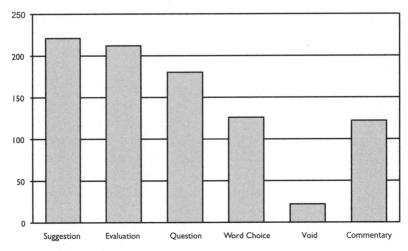

Figure 1. Frequency of response types

In responses to essays produced later in the semester, such comments were infrequent.

We were particularly vigilant for those kinds of comments that Nancy Sommers has labeled "not text-specific," those comments that "could be interchanged, rubber-stamped, from text to text" (152). Void or vague comments like "good" and "OK" do not help students identify the strengths and weaknesses of their draft. Moreover, such comments suggest a cursory glance at a text. We were encouraged to find that the numbers supported our survey findings—students offered relatively few void comments. We also realized that the void comments were not, in fact, rhetorically empty. They contributed to the developing community; the occasional "good job" connected writer and respondent and encouraged the writer to continue the revision process. ORG participant Bharat, for example, connects his void comments to more substantive evaluations or suggestions. In a comment to Louise, he writes, "*This is a good point* but it is repeated from the previous paragraph, perhaps put other evidence in here" (emphasis added). By combining vague yet encouraging responses with more specific and targeted feedback, he suggests that he wants to establish a personal connection with each author and create a more receptive environment for his ideas. In combination with other types of response and in moderation, these comments were effective.

Table 2
Types of ORG Responses

Type	Definitions	Student Examples
Question	Respondent asks for further clarification of ideas. *Closed:* required yes/no or single-word response *Open:* required further, detailed explanation; not answered by yes/no or a single word	*Closed:* Wife battery would not be an issue if the family is constituted of two or even more parents of the same sex [[Wouldn't this cause same-sex battery?]]. *Open:* prevent guns from getting into the wrong hands [[and how will this be done?]]
Suggestion	Respondent offers alternative approach.	United States is the leading cause of accidental death. [[If you give some statistics, it may make your argument stronger.]]
Evaluation	Respondent judges particular elements of author's text.	The core teaching of Confucius, *one of the four greatest sages in mankind's history* [[too sweeping of a statement]]
Word Choice	Respondent comments on surface-level issues (e.g., spelling or word choice).	be argued that advertisements on its [[their]] own are actually depicting a real threat to the public
Void	Respondent marks text with a positive adjective that is typically not followed by any specific element.	Also, gay couples raising children would provide diverse, less restrictive family forms, and therefore it would be beneficial to society because it wouldn't force conformity. [[good]]
Commentary	Respondent makes an observation on the content of author's essay, most often using an "I" statement.	Johnny now takes Ritalin. [[I like the way you set the mood and show the social problem in a personal, easily identifiable way.]]

Of the remaining types of responses, commentary responses (most often represented by "I" statements) were not among the top three forms of response; as a group, these writers offered only 122 commentary responses out of 893 total responses. Yet commentary did play a significant role. In combination with their suggestions and honest questions, commentary provided writers with an authentic audience response. On the survey, several students credit the ORG for allowing writers to share "multiple perspectives." Respondents' use of "I" statements made concrete the community that was reading and responding to the texts.

André offers a response to Yan Lin about her first paper that show-cases the rich sense of audience the "I" statements, in combination with other responses, can afford.[7] He explains:

> Good thesis, but I have a hard time seeing the focus of the topic at hand. Where is the private trouble? Is it in the immorality perceived by the public, or in the juxtaposed point "conservative social policies and attitudes"?

Notice the relation among the evaluation at the start of this feedback, the commentary in the form of an "I" statement, and the two questions: each seems to build on the other. Additionally, after the "I" statement, André links his questions specifically to Yan Lin's text. André's voice is clear; so is his attention to Yan Lin's text and his suggestions for revision. Even if Yan Lin does not agree with André, she can be certain that he has considered her text carefully and offered feedback in earnest.

Overwhelmingly, student comments are either suggestions or evaluations, both of which indicate the ORG's community-building potential. When making their suggestions, students range from the more tentative, as when Julie says, "The sentence *does not really* connect to the previous one, *maybe* you can add 'however,'" to the more directive, as when Louise bluntly states, "*Make this* arguable, schools must estabalish after school programs because" (emphasis added). In both cases, students do more than just state that the original version does not work—they offer concrete alternatives for making the claims more effectively. Their level of detail here demonstrates their commitment to one another's papers and, ultimately, to their community.

Students also combine their suggestions with both implicit and explicit evaluations. For instance, Suraj tells Julie that she has a "good thesis" but that it "should be incorporated in the first paragraph." Terrence tells Jusheng that it would be "more convincing" to add "facts instead of making up a scenario." Rather than just mandate change, many students gave a rationale to the author to support their suggestions, which reinforced the sense of congenial conversation in the asynchronous exchange. Notably, it was not all positive criticism—Terrence's comment suggests that he felt the example Jusheng offered was not as convincing as it could be. Yet instead of simply dismissing Jusheng's efforts, Terrence offers him a new approach.

All students who provided marginal comments included some evaluations. In doing so, these students established a degree of authority—even the respondent who offered the fewest evaluations was willing to take this risk. What strikes us is not only the commonality of these writers' evaluative comments but also the way they used these comments. Of the 212 evaluative comments made by the class, 142 were made in combination with a suggestion, question, comment, or void comment. For instance, Julie writes to Adrian in response to his second paper, "Clear thesis! Add more analyze about why the use of fear is unethical and immoral." This group's commitment to offering honest feedback along with revision suggestions points to their authority as writers, as respondents, and as members of this writing community.

Finally, many respondents asked questions as part of their feedback; what struck us as meaningful were the types of questions asked and how they were posited. Seventy-three percent of all questions asked were open-ended, inviting writers to clarify their ideas. Most often, students asked questions in the context of another comment. André, for example, responds to Bharat's third paper by commenting and asking, "Your thesis is a bit broad. You're basically just rephrasing the prompt into an answer. What specific changes would be beneficial? Focus on specifics rather then everything." Like many of his peers, André makes judgments but in a supportive way—he follows his judgments with an open-ended question and a specific suggestion, indicating his involvement with Bharat's ideas and his rhetorical approach.

In crafting open-ended questions such as these, the respondents made clear their engagement with their peers' texts. Their questions appear to represent honest questions, questions to which they would truly appreciate answers. Yet even the closed-ended questions, which represent only twenty-seven percent of the questions, proved productive. By placing these questions in proximity to other response types, respondents were clearly committed to helping their peers achieve clarity in their texts.

Ultimately, the students' feedback to one another reifies their survey responses. As digital peer respondents, they created a writing community by providing feedback that is both honest and supportive. Even more, the frequency of the useful and useless comments suggests that these writers used this ORG as a place to experiment—a sure sign that this space is a constructive place for emerging writers.

Getting an ORG Started

To assist you in designing your own course-based ORGs, below are five key steps, organized chronologically. Technology issues should, of course, be resolved as early as possible to avoid any potential challenges. Notably, students should be introduced to the language of response before setting up the groups. We have found this order useful because it provides time to get a sense of the demographics and skill levels of the class.[8] Finally, a short debrief can be extremely useful to cement students' responding skills.

1. *Technology.* Choose the technology platform that best complements your campus and students' technology literacy and access. Students can use e-mail accounts, e-mail distribution lists, or, if possible, file exchange programs (e.g., *Blackboard* or *WebCT*) to exchange essays.
2. *Language of response.* Introduce students to the language of honest questions and "I" statements over the course of an entire class period (see app. 1).
3. *ORG Procedures.* Provide students with a handout explaining ORG procedures. This will reduce, but not completely eliminate, technical glitches. Instructors may choose to provide students with alternative response opportunities (conferences with instructors, writing center visits) in case of technology problems.
4. *Response groups.* Set up response groups. Groups should include three to four heterogeneous students with diverse skill levels (if possible). These may be set for the entire quarter or semester, or they may change membership with each assignment.
5. *Follow-up and debrief.* Review student responses after the first assignment to confirm students' comprehension of the useful types of comments. Conduct an in-class activity with examples from the first ORG to reinforce the more effective responses (see app. 2).

Ensuring Successful ORGs: Q and A

Here we address some pressing concerns about implementing ORGs into your classrooms.

If I'm not very conversant in technology, how difficult will this be?

As you make an initial foray into the use of technology in the classroom, you will find ORGs to be a step in the right direction. Because ORGs work on a variety of platforms, including e-mail, many instructors use software supported by their institutions. Moreover, since ORGs do not compel instructors to move from face-to-face to exclusively online instruction, faculty members who are searching for an introduction to technology in their classrooms may find this a safe way to experiment. Finally, those instructors who are comfortable sharing authority in the classroom may find that they have students in their class willing to set up their ORGs or to instruct the class in particular platforms.

If my students are not very conversant in technology, won't this threaten any progress I've made with my high-anxiety students?

Because most students will have at least a working knowledge of sending and receiving e-mail, you may choose to start with this technology. Once students have been introduced to this technology, high-anxiety students can flourish with the added level of distance. They may have little to say in face-to-face response groups, but in online spaces they are able to comment freely without fear of censure or ridicule.[9]

Won't my students go off topic or give useless feedback without the necessary supervision?

Our experience suggests that students are ready for this responsibility. Students' level of commitment will vary, of course, but most of our students gave feedback that demonstrated a sense of accountability to their peers.[10]

Our hope is that our case study, along with the practical suggestions we offer for implementing this pedagogy, encourages you to experiment with online response groups. Many instructors already include some version of peer response as part of their pedagogy. By conducting this activity online and structuring it appropriately, you will begin to move your students toward a new level of technological literacy. Like Breuch, we argue that as instructors, we have a professional obligation to teach technology literacy; online response groups are one transitional way to accomplish this goal (130). We look forward to sharing other strategies as you explore your new ORG communities.

Notes

1. This is an excerpt from a *Blackboard* synchronous response group discussion. Students provided us with written permission to use their responses and

writing in this case study. We have not corrected any grammar and spelling errors in the students' feedback.

2. Some key articles in writing center research include Bruffee, "Collaborative Learning" and "Peer Tutoring"; DiPardo; Harris; Lunsford; North.

3. For texts that showcase well-established theory and practice on in-class face-to-face writing response and suggest the relation between writing center and face-to-face response theory and pedagogy, see Barnard; Elbow, *Writing without Teachers* and *Writing with Power*; Gere; Spear.

4. Breuch; Breuch and Racine; Harris and Pemberton; Hawisher and Sullivan; Hobson; Inman and Sewell.

5. We'd like to thank Dave Neary for his generous assistance with formatting our tables and figure.

6. For the purposes of this study, we have identified as "surface-level" those issues that refer to errors in grammar and syntax and as "global-level" those issues that refer to the content or rhetorical elements (e.g., organization, argumentative force, support) of the essay.

7. Of the 122 commentary statements offered by the class, 103 were surrounded by other types of feedback.

8. See Breuch; Monroe; Richardson; Sommers; Straub.

9. Like our case study, Mark Mabrito's "Electronic Mail as a Vehicle for Peer Response" also makes this point. With practice, ORGs offer a level of comfort that can translate into more productive in-class relationships for low- and high-anxiety writers and respondents alike.

10. Lee Honeycutt, in his article "Comparing E-Mail and Synchronous Conferencing in Online Peer Response," also found asynchronous online response to be productive for student writers.

11. Developed in consultation with Michelle Mullen from the San Dieguito Academy and the College of Education at California State University, San Marcos (see Mullen).

Works Cited

Barnard, Ian. "Whole-Class Workshops: The Transformation of Students into Writers." *Issues in Writing* 12.2 (2002): 124–43. Print.

Breuch, Lee-Ann Kastman. *Virtual Peer Review*. Albany: State U of New York P, 2004. Print.

Breuch, Lee-Ann Kastman, and Sam J. Racine. "Developing Sound Tutor Training for Online Writing Centers: Creating Productive Peer Reviewers." *Computers and Composition* 17.3 (2000): 245–63. Print.

Bruffee, Kenneth A. "Collaborative Learning and the 'Conversation of Mankind.'" *College English* 46.7 (1984): 635–52. Print.

———. "Peer Tutoring and the 'Conversation of Mankind.'" *Writing Centers: Theory and Administration*. Ed. Gary A. Olson. Urbana: NCTE, 1984. 3–15. Print.

Coogan, David. "Towards a Rhetoric of On-Line Tutoring." *Writing Lab Newsletter* 19.1 (1994): 3–5. Print.

DiPardo, Annie. "'Whispers of Coming and Going': Lessons from Fannie." *Writing Center Journal* 12.2 (1992): 125–44. Print.

Elbow, Peter. *Writing without Teachers.* New York: Oxford UP, 1973. Print.

———. *Writing with Power.* New York: Oxford UP, 1981. Print.

Gere, Anne Ruggles. *Writing Groups: History, Theory, and Implications.* Carbondale: Southern Illinois UP, 1987. Print.

Harris, Muriel. "Collaboration Is Not Collaboration Is Not Collaboration: Writing Center Tutorials versus Peer-Response Groups." *College Composition and Communication* 43.3 (1992): 369–83. Print.

Harris, Muriel, and Michael Pemberton. "Online Writing Labs (OWLS): A Taxonomy of Options and Issues." *Computers and Composition* 12.2 (1995): 145–59. Print.

Hawisher, Gail E., and Patricia Sullivan. "Women on the Networks: Searching for E-Spaces of Their Own." *Feminism and Composition Studies.* Ed. Susan C. Jarratt and Lyn Worsham. New York: MLA, 1998. 172–97. Print.

Hobson, Eric H., ed. *Wiring the Writing Center.* Logan: Utah State UP, 1998. Print.

Honeycutt, Lee. "Comparing E-Mail and Synchronous Conferencing in Online Peer Response." *Written Communication* 18.1 (2001): 26–60. Print.

Inman, James A., and Donna N. Sewell, eds. *Taking Flight with OWLs: Examining Electronic Writing Center Work.* Mahwah: Erlbaum, 2000. Print.

Lunsford, Andrea A. "Collaboration, Control, and the Idea of a Writing Center." *Writing Center Journal* 12.1 (1991): 3–10. Print.

Mabrito, Mark. "Electronic Mail as a Vehicle for Peer Response: Conversations with High- and Low-Apprehensive Writers." *Written Communication* 8.4 (1991): 509–32. Print.

Miraglia, Eric, and Joel Norris. "Cyberspace and Sofas: Dialogic Space and the Making of an Online Writing Lab." Inman and Sewell 85–103.

Monroe, Barbara. "The Look and Feel of the OWL Conference." Hobson 3–24.

Mullen, Michelle. "How to Respond to Student Writing." CAPI Summer Institute 2000. California State U, San Marcos. 3–9 Aug. 2000. Workshop.

North, Stephen. "The Idea of a Writing Center." *College English* 46.5 (1984): 433–46. Print.

Richardson, S. "Students' Conditioned Response to Teachers' Response: Portfolio Proponents, Take Note!" *Assessing Writing* 7.2 (2000): 117–41. Print.

Sommers, Nancy. "Responding to Student Writing." *College Composition and Communication* 33.2 (1982): 148–56. Print.

Spear, Karen. *Sharing Writing: Peer Response Groups in English Classes.* Portsmouth: Boynton-Cook, 1988. Print.

Straub, Richard. *A Sourcebook for Responding to Student Writing.* Cresskill: Hampton, 1999. Print.

Appendix 1: The Language of Response

Lesson Plan

Materials

"Language of Response" handout (see handout 1); "Responding to Writing" activity (see handout 2); one-page writing sample excerpted from a student text

Goals

Introduce student writers to a language of response; allow students to practice using this language with their papers.

Class Description

In this class, students conduct peer reviews online. This review system only works when all students participate. As such, students should receive points for submitting a draft as well as points for each draft commented on. If, for some reason, a student does not submit a draft, points can be accumulated by taking a draft to the writing center. Students should be aware that the writing center visit will only count for points if their peer did not submit a draft; students cannot attend the writing center in lieu of commenting on peers' essays.

Class Discussion

Introducing Useful and Useless Comments

The instructor can begin by asking students to recall a paper that they spent a good deal of time writing and on which they received suggestions for revision from a peer, teacher, or friend. Students can then reflect on the feedback they received and create a chart with two columns: "Useful" and "Useless." Students should jot down at least three useful and three useless comments they received and then share these comments with the class.

After students have completed their charts, the instructor can collect the feedback to create a class chart. (We have used transparencies to record this feedback.) The instructor can then read the class list back to the students and ask them to describe what the class is reporting as useful and useless feedback.

Linking Students' Comments to the Research

In a minilecture, the instructor can link the students' comments to the research. (Note: Students' feedback to the first activity will most likely reinforce the research findings. Tell students this.) The instructor can then present commenting as a genre for which teachers and students usually receive little training. Finally, the instructors can review the research findings:

Comments often take students away from their own purposes as writers; comments from teachers often do this.
Comments are often not text-specific but generic, rubber-stamped comments.
Writers often feel that they are not receiving genuine feedback (see Sommers).

The goal of respondents should be to give writers "an inherent reason for revising" (Sommers 151).

Providing the Desired Feedback

For this topic, the instructor can distribute and discuss the "Language of Response" handout, the writing sample, and student-generated samples of responses that use "I" statements and honest questions, if available. Students can then be asked to respond to the writing sample by doing the following:

Putting squiggly lines under words, phrases, or sentences that are particularly effective.
Putting flat lines under words, phrases, or sentences that are unclear.
Asking at least one honest question in the margins about each paragraph.
Writing a brief letter to the author of the writing sample using "I" statements and honest questions.

After students have reviewed the writing sample, the instructor can ask students to share examples of words, phrases, or sentences they marked. Two or three students can share their letters with the class. The instructor can then discuss each letter in turn, encouraging the class to offer revision suggestions for the letters.

Practicing the "Language of Response"

The instructor can move the class to the computer lab, where he or she can distribute and facilitate the "Responding to Writing" activity.

It may be helpful to conclude this lesson with a question-and-answer session with the class.

Handout 1, Language of Response

As a respondent . . .

1. Before you begin sharing work with a peer, get to know each other a bit as writers.
2. Discuss and agree on the "rules" that you and your peers want to use as respondents.
3. Focus on your response to the text.
4. Don't talk about the writer. Talk about yourself and how *you* responded to the piece (see suggested techniques below for using "I" statements and honest questions).
5. Ask questions about things you don't understand.
6. Be specific with your comments.
7. Use examples of things in the writing that made you feel the way you do.
8. Share your feelings truthfully.
9. Have more than one thing to discuss.
10. Give the type of responses that you want to receive.

Use "I" Statements (Let the writer know you responded)

Helpful things to say	*What not to say*
"I wanted to hear more about . . ."	"I think you should change . . ."
"I wasn't interested until you wrote . . ."	"I felt you did a good job with . . ."
"I didn't understand why . . ."	"I believe you should . . ."
"I was excited, confused, irritated (etc.) when . . ."	"I thought your letter/memo/e-mail was pretty good."

Ask Honest Questions (What do you really want to know that you don't already know?)

Helpful things to say	*What not to say*
"Why did you mention . . . ?"	"Don't you think it would be good to . . . ?"
"What happened to the information from . . . ?"	"Wouldn't it be better if you . . ."
"Who did you intend as the primary audience?"	"Why would anyone want to read . . . ?"
"Where did you provide the details about . . . ? I must have missed that part."	"Why not cut the part about . . . ?"

Handout 2, Responding to Writing

Preparing Your Text for Feedback

1. Let's begin by getting your writing sample prepared to exchange with a peer. Access a copy of your essay, and open your document.
2. At the top of your document, insert the following questions and respond to them: What is the assignment prompt or goal of the text below? What specific question(s) do I have of the respondent to my text about my text?
3. Save your document with a slightly revised name. If, for instance, your document was saved as Vargas.doc, save it a second time as Vargas_revision1.doc. This new name will help you keep track of the original document and the subsequent revisions.
4. Change seats or digitally exchange your work with a peer. You should now see your peer's writing on the screen.

Responding to a Colleague's Text

5. Review the "Language of Response" handout. Keep the idea of "I" statements and honest questions fresh in your mind.
6. Review the responses your peer provided to the questions noted in step 2. If you have questions or comments about his or her response, indicate so by including that feedback in his or her document.
7. Skim the body of the text once. Then read the text and insert your comments using brackets and bold [[i.e., **You want your comments to be eas-**

ily discernible from the body of the text.]]. In addition, I encourage you to indicate successful and less successful words, phrases, sentences, or passages by marking those sections using the heart-flutter/flatline system—that is, *italics* and <u>underline</u>.

8. At the end of the text, write a brief letter to the writer. Remember, you are *not* grading the paper. Your goal in this letter is not to justify a grade. Your goal is to provide honest feedback for the writer. What makes sense to you? Where did you get lost? Are there particular words, images, or ideas that strike you in particular now that you are reflecting on the piece? If so, say so. We encourage you to consider quoting words or phrases from the writer's text in your letter. In this letter, remember that you are a writer writing to another writer, not a teacher writing to a student.

9. Save your additions to this document and send the work back to the writer or return to the computer with your work.

Understanding the Feedback to Your Text

10. Review the feedback from your colleague. Think of one question or comment you have about the feedback, in preparation for a group discussion.

Break-Out Discussion Activities and Questions

11. What did you learn about responding online?
12. What impact do you believe the online feedback will have on your text?
13. How useful is this feedback compared with a face-to-face environment?
14. When will you want to use online feedback? Face-to-face feedback?

Appendix 2: ORG Response Debrief

Goals

Allow students to see multiple examples of feedback; encourage students to articulate the characteristics of effective response; help students generate a rubric for themselves to use when formulating feedback.

Class Presentation

Instructors can introduce the follow-up activity by asking students to find at least three specific examples each of useful and not useful feedback. Once students have located three clear examples of each, they should type them on a separate sheet of paper, taking care to mix useful and useless together without identifying them as such.

Students should be encouraged to maintain anonymity—they should understand that the follow-up activity is meant not as a reward or punishment for ORG work but as a way to produce consistency in ORG responses.

Class Activity

In class, instructors can have students get into small groups of three or four students, reminding them that their group should consist of entirely new peers—they should not be in groups with any of their ORG respondents.

Each group can then read the examples on their list. Groups should determine if the example is a heart flutter (i.e., useful feedback) or a flatline (i.e., useless feedback). Groups should discuss what characteristics they note with both types and should try to reach consensus as to what makes a comment or question useful or useless.

Once groups have reviewed their lists, instructors can have each group share with the class one to two of their heart flutters and flatlines. As they read, record their responses on the board as either useful or useless.

Next, students can review the two lists generated by the class. Instructors can discuss the characteristics of each type with the class. Ideally, students will begin to generate a rubric for themselves that they can use when formulating their own feedback.

Nike Arnold

Language in Action: Supporting Foreign Language Literacy Development with Online Discussions

The following case study describes the integration of online communications into an advanced foreign language class, giving university students an opportunity to interact with native speakers. After describing the setup of this project, I explain the practical and pedagogical reasoning behind its design, then how the online discussions were used for instructional purposes to fit into a literacy-based curriculum.

Description of Online Discussions

The online discussions described here were integrated into a third-year German composition and conversation class, which had an enrollment of fifteen students. As for many foreign language classes at this level, the students formed a rather heterogeneous group of different ages (ranging from early twenties to late forties) and levels of language ability (including a heritage speaker, several students who had lived in Germany, and others who did not start learning German until college).

Apart from essays, tests, and other assignments, the assessment for this course included a portfolio based on three asynchronous online discussions (worth twenty percent of the final grade). At the beginning of the semester, students wrote two entries for their portfolios: a reflection of their image of Germany and Germans (in English) and a list of ten questions for the online discussions. Students were encouraged to ask the virtual guests from Germany anything about German culture in which they were interested.[1]

Before the start of the first discussion, students spent part of one class period in a training session on how to use the discussion board. In addition, they were provided with a list of useful German expressions and given very specific guidelines reflecting my expectations for the discussions. Students were expected to actively participate during each discussion by posting several messages (e.g., asking questions, commenting on other messages, or adding follow-up questions) as well as reading the postings of the guests and other students. The goal of the online discussions was communication, not one hundred percent accuracy,[2] and the use of English was unacceptable. To facilitate interesting discussions, the virtual guests were encouraged not to limit their participation to just answering the students' questions. My own participation, however, usually consisted of only a welcome message.[3]

Throughout the semester, students participated in three online discussions, each with a different guest from Germany. The discussions were conducted outside class using the discussion board feature of the course management system *Blackboard*. They took place in one large forum so that every student interacted with each of the three guests between Monday and Friday. Unlike chats, asynchronous computer-mediated communication is time independent, meaning that participants read and write messages whenever they log in to the forum. Five students were selected to begin each discussion by posting their first messages by nine o'clock on Monday morning—that way, the guests knew when to log in to read the first postings.

While the electronic discussions took place outside class, they were integrated into classroom instruction: students brought up any issues they found interesting or surprising or had questions about and analyzed select messages in terms of language use.

After completion of all three discussions, students added to their portfolios a reflection about what they had learned about Germany and Germans, a reflection describing any insights they had gained into the nature of the German language (both in English), and six of their best postings to the discussion board.

Practical and Pedagogical Design Considerations

Certain aspects of the specific design of this online discussion board activity were influenced by practical concerns. While other projects have teamed up each student with a native speaker, which can be difficult to set up or maintain, the discussions described here took place in one large forum where every student interacted with each native speaker. As a result, students were exposed to different points of view and styles of communication, which supported their literacy development. This one-to-many setup significantly reduced the number of native speakers needed for this project, which meant that I was able to ask personal friends and relatives in Germany to participate.[4]

The discussion board feature of *Blackboard*, which is available to all instructors at our university, was used as a platform for the online discussions. It is very user-friendly for both students and instructors, requiring only basic computer skills (even for setting up discussion forums).

While it is necessary to consider practical issues like the ones mentioned above when deciding how to use instructional technology, pedagogical issues should be the dominant factor influencing course design. For this particular class, using online interactions promised a variety of pedagogical benefits. First, computer-mediated communication gave students the valuable opportunity to connect with several native speakers of German, which can be difficult in a state like Tennessee. Second, computer-mediated communication seemed an ideal tool for a heterogeneous class like this one, where students with immersion experience often dominate oral classroom discourse. Providing a time-delayed and more anonymous form of communication (Roed), electronic discussion boards tend to have a neutralizing effect on student participation (Shetzer and Warschauer 173) by encouraging even reticent foreign language learners to contribute (Warschauer). Learners do not have to find the right moment or strategy to take the floor but can join the discussion at any time. Also, students can take as much time as necessary to compose and understand messages, which can make communication with native speakers less stressful. The third reason for using computer-mediated communication relates to its popularity in today's world, making it a medium with which many students are familiar and comfortable. In addition, it has become an important form of communication in its own right with unique stylistic and sociolinguistic conventions (Shetzer and Warschauer 173). Real-world applications of a foreign language are likely to include computer-mediated communication; students studying or interning abroad, for example, will probably use e-mail to communicate in the foreign language with their professors, classmates, or colleagues. Therefore, foreign language classes should also build learners' electronic literacy: "The development of literacy and communication skills in new on-line media is critical to success in almost all walks of life" (Shetzer and Warschauer 171).

In terms of pedagogical frameworks, this particular implementation of computer-mediated communication reflects a communicative as well as literacy-based approach to foreign language teaching. It fits into communicative language teaching because learners are engaged in communication, in real-world tasks as well as in meaningful and authentic language use (Hadley 117). But these online discussions also promoted learners' foreign language literacy.

Richard Kern has defined literacy specifically for the context of academic foreign language education based on linguistic, cognitive, and sociocultural strands:

> Literacy is the use of socially-, historically-, and culturally-situated practices of creating and interpreting meaning through text. It entails at least a tacit awareness of the relationships between textual conventions and their concepts of use and, ideally, the ability to reflect critically on those relationships. Because it is purpose-sensitive, literacy is dynamic—not static—and variable across and within discourse communities and cultures. It draws on a wide variety of cognitive abilities, on knowledge of written and spoken language, on knowledge of genres, and on cultural knowledge.
> (*Literacy and Language Teaching* 16)

On the basis of this conceptualization of literacy, Kern has formulated seven curricular principles: literacy involves interpretation, collaboration, conventions, cultural knowledge, problem solving, (self-)reflection, and language use (16–17). To address all these aspects of literacy, learning activities should include situated practice, overt instruction, critical framing, and transformed practice (133).

Naturally, the implementation of online discussions described here cannot address all these principles and components of a literacy-based curriculum,[5] but it does incorporate several important features of foreign language literacy as described by Kern. The actual electronic exchanges between learners and native speakers reflect literacy's "macroprinciple" of communication (17). Engaging students in reading and writing as authentic acts of communication, the online discussions allowed them to explore the social dimension of writing by writing for a specific audience (45). As a result, this activity did not treat reading and writing as discrete and sequential skills, which is common in traditional classrooms. Instead, they were related and recursive tasks, an instructional approach advocated by Kern to build foreign language literacy (131–32; Kern and Schultz 382).

The electronic exchanges also provided a valuable opportunity for situated practice, an important curricular component of Kern's literacy framework, which relates to the seventh principle: literacy involves language use (*Literacy and Language Teaching* 17). Immersing students in language use, the online interactions focused on "communicating in the here and now" without conscious reflection or analysis (133). Yet students did also reflect on the electronic discussions. A variety of follow-up classroom activities engaged learners in reflection, which will be described in detail in the following section.

Revisiting the Electronic Discussions for Literacy Development

The students and I were able to revisit the online discussions for analysis and reflection by using the archived message transcripts. The classroom activities described below are examples of overt instruction (focusing students' attention through scaffolded learning activities) and critical framing (stepping back from immediate language use to analyze it), two components of a literacy-based curriculum (Kern, *Literacy and Language Teaching* 133). Rereading the discussions with a focus on language use—instead of the focus on informational content of the initial readings—reflects Kern's goal of "enveloping the *textual* within a larger framework of the *communicative*" ("Literacy as a New Organizing Principle" 47). Instead of looking at a text as an isolated artifact, these reflective exercises focused on the communicative interactions among text, writer, and reader (Kern, *Literacy and Language Teaching* 16).

The topics addressed during these classroom discussions further reflect a literacy approach. To focus on the surface structure of messages, students analyzed several native-speaker messages in terms of cohesion, that is, the semantic and syntactic relation between words (e.g., pronouns and their referents). This feature tends to give texts a dense structure, making them difficult to process for foreign language learners (Kern, *Literacy and Language Teaching* 79). Cohesive devices can be especially difficult for American learners of German because of the grammatical gender of inanimate objects. The activity directly followed one of Kern's suggestions for addressing the linguistic dimension of literacy: students underlined all pronouns and other cohesive devices in several native-speaker postings to then identify their coreferents. This exercise also built learners' discourse competence, an important goal of communicative language teaching (Hadley 6). Below is the translation of a message used for this activity (italics indicate cohesive devices):

> The Green Party *here* is really great. I am a big fan of *them* and have always voted for *them*. Especially Joschka Fischer (*who* is currently foreign minister) and Jürgen Trittin. *These people* are really getting things done here—*that* is especially important in terms of environmental issues. I also like organizations like Greenpeace—*have been a member for years*.[6]

Going back to the written records of their exchanges with the virtual guests also allowed students to fine-tune their initial interpretations. To encourage this type of analysis, students were asked to formulate their first impressions of the tone of select native-speaker postings before finding words and expressions to support this interpretation. The message quoted above was a reply to a student's question about the guest's personal opinion of the Green Party in Germany. Using the German equivalents of expressions like *great, a big fan*, and *very important* gave the guest's reply a very passionate tone. When asked about the typical age for Germans to have children, the same native speaker expressed much less conviction. Instead of making sweeping generalizations, she framed her answer with expressions such as *many, most of the time*, and *I believe* to report trends in German society. After this analysis, students composed replies to a question about American society to practice the conscious selection of words in order to give messages a distinct tone. This again illustrates the overlapping treatment of reading and writing of a literacy-based classroom (Kern, *Literacy and Language Teaching* 132)—in this case, reading and analyzing the postings of others was used to inform students' own writing. In addition, this activity engaged students in transformed practice, one of four components of a literacy-based curriculum: writing based on reading (133–34).

Classroom activities also focused on Kern's third principle, which states that literacy involves conventions (17). While reading and writing are based on cultural conventions, these "rules" are not static but evolve through use as language users modify them for their own purposes. To reflect on how discourse is constructed, a task targeting the sociocultural dimension of Kern's notion of foreign language literacy, students analyzed the structure of select messages from the second guest. While they all followed a similar pattern (salutation, answer to question, follow-up question, closing, signature), students noted the use of a variety of salutations and closings by this guest as well as the previous guest. Instead of making assumptions about the reasoning behind the choice of salutations and closings, we decided to ask the guest in an e-mail. Her response reminded students of the importance of register, which plays a prominent role in the German language and culture, and emphasized that linguistic form is determined not only by content but also by situational contexts (Kern, "Literacy as a New Organizing Principle" 51). Depending on her level of familiarity with the correspondent, this native speaker reported using either informal or formal expressions to begin and close her messages. She also mentioned that in her line of work (she works in an advertising agency), it is acceptable to leave out the salutation and closing in internal work e-mails, a practice she nonetheless finds somewhat rude. Electronic correspondence with other agencies, however, should always include these elements and be signed with the sender's full name, not just her initials. In addition, she explained that she often avoids formulaic closings to add a personal touch. Instead of using the German equivalent of "kind regards," for example, she might use a more creative closing like "sunny greetings from the Rhine River." This guest's explanations illustrate the important role conventions as well as individual style variations and preferences play in shaping discourse. They also show why it is important to shift the focus of language instruction from prescriptive norms to appropriateness of use, as advocated by Kern ("Literacy as a New Organizing Principle" 46). Through this activity, students were made aware that texts do not exist in isolation but have communicative effects and consequences (Kern, *Literacy and Language Teaching* 16). Leaving out a salutation, which some consider an acceptable practice, can have unwanted effects on the reader.

Another valuable example for this type of literacy-based exploration pertains to the use of capitalization by two of the three native-speaker guests. The first guest's lack of capitalization of nouns violated formal orthography rules of German, a feature brought up by the students during class discussion. Again, we took the opportunity to ask the writer directly. She explained that not having to capitalize any words allows her to type faster. This is a common and acceptable practice for electronic business communication, and a few advertising agencies even require their employees to avoid capitalization—in her eyes a ridiculous policy.

A second violation of orthography rules brought up by the students was the capitalization of the German pronouns for *you* and *your* by the second guest, which contradicted what students had learned from their textbooks. I explained that German spelling rules had just recently been revised not to require capitalization of these words. Therefore, this native speaker's capitalization of these words could be either an old habit or a conscious violation to preserve the respect that the capitalization expresses for the addressee. Interacting with three different native speakers made individual (electronic) communication styles visible, showing students that language use goes beyond formalized norms.

Classroom discussions also promoted students' literacy development by addressing Kern's first principle, which states that literacy involves interpretation (*Literacy and Language Teaching* 16). In a literacy framework, meaning is viewed not as the inherent property of a text but rather as something that emerges from the relations between readers, writers, and texts (Kern, "Literacy as a New Organizing Principle" 45). Commenting on the issue of women in the workforce, for example, a student mistranslated the word *revolution*—the English word has two separate meanings (a sudden, radical change or the motion of a body around an axis), which have different German translations (the cognate *Revolution* for the former and *Umdrehung* for the latter). Intending to talk about the change in women's roles due to the women's movement, the student erroneously used the German word *Umdrehung*, resulting in a nonsensical message. But the native speaker used interpretation and context clues to make sense of the student's message: "Hm, I'm not sure what you mean by *Umdrehung*, I guess something like *Revolution*." This potentially problematic exchange was easily resolved and could be used for classroom discussion to illustrate the cognitive dimension of literacy:

> Reading is a *thinking* process through which readers must relate the written symbols they perceive to their knowledge of language . . . and of their world, in order to bring meaning to a text. Reading therefore does more than establish links between words and referents; it requires prediction, inference, and synthesis of meaning.
> (Kern, *Literacy and Language Teaching* 29)

A follow-up activity was designed to further raise students' awareness that there is not a one-to-one correspondence between English and German words. After drawing their attention to the native speaker's successful use of interpretation and negotiation of meaning, students were asked to make a list of the different meanings of the English word *hit* (e.g., verb, noun, literal versus figurative meanings, idiomatic expressions).

The activities described above show that structured guidance in revisiting online discussions can provide learners with "new insights into the multilayered social dimensions of language use" to promote foreign language literacy (Kern and Schultz 386).

Student Contributions and Reactions

The number of messages posted on the discussion board was almost evenly split between the fifteen students and the guests, increasing from each discussion to the next. The numbers below show that students and guests engaged in active exchanges:

> Discussion 1: 23 student messages, 21 guest messages
> Discussion 2: 33 student messages, 31 guest messages
> Discussion 3: 35 student messages, 33 guest messages

Students' reactions to the online discussions and portfolio were very positive, which became evident in their responses to a multiple-choice survey administered at the end of the semester. The average ratings for the nine survey items, listed below, show that students really enjoyed the online discussions with native speakers (strongly disagree=1; strongly agree=5).

> I enjoyed the online discussions with people in Germany. 4.40
> I liked the discussions because I could include topics I was interested in. 4.60
> I learned new things about German culture and everyday life from these discussions. 4.33
> My view of Germans and Germany has changed because of these discussions. 3.93
> I learned new things about how the German language is used for communication. 4.73
> I learned new German words and expressions from the postings by the German guests. 4.67
> The portfolio provided an opportunity for reflection. 4.20
> The portfolio is a good reflection of my learning progress this semester. 3.93

> I like the portfolio because every student is graded on his or her own
> goals and progress. 4.20

Students appreciated the opportunity to address topics they were interested in, which proved valuable for a heterogeneous class composed of students who had lived in Germany as well as students who had never been there. Students addressed a wide variety of topics, such as politics, religion, education, and daily life, inquiring either about guests' personal opinions and experiences (e.g., "What do you like best about Germany?") or Germany as a whole (e.g., "What is the relationship between East and West Germans?"). Some students even brought up the same questions with several guests to compare their answers, something that would not have been possible had they been teamed up with one native-speaking partner. Students were interested not only in learning more about Germany and Germans but also in finding out how Germans view the United States and Americans (e.g., "What do Germans think about the presidential election in the US?").

In addition, students felt that the electronic exchanges were a valuable learning experience. Of the fifteen students, 73% strongly agreed and 27% agreed somewhat with the statement "I learned new things about how the German language is used for communication"; this statement received the highest average of all items included in the survey. This response illustrates that students perceived the online discussions as highly beneficial in terms of literacy development.

In their portfolio reflections, students commented in more detail on the electronic discussions and related in-class activities, and these responses were also very positive. Some comments show that students realized that they could successfully communicate, which allowed them to become more self-confident in their proficiency in the foreign language. These affective benefits were among the initial reasons for incorporating computer-mediated communication into this class and might be a result of the discussions' focus on communication, which eased students' preoccupation with form and underscored the value of communicative strategies. This step helps build strategic competence, which plays an important role in communicative language teaching.

Using the German language for real conversations with native speakers also seemed to remove some of the artificiality of formal classroom instruction, hence providing a different type of learning that really reached the students. This made the foreign language come to life for the students and let them experience a new side of it—daily colloquial use. Again, students showed an awareness of issues relating to literacy: through these exchanges and activities, students reported gaining a new awareness of language use as dynamic and contextualized.

As illustrated above, online discussions combined with reflective activities guided by the teacher can be used successfully as one component of a literacy-based curriculum to "focus students' attention on the interactions between linguistic form, situational context, and communicative and expressive functions" (Kern, "Literacy as a New Organizing Principle" 51). Specifically, computer-mediated communication can function as a vehicle for addressing the linguistic, cognitive, and sociocultural dimensions of foreign language literacy as defined by Kern (*Literacy and Language Teaching* 25–39). This case study also provides concrete examples for activities that match all curricular components to address learners' literacy needs: situated practice, overt instruction, critical framing, and transformed practice (Kern, *Literacy and Language Teaching* 133–34). Moreover, students were engaged in as well as analyzed the genre of electronic communication, which promoted their electronic literacy.

During classroom discussions, students brought up issues related to conventions of language use, an important component of foreign language literacy. Yet these issues focused on orthography, arguably the most eye-catching aspect of a language's surface structure. But the careful guidance of the instructor can focus students' attention on less visible aspects to further sensitize them to language as dynamic and interactive, thereby fostering their literacy development. After only three electronic discussions and several related activities, students felt that they had gained a new understanding of how language works. To build on this new knowledge, in the next instructional phase, students should engage in language production tasks where they can actively apply it. It is also important to include learning activities targeting aspects of literacy that are not addressed by online discussions like the ones described here, such as literary and aesthetic aspects of foreign language reading, writing, and speaking.

Notes

1. Students were advised, however, to avoid trivial information questions whose answers they could easily look up.

2. Unlike the online discussions, other assignments, such as essays and homeworks, did include a focus on form and accuracy.

3. In two of the three discussions, I contributed an additional message: a German cartoon illustrating one of the discussion topics and an answer to a question that nobody else could answer.

4. Working with friends and relatives was also beneficial because I knew that they would be reliable and contribute appropriate and insightful postings.

5. It ignores, for example, the literary aspect of literacy, which can be addressed in other parts of the course.

6. All translations from the German online discussion into English are mine.

Works Cited

Hadley, Alice Omaggio. *Teaching Language in Context*. 3rd ed. Boston: Heinle, 2001. Print.

Kern, Richard. *Literacy and Language Teaching*. Oxford: Oxford UP, 2000. Print.

———. "Literacy as a New Organizing Principle for Foreign Language Education." *Reading between the Lines: Perspectives on Foreign Language Literacy*. Ed. Peter C. Patrikis. New Haven: Yale UP, 2003. 40–59. Print.

Kern, Richard, and Jean Marie Schultz. "Beyond Orality: Investigating Literacy and the Literary in Second and Foreign Language Instruction." *Modern Language Journal* 89.3 (2005): 381–92. Print.

Roed, Jannie. "Language Learner Behaviour in a Virtual Environment." *Computer Assisted Language Learning* 16.2-3 (2003): 155–72. Print.

Shetzer, Heidi, and Mark Warschauer. "An Electronic Literacy Approach to Network-Based Language Teaching." *Network-Based Language Teaching: Concepts and Practice*. Ed. Warschauer and Richard Kern. Cambridge: Cambridge UP, 2000. 171–85. Print.

Warschauer, Mark. "Comparing Face-to-Face and Electronic Discussion in the Second Language Classroom." *CALICO Journal* 13.2 (1996): 7–26. Print.

Gillian Lord

Aymara on the Internet: Language Education and Preservation

In his discussion on humanity's fascination with the search for the "perfect language," Umberto Eco quotes the Jesuit Ludovico Bertonio in his early-seventeenth-century assessment of the Aymara language as so nearly perfect that some at the time suggested it was an artificial invention. Eco goes on to claim that Aymara, based on a three-value logic (rather than the Aristotelian two-valued logic systems common among most languages), is capable of expressing subtleties that require complex circumlocutions in other languages, to the extent that some have suggested Aymara be used to resolve the linguistic problems associated with computer translation. While I leave to Eco and other experts the question of a perfect language, Aymara nonetheless provides us with an intriguing study from a cultural, linguistic, and pedagogical standpoint.

The Aymara people have lived in the Andes for over two thousand years, according to many historians ("Aymara"). Today, Aymara is the indigenous language of approximately three million inhabitants living in Bolivia, Peru, and Chile, as well as other regions in South America. Despite its history and continued use, the language has received relatively little attention in the United States academic community. Recent reports on major media outlets such as National Public Radio's *Weekend Edition* and the *New York Times* have highlighted one fascinating linguistic aspect of this language: that to the Aymara, the future cannot be seen or predicted and therefore necessarily lies behind us; the past and present, since we have lived them or are living them, are known to us and lie before us ("For the Aymara"; Gorman). This essay describes one effort to bring the Aymara language and culture to a wide audience, for educational purposes as well as to ensure the preservation of this stimulating language.

Why This Project and Why Now?

Aymara has only received attention in the United States academic community from a handful of linguists focusing on indigenous languages and in the occasional language class. Furthermore, the number of native speakers of Aymara is declining as the need to be proficient in Spanish (and other languages) grows with the globalization of even remote areas. The Internet offers the opportunity to expand Aymara teaching in the Andean region and beyond, and the goal of the *Aymara on the Internet* project is to address the issues of language revitalization and language education by teaching the Aymara language and culture to a large and diverse audience of users worldwide. Using a comprehensive Web-based self-instructional program, the course is set up for the learner to listen to, view, and observe language in use, to understand the syntactic and morphological components of the language, and to recognize important cultural symbols, practices, and artifacts. This essay examines the project in detail, beginning with a description of the original materials on which the program is based and the changes that were necessary to update and digitalize these materials from a pedagogical as well as a technological standpoint.

The Materials, Old and New

This Internet course is based on existing print materials created in the 1970s by Martha J. Hardman at the University of Florida, consisting of twelve trilingual units based primarily on dialogues with accompanying exercises, tests, cultural notes, and audio materials (Hardman, Vásquez, Yapita Moya, Briggs, and England). The materials were designed to form the basis of a four-semester intensive language class Hardman and others offered regularly at the University of Florida for some thirty years. The prevailing language pedagogy at the time was the audiolingual method, which was based on the tenets of behavioral psychology and stressed memorization of phrases and dialogues and repetitive drills (see Skinner). The classroom activities that accompanied these materials, however, emphasized spoken communication and carrying out real-life tasks such as shopping and counting money.

Part of the challenge of creating this Internet course was updating these materials to reflect current pedagogical trends while maintaining the quality and integrity of the original work. We have also had to redirect the course to a much broader spectrum of potential users, from classroom learners to heritage speakers and from linguists to anthropologists.

New Pedagogies and Technologies

The pedagogical changes needed center on two issues. First, dialogue memorization and substitution drills are no longer widely used by foreign language pedagogy experts, who opt instead for communicative task-based approaches. While the latter focus was accomplished through the teacher-student interaction in the administration of the original materials, the challenge has been ensuring a communicative focus to the computer-driven exercises in the present course. Second, then, the delivery of the materials had to be modified. Many researchers have commented on the need to find an appropriate online pedagogy that can make up for the lack of a live teacher and dynamic classroom interaction while still maintaining sound pedagogical practices and accomplishing the goals of the pedagogical enterprise (Kern, Ware, and Warschauer; Thorne). This project takes as its foundation an approach Jozef Colpaert terms "affordances-based" (478), that is, an approach that evaluates the potential of new technologies to enhance language learning and teaching.

Taking this approach as our foundation leads us to the next crucial question: What technological tools should we use, and how can we best use them? The affordances-based approach essentially focuses on models of best practices. Following Uschi Felix, we take "best practice" to mean "using the most appropriate tools to their best potential to achieve sound pedagogical processes and outcomes" (8–9). These considerations led us to the choices we have made regarding the tools and design of the project.

Database and User Interface

This project takes an innovative approach to the design and dissemination of online educational content by storing all content in a learning object database on the back end, from which it can be called up to the Web site when and where it is needed. Using state-of-the-art instructional design techniques, material is linguistically coded into the database so that it is available on an as-needed basis in the program. Information is stored on various levels, from the morpheme-analysis level to the dialogue level. From the database, a learner can see an Aymara sentence, listen to how it is pronounced, view a digital image portraying that sentence, see both the English and Spanish glosses of that sentence, and click on the elements of the sentence to see its structural breakdown (fig. 1). All elements stored in the database (morpheme, word, phrase) are linked to both a dictionary and a concordance that shows all the instances of that item throughout the entire program.

Of course, for the average language learner, the database may provide too much information, while a linguist will be looking for just this level

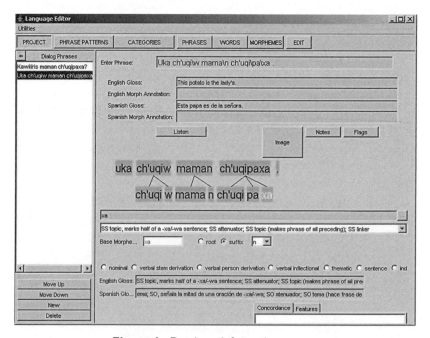

Figure I. Database information screen

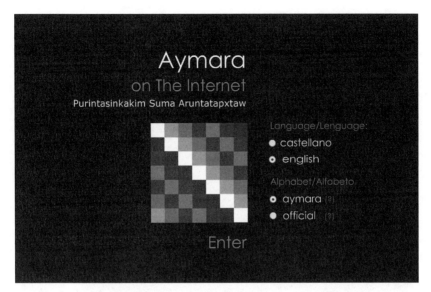

Figure 2. *Aymara on the Internet* welcome screen

of detail. Therefore, the interface is carefully designed to present the needed material in a clear fashion, while making the advanced options available to those who wish to pursue them without overwhelming other users. While the database itself stores and codes the information, a rendering engine calls up this material and presents it in a user-friendly interface using *Adobe Flash.*

Project Overview. Learners first encounter a welcome screen (fig. 2) that prompts them to choose either English or Spanish as the language of instruction. This option ensures that university students in the United States and South American heritage speakers of Aymara will have equal access to the materials in a language with which they are comfortable. From the introductory screen, learners are presented with an overview of the components of the course (fig. 3). A menu bar on the left side of the screen directs them to sections explaining the goals and the history of the materials and gives detailed technical and pedagogical instructions about how to use the program. Here also is where the learner finds links to other resources such as a trilingual online dictionary and references to journal articles and other publications for those who want to carry out further investigations. Another crucial element presented here is the preface of

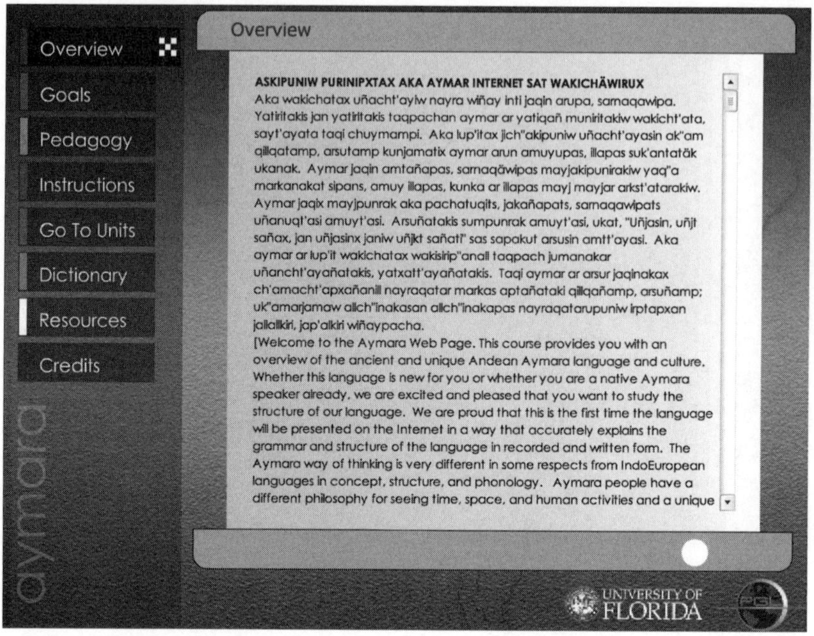

Figure 3. Program overview page

introductory materials, which provide basic information about the Aymara alphabet and its pronunciation as well as an introduction to some basic linguistic concepts the user will need to understand before proceeding through the materials. The materials we created for this project are based, whenever possible, on the original materials but still keep in mind the updated pedagogical and cultural goals.

The other option that learners encounter from this screen is the "Go to Units" button, which takes them to the launch page for the twelve units of the program. The beauty of the database design is that the interface frame is virtually identical throughout each of the units, and the only thing that changes is the specific content called up from the database. Each unit contains several pedagogical modules.

Cultural Notes. The cultural notes for each unit existed in the original materials, but only as part of the instructor's resource manual, not as material readily available to the students. They are now presented as the first segment of each unit, providing its overriding theme. This unitwide unification has helped bring the materials closely in line with current trends in contextualized and task-based instruction. The cultural notes conclude with questions for the learners, encouraging them to consider the topic in terms of the five Cs of the National Standards in Foreign Language Education Project: communication, cultures, comparisons, connections, and communities. These open-ended questions ask the learners to draw comparisons between their own culture and the Aymara culture, to consider in what ways the norms discussed are similar to their own, and so on. There are no right or wrong answers to these questions; the program simply suggests that users think about them to encourage a learner-centered approach to the material. The cultural notes also serve as an introduction to the dialogue of each unit.

Dialogue and Analysis. Each unit still centers on the dialogue, but the dialogue is now introduced in cultural terms and with a series of questions for the students to think about as they listen, thus providing much needed prelistening scaffolding and continuing to emphasize the five Cs (Fitzgerald and Graves). Further, the interface requires that students proceed through the dialogue in a series of steps: first, viewing the slideshow of authentic images that accompany the dialogue as they listen; second, listening to and viewing the slideshow while the lines of text appear on the screen (as shown in fig. 4); and, finally, reading only the text as they listen to the dialogue a third time (as shown in fig. 5), again promoting a scaffolding sequence.

Only after students have completed these three steps do they go on to the "Analysis" section, which breaks down the utterances from the dialogue in lexical and morphological chunks based on data contained in the database. The analysis level allows students to begin to study and understand the structures that are treated actively throughout the grammar presentation of the unit.

Grammar Explanation. The original materials, as they were used in the classroom, relied on the grammatical expertise of Hardman and the other trained instructors, who explained the structures in the dialogue based on their own knowledge and through repetition and substitution exercises. The online format of the current course, however, could not assume that learners would pick this grammatical information up on their own, so we had to create a series of grammar explanations to accompany each

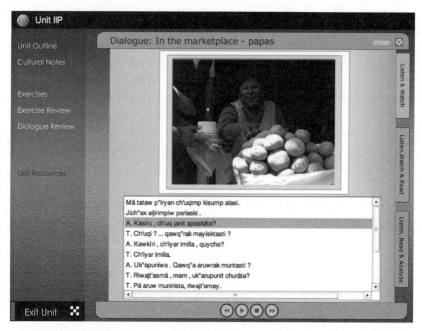

Figure 4. Listen to, watch, and read the dialogue

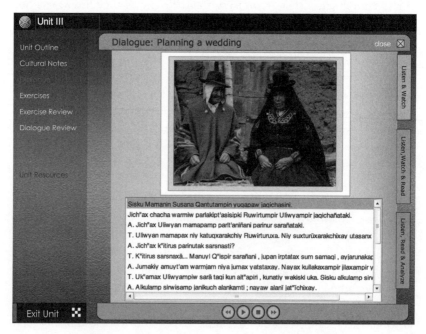

Figure 5. Listen to, read, and analyze the dialogue

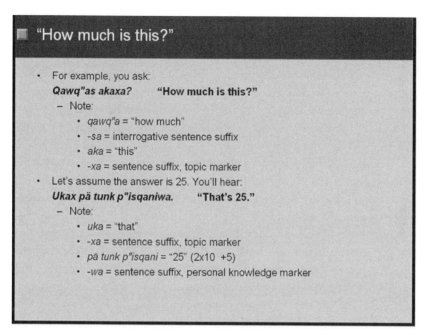

Figure 6. Grammar presentation

unit. A unit consists of three to six sets, each of which focuses on a particular structure of the language, such as verb conjugations or possessive constructions. The presentations are created with *Microsoft PowerPoint* and are then converted to image files with *Adobe Captivate*, allowing us to take full advantage of animation and colors to highlight important points and discuss morphemes and suffixes, among other features (fig. 6). Learners progress through the presentations at their own pace. Each set presentation serves to prepare the students for the exercises that accompany that set.

Exercises. The exercises in the original materials were essentially substitution drills. Most language teachers today scorn this kind of activity; however, we have chosen to keep the basic structure of the exercises for two reasons. The first is the difficulty of the Aymara language for speakers of English and Spanish. The verb person in Aymara is different from that in English and Spanish (there are four persons, the fourth being a "we" that obligatorily includes "you and I"), and verb forms include both subject and complement in their conjugations. Aymara tenses do not match up to our accepted notions of present, past, and future but rather mark the data source (e.g., truth, not truth, personal knowledge). To further complicate the situation, Aymara is considered an "inflective" language, making use of complex suffixes and subsequently extensive morphophonemic modification (Hardman). Therefore, the learner of Aymara needs extensive repetitive practice with these aspects, in addition to meaningful and contextualized opportunities to study the language, which are provided elsewhere in the materials.

The second reason we have chosen to maintain the automated nature of the exercises was out of technological necessity. Because this is a standalone program, there is no live teacher monitoring and correcting student exercises continuously, so that the program itself must be capable of creating and correcting all exercises. The database generates exercises based on the grammatical structures taught in the presentation and is then, if necessary, capable of generating both a series of cues to help the learner identify the correct answer and intelligent feedback regarding which aspects of the learner's answer need correcting. In this way, the learner progresses through the exercises that, although not contextualized and personalized to each learner, do provide a solid working base for the structures required to become proficient in Aymara. The final exercises in each set offer the learner new dialogues to listen to and analyze, based on the theme and structures of the unit. Students can thus synthesize all the linguistic information they have learned to this point while maintaining the cultural theme of the unit.

Enhancement. The concluding portion of every unit brings the focus back to the learner and away from the mechanical drills of the exercise portion. This enhancement section has been created specifically for the online materials and focuses on the five Cs of the Standards. Learners are given further ideas, suggestions, and activities to continue their Aymara study beyond the unit. Web sites are given for further reference and exploration, and project ideas are suggested. Here is where we try to take into consideration all possible users of the site; some will be in South America and will have the opportunity to interact with native Aymara speakers, while others will have to resort to Internet searches or find language partners through other avenues. All users, however, will end each unit with a comprehensive understanding of what they have learned of the culture and the language and with a broader perspective of their own language and culture.

Outcomes and Expectations

It is expected that learners will come to the course with different social and geographical backgrounds, different linguistic experiences, and different educational accomplishments, all of which will shape their own goals for using the program. A diligent language learner can expect to achieve intermediate proficiency in reading, writing, and listening on completion of the program. Other users who approach the site for reference or general information will have an enriching multimedia experience that explores the land, the people, and the culture.

Where Do We Go from Here?

At the time of this writing, the complete Aymara program has been launched both in the United States and Bolivia and is now freely available to all users at http://aymara.ufl.edu. The program is available both in English and in Spanish; the user chooses the language at the welcome screen. In addition, we offer the interface using the two alphabetic systems that are currently in use for the Aymara language. The Aymara alphabet was developed in the 1960s by Juan de Dios Yapita, an original creator of the materials that are the basis of the program; his intent in devising that system was to represent the phonetic properties of the language as accurately as possible. The government later developed what they called the official alphabet, which is virtually identical to the Aymara alphabet save for one minor difference regarding the representation of aspirated consonants. (See the program overview for more details on the two alphabets and their development.) The project uses both alphabets to avoid making a political statement by choosing one over the other.

We are anticipating a continuation of our funding to cover the next phase of the project. Additional resources at this phase will be used primarily to enhance the exercise sections of the course. We are exploring tools that would enable learners to record their answers orally, play them back, and then compare them with a native Aymara model. Moreover, the versatile database structure enables individuals or institutions to access and recombine data to meet the demands of their particular research, whether instructional or institutional.

No matter what the future holds for this project, it has proved quite exciting. *Aymara on the Internet* has brought together experts and content specialists from a variety of fields who have had not only to learn from each other but also to push themselves to acquire new skills and find new ways to create and present language-learning pedagogies and technologies. The future of Internet language teaching will undoubtedly see this kind of collaboration more and more frequently. And students of Internet language courses will undoubtedly continue to benefit from this kind of collaboration.

Note

This project is funded by a grant from the United States Department of Education, through the Partnership in Global Learning (Title VI) at the University of Florida. It involves the expertise and collaboration of numerous individuals. In addition to the expertise and content provided by M. J. Hardman, the project also involves the collaboration of numerous individuals. The grant coordinator is Elizabeth Lowe of the Partnership in Global Learning. Sue Legg is the project manager and data-entry coordinator and is in charge of project evaluation. From the University of Florida's Center for Instructional Training and Technology come Marcela Pineros (the instructional designer and Web developer) and Albert Banks (Web developer and *Flash* programmer). Howard Beck is the creator of the *Lyra* ontology system and is responsible for database programming. Gillian Lord serves as the pedagogy expert, specializing in technology in language education.

Works Cited

"Aymara Ethnic Group." *Wikipedia.* 10 Nov. 2008. Web. 20 Nov. 2008.

Colpaert, Jozef. "Pedagogy-Driven Design for Online Language Teaching and Learning." *CALICO Journal* 23.3 (2006): 477–97. Print.

Eco, Umberto. *The Search for the Perfect Language.* Cambridge: Blackwell, 1995. Print.

Felix, Uschi. *Language Learning Online: Towards Best Practice.* Lisse: Swets, 2003. Print.

Fitzgerald, Jill, and Michael F. Graves. *Scaffolding Reading Experiences for English-Language Learners.* Norwood: Christopher-Gordon, 2004. Print.

"For the Aymara, Future Is Then." *Weekend Edition Saturday. National Public Radio.* Natl Public Radio, 12 Aug. 2006. Web. 20 Nov. 2008.

Gorman, James. "Side Effects: Does This Mean People Turned Off, Tuned Out and Dropped In?" *New York Times.* New York Times, 27 June 2006. Web. 20 Nov. 2008.

Hardman, Martha J. "Aymara and Quechua: Languages in Contact." *South American Indian Languages, Retrospect and Prospect.* Ed. Harriet E. Manelis Klein and Louisa R. Stark. Austin: U of Texas P, 1985. 617–43. Print.

Hardman, Martha J., Juana Vásquez, Juan de Dios Yapita, Lucy T. Briggs, and Nora England. *Aymara: Compendio de Estructura Fonológica y Gramatical.* La Paz: Instituto de Lengua y Cultura Aymara, 1988. *Instituto de Lengua y Cultura Aymara.* Web. 15 Oct. 2006.

Kern, Richard, Paige Ware, and Mark Warschauer. "Crossing Frontiers: New Directions in Online Pedagogy and Research." *Annual Review of Applied Linguistics* 24 (2004): 243–60. Print.

National Standards in Foreign Language Education Project. *Standards for Foreign Language Learning in the Twenty-First Century.* Lawrence: Allen, 1999. Print.

Skinner, B. F. *About Behaviorism.* New York: Vintage, 1974. Print.

Thorne, Steven L. *Internet-Mediated Intercultural Foreign Language Education: Approaches, Pedagogy, and Research.* University Park: Center for Advanced Lang. Proficiency Educ. and Research, Pennsylvania State U, 2005. *CALPER.* Web. 24 May 2006. CALPER Working Paper 6.

Douglas Morgenstern

MITUPV: Language, Media, and Distance in an Online Community

Blended by Ambition

The MITUPV Exchange (http://mitupv.mit.edu) is the online component of a blended language-learning course, 21F.703 Spanish 3 (first-semester intermediate level), offered at the Massachusetts Institute of Technology (MIT). Work with the Web site encompasses twenty-five percent of the course. Students exchange text postings and multimedia materials with undergraduate and graduate students at the Universidad Politécnica de Valencia (UPV) in Spain (some UPV students are learning English, but project participation is less formally integrated into their classes). The bilingual Web site is set up as a virtual university that deals with academics, social life, and cities. The beta phase of MITUPV occurred in fall 2000 and was completely functional in February 2001. The project has since continued without interruption, although activity ceases in the summer. There has been participation during certain semesters from students at other universities, including the University of Cambridge, Universidad EAFIT, Universidad de Valencia, and University of Texas, Austin.

Unlike other telecollaborative language and culture projects, access to the MITUPV community is not restricted to students and faculty members from partner schools. There is no password protection, and registration is required only for uploading multimedia, creating a biography, posting text messages, and accessing chat. Anyone can view all the content, whether by browsing bulletin boards or downloading video files. Unlike certain types of distance education courses and other online environments, MITUPV does not allow participants to post anonymously or to mask their identities.

The project was written up in *Wired News* in 2002 (Mayfield); in 2003 my project counterparts in Valencia and I coauthored an article for the print journal *Syllabus,* now available online as *Campus Technology* (Morgenstern, Plasencia, and Seiz). MIT's *OpenCourseWare* initiative published Spanish 3 materials, including information about MITUPV (Morgenstern). Unrestricted access, combined with publicity generated by these and other sources (blogs, newspaper accounts in Spain), have resulted in a hybrid exchange. The interchange among specific universities is plugged into a larger global community from which, for instance, students residing in Asia often register.

The MITUPV Exchange is the largest project of its kind: as of February 2009, almost 3,800 registered members have participated, as have unregistered users, in more than 640,000 sessions. The "People/Gente" section includes more UPV than MIT students, and there is a substantial number of participants from neither school. The Web site contains 6,500 uploaded multimedia objects, consisting mainly of photos and videos. Because many videos are in multiple formats, individual videos total perhaps 1,000. Community members create all content. The pedagogical orientation is decidedly bottom-up; the structure of the virtual university, rather than top-down teacher-generated topics, determines participation. Students are given one basic objective, to extend the life of this virtual community by providing content. Although sometimes postings refer to archived material, every semester brings new postings from the registrants.

MIT's Spanish 3 course normally offers three sections in the fall and two in the spring of about sixteen to twenty-two students each, all of whom participate in the project. Spanish 3 has been cotaught by a series of colleagues (Soledad Fox, José A. Ramos, Ricardo Gessa, Lissette Soto, and César Pérez) who bring their perspectives to their activities in MITUPV. Ramos, for instance, who graduated from MIT in mechanical engineering, brought a unique perspective to his activity in MITUPV. Project-related course work consists of creating a biography and accompanying photo, shooting an original video, commenting on photos and videos submitted by students from UPV and MIT, participating in text-based bulletin boards and in a video-chat session, and giving oral and written reports. Most engagement with the project takes place outside class.

Nobody Expects the Spanish Inquisition

The above section title resonates only for readers familiar with Monty Python. In general, context consists of prior experience and accessibility to new, often unexpected, information. The MITUPV Exchange offers a space where meaning depends on cultural context and interpretation is generated at least partially through discourse. Students represent themselves, their university, and, at times, broader entities such as their region or country and interpret the text postings and multimedia objects submitted by others. Linguistic orthodoxy commingles with heresy. Contributors are asked to use both the target language and their native language in written and multimedia contributions, but compliance is not universal. Some students create a dual message aiming for the same content in both languages, while others vary the content. Errors are considered part of learning and are usually left uncorrected. When I do correct them, I often e-mail students, pasting in their original text and the revision. In years when many UPV students were in English as a foreign language classes or when Colombian students from the Universidad EAFIT participated, I followed the same procedure with those groups. The resulting mix of authentic interlanguage discourse and teacher-corrected language is grounded as much in pragmatism as in intentional pedagogical strategy.

If It Moves, Shoot It

In addition to the anchoring theme of MITUPV, a virtual university, what sets this project apart from other telecollaborative undertakings is its focus from the outset on multimedia, especially digital video. Students determine the content of their own biographies, which appear in the "People/Gente" section and are sometimes accompanied by photographs. The tone of these biographies ranges from straightforward and serious, including comments about divorce and religious devotion, to whimsical, with stylized photos or cartoon characters substituted for portraits. At UPV, most of the videos have been shot, edited, compressed, and uploaded by the project cofounder Adolfo Plasencia, who directs that university's master's in multimedia program. His videos are polished, with background music and titles. He also uploads elegant photo collages of video scenes. Other videos have been created by the English as a foreign language teachers Rafael Seiz Ortiz, Ignacio Gil, Pilar Conesa, Elena Benito, and their students. When there was participation from the University of Cambridge and the Universidad EAFIT, students and language teachers there followed similar procedures.

At MIT during the first year of the project, I accompanied students to their athletic events, engineering project demos and dorm tours, and shot the videos myself before editing, compressing, and uploading them. This method allowed me to ask for retakes for segments in Spanish when students made severe errors but also entailed reduced access and authenticity. Subsequently students, including those in sections I do not teach, borrow mini digital video cameras from our language lab and return the cassettes to me, sometimes with editing requests. The determining limit is file size. To maintain acceptable audio and video quality, I usually edit the source video (which can be as long as sixty minutes) to approximately three minutes in length. In a few cases, MIT students take charge of all aspects of video creation and production. Results vary, but these videos are often considerably more appealing and technically complex than those I edit.

UPV photos and videos are varied in content, including the buildings of the renowned Valencian architect Santiago Calatrava, the Fallas celebration (costumes, floats, fireworks), original art works, Campus Party (a huge networked computer event), and industrial design experiments. An interview with an art student from the north of Spain studying in Valencia reveals her professional aspirations and demonstrates her technique; the combination of image and language allows a brief art demonstration to serve linguistic and cultural purposes. A photo of a Spanish water jug elicits comments about form, function, and history. Plasencia's interest in technology and humanism and his work in online and television journalism often lead to additional themes. Other UPV faculty members, including scientists and artists, participate. Students from the rest of Europe and from Latin America attending UPV produce videos with richly layered cultural perspectives, as do MIT's international students. Occasionally students from both institutions create a work of fiction rather than a documentary.

MIT videos include experiments, aspects of residential life, cultural activities, engineering contests, volunteer projects in the community, and sporting events in MIT and in Boston. Students travel with their camera outside Massachusetts or incorporate footage taken previously in other countries. Some videos demonstrate exceptional musical prowess. There are a few videos with journalistic import, such as one from 2002 by the son of a New York City firefighter witnessing a September 11 Memorial Day service and another in which a student documented her participation in a Miami protest against globalization (tear gas one day, a trip to the beach the next). Apart from their value for the project, videos created at MIT offer a unique archive of its student life during the last nine years.

We also arrange a synchronous event for each MIT class, using *Apple iChat*, with groups of UPV students. Differences in time zone and accessibility make this activity much less frequent than asynchronous communication.

Fearful Symmetry

Unlike the nameless creator in William Blake's "The Tyger," very mortal hands and eyes frame our project's asymmetry: we are fearful of asymmetrical participation among students. Those in North American universities tend to spend more time online and have greater access to their university's computational infrastructure—and to high-speed connections in general—than their counterparts in many other countries. Academic calendars are different, and students in Spain enjoy more holidays and vacations during the school year. Teachers in Spain who participate in projects of this kind receive fewer professional benefits than do those in the United States. As a result, biographical information is incomplete, bulletin-board questions go unanswered, and multimedia uploads fail to receive comments. One solution would be the inclusion of additional universities from Spain and Hispanic America. The failure to accomplish this goal on a long-term basis is owing not to any lack of effort by those of us involved in the project but rather to difficulties arising when universities change their curricula, underreward faculty members for their efforts, and make do with an inadequate technological infrastructure for students.

Historical Context

Even before the advent of the Web in the early 1990s, language teachers looked to technology to enhance classroom-based teaching and learning.

It became apparent that video, first available in analog form with the VCR, was a medium particularly well-suited for this purpose. The microcomputer initially returned the focus to text, but soon digital multimedia allowed learners to access graphic and photographic images, text, audio, and video of varying degrees of interactivity. E-mail and other telecommunicative tools allowed expansion of the pen-pal model already familiar to teachers. As the Web matured in the beginning of this century, presentational aspects (the browser) were complemented and at times eclipsed by explorational aspects (the search engine).

Currently two significant developments, made possible by increasingly rapid interconnectivity and more uniform interoperability among devices, offer glimpses of continued large-scale transformation. The first development is the emergence of digital video as the dominant online medium for transmission of compelling content. The second phenomenon, sometimes referred to as Web 2.0, is the expansion of the original microcomputer–Web page paradigm to include social networking (such as blogging and podcasting) available on additional platforms (such as iPods and cell phones) and in new physical environments (such as neighborhoods and cities with wireless capabilities). These phenomena begin as discrete entities but end up converging. For example, the predominance of video and the importance of searching have joined in the emergence of video search functionality. Increased speed and interoperability have facilitated the viral spread of content (such as homemade videos of individuals lip-synching to popular songs) through stationary and portable devices. With the availability of small, unobtrusive, and inexpensive devices that can record and transmit digital audio, photos, and video, previous distinctions between creators-providers and recipients-consumers are less sharp. User-generated content has proliferated across media.

Project Origins and Expectations

As a foreign language teacher interested in developing projects in the post-Web era, I took into careful consideration the expectations and desires of students. My experience with previous projects and with classroom materials convinced me that video was a rich and effective medium for transmission of linguistic and cultural content. I also had developed non–technology classroom simulations since 1981. The particular activity potentially most suitable to a telecollaborative project between two universities was *La universidad utópica*, used since the mid-1980s with my

Spanish 3 students. Students work individually and in groups to rank features of a new imaginary university. The text handout received by students and a brief video clip of the activity are available on the Spanish 3
MITOpenCourseWare site under "Assignments" (Morgenstern).

Opportunity also played a part in the genesis of the project. As a result of previous e-mail contact with Plasencia about an unrelated matter,
in early 2000 we adapted the "utopian" university concept to a virtual
collaboration between both institutions. Then, bypassing a long development cycle typical of humanities projects, an MIT Web design class tai-
lored to the creation of virtual communities, 6.171 Software Engineering
for Web Applications (taught by Harold Abelson and Philip Greenspun),
programmed MITUPV in one semester (fall 2000). The two undergraduate student programmers, Aimee Lee and Kathy Lee, supervised by the
teaching assistant Bryan Che, received substantial input from students in
a fifth-semester MIT Spanish class I taught at the time. This collaboration brought new perspectives to the design, resulting in features such as
a "People/Gente" section with biographies and photos created by users.
This idea was implemented four years before *Facebook* emerged as a Web
phenomenon in 2004, first in Harvard and then at other universities, linking photos and text descriptions of undergraduate students as part of a
vast social community.

Navigation and Technical Aspects

The overall Web site design follows a minimalist aesthetic. The opening
page displays the university categories and alternating photos of both universities. Moving the cursor over the category titles changes them from
English to Spanish. One way to access materials is through "What's new
/ Novedades," whose recency can be configured from one day to ninety
days (any number of days can be entered by hand in the URL). The uploads, links, and comments appear with the name of the community member and the date of submission, and sequencing begins with the most recent.
Another navigational path is through individual categories. For instance,
under "University," one can click on "Academics," which leads to a page
that, as with other categories, follows a uniform pattern. The bulletin-board
messages posted in each category are at the upper left, the links to exterior
Web sites at the upper right. Archived material is available through links.
Scrolling down reveals the "Multimedia" section. Uploading of multimedia is intuitive but requires an accompanying text caption. Choosing

"View all" leads to the pages of the multimedia archives. "Academics" contains more than fifty archived pages, and the oldest pages date from the beta version in fall 2000, when all multimedia were listed under this category.

Apple's powerful and easily learned *iMovie* is used for video editing at MIT by me and at UPV by Plasencia. Compressing edited video to yield an uploadable file with *Terran Media Cleaner, Apple QuickTime Pro*, or *Telestream Flip4Mac* is slightly more challenging. *Windows* applications are often used by other community members. Most of the videos appear in both *QuickTime* and *Windows Media* versions and can be viewed in the Web page or downloaded, depending on the browser configuration. Originally we considered streaming videos, but acquiring infrastructure support was too complicated.

Results

The following conclusions arise from observations of online behavior as well as what MIT students communicate about their experiences in class discussions, oral and written reports in Spanish, and written anonymous evaluations in English. Feedback from UPV students has been less systematic.

Principal gains have occurred in vocabulary acquisition, listening comprehension, and especially cultural knowledge. Slight improvement in speaking might have taken place through the creation of videos, especially when students did multiple retakes to remedy their errors. Cultural knowledge increases, sometimes in the form of simple transference of information, at other times as a result of a longer reflective process in which students, while representing their lives and universities, come to realize the inadequacy of mapping, from one culture to another, what they assume to be universal constructs. As in other telecollaborative projects of this nature, there has been an interplay of cultural awareness and propagation of stereotypes. When, for example, a video of a small-town bullfight was uploaded from Spain, an MIT student posted a comment questioning the morality and purpose of this Spanish tradition. The reply from a UPV student was a strong condemnation of bullfighting. Another example was a prolonged discussion of the Macrobotellón, street-drinking parties attended by huge numbers of youths in various cities in Spain protesting steep cover charges at discos and bars. The interchange on this topic started with postings of photos and videos, was followed by text comments, and continued during the spring 2006 video-chat session. MIT students were privy to discrepancies of interpretations among UPV students as they commented on variations in policy by regional governments and mainstream media representations of this societal phenomenon.

University life is a theme of immediate accessibility and interest to students. The flexibility of the design permits the inclusion of additional, indirectly related topics, such as photos or threaded discussions about the 11 March 2004 terrorist attack on Madrid or about the Iraq war, which provoked a substantial number of postings and even prolonged debate. The systematic exchange of information and opinions about engineering, science, architecture, art, music, sports, politics, and other topics provides successful examples of content-based learning, where students transcend the physical and curricular bounds of a language class. An MIT student encounters the notion of fractals for the first time in a UPV work of art. A UPV student's preconceptions of ethnicity in the United States are challenged by a photo of the MIT symphony orchestra.

The MITUPV Exchange offers a discursive environment situated somewhere between a traditional university language-learning course and a study- or work-abroad experience. The Web site, compartmentalized and classified by category, approximates the serendipitous nature of authentic language immersion. The student meets with complex and even incongruous textual and visual arrangements, especially when using the popular access route, the "What's new / Novedades" section. Here one finds long lists of disparate multimedia objects: political protest paintings from Argentina; a strange old car in Egyptian traffic; a volleyball tournament at the University of Pennsylvania containing an interview with a Polish student who lived in Barcelona; cascading still photos of a solemn religious procession in Andalusia, set to music; a kitten in a dorm room; the Boston marathon; a robot construction project; the ocean at twilight. As when entering an urban magazine kiosk, all these elements compete for attention and lead one down different paths. Students make choices and take chances.

Sometimes the choice leads from virtual to physical interaction. An MIT undergraduate who participated in 2001 subsequently became a medical student and spent her summer conducting research in a scientific institute in Valencia. A former Spanish 3 MITUPV community member encountered UPV students in France in an alternative-fuel-vehicle design contest; three of these students spent a summer at MIT participating in a multischool project. Other MIT students have contributed to the Web site during a study-abroad experience in Madrid or during volunteer service in Ecuador.

All required class-related projects are somewhat coercive and artificial, but having an obligatory interchange between groups of students in different parts of the world develop gradually, starting with elements that foster social cohesion, has turned out to be a natural and effective way to foster meaningful interaction in this kind of virtual community. Most MIT students concur with this view, although there have been exceptions. One student told me that he already was a member of too many virtual communities. Other students asked exactly how many postings and uploads they should contribute each week. Another objected to being forced to communicate with "random" people. Counterbalancing these examples are instances where participation occurs beyond course boundaries. Long after the spring 2006 semester classes and exam period ended and grades were submitted, an MIT student posted a comment to a video that had just been uploaded by a UPV student. Also, when accessing the "Who's online now?" feature in the "People/Gente" section, I have been heartened to see the names of MIT and UPV students who participated in the project years earlier.

Multimedia, especially when created by peers, is crucial in motivating student interest. Most students rank viewing MITUPV videos created by others and making their own videos as especially valuable. Many students cite the synchronous video-chat experience as a high point, although when pressured to express themselves coherently in real time, they are sometimes discouraged by their limitations. The most successful video chats result from a combination of an appealing topic and a mix of students who have established online rapport through text and multimedia exchanges earlier in the semester. Personality and group chemistry also influence outcomes. A concomitant benefit is that the project promotes attention to media and exposes students, experientially if not formally, to the concepts underlying media literacy. Having as one of my counterparts a colleague whose field is media rather than language teaching is also beneficial. Plasencia constantly pushes the envelope toward experimentation. This mix enhances the professional development of all the faculty members involved in MITUPV.

The model for a typical foreign language multimedia project—whether delivered by CD, DVD, or the Web—is to create or obtain photos, audio, and video; supply contextual information and activities; and use the project until the multimedia content becomes outdated. Apart from possible hardware or software obsolescence, sustainability and exportability are not serious challenges. This situation applies to telecollaborative projects based on e-mail exchanges as well as voice-recording and voice-sharing technologies. In contrast, sustainability and exportability are significant issues for MITUPV. A faculty member at each participating campus must be responsible for video postproduction. At UPV, the role of Plasencia is exceptionally labor intensive. At MIT, it is common for me to receive several digital video tapes in one afternoon, then teach an evening class, and finish postproduction and uploading by three the following morning. Colleagues have suggested that I outsource the editing and compression tasks to a technician, but processing these videos entails pedagogical considerations and is best left to the teacher. I eliminate and reorder segments on the basis not only of visual and audio quality or aesthetic criteria but also of the student's performance in the target language and even in the native language. I also take into account the welfare of the student and of MIT, as, for instance, when editing a video of a fraternity party. The project has added new dimensions to our roles as teachers, since we share community membership with students but also mediate their input. The teacher's labor-intensive role might be reduced in the future, with consequences for sustainability and exportability, if more students arrive well-versed in digital video production or if some other development permits autonomous multimedia creation. Even then, however, exportability may be limited because many teachers feel more comfortable working with projects that provide instructional templates and offer enhanced predictability and teacher control.

Recommendations

Readers who contemplate developing a telecollaborative project for language classes should certainly investigate *Cultura*, developed by Gilberte Furstenberg, Sabine Levet, and Shoggy Waryn, and consult publications that focus on this relatively new field (Belz). Second language acquisition research generally uses observable online behavior as the basis for hypothesis construction. There are claims that such an approach neglects students who are attentive but learn without participating overtly (Gulati). Social online interaction may vary according to culture (Kim and Bonk).

My other recommendation is to consider incorporating the best features of the MITUPV Exchange paradigm: joint teacher-student conceptualization and design; a rapid implementation cycle using open-source

applications; user-generated multimedia content; social-cohesion mechanisms operating in a bottom-up approach; a mixture of navigational paths,
some by topic, others by recency; involvement of faculty members from
diverse fields. From a vantage point in 2009, I also recommend features
not implemented nine years ago: powerful text and multimedia search functionality, mechanisms for students to correct their input after posting, a
design that can be easily altered to incorporate Web 2.0 technologies, and
integrated media-literacy instruction. And, of course, something ambitious:
multimedia annotating and restructuring capabilities. A student presents
a media object and another student (or teacher) thousands of miles away
inserts links, text, audio, graphics, photos, or video; rearranges segments;
transforms the original—responding with words and images that question, reveal, delight, and mystify.

Works Cited

Belz, Julie A., ed. *Telecollaboration.* Spec. issue of *Language Learning and Tech-
    nology* 7.2 (2003): 1–172. Web. 13 June 2006.
Gulati, Shalni. "Constructivism and Emerging Online Learning Pedagogy: A
    Discussion for Formal to Acknowledge and Promote the Informal." *Education-
    Line.* U of Leeds, 6 May 2004. Web. 13 June 2006.
Kim, Kyong-Jee, and Curtis J. Bonk. "Cross-Cultural Comparisons of Online
    Collaboration." *Journal of Computer-Mediated Communication* 8.1 (2002): n.
    pag. Web. 13 June 2006.
Mayfield, Kendra. "College Kids: A Day in the Life." *Wired News.* Condé Nast,
    5 Nov. 2002. Web. 13 June 2006.
Morgenstern, Douglas. "21F.703 Spanish 3, Spring 2006." *MIT OpenCourse-
    Ware.* MIT, 2006. Web. 13 June 2006.
Morgenstern, Douglas, Adolfo Plasencia, and Rafael Seiz. "Students as Designers
    and Content Creators: An Online Multimedia Exchange between the U.S.
    and Spain." *Campus Technology* 1 Nov. 2003. Web. 13 June 2006.

Part III

Case Studies in Literatures

Kathleen Fitzpatrick

The Literary Machine: Blogging the Literature Course

During the fall 2003 semester, I taught an advanced undergraduate seminar entitled The Literary Machine: Writing in the Human/Computer Interface. This course, in which ten senior English majors enrolled, proposed to explore the relation between the human being—and humanism—and contemporary computer technologies, particularly as they are imbricated in literary representations of computers, newer computer-mediated forms of literature, and theories of new media and their connections to and disconnections from older cultural forms. As part of this course's work, I asked the class to participate in a group blog. I hoped that the blog would offer students a space in which they could delve into, on an ongoing and somewhat informal basis, the materials and ideas they were encountering in the course. I also imagined that the blog would situate students in the human-computer interface that the course was exploring by asking them to confront the ways that computer mediation affected their reading and writing. I have used blogs successfully in a range of other courses since then, but I have chosen to focus on this course—a partially successful first stab at incorporating student blogging into my teaching—to explore the full range of successes and failures of this experiment. The blog produced some exciting interactions among the students, as well as some innovative

205

uses of the technology. Yet the ways that the blog failed to obtain a full purchase with the students led me to some conclusions about the importance of the instructor's role in the course blog and the ways that blogging needs to be fully integrated into a course's structure.

A blog, or "weblog," according to the most basic, stripped-down definition, is "a frequently updated website consisting of dated entries arranged in reverse chronological order" (Walker). Blogs can be created by individuals or by groups; they focus on subjects that are personal, political, journalistic, technical, academic, or, often, random; their posts can take a link-and-comment form or be more essayistic; they often include multimedia content, including images, audio, or video. Perhaps the most important feature of blogs, however, is the comment function: most blogs provide readers with the ability to respond to and discuss posts, and it is this space for interaction among readers and writers that makes the blog, as a form of social software, such a useful teaching tool.[1]

Many other forms of computer-mediated communication, including bulletin boards and e-mail discussion lists, lend themselves to student interaction and discussion, of course. The blog differs from those other forms, however, primarily owing to its architecture; the hierarchy of post-and-comment is much more pronounced in a blog, since only the original posts appear on the front page of the blog and the discussion of each post takes place offstage, on a secondary page. One result of this structure is that authorship of a blog post is more significant, more substantive, than authorship of the original entry of a bulletin-board thread; the post somehow belongs to its author in the way that a thread on a message board or an e-mail discussion list never does. Thus students need to be focused in their original posts, to think through what they would like to say in a way that is more coherent and developed than a bulletin-board thread or an e-mail message but less so than a full essay. The comments sections of blogs frequently bear much in common with bulletin boards, but their relation to particular posts makes it clear that there is something particular they are responding to, and thus the comments on any given post tend to be a bit more focused than bulletin-board threads are. Such an organization of primary posts and related discussion often allows students to test out ideas that they will later develop into longer essays.

Blogs also differ from discussion boards and lists by providing for a kind of narrative development and coherence over time, since the reverse chronological order of posts reveals a growth of ideas and recurrence of points of interest. Students are able to link directly to earlier posts and comments, allowing ideas to gain complexity through their interrelation. Finally, though they can be password-protected, blogs are generally far more public forums than bulletin boards or e-mail discussion lists are and are thus more akin to a student-run magazine than to a private distribution list. As a result, a course blog can often develop a public readership, and the comments of non–class members can encourage students to think critically about the question of audience as they write.

I began blogging in June 2002, on the heels of finishing the major work on a book manuscript. In writing that book, I had accumulated a number of small questions that I wanted to discuss but that I knew would never attain the heft required for an article. Faced with a years-long wait for the appearance of the finished book (and an even longer wait for any reader response) and needing more immediate conversation and feedback than traditional scholarly publishing allows, I started a blog that enabled me to build a network of colleagues with whom I could regularly discuss pedagogical issues and ongoing projects (Fitzpatrick). Excited by the ways that blogging had energized my writing life, I decided in fall 2003 to set up *The Literary Machine*, a group blog for my senior seminar on which all ten students would have full posting privileges; I hoped that the class would find the form as engaging as I did. I intended this blog to take the place of the reading responses or other short pieces of analytic writing I ordinarily assign, encouraging students to direct those often interesting readings of our course texts to one another, rather than solely to me. In addition, the blog would allow students to continue conversations outside the class's parameters, both by opening the "twenty-four-hour classroom" and by encouraging students to bring material related to the course to the attention of their peers through links. Perhaps most important, I meant for the blog to model the material that I was teaching, which focused overwhelmingly on the kinds of changes that computer-mediated communication has introduced into contemporary writing; I hoped that students would be a bit reflective about how their own writing was affected by the process of blogging.

Some of my blogging colleagues have used their own blogs as pedagogical tools, engaging and directing students through their posts on the subject matter at hand, encouraging student response in the comments. I decided, however, in the early days of this pedagogical experiment, to keep the class blog separate from my blog. This decision stemmed in part from my desire that my students blog on their own terms, in their own space, and in part from my sense that the class blog could be more focused than it would be if it were nested in the wide variety of issues my blog engaged. I was also nervous, as an untenured assistant professor, about the potential consequences of allowing my blog, which I hoped could remain at least somewhat personal, to become a part of the official record of my employment. Thus I hosted my blog on an outside server, and though I knew that some of my students had discovered and were regularly reading my blog, I never discussed it in class. In retrospect, my blogging might have provided a useful model for the class, and I have since become brave enough (and tenured!) to discuss it freely. At the time, however, the distinction between my blog and my class's blog seemed necessary.

In any case, after a few glitches in setting up our *Movable Type* installation, I opened the blog for business two weeks into the semester, demonstrating the software in class and giving students the log-in IDs I had created for each of them. In the introductory post on the blog, I informed the students of my hopes and expectations:[2]

> I'll be posting here as well—thoughts that occur in the off hours, links to various resources, and so forth. I've also built a blogroll for us (the list of links on the left). Do some exploring, and bring us back good examples of blogs that we should be reading.
>
>   My expectations for your writing here are as follows: each of you should post (at least) one new entry each week, and should respond to (at least) two of your peers' entries each week. Your posts should be thoughtful, interesting, and well-written. Attention to grammar, spelling, and other conventions of writing is a must.
>
>   Finally, remember: we're carrying on a conversation with one another here, but we're doing it in public. Be generous, and keep your broader audience in mind. ("Welcome!" 15 Sept. 2003)

While these expectations and desires seem relatively clear in retrospect, there were two specific problems with the way they played out: first, they needed much more frequent recapping to stay fresh in my students' minds; somehow, the new form of the blog simply did not register with them as a course requirement the way a weekly printed reading response would have. And second, my students were at this stage pretty unfamiliar with blogs and blogging and so were not sure what a good blog post might look like. My plan was to attempt to communicate the forms and uses of blogging by example, hoping that my students would come to their own conclusions about the form and its effects on their reading and writing practices without my leading them too directly to my own ideas. Accordingly, I said nothing in this initial post about the kinds of self-reflection that I hoped the blog would inspire; failing to indicate that desire, however, resulted in an entirely unsurprising failure in its fulfillment.

Operating on the hope that this modeling would suffice, I posted the next entry to the blog two days later. Referring to a conversation in class about Alan Turing's proposed test of computer intelligence, I linked to the Loebner Prize Web site, on which information about the annual competition for chat bots was posted, again asking my students to post links to other sites with useful information for us to consider ("Turing/ Wiener," 17 Sept. 2003). Audre, the only student in the class with any previous blogging experience, left a comment a few hours later, linking to the most recent prize-winning bot and teasing her classmates by saying that "after this experience with Alice, I have to say, I'm more convinced than ever that you're all automatons" ("Turner/Wiener," comments). No one rose to the bait, however, and any potential conversation short-circuited. Another student, Veronica, later followed up with three more comments, but the first of those comments came eight days later, and the other two another two weeks after that; by that time, the discussion had moved on.

The next top-level post, which appeared half an hour after Audre's comment, was a relatively long entry—a mini essay—from Patrick on the origins of contemporary cognitive science, particularly John Searle's "Chinese Room" thought experiment ("The Argument from Consciousness and the Machine/Human Divide," 18 Sept. 2003). Patrick ended this post with an extended series of questions:

> I am not sure that I accept Searle's argument, but it is an interesting approach to forming a distinction between machine processes and human thoughts. Do you all think that thinking and consciousness can ever be achieved by machines? Are these terms loaded with connotations of "what it means to be human" and thus unfair to apply to machines? Despite the complexity of a given machine, is this a problem of type rather than degree? In other words, is consciousness or experience a uniquely human attribute? Or, on the other hand, are humans (in a sense) just extremely complex machines? . . .
>
> . . . Is our "humanity" at stake in understanding the mind in terms of computing machines? What are the implications of this discussion for writing, creativity, and the idea of (inter)textual "networks"?

These questions were precisely the core questions on which the course was focused. Unfortunately, no one followed up Patrick's post with any discussion—including me. My sense was that if I became the first to comment on every post, I would run the risk of inadvertently silencing the class, since the students might begin to write to me, not to one another. Instead, I decided to wait and see if anyone else would respond. Unfortunately, what often works in the classroom—waiting patiently, after asking a question, until everyone starts squirming and someone finally speaks— does not work as well on the Internet, where silence is much harder to read and very easily ignored.

The next post, four days later, came from me. Again, I closed with questions; again, there were no takers ("Remedios Varo," 22 Sept. 2003). Later that morning, during class, I prodded the class to remember their posting and commenting requirements for the semester—a prodding, as it turns out, that should have been repeated much more frequently during the semester.

That day, we discussed Raymond Queneau's *Cent Mille Millards de Poemes*, and the following evening, in response, Audre posted links to a number of online Queneauvian sonnet generators ("No Scissors, but We Can Still Play," 23 Sept. 2003). I decided to respond first, to see if I could trigger some conversation; my response was followed a couple of hours later by a response from Patrick. At this point, then, eight days into the experiment, only three of ten students had participated in the blog. We did have, however, a guest: François Lachance, a regular reader of my blog, had been following the students' posts thus far and, with my blessing, left a comment about his experiences with the sonnet generators. But the conversation died there.

After another two days had passed, Veronica posted a top-level entry, including an excerpt from an interview with Ted Nelson, exploring the ways that his ideas about hypertext and its relationship to his nonlinear thought processes helped her understand her own struggles with dyslexia and making herself understood in writing ("Hypertexts and the Politics of Writing," 26 Sept. 2003). Fascinatingly, Veronica went on to become one of the blog's most prolific posters and commenters; though she never said so overtly, my suspicion is that the electronic mode removed some of the pressure that she had felt in the past in print-on-paper assignments, freeing her to write and contribute more frequently.

Veronica took the lead on the next post as well, creating one of my favorite posts of the semester; in class that day, we had played with an aleatory writing game in which each word in a given line of a poem begins with the letters that spell out the last word in the line before. Veronica proposed that we compose another such poem, starting us off with the title "Senior Year" ("Oulipo Poem," 26 Sept. 2003). Audre, Patrick, and I were the first three respondents, but, at last, four other students (Alex, Emily, Evan, and Joy) then joined in, posting for the first time. The poem only lasted those eight lines, but it was far and away our most successful use of the blog thus far. Since all the students in the class were seniors, their common interest in this transitional period in their lives may have produced some of their engagement. Moreover, Audre's first line for the poem, "Young, eager, and restless," alluded to a quotation from a past president of the college that is inscribed on the college gates, insisting that only the "eager, thoughtful, and reverent" may pass through. These two connections, I thought at the time, produced a personal engagement with the post on the part of the four new commenters. What may have been more important, however, was the aleatory nature of the game that we were playing; because there were rules for the poem, rules that had been clearly communicated to the students, they felt safe in commenting on this post. The open-endedness of the blog and of the previous attempts at discussion had left the students uncertain about how to begin.

As this poem was being composed, however, our class work had moved on; we were now reading Italo Calvino's *If on a Winter's Night a Traveler*. Our conversation in class that day had focused on the repeated scenes of violence that accompany the interpretive act in Calvino's novel, and with that in mind, I linked the students to *Skin*, the project recently announced by Shelley Jackson, for which she sought participants willing to become part of an "embodied story" by having one word (and perhaps a punctuation mark) tattooed upon them. In my response I suggested:

> This . . . project . . . seems to me to do a double violence to the idea of readership—both physically carving the text itself into its ostensible audience (arguably "demoting" them to the unconsciousness of inscription itself) while simultaneously reserving all the pleasures of reading to the author.
> ("On Reading, Writing, and Violence," 27 Sept. 2003)

The two students who responded—Alex and Whitney, who was posting for the first time—both took issue with the project's stated aims. Alex disputed the notion that *Skin* could constitute a "text," given its distributed form:

> Projects like this force us to ask: to what degree can a text be fragmented and still be considered a text? We seemed to have no problem considering Calvino's fractured narrative techniques, or Pynchon's fragmented sense of objectivity as part of single texts. But what happens when the text itself is fractured. Can a hypertext website be said to form a single "text"? Is the library card catalogue a text? What about the entire internet? ("On Reading," comments)

Whitney further objected to the idea that the participants in Jackson's project could be considered the embodiment of words, rather than the surface on which they were inscribed, finally concluding that "we could do a whole course on this project alone. Can we talk about this in class?" ("On Reading," comments").

Such engaged responses, as well as the fact that, over the next three days, there were four new top-level posts (one each from Alex, Whitney, Joy, and Emily), encouraged me to believe that the blog had finally broken through and found purchase in the class. Comments were sparse, still, but by the end of September, in the first two weeks of the blog's life, eight of ten students had posted, and their posts were interesting and insightful, raising questions that we later took up in class discussions, when they did not get much back and forth online. While the volume of posts and comments was not what I had hoped for, it seemed to be on a steady incline.

As it turned out, October was the most active month on the blog, with fifteen top-level posts and a total of twenty comments, but even this level of activity fell far beneath my expectations; had all ten students participated at the level I had originally hoped for, there would have been closer to forty top-level posts and eighty comments during the month. As it was, a ninth student did later join the conversation with one top-level post (the tenth never posted or commented at all during the course of the semester). Patrick was far and away the most prolific poster, with four posts and two comments in October; Audre was not far behind, with three posts during the month, but was also a prolific discussant, leaving six comments. Veronica posted three times and left three comments, and Whitney, Joy, Chris, Alex, and Emily each posted once. Evan, finally, never created a top-level post but did leave a comment.

November saw a significant reduction in the number of posts—a mere six for the entire month—but an increase in discussion on each of those posts, with seventeen comments in total. Posts trickled to a stop mid-month, however, as the students became increasingly involved in their independent projects for the course, and the last three posts on the site (which include a lone post from December) had no comments whatsoever.

What happened? I believe the blog's rapid decline was primarily owing to instructor miscalculation: though I read the blog assiduously and though I often brought up blog posts and discussions in class, my last presence on the blog, either as a top-level post or as a comment, is dated 28 September. Because I felt the class had the blog operating smoothly, I absented myself from it, hoping that my students would feel free to make the space their own; instead, as I later learned from their course evaluations, they felt somewhat abandoned, as though I had lost interest in the project. This was a shame, in more ways than one. My students really had begun to get invested in communicating with one another through the blog, but their sense that I was not that involved allowed them, when the semester got busy, to see the blog as optional. More important, the blog had begun to develop some quite provocative conversations, drawing in readers from outside our classroom community, and when the blog died, those conversations died as well. The most significant example of this kind of conversation began with a post from Audre, in which she directed the class to an online version of one of the first pieces of interactive fiction, created during the 1970s, *Adventure*, asking what the experience of playing such a text-only game was like for the *PlayStation* generation ("Adventure," 11 Nov. 2003). Emily responded with a fairly detailed analysis of her experience with the game, pointing out that "in certain ways I feel that this archaic game is more complex and makes better use of the electronic medium than much of the more literary (and more recent) hypertext/e-fiction we've read in class," particularly noting that the "sense of play and interaction" of the game was important to her, finally asking whether "hypertext really engages this quality of the electronic medium—if not, can this quality ever be effectively incorporated into literary hypertext?" ("Adventure," comments). This comment drew a response from Dennis G. Jerz, a leading expert on such interactive fiction, who seconded Emily's sense of *Adventure*:

> [W]hile there are plenty of text-adventure games that don't do interactivity very well, it's probably easier for a lone programmer/author to create the illusion of interactivity in a text environment than it would be for the same programmer to create the same sense of immersion in a visual and audio environment. ("Adventure," comments)

The excitement of this moment—having drawn one of the world's experts on the subject of our class discussion into conversation with us—was unfortunately lost, since my disappearance from the scene left the students without anyone to indicate how significant this bit of interaction was.[3]

Thus the primary lessons I learned from this first foray into using a blog as part of my teaching were about my responsibilities: I needed to prepare the class for blogging by introducing them to blogs and their uses in class before turning them loose with the software; to remind the students, frequently, both in the classroom and on the blog, of my expectations for their participation; to participate actively, not just as a reader but also as a contributor, while being careful not to allow my presence to dominate the blog or let the students off the hook. In ensuing semesters, I put these lessons to work, in classes with similar group blogs and in classes with individual blogs; each time I have used blogs in this way, I have improved the results, both in terms of quantity and quality, since a greater percentage of the class achieves a level of investment in the blogging process. One baseline has remained, however: on average, ten percent of the students in a class with a blogging requirement will participate only marginally or not at all.

This failure to participate in the blog, I believe, has less to do with the blog form than it does with the host of other reasons for general student nonparticipation that also arises in technology-free classes, given the correspondence I have found between the failure to blog and the failure to complete other assignments. A small subset of otherwise strong students are made nervous by the new form, unsure of its parameters, uncertain of its audience, uncomfortable with its public nature. In recent semesters, I have attempted to assuage their concerns by requiring all my students to blog under a pseudonym, such that their identity will be known to the members of the class but not to the outside world. As I explain to them, anything associated with their names will have a surprising durability on the Internet, and I want to ensure that they are free to experiment—and, indeed, to make mistakes—in their blogging without fear that some future employer running a background check will happen onto the site and potentially hold them accountable for youthful errors and indiscretions. This policy reassures some nervous students, but others, including the less technologically sure, require additional assistance in building their confidence in such online activities.

I have used class blogs since then in two very different registers. In some classes, such as Introduction to Media Studies, blogs are a form of course management software that deliver content to the students. In other courses, such as a course on new media theory that I taught in fall 2005 or Writing Machines, which I taught in fall 2006, I have asked students to maintain their own blogs and have built a central course aggregator that draws their disparate posts together. Now when I ask my students to blog, I am careful to give them a clear sense of my expectations for the frequency of their posts and then to let them know throughout the semester how they are performing in relation to those expectations. I show them many sample blogs, to give them a sense of the range of topics and tones that good blogs can espouse, and I explain my hopes for the kinds of posts that they will produce. I generally require my students to post to their blogs two to three times a week and ask that at least one of those posts be a direct response to the reading assignments; the other posts, I tell them, can focus on anything that is of interest to them—links to related Web sites or news items, responses to class discussion, thoughts about the research they are doing toward their term papers, early drafts of material that will wind up in their essays. Such suggestions, which by no means exhaust the field of good blog fodder, give the students a sense of where to begin, helping them avoid the too common "blogger's block" felt by those who are uncertain whether their thoughts are interesting enough to warrant posting.

What the students who participate in such blogging experiments are able to accomplish is dramatic: they write to and for one another, rather than solely for me; they test out ideas that later find their ways into term papers and projects; they continue conversations long after a class session has ended; they find connections between the work done in the literature classroom and the surrounding culture. Most exciting for me, the students in my fall 2003 class remembered the experience clearly and fondly, three years later, when I wrote to ask their permission to quote them in this essay. The blog caused their work in the course to obtain a public life and a durability in ways that little traditional course work can. In the semesters since then, as I have been able to put the lessons that I learned from this first experience into practice, the excitement for both me and my students of seeing their intellectual work take public flight has only grown.

Notes

1. For further exploration of the relation among social software, education, and the "read/write web," see Richardson.

2. All postings from the class blog, *The Literary Machine*, can be found by date in the archives at http://machines.pomona.edu/170J-2003.

3. By way of contrast, one might explore how Chuck Tryon responded when his first-year composition class's blog suddenly became a topic of conversation amongst the blogs that the course was studying.

Works Cited

Fitzpatrick, Kathleen. *Planned Obsolescence*. Fitzpatrick, 2008. Web. 24 Nov. 2008. Personal blog.

The Literary Machine: Writing in the Human/Computer Interface. Pomona College. Pomona Coll., 2003. Web. 24 Nov. 2008.

Richardson, Will. *Blogs, Wikis, Podcasts, and Other Powerful Web Tools for Classrooms*. Thousand Oaks: Corwin, 2006. Print.

Tryon, Charles. "Using Blogs to Teach First-Year Composition." *Pedagogy* 6.1 (2006): 128–32. Print.

Walker, Jill. "Final Version of Weblog Definition." *Jill/txt*. Walker, 28 June 2003. Web. 31 Aug. 2006.

Haun Saussy

The Literal and the Lateral: A Digital Early China for College Freshmen

As someone who works in comparative literature, does most of his "comparing" with Chinese literature and history in mind, and often teaches big courses for nonmajors, when I first heard about hypertext I thought it would solve all my routine pedagogical problems and let me move on to the important ones. The routine problems loom large for the teacher of a basic Chinese civilization class. The texts available in translation go in and out of print, and their quality varies enormously. The different romanization systems confuse students, who cannot reasonably be expected to recognize or remember that Chou Kung (in Wade-Giles transcription) is the same as Zhou Gong (in pinyin), let alone 周公. The many homonyms, or near homonyms, in this tonal language usually defeat even those students who put in the effort to remember who Zhou Gong, Gong Gong, Wen Wang, Wu Wang, Cheng Wang, and the bearers of twenty or thirty other two-syllable names were. The twenty-five traditionally recognized dynasties, the many philosophical schools, the eighteen (pre-1911) provinces, the countless cities, mountains, and rivers quickly take on the look of a heap of smooth mah-jongg tiles engraved with elusive symbols, and then the uninitiated student gives up and drops the course. Students of Chinese background in the same class pose a different challenge: they often bring with them preconceptions acquired at an early age from relatives or primary school texts, and these representations are something they simply know and have never had to consider debatable propositions; the non-Chinese teacher who offers a different view on the hallowed story may appear to them ignorant or arrogant. Neither of those two impressions will sweeten the classroom atmosphere, given that students in the early-twenty-first-century United States are trained to tiptoe carefully around the ethnic, religious, or political identities of their classmates and quickly sense a smoldering issue. When one group of students feels unable to acquire the basic vocabulary needed to take part in a discussion and another group is suspicious of the questions thrown out to start the conversation, a thick silence may take over.

In a lecture class, the same puzzlements and suspicions apply, but the teacher may discover what went wrong only after the midterm exam, when the worst sufferers—and who hath need of the physician, but they who are sick?—have looked at their first grades and left.

The frustrating thing about these obstacles, whose unyielding solidity I have confirmed more times than I care to enumerate, is that they occur on a low level of cultural competence: transliteration, pronunciation, dramatis personae, markers of space and time. They work so effectively to discourage all but the inspired few from going further into Chinese studies that the beginning-level course hardly has a chance to do what college humanities courses are designed to do, that is, raise far-reaching questions of value, narrative, desire, law, action, difference, purpose, and the like through the careful reading of texts in their historical setting. (The lecturer, of course, gets there. The question is whether the lecturer brings the class along.) Three hundred years of practice have smoothed the way for the teacher of Plato, Dante, or Mary Wollstonecraft in the English-speaking world. It might take another hundred or so for Chinese antiquity to be seen as something other than Chinese, an exotic weirdness or dab of ginger included on the syllabus for the sake of contrast (possibly even, at that, a covert advertisement for the familiar joys of Aquinas or Burke). But the teacher who believes in the importance of the subject will want to speed the process up.

Of course I exaggerate. There are always monolingual students who fall under the charm of Laozi or Zhuangzi, whose moral quest finds a partner in Confucius or Mencius, who recognize the elusive flash of similitudes in a stanza from the *Shi jing* (*Book of Odes*). But the monolinguals often remember the lesson but forget the fable, take away an impression but do not remember the names, the dates, or the places; whereas for Chinese speakers, the particulars and where they are set on the great background of history matter, as it matters to most people in European culture whether a given prophecy is Ezekiel's or William Blake's. If Chinese culture matters only as fable, as metaphor, it is not quite serious enough to deserve a place in history, in the chains of cause and effect that somehow produced us. So the obstacles of vocabulary, identification, and pronunciation, trivial as they are, add up to a question about what really matters—just the sort of question teachers can ask in a freshman humanities course and possibly nowhere else in a college education without sounding foolish.

Hypertext, I thought, would enable me to vault over these trivial questions and get to the deeper ones: How is this passage constructed? Who has the point of view and why? What is it arguing for and against? What does it preemptively exclude? How might it have been written if it had started from different assumptions? By clicking on a word or a name, the student could quickly (and without making a show of ignorance) access a definition, a genealogy, a time line, or a related text. Chinese speakers could jump to the same passage in the original. Neither action required me to be at the student's elbow. As the World Wide Web grew in size and refinement, it became possible to imagine hypertext links that spoke, by opening up a little sound file that would present to the ear the differences between the Gong Gongs, Zhou Gongs, and Cheng Wangs so confusing to the eye; image files that would illustrate every unusual object; and windows that would send straight to the instructor the pleas for help of the lost.

I got a chance to test this daydream when a member of Stanford University's committee charged with revising the freshman Cultures, Ideas, and Values (CIV) requirement invited me to join some colleagues I had never met and with them design a new sort of humanities course. Cost would be no object, it was implied, and many digital toys would be put at our disposal. Brilliant graduate students in engineering, computer science, and our own departments would collect our hot air and condense it to practical lines of code. We would have a summer of paid research to work out our syllabus and then, on day 1 of classes, invite our captive audience "to boldly go" on a star trek where no Stanford student had gone. I could not imagine refusing.

The Stanford humanities requirement needs some explaining. A longstanding yearlong freshman course in Western civilization had finally been brought down in the 1980s by a campaign much talked about and caricatured in the press. Numerous cultural warriors of the left and right had cut their teeth in those battles, trading accusations of ethnocentrism and superficial relativism. A patient faculty committee worked out a decentralized solution called Cultures, Ideas, and Values. Under the CIV system, departments of humanities and social sciences petitioned the decanal committee to establish and run their own tracks of freshman study, each track being expected to include materials exhibiting a diversity of cultural and historical points of view. By 1997 the burdens of this system on the relatively small departments were becoming obvious. The revision of the freshman requirement set forth in that year established a program office charged with supervising and supporting courses that were to be created by teams of people from more than one department. A diversity of disciplines was now as important as a diversity of cultures (the obligatory reference to which had led, under CIV, to some strange yet predictable syllabuses: Confucius taught everywhere in translation, heavy reliance on the *Popol Vuh* and *Things Fall Apart*, little attention to linguistic specificity). CIV had presented its set of opportunities; those of the new Introduction to the Humanities (IHUM) program were there for the opportunistic to discover; and I was curious to see what interdisciplinarity would become in the setting of a first-semester freshman course.

My colleagues were Larry Friedlander of the English department, Shakespeare director and ponderer of the Abrahamic tradition, and Tim Lenoir, a historian of science whose consuming interest just then was a fabulous prosthetic apparatus that allowed surgeons to operate on patients half a world away, through force-feedback and instantaneous 3-D modeling. We gave the course the provisional and inclusive title The Word and the World. The IHUM rules allowed us just five texts for the ten-week quarter. We settled quickly on the Book of Genesis, *Hamlet*, René Descartes's *Meditations*, and the movie *Blade Runner* as works that came together around some common problems of selfhood, action, and intention. They might in fact be set up as a history of the Western soul, from beginning to probable end. We also agreed that we wanted to do something with an East Asian text—why not something from a Buddhist tradition that balked at the reality of the self and categorized the soul as belonging rather to the problem than the solution? I went home and spent several days looking at likely candidates. The *Lotus Sutra*? The *Platform Sutra of the Sixth Patriarch*? *Journey to the West*? All were beautiful, complex, and had much to say to the other texts, but *Journey to the West* could only appear as a snippet (a few chapters taken from Anthony Yu's stout four-volume translation), a concession I was reluctant to make, and the two Buddhist sutras were too much in the form of lectures, interrupted, to be sure, with beautiful analogies and fragments of dialogue, but I was afraid the students would see them as formally identical to the *Meditations* (and disregard the big differences). The legs of our table kept migrating all to one side; we needed something that would stand apart and hold the whole thing up.

Our four agreed-upon texts were all about finding, making, or confirming a self—that was easy to see. They were also all in some way about, or involved, transfers of power, the matter of kingly epics ever since the scribes wrote on clay. And in every transfer something went wrong: Sarah laughed, the Ghost cried foul, Descartes did not entirely protect his argument from uncooperative corollaries, and so forth. As I fiddled with this idea, a Chinese corresponding text came to mind, the *Shang shu* 尚書, or *Book of Documents*, one of the Classics honored since antiquity but the one that had, as scholars had admitted for centuries, a few things wrong with it. Its date was uncertain, somewhere between 1000 BCE and 200 CE, if all the scholarly opinions were taken into account. Many of its thirty-odd chapters concerned legendary and unverifiable happenings; others had been bitterly contested by sages of antiquity who thought the Classic's history was all wrong. One edition that prevailed for some six hundred years was later shown to be a forgery, and some two thousand years ago a contest between two schools of thought had left the book separated into two strata, of which one or the other was always suspect. It would be impossible to make everyone read all thirty-eight chapters in either of the two existing English translations, both by great scholars—James Legge and Bernhard Karlgren—but both practically unreadable, Legge's for its King James manner and Karlgren's for its numbing parenthetical precisions and qualifications. I would have to choose a subset of chapters and make a new translation; and this time the easiest way to put the results in front of our ninety students would be to publish it on the Web.

I had dealt with some chapters of the *Shang shu* in my dissertation, back in the pre-Web days of 1990, so I had a sense of where to begin. The most often argued-over section of the book, the chapter rejected as history by no less an authority than Mencius, is a battle that occurs at the transition point between the Shang 商 (traditional dates 1766–1122 BCE) and Zhou 周 (1122–256 BCE) dynasties. According to the history

222 The Literal and the Lateral

given us in the *Shang shu* and later sources like the *Shiji* 史記 ("Records of the Grand Historian") of Sima Tan 司馬談 (d. 110 BCE) and Sima Qian 司馬遷 (c. 145–c. 86 BCE), Zhou Xin 紂辛, the last king of the Shang dynasty, was cruel and depraved and enjoyed torturing his subjects, especially officials who dared to remonstrate against his wicked ways. One of his feudal subordinates, Lord Wu 武 of the Zhou people in the northwest part of the realm, suffered to see the condition of the once great Shang and regretfully took on the burden of righting the world. The battle between Wu's army and that of his hierarchical superior Zhou Xin was said in an early version of the *Shang shu* to have caused so much blood to run that "clubs and pestles floated about."[1] This passage scandalized the great philosopher Mencius (fl. 320 BCE). He declared it had to have been a historical fabrication because a true king like Wu must have been able to conquer violence without violence. "Rather than accept everything in the *Shang shu*," said Mencius, "it would be better not to have the *Shang shu* at all!" (Lau 194; my modification of trans.). There at any rate was one case of the "something wrong" that flashes across the transfer of power. It gave me something to work with.

The scandalous chapter is "Wu cheng" 武成 ("The War's Completion"). In a further complication in the reception of the chapter, one of its major interpreters, the philosopher Zhu Xi 朱熹 (1130–200), declared in his commentary to the *Shang shu* that the chapter had fallen out of its proper arrangement. A student of Zhu Xi reshuffled the sentences of the chapter to make them follow a strictly chronological order—thereby making obvious, to those who might not have noticed, that the earlier arrangement began with the end of the story, recounting Wu's triumph and the victor's humble sacrifices to heaven well before mentioning the bloody event itself.

These puzzles in the text, its meaning, and its reception shaped the *Shang shu* Web site we built that summer as a subset of the general Web site for the course. Although I had a sense of the conceptual anchors of the text as I wanted to present it—which would become the turning points of the student assignments to be built into the electronic text—the actual shape of the work, in all its electronic materiality, only emerged through discussions and testing with our splendid team of Web designers.[2] Various combinations of our group members worked on the sites for Genesis, *Hamlet*, *Meditations*, and *Blade Runner*. We were all back in school and learning from one another.

Figure 1. *Shang shu* site index page

Sponsorship for our Web design enterprise came from the Stanford Learning Lab.[3] The lab also supported George Toye's team creating *Pan-fora*, a threaded chat board that we would use as a semipublic extension of small-group discussions (all messages were open to every student and faculty member in the class but not to outsiders; messages could be re-grouped instantly by date, topic, sender, or assigned section). Essays and ungraded reaction pieces were submitted through the Web, by clicking and uploading—a relatively new interface in 1997.[4]

The medium gave us the opportunity to do almost everything I had dreamed of doing with the granular preliminaries to Chinese cultural literacy—namely, get them out of the way and into working knowledge, or, in computerspeak, to front-load them. The main page offered the revised translation of the *Shang shu* text (fig. 1). Next to all Chinese words were little megaphone icons that, when clicked, opened a sound file of a voice pronouncing the word or, in one case where rhyme and cadence were important, a whole passage in modern Mandarin. (Philological accuracy in the shape of reconstructed archaic Chinese would have scared off even the fluent Chinese speakers.) Where a sentence needed explaining, it was un-derlined: a click brought up a sidebar with a gloss signed by me, Mencius,

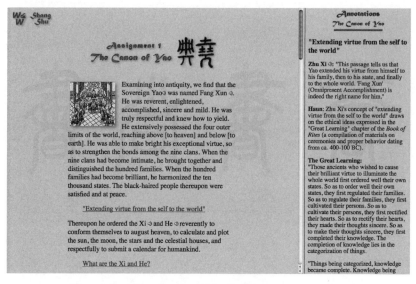

Figure 2. "The Canon of Yao," with commentary bar

Zhu Xi, or some other momentary authority (fig. 2). We gratefully took advantage of the networked outside world: place-names linked to maps and, in some cases, to the promotional Web pages of Chinese towns. Bronze cauldrons and weapons sat ready for inspection on museum Web sites, even one vase that rotated in *Quick Time*. Scans from the Hoover Institution's fine late-Qing woodblock printing of the *Shang shu* with its eloquent illustrations provided visual punctuation (fig. 3).

At times, worried that the ancient text sounded too austere, we pushed user-friendliness to the point of invading personal space: "Want to know more about Gong Gong?" asked a line of underlined text interrupting the chronicle, and a call-out offered to tell all on "The Scandal Surrounding Shun's Marriage." Multiple and divergent views from either the classics or their postclassical commentators were all to the good, and we foregrounded them, anticipating that they would help break down the expectation of a single, indissoluble, culturally authentic truth about ancient China that the later-born and foreign-born could never intuit. Most of the people who since antiquity had added footnotes to the *Shang shu* had felt themselves to be remote from the text in one way or another, and they wrote to shorten the distance. Our glossing showed that the tradition was a conversation. Rather than put the ancient text at greater and

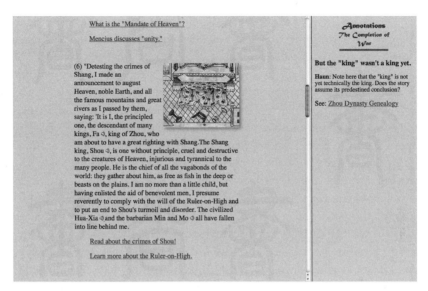

Figure 3. "Completion of the War," with commentary and clickable illustration

greater removes, glossing brought the text ever closer—at least, that is what I felt it was meant to do, as I have always felt it does in the elaborate, meticulous, argumentative annotation of the Chinese histories and classics. We were electronically "remediating" that experience for our audience (Bolter 23).

Some of these things might have been done on paper, but much more awkwardly. I could have written introductions, added footnotes, clipped and pasted parallel passages, and included phonetic guides, maps, and pictures. The hypertext medium, however, allowed me to plan the reader's trip through the text: to bring certain things up simultaneously, to delay other things, to interrupt, or to be discreet. We sometimes express the difference between electronic and paper texts as that between simultaneous and linear media. To tell the truth, it is rather that an electronic medium gives us the chance to decide how many things to put in the visual space (and click space) that makes up the reader's present; at times we will want a linearity even stricter than that of the book (whose codex form always allows a disobedient reader to flip ahead to page 203 or back to the last time Ogdred Weary's sofa was mentioned).[5] And when the tracks lead inexorably onward to a box marked "Assignment," we can even refuse to let the reader go on until the homework is handed in.

The Web site took shape, then, as follows. A splash page offers three points of entry into the *Shang shu* text. From the first entry point, a short introduction gives the barest of backgrounds into the time and place of the *Shang shu* and suggests ways of reading it (as history, as mythology, as moral fable). With another click, the reader is now in the text itself: the two chapters entitled "The Canon of Yao" and "The Canon of Shun," which tell of two ancient sage-kings, one of whom was able to create order by appointing the right administrators to every department of the cosmos. The other, named only after a few deceptive candidates had shown their inadequacy, had to deal with rebellions but quickly brought the world back into balance by executing or banishing the wrongdoers. A transitional passage points out the prevalence of the questions suggested by these legends (hereditary kingship versus elevation by merit; the trust between sovereign and official; the fear of rebellion; the importance of technology) among philosophical writers of early China. At this point an "Assignment" box asked some relatively easy questions about the means of creating order envisaged by the *Shang shu*. All this was planned as one day's assignment, in preparation for the first lecture on this text.

The second assignment, appearing under its own heading on the splash page, opens with a short introduction of its own. Here it seemed well to alert students to the questions to be considered in the assignment at the end. The introductory passage says in part:

> From very early on, the story of Wu's rebellion has been faulted for two kinds of incoherence: moral and structural. We will discuss the moral problems throughout the annotations to this chapter, prompted by comments on and retellings of the tale by Mencius, Zhuangzi, Sima Qian, and Emperor Jing of the Han Dynasty. Far from settling things, the "charter" is vigorously fought over! . . .
>
> How do formal choices—for example, different orderings of the same elements—result in differences of meaning? What are the relations among artistic strategies, their effects on readers, and the moral power of history-writing?[6]

The story of Wu's successful rebellion against the Shang monarch is given in its traditional, that is, unchronological, order, with the usual illustrations, sound clips, glosses, and marginalia. At the end, peace is achieved:

> [Wu] attached great importance to the spread of the Five Teachings among the people; in his care for food, for funeral rites, and for sacrifices, he showed generosity, truthfulness, prudence and loyalty, he

honored virtue and rewarded deeds of merit. He let his robes hang down, folded his hands, and the whole world was well ordered. (*Shang shu* 1: 393)

And then, of course, the arguments begin.

In a face-to-face classroom, at this point I would have given some time to framing the issues and starting a discussion, hoping not to have to guide it too overtly. Here, though, having the prefabricated interactivity of server memory to run with, I let myself be far more directive and bossy than usual:

> Mencius takes seriously King Wu's claims to be a benevolent sovereign and a restorer of the old ways, and therefore rejects any implication that violence and bloodshed were necessary to establish Wu on his throne. But what standard is Mencius using to establish history? Isn't there something unusual in relying on what *ought to have happened* to determine what really happened?
>
> Mencius may sound like a peculiar historian, but note that in trying to make the actual conform to the ideal Mencius was simply following in the footsteps of the heroic King Wu himself. Wu represents himself as a restorer of order to the world, but leading a rebellion is necessarily a violent and disorderly act. Is there a fundamental mismatch between Wu's actions and his words? Or is the mismatch the very point of the story, as if to say that justification is always inadequate?
>
> If these are contradictions, a paradox within the story may represent an attempt to resolve them. Mencius objects to a version of the "Completion of the War" chapter that appears to blame King Wu [link here to Mencius passage] for the copious bloodshed. But the version of the chapter in our present *Shang shu*—like Sima Qian's version [link here to Shiji passage]—exonerates him by suggesting that [Zhou Xin's] army eliminated itself! Is this improbable history, or a response to a moral contradiction in history, perhaps fashioned by a reader who, like Mencius, could not reconcile the many dimensions of the founding legends of the Zhou?

Giving students this much thematic material to work with (much of it paradoxical, therefore apt to produce detailed critical argument) was a preparation for the assignment, which deals with the formal properties of narration. The assignment—this time designed as a two- or three-page essay question—presents the chapter "Wu cheng" in its traditional arrangement alongside the strictly chronological arrangement and asks, What's the difference? Given that the content is identical, the same words and sentences standing in an unchanged referential relation to their context, what is there to justify preferring one version over the other? What effects of meaning are specific to one or the other version of the chapter, but not both? In what ways are they not the same literary work, although built from the same sentences and paragraphs? The properties of the work that students are asked to examine are features that definitely belong to the literary material of the text but do not require immersion in the original language; here we have kept both untranslatability and paraphrase, the China scholar's usual twin monsters, away from the door. This situation explains my immoderate satisfaction with the way the lesson came out. Firecrackers, please, to chase the devils away.

The two lectures and two discussion sections that surrounded these assignments took care of one week of the course. The schedule then provided for weeklong units, similarly organized around electronic discussions and assignments, for Genesis, *Hamlet*, *Meditations*, and *Blade Runner*. In the sixth week, we revisited all the texts, taking them in combinations. The game was to isolate strands of formal or thematic properties in two or more of the works and correlate them so as to produce a better-rounded argument. Hamlet's and Descartes's conceptions of, and partial yielding to, insanity provide one example: to reduce them to the same theme makes both uninteresting, but to work out how the parallel paths diverge, how they result in different actions, gives us more to think about. Usurpation and taboo were the features of the *Shang shu* chapters that seemed to have the most suggestive power in relation to Genesis and the other four texts. To expand on this theme, I added a further set of readings from Chinese history reinforcing Mencius's objection with the recommendation that, even if usurpations are fated to happen, it is not advisable to talk truthfully or at all about them, and I played this view against another text by the most tactless historian of Han China, Sima Qian. That text presents Wu's rebellion from the point of view of two loyalists who chastened Wu for his lack of reverence for rank and, seeing their words fall on stony ground, fled to the mountainside to starve rather than eat the grain of a criminal dynasty. Lamenting the miserable end of these upright gentlemen (who were nonetheless on the wrong side of the new and universally acclaimed dynasty), Sima Qian questions the famous benevolence of heaven, of which the king's benevolence is supposed to be a shadow. The historian's act of questioning falls into a series, connecting with but not repeating the questions of Hamlet, Descartes, Isaac, and so forth—at least, the possibility of that claim was the wager of our course, and whether it makes sense is the test of our ability to bring a small set of Chinese texts into an intenser than usual conversation with European and American texts.

Given the obstacles to making Chinese texts meaningful (that is, a matter of concern as well as of understanding) to students outside the large piece of the world where Chinese culture is taken for granted, I have found electronic media to be a great help and ally. But it is not being electronic that makes the medium good: it is the opportunities it offers, and taking those opportunities requires design and work. In The Word and the World, I was fortunate to have Stanford's resources on my side: the course was intended as an experimental vehicle, and we had extraordinary support and hand-picked collaborators. In the far greater part of my educational-technology life that is supported by odd moments in the office between meetings or late nights and weekends at home, the class Web projects I type up and piece together, one link at a time, are far less ambitious—little more than glorified syllabi. But having lived the high life once, I know at least what I would like to be able to do.

The Word and the World Web sites were tailor-made to fit the texts and arguments we had conceived of beforehand (and continually modified in the course of implementation). In each case, we had identified pedagogical problems to be foregrounded: these problems led the design of every aspect of the sites; for the *Shang shu*, the choice of readings, the exegetical style, the division into chapters, the sequencing of readings and assignments, the connections to the other main texts for the course.

In the push to bring classrooms and their fauna into the digital age, I have seen many universities install build-your-own kits for instructional software, sometimes even requiring faculty members to use them. These Lego-style systems take the user, step by step, through a predetermined set of expected components. Drop name and title here, office hours here, picture (optional) here, first week's readings here, and so on. More sophisticated kits allow for the posting of text and explanatory notes or automate the uploading of lecture slides. These kits simplify the decision making that goes into course site design, but to a degree that no instructor could tolerate in a student paper. Like *PowerPoint*, these kits gain their ease of use by precluding most imaginable uses, by predetermining the analytic framework that will house the content (Tufte). Types of argument that lose a great deal by being presented as a major point followed by a maximum of six bulleted subpoints clash with the medium, and when the medium is a gatekeeper (as is the case for software packages channeling data to class-work servers), the argument loses the battle. Here the electronic garment has been made first, and the issues of interpretation and pedagogy had better twist and squeeze into it. I realized how different the other way was when I tried to drop my 1997–99 *Shang shu* module into a different course, a general survey of Chinese civilization. Although the points covered were all, in their way, relevant to the "Shang, Zhou, Qin, and Han Dynasties" segment of such a course, and the students were receptive to the handsome, clickable design, the ideas led in their own directions, and I was constantly aware of intellectual phantom limbs: here a parallel with Polonius cried for attention, there a digression into neo–Hollywood noir loomed. I should have taken the time to make an entirely new, *durchkomponiert*, purpose-built site for this other course.

This recommendation may sound elitist and feasible only for professors at elite universities at the rare moments when the system winks at them to go ahead. My intention is other: it is really a recommendation for someone to work at the pedagogy of pedagogy and break down the sclerotic tools of educational software into units that the nonexpert can recombine in more flexibly configurable ways to espouse the contours of the idea he or she is pursuing. We know what we admire, enjoy, and seek to encourage in student writing; why not approach our digital design projects with similar expectations? It is also a recommendation for institutions to invest in best-practice course development—an excellent way to reinvigorate the skills of experienced teachers through contact with students and novice teachers who may feel as much at home with XML as with English grammar or MLA citation style. I am still learning, in 2006, from the things I tried out in the summer of 1997, a Methusaleh's lifetime ago in the time of Silicon Valley.

Notes

1. This and all translations from the Chinese are mine unless otherwise indicated.

2. Charles Kerns led the team and worked with the group that was outfitting digital classrooms for section meetings. Sheri Sheppard, at the head of a band of engineer-ethnographers, assembled testers and scrutinized our decision-making processes (all our meetings were recorded, even a few where we fought and yelled). Carlos Seligo and Shari Epstein gave particularly good advice on building analysis into visual and procedural forms (Seligo, a critic of science fiction, and Epstein, a historian of Chinese thought, are both nimble with HTML). Jani Scandura's background in theater and the history of psychiatry led to strong con-

vergences between the *Hamlet* and *Meditations* sites. (In the second and third years of the course, we were joined by Mariatte Denman.)

3. The lab is now closed. The Stanford Center for Innovations in Learning preserves notes on the lab's work in The Word and the World.

4. This feature created our one moment of unhappy collaboration between humanists and engineers. We had specified that a certain assignment was to be completed by midnight on a Tuesday, and the engineers, taking us at our word, closed the window for submissions at 12:01 a.m. Stanford students of whatever major tend to begin their studying at two in the morning. Those who had sat down early to do their work and made their click at, say, 12:02 saw their papers vanish into nothingness. We had a lot of apologizing to do at the Wednesday lecture.

5. An anagram of "Edward Gorey," who published *The Curious Sofa: A Pornographic Tale by Ogdred Weary* in 1961.

6. This and all unreferenced quotations are taken from *Shang shu*, the instructional Web site developed by Haun Saussy et al. at Stanford University in 1997 (not currently visible).

Works Cited

Bolter, Jay David. *Writing Space: The Computer, Hypertext, and the History of Writing.* Hillsdale: Erlbaum, 1991. Print.

Karlgren, Bernhard, trans. *The Book of Documents.* Stockholm: Museum of Far Eastern Antiquities, 1950. Print.

Lau, D. C., trans. *Mencius.* Harmondsworth: Penguin, 1970. Print.

Legge, James, trans. *The Chinese Classics: With a Translation, Critical and Exegetical Notes, Prolegomena, and Copious Indexes.* 5 vols. Hong Kong: Hong Kong UP, 1966. Print.

Shang shu [The Book of Documents]. 阮元, *Shisanjing zhushu* 十三經注疏 [The Thirteen Classics, Annotated and Commented]. Ed. Ruan Yuan. 1815. 8 vols. Taipei: Dahua, 1987. Print.

Tufte, Edward R. *The Cognitive Style of* PowerPoint. Cheshire: Graphics, 2003. Print.

The Word and the World. Stanford Center for Innovations in Learning. Stanford Center for Innovations in Learning, 2006. Web. 31 Aug. 2006.

Murray McGillivray

Old English Online at the University of Calgary

Planning the Course

In February 1997, I learned that my application for Alberta provincial government Learning Enhancement Envelope funds to create an entirely online version of English 401 (Old English Language and Prose Literature) had been successful. Old English is the variety of English written before about 1100 CE, a somewhat arcane and difficult form of the language that is as inflected as German and bears about the same resemblance to modern English as does Latin to French. I would need to reimagine entirely the teaching of a subject matter that even in my own progressive classroom relied heavily on methodologies dating from the nineteenth century and inherited from my teachers.

When I applied for the funding, I had two main motivations. One was to reach new audiences for a course that each year typically garnered no more than eight or nine students who were truly committed to the subject out of a total enrollment of fifteen to thirty-five. An online course could reach students outside my institution, appeal to students who might not otherwise have considered taking the subject, provide a small source of revenue for my department, and suggest one model of remote course delivery to be used for our new branch campus in Red Deer. The second motivation was to rethink the traditional modes of instruction for the course, such as rote learning of grammatical paradigms and the "translation circle," a humiliating classroom technique in which each student is called on in turn to translate a portion of the Old English text and comment on its grammatical features, any errors being corrected publicly by the professor.

I hoped to replace the humiliation of the translation circle with an exploratory methodology driven by students' interests and to facilitate the learning of declensions and conjugations by using interactive exercises similar to those pioneered earlier in the decade by Constance B. Hieatt, Brian Shaw, and Duncan Macrae-Gibson. I suspected that with those two problematic areas of instruction improved by the application of technology and given the ease of use and multimedia capabilities of the World Wide Web, the necessity for direct personal contact with my students would be greatly reduced, particularly because I could also improve what I see as the main reason for the high dropout rate in the traditional Old English class—the experience that students have with textbooks outside the classroom.

The traditional out-of-classroom experience of students contributes more than the classroom humiliation does, I believe, to their frustration, low morale, and drop rate. Old English textbooks try to be user-friendly, but such attempts are hampered by the medium in which they exist, the codex-structured book. A typical organization of the contents of the book includes three main components: the Old English text; explanatory notes that treat the cultural, linguistic, intertextual, and other aspects of the text; and a glossary that provides definitions and grammatical information about words. The components other than the Old English text are usually elsewhere in the book, often at the end, and the notes usually precede the glossary at the very back.

Studying an Old English text in a textbook is therefore an experience totally unlike normal reading. Students must flip constantly between three different parts of the book. After having visually identified each word in the text, they turn to the glossary to look it up, then, keeping the definition in their memory, go back to the text to find their place again, then back to the glossary for the next word. Every few words, an ending needs to be looked up in the student's grammar, which may well be a separate book. Every few sentences, students must check the explanatory notes to understand what is going on. Four fingers may be required to keep open all the places a student needs.

And every step of this laborious process is subject to accident and error. The spelling system is different, so students find the spelling of a word difficult to remember while flipping to the glossary and easy to confuse with a similar-looking word once there. Grammatical inflections mean that the precise spelling in the text is most often not even a headword in the glossary (English speakers are totally confused by that). Students can lose their place in the text while dealing with the glossary, can forget the definition of the word they just looked up when searching for their place in the text again, and can forget the web of accumulated meaning when a new word comes to join a partially completed phrase.

The whole picture is not a pretty one: the combination of classroom humiliation and textbook frustration has caused generations of students to avoid Old English entirely or to drop it if they accidentally register. My goal was to improve on the traditional in-class experience of students of the language and on their traditional out-of-class experience by providing interactive and multimedia replacements for parts of both.

I began by listing the features of my classroom course that would need to be retained to make the Web adaptation of the course a success: some canonical texts, the basic rules of grammar, some cultural and linguistic understandings that my classroom teaching had tried to reveal to students. Not really sure in this new enterprise how normative my classroom practices actually had been, I also got some help by asking colleagues on my disciplinary e-mail discussion list, ANSAXNET, what the course should include. The responses did not provide all the kinds of help I wanted but did give me food for thought on one particular issue: those who were horrified that I would contemplate doing this thing were most horrified about the absence of in-class pronunciation practice.[1] I immediately revised my plans to boost the provision for sound on the planned site.

Another source of help was our institutional communications media department, which raised issues that otherwise would not have surfaced so soon. Would students be online all at the same time, allowing synchronous exchanges (e.g., chat rooms), or would they be accessing the materials at different times and therefore be interacting with one another and me by asynchronous communication (e.g., an e-mail discussion list)? Was there a way to control the technology at the students' end, or would the course need to be usable on a wide variety of machines (quite an issue in 1997)? Would the experience involve more guidance, including daily or weekly tasks, or would it allow for a freer exploration, like surfing the

World Wide Web? How would tests and other credit exercises be delivered? What would the instructor's role be if much of the content was delivered through Web pages? Could delivery software such as *Lotus Notes* or *WebCT* be used?[2]

The First Run

In fact, because of the tightness of the development timeline, some of these issues were still being explored as the course began in mid-May 1997 in our spring session, a compressed six-week semester. At that point, only the first three lessons of a planned fifteen were in existence in a form suitable for students, although materials existed ready for incorporation into some of the later lessons. The online grammar had been written but still had a few typos. Many of the reading texts had been linked to their glossaries in a standardized set of interlinked frames, in which the word clicked on by the student in the top frame linked to a glossary that displayed in the bottom frame the definition and grammatical description of the word. Most of these texts had been available for some weeks, and registered students had been urged to play around with them and browse through the grammar before the course began. They were also invited to explore the links in Cathy Ball's *Old English Pages* (which now no longer exists). Behind the scenes, the team continued to develop the course, often completing a portion hours or even minutes ahead of the time students would first access it, a process that continued for the following six weeks as the course ran for the first time.[3]

The course was designed for asynchronous access: I had theorized that students might end up taking it from different time zones and all might not be able to be "present" at the same time (over the years, I have had students from Western and Eastern Europe, Australia, China, South America, and all regions of the United States). Students communicated with one another by means of an e-mail discussion list, with me individually by private e-mail.

Assignment completion and due dates were about as free-form as is possible (following a theory of exploratory learning that seemed to be a logical corollary of the shape of the Web): while students were exhorted to try to keep to a schedule of readings and lesson completion included on the course site, they really only needed to complete the online grammar tests (called credit exercises to distinguish them from self-improvement exercises also offered on the site) by the last day of classes. The flavor of the teaching and learning philosophy that inspired the course structure in the first run is given by the introduction to the online schedule:

> This course is structured as a series of lessons, as a series of readings, and as a series of learning tasks (such as completion of particular exercises). In the schedule given below and in the lesson pages these are interrelated, but you should be aware that it is not always necessary to follow the particular order in which things are laid out here. You may, for example, find it worthwhile and challenging to try reading some of the texts before attempting the grammatical learning that the schedule and lesson plans associate with them, or vice versa, and there's nothing wrong with that. Feel free, in other words, to take charge of your own learning within the confines of the course.
> ("English 401 Schedule")

In fact, because we were still writing the course pages and making them available as the course progressed, this suggestion of freedom of approach was largely illusory during the first run, probably, in hindsight, a good thing. The students simply had to work with what we had available to give them in any given week.

There were eighteen students registered, of whom twelve were main-campus students, most of whom would have been able to take a classroom version of the course if one had been available; four were students who took the course from our satellite program at Red Deer College, an hour-and-a-half drive north of the main campus; and two were distance students (one in Massachusetts and one in Texas). One student was eight months pregnant and looking after a two-year-old and would not have been able to take a course on campus; two worked in food service and "took" the course mostly after 3:00 a.m.

I opened the discussion list conversation by asking people to introduce themselves, and although the resulting messages competed for airtime with people's technical problems (a theme of the first week), the foundations of an atmosphere of mutual respect and cooperation were laid as replies to the introductions brought out connections between students either relevant to the course content ("I took Middle English with her, too!") or completely irrelevant ("I was born in Ontario, too!").

Although I was working my fingers to the bone behind the scenes preparing the site as I went, I strove for a public persona as a relaxed, helpful, sympathetic mentor to reduce the distance between me and the individual student. It is considerably easier for a teacher to present a pedagogic persona (something I realize that not all of us will admit to having) online, where fifty-year-old truckers magically become pubescent girls, than in the physical classroom. In addition, online learning, or at least the site-centered explorational learning method I was using in this course, demands increased agency of learners and as a result requires that the professor slip into the role of mentor: the students are necessarily in charge of the project of understanding the subject matter.

The relation of students to one another changed as well. A class discussion list or bulletin board is an ambiguous space, not clearly identifiable as a version of the classroom (with its power structure and formal rules of exchange), of the study group (with its atmosphere of cooperation and academic interchange), or of the pub (where students relate to one another with only incidental reference to academic matters). The teacher can intervene gently to curb a too dramatic tendency to the last view (and certainly has a duty to intervene firmly if conversation becomes insultingly informal or verges on racism, sexism, or homophobia), but in my experience the new freedom of informal interaction with professor and fellow students allowed by this ambiguous space benefits most students, among other things by opening a space for doubts and uncertainties as well as for questions. Students who are shy and retiring in the classroom sometimes blossom in the online environment; students who are class cutups are sometimes much more reticent in an online forum.

Freedom to complete assignments in the order and according to the timetable chosen by the student may not be such a clear benefit. While some students thrive in a free-learning environment and explore far beyond the confines of the official course material, and others are organized enough to create a timetable for themselves or follow the suggested one on the site, almost all students allow freedom to slide into procrastination. In the first run of the course, there were four assignments (set translations from Old English to modern English) to be completed on "firm due dates" and seven assignments (six credit exercises and a final written project that could be a paper or a further translation) to be submitted at the student's leisure with only a "suggested date" ("English 401 Schedule"). Thirteen of the eighteen students delayed completion of all credit exercises (worth fifty percent of the final grade) until the last two days of the course, effectively turning the assignments into an examination, with very bad effect on their final grades in at least three cases and in all cases on their performance in the translation assignments, where grammatical knowledge was badly needed.

Several parts of the course were particularly successful. The heavily linked Old English texts, where every word in the text linked to its glossary entry, dramatically facilitated the reading of the Old English compared with the textbook experience of ceaseless flipping. Students responded well to the Java applet self-improvement exercises that attempted to improve on the Hieatt, Shaw, and Macrae-Gibson "Beginning Old English" interactive exercises; students especially loved one exercise not in their diskette—a simple reproduction of a deck of flash cards for Old English cases and their meanings. The e-mail discussion list was a lively place showing a high level of student engagement with the course materials, with me, and with one another; also helpful was the streaming *RealAudio* sound (once students got it going), which provided full readings in both male and female voices of several of the early prose texts in the course.

Not all parts were successful, however. The assignment timetable mentioned above was problematic; students found the off-puttingly minimal visual design of the site unsettlingly amateur; and the JavaScript testing function we had developed in-house for the credit exercises stalled on some students and was vulnerable to Web delays that resulted in automatic submission of the test and blocking of the student from further access. Glitches of the last kind, by the way, have not ceased with recent assignment of the testing function to *Blackboard*.

Subsequent Developments and Future Plans

Since spring session 1997, the online version of English 401 has been offered seven times. I was the instructor on six of these occasions; once the course was taught by another instructor when I was unavailable. A thorough overhaul of the visual aspects of the site was done in 1998 by the summer student and artist Maija Graham, who developed the graphic elements still used in the course. The testing function and student management functions were moved to *Blackboard* in 2004, after years of struggle with our homegrown testing function, though I am proud that my institution has continued to allow open access to the main sections of course materials through the English 401 Web site (www.ucalgary.ca/UofC/eduweb/engl401), which was never migrated to *WebCT* or *Blackboard*. The texts with linked glossaries were so buggy in 1997 that I offered a prize to the student who could catch the most mistakes; they were gradually revised and improved over the next few years, and a major overhaul was done in 2004. An Old English poetry course was added as a directed reading course but with the same kind of hyperlinked texts and glossaries in 2000, becoming a regular offering the following year.

I had time to make all these improvements because having the course online has consistently (after the first run) meant that it has taken me substantially less time to teach than classroom offerings. This time-savings is no doubt partly the result of choosing simple and stable Web technologies from the beginning, so that, on each run of the course, most of the site does not need revision and the time liberated by Web delivery of course content can be devoted to making improvements as well as to mentoring students.

The first offering of the course had been such an intense experience, and the technical challenges were so frequent, that it was difficult for me to reflect comprehensively for a few years on the question of general course design. But the structure of assignments was gradually revised in the direction of more guidance for students. The credit exercises may still be completed at the student's leisure, but e-mail reminders now reinforce the suggested date. Firm due date parsing exercises, in which the student has to provide a full correct grammatical description of each word in a short passage, have been added to make sure students learn their grammar on time, even if they have not completed the credit exercises at the suggested times. And the following statement has been added to adjust the implications of the free-exploration description quoted above:

> Although it will be "asynchronous", English 401 will be a "timed, progressive" course. . . . "Timed, progressive" means that although the entire Web site will be accessible for the whole duration of the course, it will be expected that students will have performed certain learning tasks by certain dates, and they will be tested on the knowledge they are supposed to have acquired.
> ("English 401 Course Outline")

I have also, inadvertently as a result of administrative decisions, experimented with class size over the years, teaching the course to as few as twelve students and as many as fifty (in two sections of twenty-five with separate e-mail discussion lists). Though all have been successful in some measure, the least successful classes were those with smaller numbers: an asynchronous conversation on an e-mail list needs to be fed with at least a message a day, or it gradually falters and then ceases. Even if a portion of the final grade is devoted to discussion participation—it becomes a big, silent, empty space that is daunting to address, rather than a helpful and friendly conversation. Since participation in the course conversation is a surrogate for sitting in the classroom, students also become detached and alienated from the course itself if the online conversation does not keep going. The opposite occurs if the group is too large. Messages more often than five a day are overwhelming for students checking in on the course sporadically, and they can clog mailboxes of students who are using a free e-mail service such as *Hotmail* or *Yahoo*, resulting in missed communications (especially damaging if instructor announcements are made through the list). Groups larger than thirty work better through a threaded bulletin-board function.

My online Old English course seems to be successful by all possible measures applied to traditional classroom courses: student satisfaction with the instruction provided (as measured by our standard university response instrument) is high; the dropout rate has remained low, in fact much lower than in the classroom version I taught; and students have gone on successfully to other medieval literature classes, to postgraduate programs, and in one case to doctoral study in Old English. Apparently, most students find the course an engaging and congenial way to approach the subject matter. But one category of student continues to concern me: the young person whose success with higher education has always been supported by classroom contact with the instructor, who is unable to revise that expectation fully, and who therefore flounders in an online course. For such students I instituted an optional face-to-face tutorial during the fall 2004 run of the course, to which only three people (of the fifty in two sections) came, but not the ones who had the problem. The next time I teach the course I will make physical attendance at some stated proportion of the face-to-face tutorials of my Web-based course a requirement (for students who are on campus).

This provision of an in-person meeting requirement seems in some ways a step backward from the original idea of a course offered entirely over the Internet, but I do not see it as an admission that purely online instruction is inadequate to the needs of learners. After all, the proportion of students who have been unsuccessful in my online course over the years is much smaller than the proportion who failed to complete the classroom version. Moreover, my online course materials, which are entirely available on the Web to everyone, are widely used for self-study by people all over the globe who frequently write to tell me about their success in using them (and sometimes the messages are in Old English!). Rather, this apparently retrograde step seeks to adapt what is overall a highly successful teaching and learning environment to the needs of a particular minority, a small contingent of learners whose own learning style requires personal contact with the instructor rather than mediated contact.

A final concession to students, and one I should have contemplated from the first, is the provision of an alternative version of the course materials as a pair of textbooks and a pair of CD-ROMs. Even my first group of students in the course wished that in addition to the online materials they could have a version of the texts to carry with them on the bus and mark up with pen or pencil and a version of the interactive materials to use when they did not have access to the Internet. I resisted these ideas for some time, theorizing that they were a symptom of students' lack of comfort with the online environment that would diminish and disappear as familiarity with the Web became widespread and more fundamental. I suggested that students who felt this way make their own printout or download to a CD. My attitude changed when instructors of Old English classes elsewhere, who were in effect using my course Web site as their text, began to ask if they could have permission to download my site and provide it to their students as a course pack. A particularly expressive class of mine demanded the same from me. Until electronic media catch up with paper forms in the areas of portability, universality of access, and user-modifiability by annotation, there is a strong case to be made for providing an alternative version using traditional technology for those who want it.

I am very pleased, however, to have reached an agreement on the textbooks (a grammar and a reader with associated electronic exercises) with a publisher who repects my desire to continue to provide my learning materials on the Web to anyone who cares to use them. I often think with particular satisfaction of three messages of thanks I have received from graduate students of English who did not have access to decent libraries or textbooks, one in the former Yugoslavia, one in Turkey, and one in a remote university in China, who would have been unable to gain any familiarity with this early form of the language without the materials I have provided. Among other advantages, online instruction has enabled me to teach people I have never met and probably never will meet (including some who live in my city) and to bring knowledge of my subject to students all over the world who would not have been able to acquire it in any other way. What started out as an experiment to expand the audience in my university for my fairly arcane subject has become rather more than that.

Notes

1. Public responses on the list can be read at *AnsaxDat*, the archives of ANSAXNET (www.mun.ca/Ansaxdat/).

2. *WebCT*, in beta at the time, offered no support for most of the things I wanted to do.

3. The team was composed of two undergraduate assistants who had taken the course in the classroom and knew Web technologies, one computer programmer who was also an English major, a master's student who could code JavaScript, and me.

Works Cited

Ball, Cathy, ed. *Old English Pages. Georgetown University*. Georgetown U, 30 Dec. 2000. Web. 5 July 2006.

"English 401 Course Outline." *Old English at the University of Calgary. University of Calgary*. U of Calgary, 2004. Web. 16 July 2009.

"English 401 Schedule." *Old English at the University of Calgary. University of Calgary*. U of Calgary, 2004. Web. 16 July 2009.

Hieatt, Constance B., Brian Shaw, and Duncan Macrae-Gibson. "Beginning Old English." Binghamton: Center for Medieval and Early Renaissance Studies, 1994. Diskette.

Martha Westcott Driver

Medieval Literature and Multimedia: The Pleasures and Perils of Internet Pedagogy

LAUNCELOT: We were in the nick of time. You were in great peril.
GALAHAD: I don't think I was.
LAUNCELOT: You were, Sir Galahad, you were in terrible peril.
GALAHAD: Look, why don't you let me go back in there and face the peril?
LAUNCELOT: It's too perilous.
GALAHAD: Look, it's my duty as a knight to try and sample as much peril as
    I can.

—Monty Python

Whether for knights of the Round Table or college professors and their students, peril and pleasure seem to go together, particularly when experimenting with applications of the Internet and other media for teaching medieval literature. Here I outline some of these in a range of pedagogical experience, including the development of the multimedia course *Beowulf* to *Lear*: Text, Image, Hypertext, taught at Pace University in New York from 1996 to 2004, and methods learned from this course and applied to two other courses (Meanings and Models of Motherhood and Medieval Women, both at Pace University). Other related experiments have included teaching Legends of King Arthur Online through a *Blackboard* interface and videoconferences run through Internet2 with Western Michigan University, in which students discuss medieval texts studied in common. When the technology works well, such experiences can create powerful networks of learning and rich intellectual exchange.

Pace University is a multicampus university serving a diverse population of students. Many are the first in their family to attend college, and many, especially at the New York City campus, where I teach, are recent immigrants. All students, whatever their major, must take a liberal arts core. This core includes courses in English composition and writing on literature and also a course in computer information systems. Thus all students studying at Pace University must learn the fundamentals of writing, research, and writing about literature, as well as take an introductory class in computing. The *Beowulf* to *Lear* course, which I developed with Jeanine Meyer, a colleague from the School of Computer Science and Information Systems at Pace University, satisfied the requirement for the study of premodern literature and counted as one credit toward a computer science or information systems elective. Drawing on a survey course I had taught for many years, we replaced or augmented some of the oral and written work with technology-based assignments.

Beowulf to *Lear* was created during the peak of the dot-com frenzy. Classes were filled to capacity and had lengthy waiting lists, mainly made up of computer science students who were interested for a variety of reasons in studying the Middle Ages (and simultaneously fulfilling their literature requirement).[1] The idea was to provide stimulating content—medieval literature and history—to students already adept with the technology. While studying traditional literary works, students used e-mail, online discussion, and the World Wide Web to create Web projects based on their reading and research. The best student work was published on our university Web site, which was overseen by a student webmaster.[2]

Adding the element of technology to the course work engaged students who might otherwise have been less than enthusiastic about a required literature class. While we taught students from a conventional textbook (*The Norton Anthology of English Literature* [Abrams et al.]) and had them take tests and write analytic and critical essays, we also asked them to revise and expand their writing assignments into Web pages, incorporating design, images, sound files, and hypertext links. Students tended to spend more time reading and considering the literary material than did students in more traditional survey classes and, with the promise of Internet publication, much more time revising their writing. The site on which their work was posted not only recorded the best work of the class but became an inspiration for students who took the course later, creating a larger sense of audience that extended beyond just one teacher or one class. Students became intensely involved with the readings and the learning process. In every class, we observed that students taught one another a range of skills, from computer technology and page design to how to read more attentively and analyze texts closely, using text, along with appropriate images and captions, to support their arguments.

The class took place in a computer classroom (and sometimes met once a week in a regular classroom as well). The computer classroom was equipped with a projection system (*Robotel*, a system commonly used in language lab settings) that allowed any single computer screen to be projected onto all screens, so that students could share and discuss the work of their classmates. Students shared their written assignments in these workshops, and all student work was previewed, during which teachers and fellow students offered praise and constructive criticism. Everyone in the class had several chances to see everyone else's work. After students, either individually or in groups, reported in class on various aspects of the medieval texts (for example, on an episode in *Beowulf* or a character from the Arthurian legends), they submitted hard copies of drafts as part of a process of writing; these were vetted, commented on, and returned for revision. Students then incorporated their essays into Web pages along with links, illustrations, time lines, and image maps. When the final drafts were handed in, projects graded B+ or better were posted on the class Web site. The posted projects also had to meet additional standards for giving credit to all sources, both verbal and visual, and being sufficiently scholarly that fair use could be applied to their electronic publication.

The success of these classes can be attributed to several factors, among them the emphasis on revision of student writing and on an expanded sense of audience. When students construct multimedia—that is, when they orchestrate text, images, and hypertext to express their ideas—they must still compose text. Lack of attention, dullness, or imbalance in a multimedia composition can usually be attributed to lack of text or poorly conceived or expressed text. Student-authors, teachers, and other readers can scan essays and page composition and readily note errors, weaknesses in the argument, lack of organization, and other problems. Further, in the process of considering a literary text and responding to it, students must choose appropriate images, balancing these with their texts and adding levels of meaning to their written responses, while keeping in mind Edward R. Tufte's maxim that "visual relationships must be in relevant proportion and in harmony to the substance of the ideas, evidence and data conveyed" (54).[3] Constructing glossaries of difficult terms found in the literature required that students select terms needing explanation. They then composed clear definitions to explain these words to others. Designing titles, backgrounds, and layout for their compositions forced student-authors to think through the message of their writings. To create a balanced, intelligent response to the literature, students had to reread more carefully not only the primary texts under consideration but also their own work.

Traditionally, students write for one person, the teacher, who is assumed to know more about the topic than the students; it is easy to understand why students are not focused on guiding their readers and helping to interpret texts for them. In *Beowulf* to *Lear*, students in the class, along with the teachers, were the immediate audience. In the many preview sessions of student work, the class and professors offered practical comments and advice: "We cannot read your text because there is not enough contrast with the background." "That image takes too long to load." "You tell us a lot about X but not enough about Y." It was also genuinely easy to make positive comments about the work: "That illustration powerfully introduces your subject matter (be sure it is properly cited!)." "You have compiled an amazingly detailed bibliography!" "Show everyone how you incorporated that time line." Such student assignments create many possibilities for being positive, which, in turn, help both teachers and students convey suggestions for further strengthening the work. With the possibility of their work being posted on the Web and therefore available to the world, students revised, edited, and expanded their essays and created some imaginative page designs to reflect their critical responses to the literature.

After the dot-com bust, fewer students chose computer science and related fields as their major, and my coteacher, Jeanine Meyer, moved on to another job at a university closer to her home. Fewer students enrolled in *Beowulf* to *Lear*, and almost none knew anything about creating a Web site, though students remained adept at surfing the Internet and using e-mail. It was time to take the lessons learned from teaching *Beowulf* to

Lear and apply them to other courses. In 2001, I had already begun to develop the course Meanings and Models of Motherhood, which also required students to create Web pages as a final project, the best of which are published on the course's Web site.

Meanings and Models of Motherhood, an intensive survey course, examines motherhood as a social, historical, and literary construct, looking at representations of women as mothers from the earliest creation myths through World War II. The course counts for six credits (or for two courses); I teach the course with Nancy Reagin, a historian specializing in twentieth-century Germany and a colleague in the Women's and Gender Studies Department at Pace University. Like *Beowulf* to *Lear*, this course also develops students' familiarity with various forms of information technology and multimedia presentations. Students in the motherhood class visited the computer classroom, where we used *Robotel* to share student work—and, again, we included several preview sessions before students turned in their final Web project for the class. Whereas in *Beowulf* to *Lear* students wrote and revised four essays and their Web composition continued throughout the course, students in Meanings and Models combined their course papers, which were read by both professors and substantially revised over the semester, into a Web site at the end of term, essentially their capstone project. This class spent just a few sessions learning the basics of putting together a Web page in the computer classroom, and the students who were more technologically advanced often helped those who were less so. The class also employed a student tutor to help students individually with technical aspects of their Web pages. In this case, too, the chance of publication on the Internet inspired students to work hard on their writing and on their presentations for the course. And, since we quickly developed a substantial body of published work, students could be introduced to the Web pages of their peers at the beginning of the term, then strive to match, or in many cases to surpass, the work of previous classes.

In the early 1990s, I first experimented with stand-alone multimedia by building two projects using *Toolbook*: one on medieval women and the other on the Arthurian legends. The content and research were my own, and graduate students in the School of Computer Science and Information Systems assisted me.[4] The preliminary work on medieval women became the backbone for a course I currently teach on the subject. The first year I taught this course, with the help and support of the Center for Learning and Technology at Pace, I also encouraged students to build

Web pages that were then posted on the *Beowulf* to *Lear* site, but I have taught the course more recently without this addition. Instead, I require students to discuss writers and literary figures weekly on the class discussion board on *Blackboard*, which is sometimes shared with students outside the university.

The Arthurian legends multimedia project was also readily translated to an online course through the introduction of *Blackboard* at the university. In 2002, I received a Sloan Foundation grant to teach the course online (and as of 2006 have taught it three times). This course examines a range of writings about King Arthur and his court, from the earliest chronicle writings to the twelfth-century romances of Chrétien de Troyes and the later stories told by Geoffrey Chaucer and Thomas Malory, through a variety of modern works such as T. H. White's *Once and Future King*, Rosemary Sutcliff's *Sword at Sunset*, and Marion Zimmer Bradley's *Mists of Avalon*; students in the class also view films (*Perceval le Gallois, Monty Python and the Holy Grail*, and *Excalibur*, among others) on reserve in the library, which they then analyze in seminars posted on the discussion board.

After reading various medieval texts, including selected secondary sources on electronic reserve, and my weekly lectures posted online, students take six tests and write four papers with revisions. Tests are sometimes timed, sometimes not. They may take the form of short-answer essay, fill in the blank, or multiple choice. Some tests (like the one on Monty Python) may be taken over and over again until the student achieves a perfect score—a learning experience in itself. Other tests are taken once only and require mastery of the text and attentive reading of my lecture (and proper spelling of names and terms for the answer to receive credit). In the test instructions, students are forewarned as to which test is which. Further, I post the best student papers on a variety of subjects on *Blackboard*, and some of the tests ask questions about them as well so that students learn from reading one another's work.

With careful study of the readings, my lectures, and papers written by fellow students, the class learns about the historical backgrounds and the social contexts that inform the Arthurian narratives. With their subsequent study of modern Arthurian readings and films, students also learn to recognize contemporary as well as universal issues addressed by the Arthurian legends, including the development of the warrior code, the balance between private and public life, and shifting ideas about morality.

The course is not given in real time but can be taken at any point in the day or week (assignments are given on a weekly basis), offering a flexibility in scheduling that some students like very much. Interestingly, a number of women with small children, along with traditionally dressed Muslim women who were commuter students afraid to travel around the city after 9/11, signed up for this class, as did adult students who were working full time and some Pace students who were living in other states or in Europe. There were always a few who took the online class thinking they could somehow fit this into their busy schedules and found they could not, but most students, usually more than twenty of the twenty-five enrolled, did very well.

In 2000, I wrote part of a National Science Foundation grant to sponsor Internet2 at Pace University, which was then awarded. In spring 2002, though our Internet2 system was not yet up and running because of the events of September 11, students in *Beowulf* to *Lear* were able to discuss *Beowulf* and the legends of King Arthur through videoconferencing with students at Western Michigan University in the class Heroes and Villains. Students were excited to meet their counterparts at another institution through several of these videoconference sessions and enthusiastically shared their ideas about *Beowulf, The Thirteenth Warrior* (and other modern allusions to *Beowulf*), and the King Arthur legends. Students at both colleges discovered that many of their questions and thoughts on the medieval texts were the same. Suddenly the materials studied in one classroom became connected with those studied in another, and students recognized that studying these classics, which are known and loved by educated people, is a worthy enterprise. Undergraduate students also discovered that they could explain their ideas and opinions eloquently and intelligently to students elsewhere. When the technology worked, the exchange of ideas was electric.

In our first few meetings, the classes at Pace University were mainly composed of (very vocal) female students, while the students in the classes at Western Michigan were mainly male (and quiet). Pace students living in the New York City area represented a great diversity of ethnicities, while the Western students were mostly white Midwesterners. All the students were charming, knowledgeable, and on their best behavior when meeting their counterparts; they also had fun being on TV.

The exercise brought out competitiveness between the students, and the Pace class became extremely articulate and expressive about the texts, even more so than in the usual classroom. This energy and sudden interest in discussion of medieval texts carried over into the off-camera weekly discussions. The preparation for videoconference discussion with another class also focused attention more sharply on questions of interpretation of a range of texts. Students from both institutions were able to continue their dialogues through the Pace University *Blackboard* site. This bicollegiate experiment has been continued with many of my classes, including those on the King Arthur legends, comparative medieval literature, and medieval women, in which students also commune on several questions through the *Blackboard* interface as well as by videoconference.

The purpose of these exercises was to bring students into a larger learning community across institutions and to create cadres of student-scholars who were taught to use Internet materials and their student networks as adroitly as adult scholars do. From 2001 through 2006, I met with Paul Szarmach, director of the Medieval Institute at Western Michigan University, and worked with the graduate students who taught Heroes and Villains to create a powerful learning environment for students on both campuses. My hope was that students might be encouraged to form study networks across campuses, though this has not quite happened yet.[5]

For our later meetings with Western, Pace students participated outside class time and were very responsible and responsive. Unfortunately, in 2005 and 2006, the videoconference interface did not work very well; though tests were diligently performed by the technical staff on the videoconference and Internet2 connections between colleges, there were problems with sound and two-way communication in several meetings. The students at both institutions were, however, able to communicate and engage in lively exchange through *Blackboard*. Some of the interactions between the Pace and Western students were warmly social (linking pictures of pets, families, or sweethearts to their greetings on *Blackboard,* for example), while others were intellectually exciting (writing sophisticated responses to the reading assignments).

To create meaningful learning experiences using technology, I have found it essential to work with an enthusiastic and inspiring coteacher or colleague who is well versed in the technology and aware of both its possibilities and its limitations. Whether one is creating a class Web site or an interface between two educational institutions, it is crucial to establish networks of involvement between the professors and the technical support people at the university. Courses, like people, cultures, and cities, seem to have a natural trajectory. The approach is experimental—let us determine whether this works and for how long and then use what we learn from the experience to create new kinds of learning environments. Technology is always changing. What can we make it do? How can we use it to engage students? What did we do well? What did not work quite the way we thought? Why is this equipment not working? *Blackboard* is down! Call Verizon!

Writing recently in the *Chronicle of Higher Education*, Vartan Gregorian discussed "the knowledge that can be imparted by science and the peril that possessing such knowledge may present," calling on teachers and scholars "to make connections among seemingly disparate disciplines, discoveries, events, and trends, and to integrate them in ways that benefit the commonweal" (B4–5). In my experience, the peril lies in the technology, which remains an imperfect tool. Its mastery requires patience and a contingency plan for every lesson employing it. The preparation, whether for a videoconference or an online course, is part of the lesson, for students planning their discussion of *Beowulf* on camera or for professors working with one another and technical staff members to be sure the classes run smoothly. While the equipment may not always work very well, in this process everyone learns.

Recently, I hired a cameraman to videotape my English majors reading Chaucer aloud in Middle English—perhaps a medieval impulse to record at least a bit of the class for posterity, but mainly I wanted to make a film to show future classes that learning to read and understand Middle English is not as difficult as it might seem. I did not tell the students beforehand that they would be filmed, but, on camera as in the videoconferences, they outdid themselves. They were as intelligent, funny, and focused as, and often more articulate than, they were in the more formal classroom setting. Film seems simultaneously simpler and more complex than multimedia design, and I expect to work with people who understand film editing to craft this little project for the instruction and viewing pleasure of my future Chaucer classes. There is always something to learn, and I have been very fortunate in having helpful and inspired colleagues, knowledgeable in the technology, who have taught with me, instructed me, and shared their expertise with me and our students alike.

Notes

1. For some of these adventures in teaching, see Driver; Driver and Meyer, "*Beowulf*"; Driver and Meyer, "Engaging"; Driver, Anstendig, and Meyer. Jeanine

Meyer was initially introduced to me by Susan Merritt, the dean of the Ivan G. Seidenberg School of Computer Science and Information Systems, who has also been an important supporter of my efforts at Pace University.

2. The site maintained by students (http://csis.pace.edu/grendel) has not been updated in several years. I hope, however, to revisit and update the *Beowulf* to *Lear* course site and resurrect the course itself in another year or two, perhaps creating an interface with colleagues at universities elsewhere.

3. Students were also reminded of another Tufte statement: "Clutter and confusion are failures of design, not attributes of information" (51). This point was especially important for those students attracted to animations, which tend to lengthen loading time for the program and make the page look too busy, distracting viewers from the central emphasis on the text.

4. *The Medieval Woman at Work and at Play*, a Web site I developed with Denise Cox, a Pace University graduate student, is briefly described in Driver and McGrady.

5. For this project, I had the help of several Pace University colleagues on the technical side, including Jennifer Thomas and Jean Coppola of the School of Computer Science and Information Systems, as well as members of Pace University's educational media staff, to strengthen the technical interface and to troubleshoot technical problems for many of these classes.

Works Cited

Abrams, M. H., et al., eds. *The Norton Anthology of English Literature*. 7th ed. Vol. 1. New York: Norton, 2000. Print.

Beowulf *to* Lear: *Text, Image, and Hypertext. Pace University*. Pace U, 2000. Web. 26 May 2006.

Driver, Martha. "Medieval Manuscripts and Electronic Media: Observations on Future Possibilities." *New Directions in Later Manuscript Studies*. Ed. Derek Pearsall. Woodbridge: York Medieval–Boydell, 2000. 53–64. Print.

Driver, Martha, Linda Anstendig, and Jeanine Meyer. "Web Research and Hypermedia: Tools for Engaged Learning." *Journal on Excellence in College Teaching* 9.2 (1998): 69–91. Print.

Driver, Martha, and Deborah McGrady. "Teaching about Women with Multimedia." *Medieval Feminist Newsletter* 23 (1997): 21–23. Print.

Driver, Martha, and Jeanine Meyer. "*Beowulf* to *Lear*: Text, Image and Hypertext." *Literary and Linguistic Computing* 14.2 (1999): 223–35. Print.

———. "Engaging Students in Literature and Composition Using Web Research and Student-Constructed Web Projects." *WAC Clearinghouse*. Colorado State U, 26 Mar. 2000. Web. 15 Oct. 2006.

Gregorian, Vartan. "Grounding Technology in Both Science and Significance." *Chronicle of Higher Education* 9 Dec. 2005: B3–5. Print.

Heroes and Villains of the Middle Ages. Michigan Western University. Michigan Western U, n.d. Web. 26 May 2006.

Meanings and Models of Motherhood in European History and Literature. Pace University. Pace U, n.d. Web. 26 May 2006.

Monty Python and the Holy Grail: Screenplay. By John Cleese, Graham Chapman, Terry Gilliam, Eric Idle, Terry Jones, and Michael Palin. London: Methuen, 2003. Print.

Tufte, Edward R. *Envisioning Information.* Cheshire: Graphics, 1990. Print.

Michael Best

Seeking the Best of Both Worlds: Online and Off-Line Shakespeare

From Print to Screen

Teaching and research used to be such comfortably delineated activities. Teaching took place in the classroom, and research involved the library. The astonishing expansion of the Internet and associated electronic media has turned the desktops of students and teachers alike to portals that open on a seemingly inexhaustible ocean of data. In this transitional period, as I have been adapting to new ways of communicating with my students, my aim has been to combine the best of both worlds, the traditional and the new. Thus the courses on Shakespeare that I have developed and taught partially online in recent years have involved a combination of techniques and media. The courses are the result of an incremental evolution from print to screen over two decades, beginning well before the appearance of online software like *Blackboard* or *Moodle*, which provide templates for the development of online resources, keeping track of students' work, and online discussions. The resulting courses are accordingly attuned to my particular interests and may not be easy to replicate; I believe, however, that the experience has made clear some overall strengths—and limitations—of online teaching, as well as how the new technology can overcome some of the limitations of a traditional classroom.

Print Technology

My interest in teaching outside the conventional classroom began in the 1980s, when I was asked to create two courses on Shakespeare for the Open University of British Columbia. These courses were to be delivered by traditional distance methods, involving a printed course guide enhanced by additional readings, some audiotapes, and selected images of the plays in production. I learned that the tone of the course guide had to be conversational but not condescending and that it should prompt the students frequently with questions to stimulate their thinking. The designers of the print materials used the medium to great effect. Pages had wide margins and lots of white space, so that students could make their notes as they worked; the commentary was broken up with clear headings, occasional explanatory visual images, and illustrations of the plays in performance.

In each course guide, I created a written commentary designed to lead the students through the play, encouraging them as the course progressed to become aware of a range of current critical approaches. I supplemented the commentary with readings from both historical and recent criticism, designed to open up debate on issues of particular interest in the plays. The course package also included cassette tapes of scenes from the plays and graphic illustrations of performance, resulting in students having a rich multimedia experience, limited only by the prohibitive cost of developing copyright-free video materials or accessing those protected by copyright.

Enter Hypertext

The next stage in the evolution of the online courses came with the advent of the electronic medium and the then new concept of hypertext. The initial promise of hypertext was that it would make it possible for students to read and explore in much the same way as they think, by association rather than by linear argument. My early work in this mode is now reflected in the section of the *Internet Shakespeare Editions* site that focuses on Shakespeare's life and times. It began as a series of interlinked modules using Macintosh's *HyperCard*; the limitation of the software was such that all graphics were in black and white and sound files were rudimentary. In due course, *Shakespeare's Life and Times* was upgraded to a CD-ROM with color and high-quality sound; finally, in 1998, it was adapted to the new medium of the Web (Best, *Shakespeare's Life*).

My purpose in creating *Shakespeare's Life and Times* was to provide a kind of sandbox for students to play in, exploring the context of Shakespeare's work until they found a subject that was of sufficient interest for a research paper; each page ("card" in the original software) included a contextual link to a bibliography, so that students could graduate from the sandbox by printing out a list of books relevant to the topic and then pursue it further in the library. Students at the introductory level seldom know enough about the context of the plays to realize the range of topics available for research; if I was fully prescriptive in setting topics, students were less likely to be motivated, but if I offered them free choice, they would select the same two or three tired and obvious areas for study. The hypertextual space allowed students to gravitate to an area of significant interest to them, usually within an hour or two of exploration, and to move on to fuller research.

The Internet and Communication

While I was working to put *Shakespeare's Life and Times* on the Web, the Internet began to take over the business of communication, and e-mail increasingly made the postage stamp seem an attractive but expensive and unnecessary invention. The e-mail discussion group became a convenient and immediate way to provide the missing personal contact that standard distance education lacked. The tools for the course Shakespeare by Individual Studies—to be taken by students on or off campus—were in place: a course guide, associated readings, modest multimedia support, the resources of *Shakespeare's Life and Times* now readily available on the Web, and the opportunity for students to engage in discussion. This combination of media came at a time when administrators were convinced that online teaching would be cheaper, and just as good, as the classroom experience. Time and experience have shown that fully online teaching has some advantages over earlier methods of distance education, but it is fair to say that dreams of saving—or earning—vast sums of money have evaporated. Nonetheless, I was fortunate to receive funding to adapt my distance courses to an online environment.

The courses are designed to fulfill a need for students, mainly on campus, who are unable for various reasons to regularly attend lectures—those with jobs (an increasing number), home-care responsibilities, or the demanding rehearsal schedules that are required in the theater department. Since most students would be on campus, I was able to schedule a voluntary tutorial to allow face-to-face interaction for those who preferred personal contact with the instructor. It is an interesting comment on the limitations of classroom discussion that the tutorials start by being well attended but that the size of the group steadily declines to a determined core by the end of the course.

Instructional Media in My Shakespeare Courses

Because of the process of evolution from standard distance methods, the courses I designed used print, electronic, and multimedia technologies. I believe that the result does indeed combine the best of both worlds, using each medium for the learning experience where it excels. There is no doubt that students value the presence of a teacher as a warm body in the classroom; it is a time-tested technology, and in Shakespeare especially even a modest ham as teacher is better than any textbook or course guide. On the other hand, classroom teaching can cover a multitude of approximations if not sins. Under the expert guidance of course developers at the Open University of British Columbia, for example, I learned of the rather obvious need for a distance-education course to provide much more detail about the processes of teaching than classroom courses usually do, since the warm body is not there to answer students' queries about what the instructor wants in each assignment. Consequently, my course guide details very carefully what I expect of students in their reading, in the assignments, and in the final exam. I believe my traditional classroom teaching has benefited significantly from this awareness as well.

Print. By the time I realized that the Internet opened up new ways of engaging students, I was very much aware of the usefulness of print technology in teaching at a distance, whether that distance was the few meters that separate the teacher from a student in a classroom or the many kilometers that divide the teacher from a student on the other side of a province. In class evaluations, students routinely rate the course guide as the most useful of the resources the course provides.

Audio.   The original cassette tapes—several for each course—were superseded by CDs and have now become .mp3 files to be downloaded or distributed on a single CD. The tapes were generated in sessions with a fine group of actors from the Vancouver Playhouse and include discussions about varying interpretations of character and meaning. Students' response to them is varied; some find the tapes fascinating and useful, others are clearly less interested.

Video.   Though cost prohibits customized video for the course, the standard films of the most popular plays are readily available from the university library and from most video stores. An option for one of my assignments is to compare two video productions of a specific scene from a play. Those who work in institutions that have taken advantage of the recent offer of Films for the Humanities / Films Media Group to provide streaming video on demand will have more options (Moniz), but the ideal situation— illustrating a lecture with short excerpts from commercial videos—is still impractical because of the cost of performance rights and the intractability of copyright issues.

Electronic resources.   In both online and face-to-face classes, electronic resources are becoming increasingly the norm: course home pages, electronic discussion, and ready access to Web-based information (free or by subscription). In all my classes I use a series of pages to provide notes, readings, and active links for further research for my students. For regular classes I use Web pages rather than the whiteboard, the blackboard, or *PowerPoint* because students can access them for their own study at leisure and can see the general shape of discussion when they miss a class (see Best, "English 366C"). I routinely use online resources of various kinds, many from my *Internet Shakespeare Editions,* where original texts and sections on the Renaissance context of the works provide useful illustration for many classroom moments. I also use the *Lexicons of Early Modern English* (http://leme.library.utoronto.ca), *Literature Online* (http://lion .chadwyck.com), and the online *Oxford English Dictionary* in discussing language. In general, however, with the exception of the electronic discussion group, I have found electronic resources of this kind most useful in creating assignments.

I do not intend to consider the use of electronic discussion in detail here,[1] but I do want to point out one way in which I find electronic discussion groups especially effective. The medium encourages students who find it difficult to talk in a standard classroom situation: they have time to think and are less intimidated by other students in the privacy of their own study or a computer lab.

Assignments That Use Electronic and Online Resources

A concern in both the online and off-line world is the need to structure assignments that make it difficult or impossible for students to plagiarize. The convenience of searching on the Web for essays on familiar topics and the relative cheapness of the essays that are readily available from sites like *AntiEssays, Go-Essays, GradeSaver, EssayRelief,* and *123HelpMe* make it increasingly easy for students to take shortcuts in their assignments by getting someone else to do the work. In structuring assignments that use online materials, it is especially important for instructors to be aware of the temptations that students face. There is a real problem with plagiarism (see, e.g., Hughes; Australian Associated Press; cf. Schmidt). The challenge facing the instructor is how to shape assignments that provide a minimum of temptation for students to look for ready-made solutions and that, ideally, co-opt some of the online techniques students are familiar with. E-mail, the Web, social networks like *MySpace* and *Facebook*, and the ubiquitous cell phone have encouraged a culture where collaboration and consultation with peers are expected; perhaps, rather than resist this impulse, we should construct more assignments that benefit from collaboration (the video assignment I describe below is an attempt to move in this direction). It is equally important for instructors to structure assignments that teach as well as evaluate and to ensure that students understand clearly what objectives the assignments fulfill. I have also found that setting more, shorter assignments helps students to keep up with the course—a constant problem with students who do not have the regular stimulus of class attendance. In the heady early days of the electronic medium, I became aware of two new ways that my students could approach their learning. In principle, hypertext allowed them to explore a subject area more freely than is possible in a world of print, and the electronic space made it possible for them to use the activities more often associated with computer games to construct their own experience of a text. Time has made the first of these discoveries almost banal through the omnipresence of the Web, and the second has become a moving target that would require substantial funding to exploit fully.

Hypertext Again: Contexts

I have already discussed the creation of *Shakespeare's Life and Times* as a means of providing students greater freedom and understanding when choosing topics for a standard research paper on the social, political, or literary contexts of the plays. My objective remains to encourage students to learn to appreciate the importance of context in reading literature that embodies both a language and a culture that is in some respects radically different from their own. The development of powerful and generally effective search engines on the Web, however, has changed the way that students interact with the medium. Statistics from our site show that over half the visits we receive are from a major search engine. The resulting process is accordingly far more hit-and-miss, since inevitably a number of visitors bail out after seeing just one page. This behavior is not necessarily a bad thing; those visitors who stay have found something worth exploring, and many spend hours on the site.

The exponential development of the Web and the dominance of search engines have meant that the sandbox I created in *Shakespeare's Life and Times* has become an entire coastline—including, as well as the delight of sand and shells (to stretch the metaphor somewhat), the risk of rocks, sharks, and poisonous box jellyfish. And certainly the means and temptation to plagiarize have become far greater. The original assignment for which *Shakespeare's Life and Times* was designed was simple: explore, choose a topic, get approval from me, go to the library, and write a research paper. Now, however, stimulated in part by the all-too-available opportunities for open-ended assignments to be abused by plagiarism, I have changed tactics. I select a limited choice of specific scenes from one or two plays and ask students to show how a knowledge of the early modern context—social, political, historical, literary—enhances our understanding of the scene. I provide them with links to major resources like the "Life and Times" section of *Internet Shakespeare Editions*, so they are free to play in the sandbox or go to their favorite search engine or straight to the library.

A sandbox provides a comforting sense of control; children are safe within its confines, and we can regulate what toys they play with. As our students move on to the widening shoreline of the Web, we lose control over the materials they access and are more likely to be afraid of the shoals and sharks than to celebrate the wide stretches of beach. We become mentors of adults rather than the supervisors of children. For this reason, we must be aware that, although our students are comfortable with computers and would think of themselves as Web-savvy, most students in the humanities are far from computer-literate or even Web-literate. We need to give them the tools that will allow them to make the best use of the medium and to show them how to find the data necessary for a critical evaluation of the sites they find. I make no conditions on their choice of sources of information, online or off-line, so long as they can demonstrate that they have checked for the kind of information that indicates whether the source is reliable. Even *Wikipedia* can be a useful starting point, if students are aware of the radical unevenness of its entries. I think it important to co-opt rather than resist materials of this kind; accordingly I take a passage from the *Wikipedia* and discuss its strengths and weaknesses. Then again, not every book in our university library is current and reliable, so the electronic world is simply making more obvious and necessary the need for critical evaluation of sources.

The Computer-Gaming Environment for Teaching

Another of my objectives in teaching Shakespeare is to encourage students to respond to the plays in performance and to appreciate the range of possibilities that the text offers actor and director. Comparison of two video productions of the play is one way of exploring performance, but it is in essence a passive reaction to the work of others rather than an active response to the plays. I work to reduce the passivity of this assignment by encouraging students to view the videos in groups and then discuss the performances together before submitting their essays. I find that they disagree with one another enough that there is little likelihood of the collaboration reducing the value of the work of any one student. In another approach designed to ensure a more active engagement, I spent some years in the local development of a software program, *Scenario*, that provided a virtual stage where students could block a scene from a Shakespeare play. While it was initially a very successful teaching tool, the longer-term experience has been instructive regarding the current volatility of the medium.

Scenario is designed to put the student in the director's chair. Choosing characters, props, and sounds from menus, students create a series of frames that show where on stage actors should be for sections of the script. They are invited to discuss their choices, since each frame provides the opportunity for written comment. Students then submit the assignment as an attachment that is loaded into the instructor's copy of the program; this can then be commented on, either frame by frame or in summary, and returned. For three or four years the program worked well, and students found it a stimulating and valuable exercise in translating the play from page to an imagined and partially virtual stage. But time has caught up rapidly with the technology; the graphics, initially eye-catching, now look rudimentary, and their level of manipulation has become almost comically limited. Unfortunately the cost of upgrading the program is prohibitive, since a modern student audience will legitimately expect something that looks and feels like the games they encounter in their relaxation time.

Nonetheless, I believe that the environment of computer gaming is a potentially rich source of many different kinds of learning experiences for our students, although the challenges are considerable. The rapid development of gaming software means that the creation of games is expensive and that older games become rapidly outmoded; in addition, the academic community, especially at the university level, is inevitably resistant to anything that looks like too much fun. Jerome McGann has suggested ways in which the structures and rhetoric of certain kinds of computer activities related to games can be put to use in learning; "within the framework of the traditional goals of humanities education," his aim is "to promote rigorous as well as imaginative thinking." McGann's initiative, using text rather than graphics, is a welcome sign of what the future may hold in this area. The difficulty of developing academically inspired games that hold the student audience is illustrated by a well-funded initiative at Indiana University, where a game called *Arden, the World of Shakespeare* failed because, as its creator admitted, "it's no fun" (Naone).

Using Online Resources

An assignment I routinely set my undergraduate students is an adaptation of the old standard, a close reading of a short passage from one of the plays we are studying. The objective is a vital one, to ensure that students can read the plays insightfully and confidently on their own. A significant advantage here is that Shakespeare provides enough rich passages that the assignment can be changed each year and old essays will not be recycled. The online environment provides some powerful tools for students to familiarize themselves with as they look for explanations of words in the set passage (and for variations in the meanings of common words over time). Some resources will require institutional subscriptions: the online *Oxford English Dictionary* (*OED*) is a good example, as well as the larger *Oxford Reference Online*. More interesting is the opportunity that students have of exploring primary sources. I have found two resources to be of particular value here: the *Lexicons of Early Modern English* (*LEME*) and ProQuest's *Literature Online* (*LiOn*). *LEME* provides a free version as well as a more sophisticated set of tools by subscription; it is a fascinating resource for understanding how lexicographers of the period saw language and often provides concise lists of what were seen at the time as synonyms. For the effective use of *LiOn*, students will need a demonstration or careful instruction on searching. This tool gives students the opportunity to gather linguistic information about words in the passage in much the same way as the original readers for the *OED* but with a fraction of the time invested. It can be a revealing exercise to look behind a work like the *OED* to see the raw material from which it was compiled; especially in Shakespeare studies, often the compilers of the *OED* were driven by what they took to be Shakespearean meanings, a process occasionally revealed by a search on *LiOn* or *LEME*. While I introduce students to these remarkable resources, I also warn them of the limitations of sites like *SparkNotes*, which provide seductively simple explanations of passages but do not invite the exploration of the ambiguity and uncertainty inherent in the originals.

A variant on the assignment of a passage for close reading that I have had success with depends on the ready availability of source texts on the Web: asking students to edit a short passage, explaining words and phrases to help a student at a level just below their own understand it fully. The *Internet Shakespeare Editions* provides old-spelling diplomatic transcriptions of all the plays and poems of Shakespeare, which I have used to set passages of thirty to forty lines for students to edit. In a further check to ensure that students do their own work, I have set different passages from a given play for classes of up to forty students. Again, it is important to provide detailed models for them to follow, since at the undergraduate level they will be familiar only with editions like the Norton, Bevington, or Riverside, which provide basic glossing rather than the fuller exploration the electronic resources make possible. At the end of the day, a class will produce something like an edition of a whole play. At the cost of some hours of programming, I have posted this version of the play for the class to enjoy.

It will be clear from the examples I have cited that assignments can teach as well as evaluate. Just as the best teaching online blends technologies from traditional and electronic media, the most effective evaluation of students' work provides a variety of tasks that demand different skills, not all of which involve a traditional thesis supported by a linear argument.

Marking Papers in Electronic Format

Electronic marking is becoming easier, though it can become even more demanding than marking in hard copy. My students approve of electronic marking because they can read my typing more readily than my handwriting. The simplest method is to use a standard word-processing program (such as *Microsoft Word*). I ask students not to use the built-in footnote function of the word processor so that I can use it for my comments; I also use *Word*'s highlighting feature to draw attention to the passage or word I am commenting on. *Word* also provides an annotation feature and the ability to track changes, but I have found these less reliable since they may not function in the same way for the various versions of *Word* that students will be using. For those who use the *Windows* operating system, *Markin* is a flexible and intuitive program for marking student work. It allows markers to insert annotations into a student's paper and to export the result as a word-processor file or a Web page. Markers can also assign categories to the kinds of errors or comments they make on the papers, and the program will summarize these when the paper is finished; the result is that students can at a glance see where they most need to focus their work for improvement.

The Good, the Bad, and the Inevitable

It is fair to say that, in its current stage of development, the electronic medium combines the good, the bad, and the inevitable. And discussion of teaching—online or off-line—must start with an acceptance that students will use their computers for research online long before they force themselves to go to the library; as teachers, we need to take advantage of the new shape of research. Whether a course is offered in a traditional classroom or online, we need to anticipate and exploit our students' propensity for online activities. Here I highlight communications with students, discussion, and assignments that take advantage of the best of the medium.

The difficulties faced by these working in the medium are threefold: the issue of plagiarism, the cost of developing online pedagogical materials, and the problem of a moving target as the medium evolves. Plagiarism is as much an issue for classroom teaching as for online courses, and I believe that the answer lies in modifying our accustomed models for evaluating students. The cost of developing quality materials for online teaching is a major problem, especially since there will be no pot of gold at the end of the process. The Open University of British Columbia helped me develop my distance course, the Provincial Government of British Columbia provided funding for teaching relief to allow me to adapt to an online format, Athabasca University gave funds to convert *Shakespeare's Life and Times* from CD-ROM to the Web, and the University of Victoria offers both the infrastructure and the opportunity to teach the resulting courses. Although I was fortunate enough to receive funding from various sources, I see no obvious way to ensure that there will be adequate funding to support online courses. Nonetheless, I am convinced that these courses reach an audience of students, on or off campus, who would otherwise be excluded from learning.

Perhaps the most challenging issue for a course developer is trying to hit moving targets, technological and academic. As technology changes, materials either become ineffective (as the example of *Scenario* shows) or require conversion, as with the CD-ROM *Shakespeare's Life and Times* and the cassette and CD audio materials that must be upgraded to .mp3 podcasts. I would, however, make a cautiously optimistic observation that the speed of change may be slowing as Web browsers and operating systems stabilize. Academic materials also have a limited shelf life; written materials created for an online course need regular updating as the readings become dated or new approaches become more important. In addition, teachers prefer different approaches, so courses aimed at advanced students tend to be highly specific and are unlikely to be adopted by a range of teachers or institutions. One solution might be to develop interchangeable course modules, with some kind of resource library of articles and discussions cleared of copyright that teachers could tap into.

Finally, I would like to focus on the positive developments made available through online instruction. The increasingly universal adoption by our students of electronic media provides both an opportunity and an incentive for the integration of online activities and resources into our teaching, whether in the classroom or in individual study. Especially for institutions that subscribe to major online repositories, there are resources of unparalleled richness for our students to access. In an extension of the classroom handout and discussion, the Web offers a method of communication that is both effective and democratic, giving a voice to the previously silent members of our classes. From the now essential word processor to the way the computer connects students to the electronic shoreline beyond the sandbox we create in the classroom, online teaching makes it possible for our students to work at the times and places that are available to them, in lives that are increasingly cluttered with the need to make a living, care for others, or multitask in other ways we may regret but cannot reasonably expect to change.

Whatever the future may hold, perhaps as gaming technology becomes available for genuinely educational experiences, as we move toward the "24-hour school with no traditional classrooms and where students use mobile phones and laptops to learn" (Edwards) or as electronic paper makes the computer at last as readable as a printed page, I suspect that the distinction between online and off-line teaching will eventually become moot. The best of both worlds will simply become the best of an integrated world, as transparent to both teachers and students as print was a generation ago.

Note

1. I have written elsewhere of my experience with it (Best, "Teaching"), and the topic is well covered by other contributors to this collection.

Works Cited

Australian Associated Press. "Four out of Five Uni Students Cheat: Study." *Sydney Morning Herald*. Sydney Morning Herald, 1 Aug. 2002. Web. 22 Oct. 2006.

Best, Michael. "English 366C, Section F01: Home Page." *University of Victoria*. U of Victoria, 28 Nov. 2008. Web. 9 Dec. 2008.

———. *Shakespeare's Life and Times: Home Page. Internet Shakespeare Editions.* U of Victoria, Nov. 2005. Web. 20 Oct. 2006.

———. "Teaching Shakespeare to Judith: Gender Politics in Distance/Online Teaching." *Working Papers on the Web* 4 (2002): n. pag. Web. 4 Dec. 2008.

Edwards, Hannah. "E-volution of Schools." *Age*. Age, 9 Oct. 2006. Web. 22 Oct. 2006.

Hughes, Julia Christensen. "Academic Misconduct Major Problem in Canada, Study Finds." *University of Guelph*. U of Guelph, 29 Sept. 2006. Web. 4 Dec. 2008.

Internet Shakespeare Editions. Ed. Michael Best. U of Victoria, 2005. Web. 21 Oct. 2006.

McGann, Jerome, with Johanna Drucker and Bethany Nowviskie. "IVANHOE: Education in a New Key." *Innovations*. Spec. issue of *Romantic Pedagogy Commons* Ed. Laura Mandell. December (2004): n. pag. *Romantic Circles*. Web. 15 Oct. 2006.

Moniz, Paul. "Films Media Group Launches FMG ON DEMAND." *Films Media Group*. Films Media Group, 15 Sept. 2005. Web. 20 Oct. 2006.

Naone, Erica. "Virtual Labor Lost." *Technology Review*. MIT, 5 Dec. 2007. Web. 31 Mar. 2009.

Schmidt, Sarah. "Young Profs Don't Fear Internet, Study Shows." *Vancouver Sun* 21 Oct. 2006: A14c. Print.

James Fitzmaurice

Writing, Reading, and Asynchronous Spontaneity in the Online Teaching of Shakespeare

Many people would say that certain elements are likely to be lost in discussions when a class on Shakespeare is shifted to the Web. I would agree that quick back-and-forth dialogue often is lost but would assert that there are important gains to be found in considered written expression and in thoughtful, text-based reading. I would go on to claim that spontaneity, instead of being lost, can become asynchronous, a situation that might seem impossible on the face of it but that I examine in this essay.

The two classes I discuss are English 335, an undergraduate Shakespeare survey, and English 553, a graduate Shakespeare seminar. I have offered both in face-to-face format on numerous occasions. I taught the two Web versions for Northern Arizona University (NAU), and both are also taught face-to-face by other NAU instructors. I offered the Web survey, capped at thirty students, in fall 2004 and the Web graduate seminar, capped at twenty, in spring 2005. Each was a single online section, and each was fully subscribed. According to rules developed by the literature area at NAU, no on-campus students were allowed in either class. All class members were enrolled in a distance-education scheme that included about five thousand students, mostly scattered within the state of Arizona. There is no distance-education major in English, so my undergraduates came from other disciplines, especially education. There is a distance English master's program, though much of it is taught face-to-face at remote sites. All these students were free to use hardware at remote sites, mostly at community colleges. In practice, however, most students worked from home or from their places of employment, and I was warned not to expect students to have more than dial-up connection speeds. I allowed students to choose their own texts and directed them to *The Complete Works of William Shakespeare*, a powerful tool on the Web. I provided course content in the form of noninteractive learning modules on the plays. I graded discussion posts, which were required, and did not use exams, though there was other written work in both classes. I taught the graduate class in *WebCT Campus Edition* and the undergraduate class in *WebCT Vista*. In both these versions of *WebCT*, it is possible for an instructor to track who read how many discussion posts but not which posts were read.

Since about 2000, faculty members across NAU have been strongly encouraged to develop Web courses and have been given released time from teaching to do so. Faculty members have been given instruction in *Dreamweaver* and have been given Web support by way of a helpline. I found that hours spent on the two Web courses exceeded time spent on comparable face-to-face classes, in part because students do not make much use of face-to-face office hours. Be this as it may, I would imagine that Web-class workload fluctuates according to an instructor's willingness to attend to discussion.

Student writing in a Web class can be stimulated by thoughtful, text-based reading and more so by reading discussion posts than by reading content modules, or lectures, as these modules are sometimes labeled. Considered writing and thoughtful reading, together with asynchronous spontaneity, sometimes coincide for good effect. By spontaneity in posts, I refer to those messages that are composed quickly, though not always without a cursory edit for typos, omissions, and so forth. In a merely spontaneous and asynchronous post, one student may simply agree with or thank another as with the following item from the graduate class: "Thank you for posting that! I really enjoyed it and will find it useful someday (cross my fingers). I appreciate it very much."[1] In a considered spontaneous post, by contrast, a student brings an important remark or maybe a substantive question into the dialogue. Such premeditation as there is in a considered spontaneous post comes from a student's mulling over a problem in advance and then, perhaps unexpectedly, stumbling on an opportunity to comment on the problem in a way that is not fully formed or finalized. Such was the case to a greater or lesser degree with many posts from a graduate student who made five originating posts and seventy posts as responses. I examine two of his seventy, mostly brief responses, beginning with one in which he replies to someone who had mentioned the French philosopher Michel Foucault in the context of a discussion of *Hamlet*: "True Foucault leave[s] little room for individual genius." Should there be any doubt, let me state that this one line is the whole of the post. The student who wrote it probably gave it a quick look after its composition, missing the typo in "leave" but making a substantive observation about a topic that was too difficult or dangerous for many other members of the class to address. The same student posted a second time some two minutes after the first post, clear evidence that the first post, at least, was speedily composed. The first post reads as follows: "But what happened to Hamlet . . . his father, a King, murdered by his Uncle, who quickly marries his all-too-willing mother . . . is so unusual that I don't know that Hamlet has any kind of norm to follow." The student uses two sets of three dots to suggest a pause in thought, a parenthetical remark, and then a resumption of thought. He also is genuinely tentative in his "I don't know." He is not undercutting a good argument, as sometimes happens in student posts. There is both considered asynchronous spontaneity in the student's post and an attempt by the writer to suggest that spontaneity in writing by using the ellipses. The *Hamlet* discussion carried on with many students after I had finished grading it. These students simply could not put the discussion away as a task that had been completed, perhaps because they enjoyed the considered spontaneity of the exchange. I certainly did.

The graduate student who made the seventy posts was, of course, unusual. Half of the twenty students in his class made between fifteen and twenty-nine posts during the semester, within the norm for the course.[2] These graduate students were careful to meet the writing requirements of the course: what they posted was written in clear, idiomatic English; demonstrated a knowledge of the details of the plays in question; and showed at least some original thought. Posts from this group were probably written less quickly and more formally for the most part, though many of these students were caught up in particular discussions in a spontaneous way from time to time. As a group, however, they were less engaged than the seven students who made thirty or more posts. These seven students set the pace for the class and usually checked in several times each week, sometimes daily. The remaining three students simply met or tried to meet the minimum standards for number of posts. I hasten to add that as a general rule a small number of very good students do not like to engage in spontaneous posting and prefer to offer what is highly polished and not in the least off the cuff. One such undergraduate student began by posting only once for each discussion topic but did so in a well-researched, highly articulate, and longish piece of writing that she also attached as a *Word* file. Later in the class, she found herself making additional brief posts but was still quite formal. My sense is that she wanted to write spontaneous posts but just was not the sort of person to do so easily.

I checked in with both classes very nearly every day, including weekends, and posted often, if only to write a line or two. I was, as might be imagined, the head enthusiast. Students, of course, caught on quickly that they were likely to receive a response from me within twenty-four hours, so they were tempted to check back sooner rather than later after posting. Some were drawn into discussion that way. Unsurprisingly, there were many who had or developed an interest in Shakespeare that went beyond merely collecting credit toward a degree. These students were, I think, the easiest to draw into a discussion that was largely spontaneous. I tended to count the students who posted a great deal as my allies in helping make class discussion valuable, but the serious lurkers were allies of another sort. They were able to help make the class a success just by writing well and by demonstrating good attitude in the few posts that they made. One lurker read more than 900 out of 996 posts made in the graduate seminar and was simply a quiet participant.

I try to appear to be spontaneous in my posts most of the time and rarely put up long treatments of any topic. If I find myself rambling during composition, I will often cut down what I have written. Sometimes my posts are less than considered in that they simply thank someone for this or that contribution to the class, but I do try to say something substantive on a regular basis. Spontaneity, of course, can be a dangerous thing. A quick reply in a face-to-face class can land an unwary teacher in trouble if it is offensive or perceived to be so. A face-to-face teacher is able to see reactions and immediately apologize or backtrack before any permanent harm is done. In an online class, detecting adverse student reaction is harder to do. I have had a few brushes with trouble based on spontaneous posts that I have made, though nothing very serious. In the undergraduate class, for instance, there was a student who wrote about the religious persecutions of the sixteenth century, concluding with the observation that at least the outcome was a Protestant England that endures today. Although she did not specifically write that she was happy that England is not a predominantly Catholic country, that was the clear implication, and I felt that I could not simply ignore what she had written. She was being, I thought, offensive to Catholics in the class, though unintentionally so. I replied to her with the following post:

> I am not so sure that Protestantism was such a good thing to mix with government. England got better, in my view, when religion was phased out as a qualification for public office. And, for a time there were Protestant and Catholic colleges. Glad that is gone, mostly. Otherwise a lot of good Catholics and others would not be able to attend Oxford and Cambridge, which is what happened in the 19th century.

I dashed off this post quite quickly, though aware that it might cause my student some discomfort by exposing her assumptions regarding religion. That exposure needed to be undertaken if for no other reason than to forestall any chance of a contentious discussion about what religion might be most or least desirable. I went on to write to the student privately and very briefly, to assure her that I did not intend that she be hurt personally: "Hope I did not sound too gruff or grouchy in my post on Protestants and Catholics. Did not mean to be."

In the public post, I intended to sound formal and less spontaneous. I can see how the speed of my reply may have made what I wrote a little less accurate than what I would have liked. To be more accurate, I should have said that religious qualification for Oxford and Cambridge only ended after the time of Gerard Manley Hopkins, who was expelled in the second half of the nineteenth century from Oxford for converting to Catholicism. During and before the time of Hopkins, an Englishman could not be a Catholic and attend Oxford. The private note to the student was intended to be far less formal and quite spontaneous. It was at least brief. The student never replied directly but did write in the wrap-up to say how much she liked the class.

On another occasion, I found myself unexpectedly having to do some explaining as a result of a spontaneous post that I made in discussion. A student, in assessing the plot of *The Tempest* in the undergraduate class, suggested that the bloody-minded Antonio should not have escaped punishment and that Shakespeare was, in essence, "soft on crime." I teased the student that she was taking a "neocon" position, and she wrote me privately to ask what a "neocon" might be. My reply, defining the word neocon, was more formal. Once more, the student did not reply to my private message, but she did have pleasant things to say about the course as a whole in the wrap-up.

I like to quote passages from Shakespeare in online discussion and then ask a very specific question or two to reinforce students in the practice of thoughtful, text-based reading. Some students need little encouragement to quote from the text and are already careful readers, such as one student in the graduate class who, in the extract below, commented on Falstaff in *Henry V* by using material from *Henry IV, Part 2*.

> In the last section of "Henry IV, Part II," [a dancer] states:
> If you be not too much cloyed with fat meat, our humble author will continue the story, with Sir John in it, and make you merry with fair Katharine of France: where, for any thing I know, Falstaff shall die of a sweat, unless already a'be killed with your hard opinions; for Oldcastle died a martyr, and this is not the man.
> So, it would seem that Shakespeare would have at least brought this character into "Henry IV." Falstaff is and was a popular character for actor and audience alike. Prince Hal (Henry) and Falstaff had developed a relationship. It would be dramatically more powerful to bring Falstaff into "Henry V" so the audience can sympathize more with his death. Instead, he is conspicuously absent and isn't killed off until II.iii. How much sense does this make for someone not familiar with Falstaff in the previous plays? I'm curious as to why Shakespeare would bother. Indeed "The King has killed his heart" (II.i.91) and this is Henry's play. I just can't grasp why Shakespeare would carry over so many characters (Hostess, Bardolph, etc.) and leave Falstaff, of all people, out.

This is a post in which reading the play as written, rather than viewing a performance, takes precedence. The text drives the analysis. The student is thoughtful about what is happening in the realm of character and, in consequence, is aware that Shakespeare knew how important Falstaff was to audiences. The student rightly asks why Falstaff did not appear in *Henry V*. It is highly unlikely that a face-to-face graduate student would have made copies of the dancer's epilogue on Falstaff and passed them out to everyone in a class. To do so would tend to make the student seem to be a little too keen. In the online graduate seminar discussion, however, inclusion of long passages was not unusual. Those students who included such segments of text, far from being understood as too keen, were often thanked by others in the class. Very occasionally, face-to-face graduate students direct a class to a key passage in the shared paper text and proceed to reading aloud, but almost never from a play other than the one under consideration, as was the case just cited. It is far easier to offer a reading of a text from one play as a springboard to discussion of another in an online discussion. Indeed, it is far easier to offer long segments of text online generally.

I frequently remind my students that they can use the online *Complete Works of William Shakespeare* for searches. This Web source (although now superseded by the *Internet Shakespeare Editions*), created by the Massachusetts Institute of Technology many years ago, is a wonderful reading tool on at least two accounts. It is a good passage finder; when one has read a play and needs to check wording on a few lines, the traditional method is to page through one's text and look for the lines. I have used *The Riverside Shakespeare* for years and know the position on the page of many key passages. This fact of memory, no doubt common to anyone who has taught Shakespeare in whatever text, comes in handy while one is in the middle of a face-to-face discussion. Once the line is found, students are informed of its page and line numbers or simply act, scene, and line. After that, the line may be read aloud extempore by teacher or student volunteer. But what of passages that one remembers and cannot find? In an online class, student and teacher alike are able to scan for segments of text. A student, for instance, may ask, as students sometimes do, "Didn't Shakespeare say, 'First kill all the lawyers'?" A face-to-face instructor probably will not be able to pick up the complete works of Shakespeare and find the line among the Henry VI plays, which are rarely taught. I am sure I could not. Such a teacher might say, as I would say, that the quotation is in among those plays somewhere. An online teacher can use the searchable text in *The Complete Works of William Shakespeare* to find the quotation quickly and comment on its context. It is not Jack Cade who speaks the line, as is often supposed, but one of his minions, Dick (*2H6* 4.2). The speaker, of course, was what we today might take to be an anarchist, so that context of the line matters in a thoughtful reading and needs to be discussed. My contrast between online and face-to-face teaching, admittedly, excludes a middle, one in which a face-to-face teacher can send students to *The Complete Works of William Shakespeare* online as an out-of-class chore. In such a case, a virtual classroom would work better than its face-to-face counterpart because it would not entail outside work. My contrast also assumes that face-to-face Shakespeare courses are not usually taught in rooms with computers and Internet connections, perhaps a bad assumption these days. Rather than be contrite, however, I suggest that the teaching of Shakespeare in high-tech classrooms is less frequent than one might hope. Such teaching is not done at Northern Arizona University, in any case.

A second use for *The Complete Works of William Shakespeare* as a reading tool involves searches that are not aids to finding lines or scenes. For instance, I suggested that a graduate student who posted about animal imagery in *Titus* conduct quick searches for words like "tiger" and "wolf" in plays other than the one under consideration. Are there more such images in *Richard III* or *King Lear* or whatever likely play? Might there be any surprises? Could a comedy or romance have more instances than any of these more serious plays? A thoughtful reader is able to ask such questions knowing that it is possible to find answers quickly. Not infrequently convenience is an aid to cogitation.

I would like to close this essay with some musing about one of its large assumptions. What, it may be asked, exactly is the value of spontaneity in class discussion, whether face-to-face or online? Presumably the answer lies somewhere in the realm of personal interaction. Personal interaction, when spontaneous, can be a powerful aid in teaching and learning. If students interact personally with one another and their instructor as a part of academic discussion, they are more likely to remember the material that they have covered than if they had worked alone. They are more apt to have an in-depth sense of the texts that they have studied. The skills honed in such an environment are more likely to stick. I myself have found that when there is strong personal interaction, I remember material more vividly and accurately, my depth of understanding increases, and my skills in interpretation grow. In face-to-face classes, personal interaction is strengthened by the physical presence of students and instructors. That physical presence involves shared jokes seen in smiles and heard in laughter. Shared emotion, including anger and even outrage, comes across through body language. In online classes, I would assert, the loss of physical presence often is replaced by a more strongly motivated group of students. Motivation is hard to measure, and many face-to-face students are very engaged. I would argue, however, that in my experience there is a greater proportion of highly motivated students in the virtual classroom than in its physical counterpart. Many online students, of course, wish that they could be present in an actual classroom and feel deprived because circumstances have conspired against them in this wish. Ironically, this desire can help create a better online environment than what these students might have encountered in a face-to-face classroom.

I do not require attendance when I teach face-to-face, and some students routinely skip classes. Some seem bent on missing one day a week on a Monday-Wednesday-Friday schedule. Although they may be good writers, they do not add to personal interaction. Occasionally there is a student who is diffident in a way that seems to be studied or perhaps derived from campus fashion. I am convinced that requiring attendance is no solution and instead works against personal interaction, insofar as that interaction is happy and positive. There are, of course, online students who do not contribute a great deal to positive personal interaction. Indeed, there are a very few who hint at being downright disaffected, but, since nobody is ever seen, their presence as sullen and unhappy creatures is minimal.

Rather, it is the happy ones who dominate online class discussion. The others are unable to influence the mood of a class by stony silence or by bored facial expressions. Many of the happy ones seem more free to discuss their personal lives in the context of academic discussion than in face-to-face classes. I know from my online discussions, for instance, that quite a few families watch videos and DVDs of Shakespeare's plays together. One mother in the undergraduate class managed to persuade her husband to watch the Kenneth Branagh *Hamlet*, an unlikely family movie in her opinion but one by which he was transfixed. Another student in the same class was a guard at a depot for trucks and often managed to find comic connections between her coworkers and characters from the plays. Although these connections were tongue-in-cheek and became a running gag, they were memorable and helped point up the details of Shakespeare's characterization. Another student in the undergraduate class, from a town just as small as Thatcher, Arizona, and just as remote from urban life, was memorable for her homey observations and her irreverent wit. I may not remember anything specific that she wrote, but, because of her, I recall vividly the conversations that class had about a set of plays by Shakespeare. The class was memorable for its view that Lady Anne from *Richard III* may have chosen to marry Richard out of canny political pragmatism rather than out of foolishness or weakness. Hers was the losing side in the war, while his won. Although there is little evidence for this position to be derived from a close reading of the play, we discussed pragmatism in the choice of spouses among the nobility at some length. My own sense of Lady Anne's supposed foolishness and weakness shifted considerably in the course of discussion.

Notes

1. I have received written permission from all students quoted to include their writing in this essay.

2. I derive my numbers from *WebCT Campus Edition*, in which the class was taught.

Works Cited

Hamlet. By William Shakespeare. Adapt and dir. Kenneth Branagh. Columbia TriStar Home Video, 1997. Film.

Shakespeare, William. *The Complete Works of William Shakespeare*. Comp. Jeremy Hylton. MIT-*Tech*, 2000. Web. 6 Oct. 2006.

———. *The Riverside Shakespeare*. Boston: Houghton, 1974. Print.

Martha Nell Smith

Enabling Undergraduates to Understand Advanced Humanities Research: Teaching with the *Dickinson Electronic Archives*

Today, I cannot imagine offering a successful course—whether a small graduate seminar or a large lecture course—bereft of thoughtful application of technology. The possibilities for use are various: peer-to-peer information exchange through which students can develop scholarly projects; digital repositories of literature, art, history, and music that can profoundly augment lectures and seminar discussions; blogs enabling daily critical responses to works under study; wikis enabling a class to collaborate on critical responses in ways unimagined even after the creation of the World Wide Web in the early 1990s. Though I am a strong advocate of using these tools for both research and teaching, I am not a technological expert. In other words, though I founded and directed the Maryland Institute for Technology in the Humanities (MITH; www.mith2.umd.edu) and am founder and executive editor of the *Dickinson Electronic Archives* (www.emilydickinson.org), I do not build software, I am not an advanced specialist in text encoding, and, contrary to what some technophiles in our profession have argued, I do not think one needs to be either of those things to use technology, and use it well, in teaching and research. My hope is that sharing some stories about my experiences will prove valuable for others, especially those who will neither darken the door of an institute for technology in the humanities nor build an online archive.

If you now holding this book in hand fit the above criteria, please do not put this wonderful machine, the primary means for knowledge transmission for the last several hundred years, down. You too can use new technologies to profound effect in the classroom. In fact, the fanciest computational software can do nothing, nothing interesting at all, unless directed and engaged by the most important software of all—that proffered by the human touch, by you. Teachers have been thoughtfully applying technologies in their instruction praxes long before the invention of the Internet, the computer, the typewriter, the pencil, even before AD and BC marked the accounting of time. Therefore, though some of my colleagues have said that there is no more important development for humanities knowledge production than that of digital studies, I respectfully disagree. Our knowledge building would be important whether we had digital tools or not. Smart classrooms, immense digital archives, speedier-than-the-blink-of-an-eye communications, and all the other amazing tools at our disposal are not interesting in and of themselves, and they cannot produce knowledge by themselves; it is what we make of them that matters.

In this instance of storytelling, I extend points made elsewhere describing and analyzing how using digital resources in my research and teaching has changed the way I work (see Smith, "Computing," "Democratizing"). At this point, reflecting on the humanities and their contribution to society and culture at large is important. The humanities are vital to the educational system Thomas Jefferson saw as necessary for achieving democracy. In fact, Americans' inalienable right to the pursuit of happiness depends on knowledge. For Jefferson, the two primary facets of education, and of learning to make knowledge, were subject matter, or the knowledge required to obtain a level of happiness, and subject method, or the processes by which knowledge is made.

Even while working as a teaching assistant, I integrated the research of my dissertation into my courses, but my methods have changed dramatically over the years. For more than a decade, I have shared my research through the *Dickinson Electronic Archives* projects, where I have been able to show rather than merely describe the signs Emily Dickinson inscribed in her manuscripts, signs that open up her exquisite poetry to unanticipated textual conditions. By 2006, I had been working online for more than a decade and a half, first through the e-mail connections that scholars on the science side of the University of Maryland had taught me about and then through the World Wide Web, which has become increasingly flexible as its use has expanded from a forum for research exchange and knowledge transfer for physicists and other scientists to knowledge exchange at all levels (from prekindergarten to institutes for advanced study), not to mention its use as a place for transactions of news, entertainment, politics, finances, families, enemies, and friends. Through these new tools, access to views I had only had in the reading rooms and special collections of exclusive academic libraries has been made possible. Though mediated through digitization, the access to those views by any student or teacher or reader with a Web browser is a very big deal. The possibility of making those views available to anyone interested in studying the writings of Dickinson (rather than relying on detailed linguistic reporting of them) was the first technological advance that profoundly influenced my teaching.

Years before I even thought of using a computer, much less of using one in the classroom as a teacher of poetry, I asked my students, "How did the poems, or rather texts, you see on the book leaf page come into being? Who made those texts?" The eager students, first stunned by the question itself, would quizzically answer, "Emily Dickinson" (or whichever poet we were reading). I pointed to the copyright and permissions page and gave a brief overview of the editors that had worked to move the handwritten works of Dickinson to the printed page. Students found this process interesting but usually dismissed it as my especial research concern rather than anything of real use or significance to them and their education. For them, there was no educational relevance in learning how and why particular books or versions of books come into being and others do not (they tended to make assumptions about a kind of magical meritocracy of authorial talent that always prevailed) or in learning how texts travel from writers' manuscript pages to the printed pages of anthologies and poetry collections.

The case of Dickinson provides a perfect opportunity for teaching students to look beyond the surface of any bibliographic page. Though she prepared at least forty manuscript volumes of her poems, Dickinson did not prepare volumes for print. She did not, therefore, see her poems through the usual stages of submission to publisher, acceptance, responses to readers' reports, final manuscript preparation, proofreading for final publication, and so forth. She left thousands of manuscripts behind for others to usher into print. Dickinson left poems in compositional stages not finished for conventional publication and in versions featuring variant words without any marked as clearly her preference. She sent others in apparently finished forms to correspondents but chose to send different versions of those finalized poems to different audiences or to record a different version in her manuscript books. Her work offers telling examples of poems in progress or of poems in conditions that appear markedly different from what readers are accustomed to seeing on the pages of an anthology or a book of printed poetry. When I started the *Dickinson Electronic Archives*, I was well aware of these facts (see Smith, *Rowing*). Since the dynamic, multimedia space of the online resource offered many more opportunities than the few halftones my publisher allowed to show rather than primarily tell and since it also made possible the kind of interactive editing I had imagined in *Rowing in Eden*, developing its possibilities was clearly the next step in both my research and teaching. In the mid-1990s, I confronted another challenge—many humanities colleagues were very suspicious of the World Wide Web and were not persuaded by the passionate arguments of pioneers such as Jerome McGann. Surprisingly, many students, even those comfortable with online gaming and other activities, were equally skeptical.

To show how the new online resources might be used, I decided to design digital samplers, or online articles, showing what can be made visible with digital tools that is not available in print. I decided to use the very familiar about Dickinson to coax readers to venture into unknown (online) territory and chose to focus on popular misconceptions about America's most well known poet. Even those only casually acquainted with Dickinson usually think they know certain facts about her: that she worked in solitude; that she tended to be morbid (and so was not particularly funny); and that she wrote little poems that, situated on the page, were surrounded by far more white space than type. These three supposed facts dictated the shape of the samplers or digital articles: "Emily Dickinson Writing a Poem," the oldest section of the *Dickinson Electronic Archives*, shows the poet at work, responding to the criticisms of her dear friend and confidante Susan Dickinson, as she writes her famous poem "Safe in their Alabaster Chambers," a poem she arguably never finished. "Dickinson, Cartoonist" shows that the poet long rumored to be morbid was in fact quite witty, even silly at times, and produced drawings and cutouts that bordered on the slapstick. "The Letter-Poem, a Dickinson Genre" shows that the poet's writings were not what most of her readers are accustomed to think of them as—pristine, clearly numbered, discrete units, easily identifiable as lyric poems. Instead, they are much more difficult to identify than her variorum and reader's editions leave one to believe.

Using "Emily Dickinson Writing a Poem," I was able to demonstrate that the identity of "Safe in their Alabaster Chambers"—any theory about its being, what the text is generically—is debatable. The poem, much circulated since the volumes of poetry were printed in the 1890s and printed during Dickinson's lifetime in the local *Springfield Republican*, is not fixed in its being. The versions that readers have encountered of the poem are not so clearly defined as those many publications of and about the poem would lead them to believe. Questions I had asked before were profoundly rejuvenated when posed in an environment of digital surrogates. How isolated was Dickinson in her writing practices, really? Is the poem under consideration by Emily and her friend Susan a two-stanza poem with four different second stanzas, as their writings and the contemporaneous printing that Dickinson saw suggest? Or is it a three-stanza poem, as rendered in its 1890 posthumous printing? Or is it five one-stanza poems? "Safe in their Alabaster Chambers" is one of four poems that Dickinson enclosed when she initiated a correspondence with the famous editor Thomas Higginson. Why might she have chosen a particular version in response to his *Atlantic Monthly* lead article "Letter to a Young Contributor"? One can see that those questions, even flattened out on the page, are important. But if you leave the page you hold now in hand and go to the online exhibition or sampler in "Emily Dickinson Writing a Poem," you will find that the questions themselves are linked to digital surrogates of the documents that inspire them, including Higginson's article. The textual conditions and situations of these writings and questions online differ from those presented in the pages of a book.

Considering the identity of the poem by using this online exhibition of the documents, readers are able to enlarge, for closer inspection, images of the marks Dickinson and others made, examine the printing of the poem in the *Springfield Republican*, and compare the handwriting in various versions to ponder for themselves whether the drafts Dickinson made are final or provisionary and are properly dated. The online resource thus provides interaction, navigation, and simulation not possible in the pages of a book. Simulation of an editor at work is especially possible in the "Interactive Explorations" section of "Emily Dickinson Writing a Poem." There, through the *Virtual Lightbox*, even beginning scholars (at the undergraduate and even the secondary or elementary levels) can simulate the work of advanced researchers to determine the relation of texts to one another poetically, chronologically, and ontologically. The *Virtual Lightbox* enables any reader to arrange and rearrange the printing Dickinson saw during her lifetime, as well as all the known manuscripts related to "Safe in their Alabaster Chambers," and thereby evaluate the meanings of individual documents and their relations to one another and to one of Dickinson's most popular and written-about poems (see also Smith and Vetter). Through the many exercises made possible by this dynamic, flexible, manipulable display of primary documents, students since the mid-1990s, working at all levels of critical inquiry, have come to understand some of the ways in which poems (and other literary artifacts) are made.

Using "The Letter-Poem, a Dickinson Genre," particularly "Morning / might come / by Accident," augments the function of literary objects as social products—made by writers, editors, compositors, copyeditors, and proofreaders working collaboratively—by showing how editors looking at the same material artifact can draw different conclusions about what they see on the manuscript page and also how predetermined notions about genre influence conclusions drawn about what is seen on the page. Editing the document that lies in the Dickinson Collection in the Houghton Library, at Harvard, to increase its general circulation in print, scholars have drawn very different conclusions about what they are seeing on these manuscript pages: Martha Dickinson Bianchi did not flatly state whether this "penciled message" is a poem or a letter but laid it out as a one-stanza poem when she quoted it in 1924 (87). Thomas H. Johnson edited it as a letter but laid all the lines including and following "Show me Eternity" as if at least part of the document was a poem (Johnson and Ward 830). Forty years after Johnson, R. W. Franklin took the lines Johnson had laid out as a poem and placed them, removed from the other lines on the physical document, in his edition of the poems (1452). Since all lines of the document are choreographed similarly, my coeditor Ellen Louise Hart and I edited the entire work as poetic and used Susan Dickinson's nomenclature "letter-poem" to describe its type (256–57). Understanding what these editors were seeing that made them draw such different conclusions would not have been possible without photographic representation of the original document, and online distribution has made this access much more widely available than would a very expensive facsimile edition in book form housed in a few libraries.

The examples recounted make clear how new media can enhance, enrich, and extend subject matter by increasing access. Even more powerful, however, is access to the other facet that Jefferson identified as a key to education, subject method. When humanists began working to produce digital scholarly editions, there were clear models for producing scholarly editions of integrity but no clear models for producing them for or with new media. Using digital media, the scholarly editions can be made perpetually updatable in ways that a book cannot. What were the implications when scholars imported into electronic editions those criteria and standards that had been established for bibliographic editions? Understanding bibliographic editions requires understanding the type of technology that the book is, inhabits, or deploys. Just before the World Wide Web became part of our daily lives, Donna Haraway observed:

> Technologies and scientific discourses can be partially understood as formalizations, i.e., as frozen moments, of the fluid social interactions constituting them, but they should also be viewed as instruments for enforcing meanings. (164)

Books record frozen social relations, points in time of critical understandings, including those regarding editorial matters.

Ron Rosenbaum's book, *The Shakespeare Wars*, recounts how scholars invest deeply in particular versions of the bard's plays, labeling some authentic and others not. A similar state of affairs exists in Dickinson studies, which some, such as Betsy Erkkila, are calling the Dickinson wars. (Elsewhere I have critiqued at length why "war" is such a wildly inappropriate term for describing critical dissensus [Smith, "Public, Private Spheres"]). Some critics are so deeply entrenched in their positions of what and how texts count as literary that they have argued that all matters about how Shakespeare and Dickinson and other writers' manuscripts are understood must be settled. Such a position claims that the social relations in and around any text must be frozen to be understood, at least to determine textual identity. Scholarly methods conceived from this perspective necessarily aim to define the authentic to produce the definitive and to do so must unnecessarily limit the authoritative. Dickinson herself wrote that "Publication—is the Auction" (Franklin 742), and many have pointed out that these critical debates, entangled as they are in the frozen social relations of bibliographic technologies, are in part created by academic capitalism that for centuries has been circulating its valuables in books. Another editorial interpretation of writings in which powerful institutions (in these instances Oxford and Harvard) have produced authoritative editions may seem burdensome, distracting, or frightening. Such reactions are not surprising when one has been accustomed to compare critical judgments in the exchange structures created by books and their production technologies. The report of judgments in print cannot be changed or substantively augmented without costly (in time, energy, money) corrected reprintings or the equivalent. From this standpoint, it is no wonder that some scholars are tempted to liken well-informed and principled editorial dissensus to war, where there must be winners and losers and some standard must prevail. In these intellectual horizons, some scholars declare that electronic editions place too much burden on the reader, who might be distracted from the poetic by paying excess attention to the trivial.

Yet recent literary criticism reveals that assumption to be a product of critical preference for the frozen social relations of the definitive edition. The access to more views of Dickinson's writings created first by a major facsimile printing in 1981 and then expanded by the *Dickinson Electronic Archives* in the 1990s appears to have liberated many readers, creating new insights, different textual pleasures, and critiques that would not have been possible without the additional views provided by these new delivery mechanisms (which can be perpetually expanded and improved). Recently, questions unthinkable when access to Dickinson's manuscripts was limited have been eloquently and generatively posed by Virginia Jackson: "Can a text not intended as a lyric become one? Can a text once read as a lyric be unread? If so—then what is—or what was—a lyric?" (6). In other words, what is and what is not an Emily Dickinson poem? Or, what kinds of poetry was Dickinson really writing? Social relations are key to Jackson's critical perspective, since she situates her speculations about Dickinson in the social relations of literary history and collaborates with new media productions. Haraway's observations about the social relations between tools and knowledge are useful to keep in mind. Technologies are formalizations or frozen social relations, but in their use, relations can be unfrozen, information unbound, and new tools developed:

> The boundary is permeable between tool and myth, instrument and concept, historical systems of social relations and historical anatomies of possible bodies, including objects of knowledge. Indeed, myth and tool mutually constitute each other. (164)

Knowledge and the tools we use to access, talk about, reflect on, distribute, and build it mutually constitute each other.

Social relations result in a book such as *The Poems of Emily Dickinson*, which is distinct from *The Letters of Emily Dickinson*. Their mutual existence demonstrates that scholars are already working collaboratively and consent to be bound by bibliographic codes. The social nature of texts has been a key concern for theorists for several decades, and, before online research archives and teaching instruments, students have understood textual sociologies to varying degrees. Yet many in literary studies have understood the sociologies of texts to be an area of critical inquiry reserved for specialists. I have found, however, that using this online resource has deepened and expanded the various classroom inquiries about texts and their ontologies so that students understand the questions previously reserved for specialists and go right to the heart of knowledge production. Without online resources, I have not been able to take students at all different levels of education this far.

The technology of self-consciousness required by viewing images of primary texts on a screen produces a healthy self-consciousness about what Jay David Bolter and Richard Grusin describe as "remediation" and what Bruno Latour and Steve Woolgar describe as "black-boxing," which occurs when one "renders items of knowledge distinct from the circumstances of their creation" (259n). In black-boxing, critical opinion becomes fact; more often than not, amnesia sets in after that factual instantiation, and, having been effectively black-boxed, fact becomes truth. The linguistic reporting on the manuscript of "Morning / might come" in the printings that made it a one-stanza poem, a letter, a letter with a poem, and a letter-poem constitutes a sort of black-boxing. Print editions cannot help black-boxing their decision-making processes. Those digital surrogates of manuscripts are obviously remediated—as printed volumes of the original writings remediate and refashion them into print objects, so electronic presentations remediate and refashion both the originals and their print translations.

As I tell my students, ways in which the remediations of new technologies unsettle our sureties about both the scholarly matters and the scholarly methods of education can be effectively exploited. But doing so requires successful application of the most important software of all—human inquiry. As I talked about plans for the *Dickinson Electronic Archives* with my colleagues and students, I concluded that two paths were before me: adopt the old paradigm and work for years developing a digital scholarly edition behind the curtain, where it would be unavailable to audiences until it was perfect. The dynamic edition would be developed following the protocols by which books are made. The alternative was to develop the digital scholarly edition publicly, sharing the production process with audiences and using that transparency as part of the critical review process. That second method, the one I used, is a new paradigm in the humanities, one that builds on the guidelines for scholarly editing established by the MLA's Committee on Scholarly Editions. Using this paradigm can reveal the processes of knowledge work to students and prompt them to ask, "How do our items of knowledge come into being, who made them, and for what purposes?"

The paradigm shift from print to digital edition will change the old truisms of scholarly publishing, the ones entangled in and by the social relations of the book:

An author's work is best when presented in a single, most authoritative scholarly edition.

Scholarly editions subsequent to such an edition are corrections and supplant what has come before.

Editors working on a single edition probably agree with one another.

In any disagreement, one party is right and all others are wrong, or at least one party is "better than" all others.

Readers and users of such editions need not be bothered with the details of judgment that went into determining what to exclude and what to include, in what order.

As far as editorial work goes, such assumptions lead to critical games of "gotcha" among editors and critics and suppress the creation and validity of different versions, which may allow that both, neither, or either might all be true. Neither faultfinding as an end in itself nor hiding the processes that determined final products is healthy for knowledge production and critical understanding.

Moving beyond the idea that scholarly conclusions can only be authentic, authoritative, and reliable when determined by a single expert or group makes it possible to bring in keen insights from people with different levels of expertise, such as the middle school teachers and students who, inspired by Dickinson's reworkings of "Safe in their Alabaster Chambers" that they studied in the *Dickinson Electronic Archives*, wrote poems of their own that extended a metaphor, just as Dickinson did in "'Hope' is the thing with feathers" and contributed them to the *Contemporary Youth's Companion* site ("Debbie").

What new methods of editing and understanding texts might, with diligent application of human software, be created in a dynamic electronic environment? Or, what lessons from and for the classroom have been described here?

An author's work does not need to be normalized; diverging views of its identity should not be excised.

Multiple authorities can be included for scholars and students of all levels to process and analyze instead of a single authoritarian view dictating what is seen and known.

Scholarly editions produced over time are not so much corrections as they are genealogical markers of what audiences could see and understand in different intellectual eras.

Editors working on a single edition need not agree with one another. Each can report what he or she sees, and audiences benefit from multiple viewpoints and levels of expertise, from critical dissensus.

Users of such editions can benefit from exposure to the details of judgment that went into determining what was worthwhile to include and can contribute to the decision-making process.

Using new media to share research findings among scholars and in the classroom enables distribution of humanities research in more interactive, rigorous, and accountable ways than traditional training leads one to think possible. It not only enables students to understand advanced humanities research but often turns them into researchers, even as the teachers and primary researchers become students. A digital environment opens up to beginners those research territories hitherto reserved for the most advanced researchers and makes use of intellectual and social networks.

Works Cited

Bianchi, Martha Dickinson. *Life and Letters of Emily Dickinson*. Boston: Houghton, 1924. Print.

Bolter, Jay David, and Richard Grusin. *Remediation: Understanding New Media*. Cambridge: MIT P, 2000. Print.

"Debbie A. Smith's Seventh Grade Class." *Contemporary Youth's Companion*. Maintained by Lara Vetter, Jarom McDonald, and Tanya Clement. Dickinson Electronic Archives, 10 Mar. 2008. Web. 6 Jan. 2009.

"Dickinson, Cartoonist." Ed. Martha Nell Smith. Maintained by Lara Vetter, Jarom McDonald, and Tanya Clement. *Dickinson Electronic Archives*. Dickinson Electronic Archives, 1999. Web. 6 Oct. 2006.

"Emily Dickinson Writing a Poem." Ed. Martha Nell Smith. Maintained by Lara Vetter, Jarom McDonald, and Tanya Clement. *Dickinson Electronic Archives*. Dickinson Electronic Archives, 1999. Web. 6 Oct. 2006.

Erkkila, Betsy. "Dickinson and the Art of Politics." *A Historical Guide to Emily Dickinson*. Ed. Vivian Pollak. Oxford: Oxford UP, 2004. 133–74. Print.

Franklin, R. W., ed. *The Poems of Emily Dickinson: Variorum Edition*. Cambridge: Belknap–Harvard UP, 1998. Print.

Haraway, Donna. "A Cyborg Manifesto: Science, Technology, and Socialist-Feminism in the Late Twentieth Century." *Simians, Cyborgs, and Women: The Reinvention of Nature.* New York: Routledge, 1991. 149–81. Print.

Hart, Ellen Louise, and Martha Nell Smith, eds. *Open Me Carefully: Emily Dickinson's Intimate Letters to Susan Huntington Dickinson.* Ashfield: Paris P, 1998. Print.

Jackson, Virginia. *Dickinson's Misery: A Theory of Lyric Reading.* Princeton: Princeton UP, 2005. Print.

Johnson, Thomas H., and Theodora Ward, eds. *The Letters of Emily Dickinson.* Cambridge: Belknap–Harvard UP, 1958. Print.

Latour, Bruno, and Steve Woolgar. *Laboratory Life: The Construction of Scientific Facts.* 2nd ed. Princeton: Princeton UP, 1986. Print.

"The Letter-Poem, a Dickinson Genre." Ed. Martha Nell Smith. Maintained by Lara Vetter, Jarom McDonald, and Tanya Clement. *Dickinson Electronic Archives.* Dickinson Electronic Archives, 1999. Web. 6 Oct. 2006.

Rosenbaum, Ron. *The Shakespeare Wars: Clashing Scholars, Public Fiascoes, Palace Coups.* New York: Random, 2006. Print.

Smith, Martha Nell. "Computing: What's American Literary Study Got to Do with IT?" *American Literature* 74.4 (2002): 833–57. Print.

———. "Democratizing Knowledge." *Humanities: The Magazine of the National Endowment for the Humanities* Sept.-Oct. 2005: 12–15. Web. 15 Oct. 2006.

———. "Public, Private Spheres: What Reading Emily Dickinson's Mail Taught Me about Civil Wars." *Companion to Emily Dickinson.* Ed. Smith and Mary Loeffelholz. Malden: Blackwell, 2008. 58–78. Print.

———. *Rowing in Eden: Rereading Emily Dickinson.* Austin: U of Texas P, 1992. Print.

Smith, Martha Nell, and Lara Vetter, eds. *Emily Dickinson's Correspondences: A Born-Digital Inquiry.* U of Virginia P, 2008. Web. 21 July 2009.

Laura L. Bush

Solitary Confinement: Managing Relational Angst in an Online Classroom

In 2005 I chose to teach my first fully online literature course. Although I had taught in technology-rich and hybrid learning environments for many years, I had avoided teaching completely on the Internet, believing it would entail significant work and resisting the loss of regular face-to-face contact with my students. Still, I knew if anyone could do it, I could. After all, I love technology, and I type really fast. When I began work on my doctorate in 1994, I gravitated toward technology as a teaching tool and soon became one of a small group of graduate students training peers to teach using computers and the Internet. After earning my degree in May 2000, I spent the next five years as a full-time instructional professional at the Center for Learning and Teaching Excellence at Arizona State University (ASU). This position gave me the opportunity to assist faculty members and graduate students across the university in integrating computer and Internet technologies into their teaching. It also afforded me the opportunity to solidify my knowledge of instructional design, including constructing a syllabus, writing learning objectives, and designing learning activities, assessment, and evaluation techniques to measure actual student learning and involvement with me. As a teacher of teachers,

I developed workshops in learner-centered and technology-enhanced instruction, all the while teaching one undergraduate hybrid business-writing course a year. Then, as now, a full-time lecturer in the humanities and arts department of ASU's Polytechnic campus, I have done a great deal of thinking about the scholarship of teaching and learning, especially online.

Writing this essay has helped me reflect critically on my development as an online teacher and explain the challenge it has been for me to translate my active, cooperative, and learner-centered philosophy of teaching to an online environment. These humanist goals are driven by my desire and responsibility to be present for students, whether face-to-face or online. Thus I work to create a learning environment, even in cyberspace, that facilitates real human interaction. I determine the value of this socially oriented teaching philosophy on a wealth of research and research-based practice in the fields of teaching and learning.[1] Nearly two decades of my own successful teaching practice further confirm the power of well-facilitated learning achieved through genuine human relationships between me and my students, enriching all our experience in a classroom.

When I began the process of developing and teaching my first online course, I was familiar with research about distributed learning, a term that encompasses both technology-enhanced learning and distance education. Nevertheless, I reviewed a number of articles, monographs, and books that further reinforced the benefits of well-designed, well-facilitated, interactive, and relationally oriented teaching and learning on the Web.[2] Seeking fresh insight about teaching in my own discipline, I also ordered a copy of Elaine Showalter's *Teaching Literature*. Her book, with its discussion of learning competencies and skills, helped me develop measurable learning objectives for a literature-based course (26–27). Writing solid learning objectives is an often neglected, even misunderstood, task, especially when instructors attempt to articulate discrete skills for literary analysis and appreciation. My adaptation and expression of Showalter's learning objectives highlights my philosophy of teaching literature in a community of learners.[3] In my ideal literature classroom, whether face-to-face or online, students engage in a variety of interpersonal events as readers and writers encountering remarkable literary texts together. As such, they are obligated by their community responsibility—and privilege—to explore and exchange interpretations of the texts with their peers, as well as with me, their teacher. My philosophical goal for these written exchanges is for students to connect with other people in interpersonal ways to influence their communities, especially their peers in my classroom.

I have taught three online courses in the ASU Department of English. The first, Critical Reading and Writing about Literature, was a foundational course for English majors that was conceived for a traditional classroom setting. Because I had already taught courses like it, I felt comfortable having this class be the first I would teach fully online. After transferring to ASU's Polytechnic campus, I made adjustments to the course and taught it fully online again. I subsequently designed and offered two additional literature courses in the following two semesters: Short Story, which I first offered as a hybrid course and then fully online, and Literature of the United States post 1860. All three courses were an entirely new preparation. I developed and taught them all online within three semesters, learning a great deal from the process—some of it quite difficult. Still, I have been able to expand and refine the major documents, learning activities, and assessment methods I began developing in Critical Reading and Writing about Literature for use in the other two courses.

I have come to two major conclusions about teaching online. First, to create significant opportunities for student learning in active, cooperative, learner-centered, and socially oriented ways, an effective online teacher must purposefully structure her courses on well-formulated learning objectives and activities, always keeping in mind the potential for mass confusion, frustration, and lawlessness in online environments. Here I share a few of the strategies I have developed for engaging my students with me and with one another by constructing well-designed syllabi, user-friendly course Web sites, and meaningful learning activities that promote interaction. My second major conclusion is that the technologies now available do not yet adequately address the human cost to me and to my students of teaching literature in a disembodied space. No technology or teaching strategy I have discovered or developed so far compensates for the profound loss my students and I experience from not being physically present with one another.

Creating Relational Opportunities for Learning Online

In *Teaching Literature*, Showalter discusses seven common anxieties shared among those of us who teach in higher education settings: lack of training, isolation, teaching versus research, coverage, performance, grading, and evaluation. Showalter explains that the first and "most profound" anxiety occurs because many of us postsecondary faculty members know we have little to no formal training as teachers. In the past, new faculty members mainly felt their way through their first teaching responsibilities, adapting pedagogies they learned from having observed the teaching methods and styles of their own teachers, either "doing unto others as was done unto us" or simply "making it up as we go along" (4).

For both inexperienced and experienced faculty members, teaching literature courses fully online only heightens these teaching anxieties. Our knowledge about teaching by way of the Internet is often even spottier than our knowledge about teaching in general. Moreover, few of us, including me, have done online learning, making this relatively new kind of literature classroom more challenging than the traditional classroom. I argue that effective online teaching of literature requires a faculty member to demonstrate competence in four distinct areas: instructional design, document design, the use of technology, and a particular field of literature, all related to the need to facilitate learning in a dynamically interactive way. I also argue that a faculty member's level of competence in any of the four areas significantly affects the success of his or her online instruction even more than in a face-to-face classroom, where the teacher may be able to wing it, play it by ear, speak off the cuff, or make it up as she goes. Regardless of how prepared a literature teacher might be to do the job, either in face-to-face or online settings, my research and experience show that one key marker of effective teaching and learning is interactivity.

Unfortunately, in online environments, teachers seldom seek out or receive much training for teaching interactively and for translating their courses online. In addition, because of the instructional design, document design, and technology-related skills necessary for success, developing the professional interpersonal skills and materials to teach literature online is time-intensive work for novices and experts alike. To address student needs and institutional demands, however, anyone willing to offer a literature course online today may be welcome to do so. While many tenure-track faculty members appear reluctant to offer online literature courses, other faculty members with the literary competence and desire to teach are usually willing. My fear is that without all four competencies, students may be untaught and justifiably confused, frustrated, or unhappy when a literature course is inadequately designed or impersonally facilitated online.

Computer and Internet Savvy: The Impersonal Challenge of Pedagogical Technique

The more ease I have achieved with new technologies and instructional design in interpersonal modalities on the Web, the more success my students experience in online learning environments. My student evaluations have been positive overall, but they have definitely improved over the three semesters I have been honing my online teaching skills. Improved evaluations over time seem like an obvious outcome, but many teachers try teaching online; receive lukewarm or poor student evaluations because they are not sufficiently prepared, trained, or supported in their efforts; and quickly give up teaching on the Web.

An effective online teacher will understand how to achieve well-organized, user-friendly Web sites and documents; be willing to learn new software features; and adapt to upgrades relatively quickly. Literature teachers should not teach in fully online environments if they are slow to pick up new technologies, have poor keyboarding skills, feel resentful about technology in general, or are not driven by the social value of teaching and learning. New teachers should develop their skills and teaching materials in hybrid classroom environments before moving to an online class. Professional development might require teachers to participate in workshops offered through the department or university to build their teaching and technology skill sets. The main challenge in online teaching is to use technology to create partnerships between a supportive instructor and a hesitant student. Without good will and significant teaching competencies, an online classroom will be fraught with frustration for students and destined for disappointment by all, including the teacher.

Although I have created my own Web sites with *Dreamweaver*, I use the ubiquitous *Blackboard* course management system, which makes it relatively easy to provide students with documents, materials, and Web resources. It also enables me to facilitate interaction and feedback through e-mail, announcements, online discussions, assignments, surveys, open-book quizzes or exams, and an online gradebook that students can access any time. The more features of this software a teacher can master over time, the better.

Balancing Student-Centered and Instructor-Centered Activity

In their book *Teaching Online: A Practical Guide*, Susan Ko and Steve Rossen encourage online teachers to balance the activities of a course between what students are required to do and what the instructor might do to provide direct instruction: "No matter what the class size, most students appreciate a balance between student-centered activities and those that focus on the instructors." According to Ko and Rossen, instructors should "contribute something unique, something students can't 'get from the book,'" but students also "respond well to an environment that asks them to be active participants in their own learning" (222). To accomplish this balance, I have been developing four activities for facilitating student learning online.

First, I use asynchronous online discussions, a student-centered activity that I begin by posing a well-focused question to ten-person discussion groups approximately every other week, depending on the course. I try through my questions to convey the value of living a responsible life in local, regional, national, and global communities.

Second, I have designed "elements logs," an activity that I require my short-story students to complete each week. Each student writes a one-page, single-spaced document listing the title, setting, point of view, central characters, plot, conflict, style, tone, theme, key passages, and a brief personal response to each story we read. I then synthesize samples of their writing to include as a major part of my minilecture covering those short stories. This compilation is one noteworthy aspect of an online literature course. Students get to see how varied others' experience and interpretation of a text can be. While I have learned to use a broad theoretical toolkit to interpret texts through multiple lenses of gender, race, and class (which I work to impart to students implicitly and explicitly throughout a semester, depending on the level and goals of the course), this step—seeing texts through the eyes of their peers—is invaluable. Reading excerpts from other students' elements logs aids students' understanding about reading, analyzing, and reflecting on the meaning we assign texts based on our own often narrow perspective.

Third, I provide students with study guides, a student-centered activity I require of my United States literature students approximately every other week when they are not participating in online discussions. In a study guide, I give students some context for the literature they will read that week, along with a number of directive questions to choose from and answer about the assigned reading. After students turn in their study guides, I synthesize samples of their work and provide insight and feedback as part of my weekly minilecture. I ask similar questions in study guides and for online discussions, but I alternate the two activities, for variety and so that students are not always required to respond to discussion group members to demonstrate their learning.

Fourth is the minilecture, a teacher-centered but student-oriented activity consisting of a scannable document I construct. This one-page, single-spaced document shares my insight about the readings for the week and my specific feedback for students based on their online discussions or answers to study-guide questions. The bulk of the minilecture usually consists of copied-and-pasted excerpts I glean and synthesize from students' writing. Students' analyses of challenging texts have been remarkably insightful and diverse, although their thinking can also be fuzzy, not grounded in the text, or unfocused. Still, I have been repeatedly amazed and delighted by what my online students have to say. Selecting key excerpts provides reinforcement and public recognition for the best of their interpretive ideas. Synthesizing those ideas can be time consuming, but the rewards and educational benefits seem worth it.

My aim in designing these four learning activities is to promote learning based on specific humanist objectives, to provide students significant personal feedback, and to offer something more than an independent-study course. Furthermore, I intend always to bring students into constant contact with my direct instruction and to value and wonder at their peers' insight.

Socially Structuring and Evaluating Online Discussions

While technologies exist to enable synchronous chats online, I abandoned chatting long ago. Chats work best among only five to seven students, and the staccato sound bites of online chatting do not promote the kind of deep critical thinking I intend to foster. In contrast, asynchronous online discussions, a core learning activity in all my online literature courses, enable groups of up to ten students to explore their interpretations of texts. I begin the process by distributing my "Guidelines and Evaluation Criteria for Discussion Forums" (see app.). This climate-setting document calls for responsible, critical discourse by putting procedures and accountability measures in place that facilitate collaborative success. Students respond well to the explicit guidelines and clear expectations, which also communicate the social and intellectual rigor of the course: our collective work matters.

Students do their most productive and engaged thinking when I formally structure their discussions. I do so based on the premise that students must write, and share that writing, to learn. One undeniable benefit of online learning is that my students must show up in writing; they cannot hide out or hide behind what other students think. Furthermore, I facilitate their discussions using key elements for effective cooperative learning: assigning them to heterogeneous groups, ensuring individual accountability and equal participation, promoting positive interdependence, and encouraging discussion roles and gambits (Ledlow, "Cooperative Learning," "Roles"; Linder and Ledlow).

Initially, I randomly assign students, mostly by last name, to heterogeneous discussion groups of ten. Before finalizing the makeup of these groups, I frequently shuffle students from one group to another to prevent a group from having students with the same first name or to balance the gender representation. I often have fewer men than women in my courses. I would, however, retain a discussion group of all women rather than assign just one man to a group, potentially forcing him into the token role of representing a male point of view. While avoiding the phenomenon of racial or ethnic tokenism when I assign students to online discussion groups is also a concern, I have paid more attention to gender diversity when I form groups since a student's race or ethnicity is often less readily apparent online. Even in face-to-face courses, distributing students into groups according to my speculative assumptions about their race or ethnicity is a problematic venture. Although I am not aware of research concerning the issue online, I believe students of color in predominantly white classrooms may be freer from the phenomenon of representing a particular racial or ethnic point of view because students online do not recognize their peers' identities by race and ethnicity as readily as they do by gender.[4] I also sometimes redistribute student groups based on writing skills, which I can begin to discern at the beginning of the semester using the students' introductions on their home page.

Besides forming heterogeneous groups, I inform students that I will hold them individually accountable for both the quantity and quality of their equal participation based on explicit grading criteria laid out in my guidelines and evaluation criteria. I have been honing these criteria over three semesters until I feel they accurately reflect the specific elements on which a student will be graded excellent, good, or inadequate. After any online group discussions, I choose eight to ten especially well-expressed responses to include in my minilecture for the week. These student responses are sometimes all I need to teach students what I want them to learn about the text. In selecting a variety of excellent responses, I reinforce the value of peers' diverse insight.

Holding students accountable for their participation relates to how I encourage positive interdependence. I formally structure discussions so that, although students begin a discussion independently of one another by posting an initial response to a well-focused question from me, they must also reply to one another's responses and questions, constructing meaningful group conversations that demonstrate higher-order reasoning rather than simple, uncritical agreement or disagreement with their peers.

To help students consider various rhetorical positions they might adopt, I provide examples of discussion roles and gambits for participating in online discussions. Defining roles such as moderator, devil's advocate, or synthesizer, as well as offering gambits or prompts exemplifying things a student might say when playing a particular role, assists students in developing effective group communication and team-building skills. Someone taking up a moderator role, for instance, might pose provocative questions, encourage people to respond, or model respectful online communication behavior, by asking for clarification or pointing out disagreements. A student in the role of devil's advocate would express opposing or contrasting points of view that encourage healthy skepticism and debate. Sometimes I assign these roles and gambits formally. Other times I merely encourage students to refer to them to learn how they might forward or complicate a critical conversation.

Finally, I can now more quickly evaluate student participation in online discussions after having articulated an explicit grading rubric that reflects both individual and collective engagements with texts. Using the grading discussion feature of *Blackboard*, which enables me as a teacher to gather all of a student's posted messages in one convenient location, I can readily examine a student's work to determine the quantity and quality of her or his participation out of fifty points overall. Since my first semester teaching online, I have whittled down the rubric. Students now accomplish excellent, good, or inadequate participation in online discussions based on the number and quality of posted messages and replies (see app.).

Anticipating, Designing, and Organizing
for Collaborative Success

I work to design and organize my courses in user-friendly ways that provide students with a consistent, common look and feel. Such a design aids them in identifying and locating course materials, assignments, and resources with relatively little outside assistance, especially after the first two weeks of a semester.

Each time I develop a new online course, I brand the site by creating a visually appealing course banner using the color schemes and cover images from texts I assign for the course. As part of the banner, I also focus students' attention on a basic premise of the course using a thought-provoking quotation. Knowing how to brand a Web site to create visual appeal and meaning online is just one Web-design skill an effective online teacher could demonstrate to communicate passionate commitment to student learning.

While some teachers might dismiss color and visual design choices as trivial, Web-design experts attest to the importance of such choices in online environments. The look and feel of an online course can enrich students' experience, not just because effective visual design looks good, but because the design and appearance of an effective Web site establishes and reinforces, rather than undermines and detracts from, the course's usability and social orientation. If teachers merely familiarized themselves with the basic Web design principles contrast, alignment, repetition, and proximity laid out in Robin Williams and John Tollet's *The Non-designer's Web Book*, they could immediately enhance their students' online experience. On her personal Web site, Williams writes, "Keep in mind that the point of eliminating bad [design] features is not just to make the page prettier, but to communicate more effectively" ("Web Design Features").

To avoid the potential for individual confusion and mass frustration, I begin designing and organizing an online course by carefully setting out the course description, expectations, learning objectives, teaching philosophy, and tone of the course through my syllabi. Clarifying the instructional design aspects of the course assists me when I organize the navigational structure of the course Web site. Thus before I have determined how I will structure literature courses within the constraints of *Blackboard*, I construct two fundamental documents my students will access before and during their online experience: the course syllabus and course schedule. Most of the documents I provide online are in *Microsoft Word*, but for the course syllabus and schedule I use *Dreamweaver* to create Web pages accessible to the public through my university Web space. Inside the private, password-protected *Blackboard* site, I place links to the publicly available Web pages. Separating a traditional course syllabus into two documents makes each Web page a manageable size for reading online. I also use logical headings, streamlined language, and nonserif, medium-sized fonts to increase the documents' readability.

To keep students on task throughout the semester, I also create weekly assignments folders, which I make available each week on *Blackboard*. By clicking on links to the course schedule and weekly assignments folders (which contain direct links to documents, external and internal links, online discussions, or assignment instructions), my students can keep track of information they should be accessing at the first level of the course Web site.

Maintaining regular submission due dates also helps keep online students on task. I establish Tuesday morning as the time when I make each weekly assignments folder available to begin a new cycle of collaborative work. I expect their initial posted message in an online discussion by Friday at noon and two replies by Monday at noon, giving me time to participate and review their work before I finalize and make available the next week's folder. Since students can be easily lost, sidetracked, or experience information overload on the Web, I work to avoid posting any extraneous materials, information, or links on the course site that might divert their attention or confuse them. The main navigation bar generally includes announcements, information about the instructor, course syllabus, course schedule, class forums, discussion forums,[5] Web resources, student Web pages, student tools, and e-mail directory.

Establishing other administrative protocols to facilitate interaction and cooperative learning has helped make teaching online more manageable and efficient than it would be without them. For example, although I encourage students to use the public "Q & A Forum" on the course Web site as much as possible, occasionally students have private questions to ask me by e-mail. To save myself some time, I request that students put the course number in the subject line of their e-mail messages so that these messages automatically get sorted in my inbox.

Devising naming conventions for files that students turn in is also helpful. I ask students to name the file as their last name, plus the initial letters of that assignment's title. Repeat assignments, like the study guides and elements logs, are numbered. I repeat the naming conventions as part of the assignment instructions and reiterate them in the area where students upload the document to the course Web site. Using this naming convention benefits me because all student files I download to my hard drive will be alphabetized in folders by the students' last name. This system makes grading and reuploading files for students more efficient.

Repeating written instructions for students each step of the way is critical. Short, straightforward names for documents, links, and areas of the course make the online environment manageable. I avoid changing, truncating, or otherwise modifying names midstream because that would confuse the students. Having to clear up administrative confusion draws precious time away from actual teaching and can become the source of both my and my students' frustration. With every course and with every assignment possible, I choose to put in the time to plan, prepare, and anticipate problems or potential confusions before they occur.

Interpersonal Teaching Online

In *I and Thou*, Martin Buber lays out the interpersonal nature and value of genuine relationships between human beings. He asserts that "[a]ll real living is meeting" (26). In the online courses I facilitate, my central form of "meeting" with students occurs primarily by way of asynchronous online discussions and e-mail.[6] While electronic meetings are real, physical manifestations of students' active presence in the course, such delayed, bodiless, faceless encounters provide limited access to what I believe Buber means by "real living." He writes, "True beings are lived in the present, the life of objects is in the past" (27). For me, the fact that my students and I can only ever leave a past trace of our thoughts, and thus a relatively limited part of ourselves in an asynchronous online discussion board, indicates that our meetings can only be read as artifacts. Therefore, electronic conversations are mere objects representing each person's historical presence, no matter how many ongoing replies we make to one another over time. On the other hand, the effect of posting, then waiting for someone else to post, and then waiting for replies, can create a feeling of mutual interest, anticipation, and identification. Still, losing people's spoken words, nonverbal gestures and body postures, eye contact, and tone of voice is a significant loss for me and my students. We cannot hear or see or touch one another as we do when we meet face-to-face.

Educational theorists examine the "transactional distance" between teachers and students in face-to-face and online environments (Moore 2–3).

This felt distance between a student and teacher is based on how a teacher structures a course and on the amount of dialogue or interaction generated between them. Depending on how a course is structured and on the degree of dialogue facilitated, a student can actually experience just as much or more distance from his face-to-face teacher than he or she does in an online classroom.

I grant that students in many face-to-face-classrooms, especially in large lecture halls, may feel a good deal of transactional distance from their teachers. I, however, have never experienced in any face-to-face class settings the same degree of distance as I have felt teaching online. For me, this digital divide is profound, further motivating the need for a socially oriented, interactive pedagogy. In my three semesters of online teaching, nothing has ameliorated my sense of isolation. I feel locked away from fellow prisoners (the students), like a captive kept without food or water in solitary confinement against her will. Many days I have wondered why in the world I ever chose to teach online. No matter how attentive to fostering real dialogue in the form of written interactions, thirty-minute conference calls, or occasional face-to-face meetings between me and my students, I still experience a palpable, emotional loss of perceived human presence and closeness that I do not experience when I teach traditional or hybrid classes.

My loss is also related to what the educational researchers Charlotte N. Gunawardena and Frank J. Zittle refer to as a lack of "social presence," a sense that people can perceive one another online as real persons who experience both "intimacy" and "immediacy." They explain:

> Two concepts associated with social presence are Argyle and Dean's 1965 concept of "intimacy" and Wiener and Mehrabian's 1968 concept of "immediacy" (cited in Short, Williams, and Christie 1976). Short, Williams, and Christie (1976) suggest that the social presence of a communications medium contributes to the level of intimacy that depends on factors such as physical distance, eye contact, and smiling. (9)

Because a technological medium such as television can "convey nonverbal cues such as eye contact and smiling," televised courses are able to generate much greater intimacy than any text-based communication I use in my online classes. After all, text is "devoid of nonverbal codes that are generally rich in relational information." It comes as no surprise to me, then, that text-driven electronic communication has a "relatively low position as a medium capable of generating intimacy" (Gunawardena and Zittle 9).

Generating my teacher immediacy for students online is equally challenging. Teacher immediacy is defined as

> both verbal and nonverbal actions such as gesturing, smiling, using humor and vocal variety, personalizing examples, addressing students by name, questioning, praising, initiating discussion, encouraging feedback, and avoiding tense body positions.
> (Gunawardena and Zittle 10)

Through announcements, online discussions, minilectures, and e-mail messages to students, I work to create a sense of immediacy when I call students by name, offer specific and positive feedback for their work, or joke with them. But, of course, I cannot generate nonverbal actions in a bodiless environment, except to offer an occasional, insufficient emoticon. Electronic smiley faces hardly capture the passion I can express in a traditional classroom. Yet my online students report I am quick to reply, personable, and attentive to what is going on in the class.

Technologists and educators in the field of online learning would likely say there are a range of solutions to alleviate my sense of solitary confinement as an online teacher. Last year, I began learning the basics of constructing a more dynamic visual- and audio-based version of my minilectures. The process of constructing such minilectures, however, even those that can be reused, is daunting. And constructing audio-video presentations contributes to greater satisfaction for online students, not necessarily for me as their teacher. In addition, such instructor-generated materials do nothing to solve the problem of losing a sense of students' social presence and immediacy.

Buber's assertions about what constitutes "real living" and "true beings" living only "in the present" capture what I experience as the central problem of the delayed, asynchronous, faceless, bodiless, and thus nonbeing of my online teaching experience. I have observed firsthand how students' posted messages and replies can influence, motivate, instruct, and even inspire other learners, including me. Unfortunately, I do not experience such interactions as "real living in meeting." What I believe is missing in the online classroom experience is what Buber calls "the lived relations" of mutuality, of real give and take (31). He writes:

The true community does not arise through peoples having feelings for one another (though indeed not without it), but through, first, their taking their stand in living mutual relations with a living Centre, and, second, their being in living mutual relation with one another. (53–54)

Living mutual relation is difficult enough in a traditional classroom. As the technological medium of computers, the Internet, and course management systems are now constituted, I experience even more significant barriers to achieving mutuality online. I am not, however, resigned and cynical about the possibility of future technologies succeeding in addressing the inadequacies of teaching literature in cyberspace. Despite my dissatisfaction with teaching courses fully online, I see where higher education is going. Arizona State University aspires to become "a New American University," where "we seek to . . . [p]rovide quality education that is accessible to a broad population" (*Arizona*). I have hope that technologies in the near future will recapture what is lost by holding class on a computer screen.

Perhaps if I offered an education mostly to students who could not get an education except through technological means, I might feel less discontented. I grant that the online courses I offer make education more possible for students who have full- or part-time jobs or who are parents with children at home. I believe that everyone deserves access to a formal education and that our society benefits from having educated citizens. Still, I also suspect that this trend toward distance education is partly due to our society's seeking another personal (and therefore impersonal) convenience. Students often hope, for example, that taking a course online might somehow be easier, especially if they can access the course any time of day or night from home. Similarly, institutions believe they could serve more students and earn more dollars by packaging as many courses and programs as possible by way of the Internet. My online classes have always filled early, whereas, because of our campus's remote location, the same classes offered face-to-face or in hybrid format might get very few students.[7]

As a humanist, I have faced a tremendous personal and rhetorical challenge in teaching online. The benefits of working mainly from home, avoiding the hassle of a thirty-minute commute, and having the option to take an afternoon nap have not yet outweighed the cost of losing a sense of connectedness with my students. I have learned a great deal from the process and would welcome the opportunity to grapple with these issues in a socially conscious and purposeful way with educators and administrators ready to do so. I know what I have accomplished so far, but obviously the impersonality of the medium requires eternal vigilance and responsiveness to manage my sense of isolation and that of my students.

Notes

1. See especially Bonwell and Eison; Bean; Millis and Cottell; Weimer; and Nilson.

2. I focused on Verneil and Berge; Vrasidas and McIsaac; the Institute for Higher Education Policy's *Quality on the Line*; Twigg; Hanna, Glowacki-Dudka, and Conceição-Runlee; and Ko and Rossen.

3. The learning objectives from the syllabus of my course Critical Reading and Writing about Literature read as follows: "After completing this course, you will be able to (1) Write a persuasive interpretation of a text with a clear controlling idea and well chosen, well organized evidence to support your argument; (2) Seek out additional knowledge about a literary work, its author, its content, and its interpretation; (3) Relate texts to one another and synthesize ideas about them that emerge from your own thinking and the interactions you have with your peers and other authors' texts or literary criticism; (4) Work with other students to hone your critical reading and writing skills through meaningful conversations and peer writing groups; (5) Explain basic aspects of at least three critical approaches to literature and apply those approaches to a text (e.g., formal, historical, biographical, cultural, psychological, or gender criticism)."

4. At least one of my online students of color purposely seemed to suppress his racial identity from other students by not including a photo of himself on his student home page. Only toward the middle of the semester in a conversation about race did he explicitly identify himself as a black man.

5. Each Discussion Forum is only accessible to the members of the group, making privacy among members of a group possible, although I as their teacher have access to all discussions.

6. I also meet by phone or in person with students who may live near ASU's Polytechnic campus. For now, though, we are a new, growing campus located relatively far out in the east valley of Phoenix, and online course offerings are popular.

7. While I feel my fears about losing personal contact with students have been realized, I do not completely dismiss the need for or value of distance education. I have recently been participating in ten-person seminars over the Internet for my own professional development. As a participant, I have appreciated and even enjoyed this delimited online learning experience. I log into the seminars using *Microsoft Live* conferencing software, and I make a free phone call to hear people's voices, questions, and comments. Throughout the hour-long seminar, the facilitator can even write electronic notes on *PowerPoint* slides. This one-stop learning session among a small group of people who are not being graded

and are not engaged in an interactive, extended learning experience with one another online is quite different, though, from a semester-long university course. Facilitating a fifty- or even twenty-five-person classroom discussion by phone would not be feasible or productive, and yet, in a relatively short time, user-friendly technologies may develop to address this instructional need.

Works Cited

Arizona State University: A New American University. Arizona State U, 7 May 2007. Web. 12 Jan. 2009.

Bauer, John F., and Rebecca S. Anderson. "Evaluating Students' Written Performance in the Online Classroom." *New Directions for Teaching and Learning: Principles of Effective Teaching in the Online Classroom* 84 (2000): 65–71. Print.

Bean, John C. *Engaging Ideas: The Professor's Guide to Integrating Writing, Critical Thinking, and Active Learning in the Classroom.* San Francisco: Jossey-Bass, 2001. Print.

Bonwell, Charles C., and James A. Eison. *Active Learning: Creating Excitement in the Classroom.* Washington: George Washington U, 1991. Print. ASHE-ERIC Higher Education Reports.

Buber, Martin. *I and Thou.* Trans. Ronald Gregor Smith. 2nd ed. New York: Scribner's, 1958. Print.

Gunawardena, Charlotte N., and Frank J. Zittle. "Social Presence as a Predictor of Satisfaction within a Computer-Mediated Conferencing Environment." *American Journal of Distance Education* 11.3 (1997): 8–25. Print.

Hanna, Donald E., Michelle Glowacki-Dudka, and Simone Conceição-Runlee. *One Hundred Forty-Seven Practical Tips for Teaching Online Groups: Essentials of Web-Based Education.* Madison: Atwood, 2000. Print.

Institute for Higher Education Policy. *Quality on the Line: Benchmarks for Success in Internet-Based Distance Education.* Inst. for Higher Educ. Policy, Apr. 2000. Web. 25 July 2006.

Ko, Susan, and Steve Rossen. *Teaching Online: A Practical Guide.* Boston: Houghton, 2001. Print.

Ledlow, Susan. "Cooperative Learning in Higher Education." *Active/Cooperative Learning: Best Practices in Engineering Education.* Center for Learning and Teaching Excellence, 2002. Web. 30 July 2006.

———. "Roles and Gambits." *Active/Cooperative Learning: Best Practices in Engineering Education.* Center for Learning and Teaching Excellence, 2002. Web. 30 July 2006.

Linder, Darwin, and Susan Ledlow. "Five Issues to Be Considered in Teambuilding." *Active/Cooperative Learning: Best Practices in Engineering Education.* Center for Learning and Teaching Excellence, 2002. Web. 30 July 2006.

Millis, Barbara J., and Philip G. Cottell. *Cooperative Learning for Higher Education Faculty.* Phoenix: Oryx, 1998. Print.

Moore, Michael G. "Editorial: Distance Education Theory." *American Journal of Distance Education* 5.3 (1991): 1–5. Print.

Nilson, Linda B. *Teaching at Its Best: A Research-Based Resource for College Instructors.* 2nd ed. Bolton: Anker, 2003. Print.

Shea, Virginia. "The Core Rules of Netiquette." *Netiquette.* Albion, 2005. Web. 12 Jan. 2009.

Showalter, Elaine. *Teaching Literature.* Malden: Blackwell, 2003. Print.

Twigg, Carol A. *Quality Assurance for Whom? Providers and Consumers in Today's Distributed Learning Environment.* Natl. Center for Academic Transformation, 2001. Web. 25 July 2006.

Verneil, Marie de, and Zane L. Berge. "Going Online: Guidelines for Faculty in Higher Education." *International Journal of Educational Telecommunications* 6.3 (2000): 227–42. Print.

Vrasidas, Charalambos, and Marina Stock McIsaac. "Factors Influencing Interaction in an Online Course." *American Journal of Distance Education* 13.3 (1999): 22–36. Print.

Weimer, Maryellen. *Learner-Centered Teaching: Five Key Changes to Practice.* San Francisco: Jossey-Bass, 2002. Print.

Williams, Robin. "Web Design Features." *Ratz.* Williams, n.d. Web. 29 July 2006.

Williams, Robin, and John Tollet. *The Non-designers Web Book: An Easy Guide to Creating, Designing, and Posting Your Own Web Site.* 2nd ed. Berkeley: Peach Pit, 2000. Print.

Appendix: Guidelines and Evaluation Criteria for Discussion Forums

Online discussion forums are informal, moderated conversations in which we discuss the texts we read to explore, examine, and develop our initial responses and understanding of those texts. Online discussions provide everyone an opportunity to express ideas and receive immediate feedback, to brainstorm and think out loud. You are welcome to write more freely and less formally than in a well-structured paper. However, please call one another by name, construct moderately clear or complete sentences, and avoid an overabundance of grammar, spelling, or typing errors that might interfere with your meaning.

Reader-Based Writing

One value I assume we share is respect for others' experiences and ideas or social positions. I also assume we share a genuine desire to learn from one another. To demonstrate these shared values, I encourage you to consider how your tone, word choice, and content may affect your readers in online discussions. Some ways people achieve responsible public electronic discourse include the following:

Calling each other by name on the screen
Using smiley faces or other emoticons if a writer's tone might be ambiguous (see http://messenger.msn.com/Resource/Emoticons.aspx)

Clarifying with someone courteously before "flaming" back a quick response

Refraining from publishing or forwarding any questionable jokes or strong language that could offend

Netiquette

Please study and follow "The Core Rules of Netiquette," developed by Virginia Shea (available at www.albion.com/netiquette/corerules.html). I especially encourage you to follow the first rule: "Remember the Human." As Shea explains, "When you're holding a conversation online—whether it's an email exchange or a response to a discussion group posting—it's easy to misinterpret your correspondent's meaning. And it's frighteningly easy to forget that your correspondent is a person with feelings more or less like your own." Effective critical readers, thinkers, and writers offer respect, even to those with whom they disagree.

Quality of Discussions

The overall quality of any group interactions—whether face-to-face or online— usually depends on the skills and performance of those willing to take responsibility for the discussion. As you post messages and reply to other students in online discussion forums throughout the semester, consider how you might informally take responsibility for performing various leadership roles in the conversation, described below.

Moderator

Poses provocative questions throughout the discussion from her or his own reading and research.

Encourages people to respond and reply; keeps the conversation going.

Models respectful online conversation and intervenes if and when a communication problem arises.

Says things like, "What do you think about . . . ?" or "That point makes sense, but could you clarify . . ." or "It seems like there's a disagreement about. . . ."

Devil's Advocate

Expresses opposing or contrasting views.

Encourages healthy skepticism and asks questions that encourage people to see issues and interpretations from diverging points of view.

Says things like, "Let me play devil's advocate . . ." or "Are you sure that interpretation is persuasive? What about considering. . . ."

Synthesizer

Notes interesting patterns of agreement or disagreement.

Synthesizes the main ideas that emerged from the online discussion by making connections among other texts or readings, experiences, fields of study, and conversations outside our immediate classroom.

Says things like, "A number of people agree that . . ." or "This issue or pattern of behavior reminds me about a concept we were discussing last week in psychology. . . ."

Sort and Collect Messages

Study the tutorial on "Sort and Collect Discussion Posts" using the *myASU Blackboard* system. If you learn how to sort and collect messages, you will be able to participate in the discussion board efficiently, and the experience will be more enjoyable.

Evaluation and Grading

You will earn overall credit for the pattern of your participation in online discussions based on the quantity and quality of your posted messages and replies using the following criteria.

Criteria for Evaluation* (Total Points Possible)

Inadequate (0–39)

Participation: frequently fails or is late to post a message under two hundred words or fails or is late to post two replies

Thinking and Evidence: summarizes rather than analyzes; evidence is absent or insufficient

Initiative and Leadership: is mostly absent from the discussion; replies don't say much more than, "I agree," "Good point," or "I disagree"

Good (40–44)

Participation: consistently posts an initial message of two hundred words on time; replies to at least two students in meaningful ways and on time

Thinking and Evidence: demonstrates good critical thinking skills by analyzing, synthesizing, and interpreting rather than merely summarizing the text; offers evidence for support, although it may sometimes be insufficient or unpersuasive

Initiative and Leadership: keeps up with the discussion and does not dominate but establishes a discernible presence online

Excellent (45–50)

Participation: always posts an initial message of more than two hundred words on time; replies to at least two or more students in meaningful and extended ways and on time

Thinking and Evidence: demonstrates excellent critical thinking skills, including logical analysis, synthesis, and interpretation of the texts; provides sufficient and persuasive evidence for support

Initiative and Leadership: offers prompt, timely, and relevant contributions to the conversation, voluntarily moderating, playing devil's advocate, or synthesizing ideas and parts of the conversation as needed

*Criteria adapted from Bauer and Anderson.

Kathy Cawsey and Ian Lancashire

An Online Poetry Course (for Carol)

Ian taught ENG 201Y (Reading Poetry), the first full-credit online course in the Faculty of Arts and Science at the University of Toronto, for three years (2001–04). To prepare for this experimental section, taken by about twenty-five students each time, he edited an online anthology of poems with twenty-six written lecture-commentaries (most of these are now on *Representative Poetry Online* [http://rpo.library.utoronto.ca/display]) and recorded thirty audio lectures. The course management system—*Prometheus* at first and then *WebCT*—delivered course content, hosted fifty-two one-hour chats that were recorded and saved, offered a bulletin board so that students could post their assignments, and administered student grades. A teaching assistant helped Ian each year, grading assignments and delivering half the chat room sessions. In 2003–04, Kathy was Ian's assistant. They met the students physically only twice, at the end-of-term examinations.

Each year Ian, his assistant, and the students weathered problems. Reaching students who had been registered in the section was hard because the Faculty of Arts and Science did not publish the course "room number" (i.e., the URL for the Web site). Some students did not even know that they had registered for an online section. The Department of English at first had to inform each incoming student of his or her choice by Canada Post. (When course evaluation time came around, the department also sent forms to students by snail mail.) The university had no laboratory that supported *WebCT* or the recording of oral lectures. Students supplied their own computers. Technical glitches occurred: sometimes some students could not access a chat, others got suddenly dropped from it, and everyone experienced minutes when the chat room screen froze.

Yet the experiment was successful. The class average was consistently higher than the University of Toronto norm, and thirty-seven percent of students earned A's in the final year. Because all lectures and chats were archived for rereading, students had access to almost every word Ian and his assistants uttered.[1] It took Ian four to five hours to prepare a thirty-minute audio segment and up to twelve hours to write a commentary on a poem. Knowing that his lectures would be subject to hard scrutiny, he polished them and looked for multimedia images (such as the Windeby Girl for Seamus Heaney's poem "Punishment") and audio (such as a recording of Billie Holiday singing "Strange Fruit," which Alicia Ostriker echoes in her poem "Holocaust"). Ian and his assistants got to know the students very well in the chats. The chat room technology leveled the playing field: no one could type more than two or three sentences at a time, and everyone could edit a contribution before publishing it. Teachers could not dominate the class, and students could contribute without stage fright. Protected in this way, students freely engaged instructors, other students, and the subject matter.

Through these chats, Ian and his assistants learned what anyone doing research in computer-mediated communication already knows: the interaction among committed students and their teachers improves markedly in a virtual classroom (chat room, bulletin board, e-mail) over what is possible in a physical classroom. Online teaching enables students to "attend" classes as well as have day jobs. No one complains about conflicts. Chats ask for everyone's intense attention while in progress, and they are often exhilarating. The students would not recognize one another on the street, but the shared online experience etches distinct human portraits in everyone's mind.

We present these portraits here. We chose the penultimate hour-long chat of 2003–04, the last chat Kathy taught and the hundred forty-ninth in Ian's three-year experiment. Kathy taught it from Cork, Ireland, on Heaney's

"Punishment," and thirteen students in Toronto participated. Together, they submitted about 240 comments in 69 minutes, or 3.5 per minute: Kathy typed 104 entries, and thirteen students typed 134 entries.[2]

Kathy joined Ian in fall 2003, since she planned to be in Ireland in the second term and participating in an online course would enable her to keep her teaching assistantship. Her computer literacy was average. She had used computers since high school, typed quickly, and was dependent on e-mail, but she knew little about the conventions of chatting. Most students were like Kathy in this respect. Unlike Kathy, who was at work on a doctoral thesis on Chaucer, only a few were English majors. Most students took the course as an elective. One student, Carol, was ill and could only take online courses.

Kathy started with doubts about online teaching. She was concerned that the impersonal, emotionally distancing medium would render her faceless and the class without personality. In a regular classroom, the teacher gets to know the extroverts; the introverts receive less attention. The online medium, to her surprise, enabled Kathy to get to know both the shy students and the extroverts better than she would have in a physical classroom. By the end of her first chat, she already had a good sense of the personalities of the students: who would make a joke to ease awkwardness, who would supply the answer to a technical question, who could be counted on to fill a silence, and who worried about the details of assignments and exams. Chat rooms also decrease inhibitions. Faceless, comfortable in their own homes, students quickly learned to tease one another, make ice-breaking jokes, and use informal language. Students developed friendships, with Kathy and among themselves. Several set up in-person study groups before the fall-term exam, despite never having met one another face-to-face. A few even sent Kathy their own poetry (one gay student came out in this way). The Whisper function of the chat room (which allows a participant to direct a comment solely to one person) had unexpected benefits. An especially shy student, who was not an English major, would Whisper a comment to Kathy to make sure it was correct before clicking <Enter>. By year's end, this student had gained the confidence to type her comments "aloud" without checking them beforehand.

Chat technology can be alienating. If the connection is slow, long pauses ensue, followed by sudden jumps in the screen as four or five comments appear at once. Even if the connection is working fine, conversation can suffer from a time lag if additional comments appear before a prior comment is handled. At about fifteen people, if all are talking regularly, the chat becomes unmanageable: too many comments flow down the screen too rapidly to process. Incoming comments and questions interfere with one's formulation of a statement. As well, some standard teaching techniques are unusable. Kathy could not catch the eye of shy students to improve their confidence, nor could she avoid those who always answered by choosing someone else. Study sessions, where the class can brainstorm, draw connections, and make lists on the blackboard, were especially difficult to do on the computer. What we thought of as the pause, waiting for students to answer a question, was perplexing. Were the students thinking, typing a long response, waiting for a slow connection, sitting there bored, or making nachos in the kitchen?

We also observed some affective issues with the students. Tone was problematic: something that was intended as a joke was taken seriously, or vice versa, in a way that would not have happened in person. Familiarity with the chat room medium, and the use of emoticons (a smiley or "j/k" ["just kidding"]) ameliorated some of these difficulties, but until a chat room screen offers video, they will remain. And whether because of the unfamiliar technology or because of the lack of face-to-face contact, Kathy encountered more anxiety in students than she had observed in other courses. Some of the influx of student e-mails arose from laziness—it is easier to send off a quick e-mail than to look something up—but in the absence of face-to-face contact, students needed reassurance, hand-holding, and confirmation of their individual importance. E-mail provided this immediacy of contact with the teacher.

Surprisingly, students never raised the issue of privacy. Over three years, no one complained that all the chat room contributions, good and bad, were archived for everyone else to read, including visitors and students who had not been at the chat. In two of the three years, Ian even let students read one another's posted essays. He deliberately supplemented his own commentaries with theirs for educational reasons. Again, no one objected, despite the fact that in Canada provincially regulated organizations, which arguably include publicly funded universities, are subject to Canada's federal Personal Information Protection and Electronic Documents Act.[3] Did students like sharing what was personal because their teachers set an example in this respect? Why did thirteen students agree to have a verbatim transcript of their last chat published and discussed here? We have no answers to these questions, but online teachers should inform students of any publication of their words, whether inside or outside the course-ware site, and allow them to opt out.

Everyone coped with the disadvantages of an online course. Some may have had specific incentives: a permanent record of all classroom conversations; easier accessibility for special-needs students; the elimination of bias due to physical appearance; and the removal of travel to class. Over the year, the class developed a high level of comfort and trust, which comes out in the following transcript of Kathy's chat on Seamus Heaney's poem "Punishment." Students are comfortable asking questions, contradicting one another, disagreeing with the teacher, taking risks, and expressing their emotions—all these wonderful ephemeral moments are caught as though in amber. At times, the chat appears to thrash, veering toward unmanage-ability, but we can clearly see that by the end the students have worked through to a sophisticated understanding of the poem.

Ian's commentary, posted earlier on the class site,[4] interpreted the poem so that students had a starting point. Kathy aimed to teach the students to work through a poem for themselves and to develop skills of critical thinking, analysis, close reading, lateral thinking (making connections to other works and events), and self-expression. To guide students thus, she avoided telling them what to think. The classroom experience had to be a group effort, not a one-way transfer of information from teacher to student. The transcript reveals how students developed some complex, subtle ideas about the poem. Kathy intervened to provide factual information, to draw out and rephrase their ideas, to add supporting evidence and ideas, and to direct their reading.

The opening chitchat about essays and the exam is omitted, as are the farewells. The rest of this chat room log has not been edited. Spelling mistakes are in the original transcript; comments by Kathy and Ian are square-bracketed in italics. Most students have read Ian's online commentary on the poem, so Kathy opens with something about the poet. She splits up her comments into several entries to imitate conversation and ensure that the lines appear on the students' screens in segments optimally sized for rapid reading rather than in large chunks that jump up suddenly. The disadvantage of this method is that interruptions can interpose themselves between the segments. Kathy and Ian both write casually to chats, without obsessing about periods, correct spelling, or consistent capitalization.

KATHY: so let's look at Punishment—what's the poem about?
PAUL: the windeby girl

CAROL: social death
CAROL: as well as physical death
HOWIE: one of the bog people
CHLOE: adultery
SARAH: public execution

> *[Kathy's general question elicits several quick responses, each of which offers a thread to follow. Kathy chooses the factual thread so that students understand the literal meaning of the poem before trying to grasp the more complex metaphorical or symbolic meanings. She praises the students, defers Carol's left-field reply about social death, and states the subject.]*

KATHY: good . . . all those things . . . let's look at the "literal" level first
KATHY: it's about a prehistoric woman who was put to death, whom archaeologists later found preserved in a bog

> *[Here Kathy basically answers her own question, making sure all the students are on the same page. Carol interrupts.]*

CAROL: emphasis on "woman"
KATHY: they speculate her punishment was for adultery

> *[Carol jumped in before Kathy could finish her summary of the poem (which then appeared in the next line), taking the class in a direction Kathy had not intended. Yet, believing this thread would be productive, Kathy allows it. She uses Carol's name in responding in the event that another comment were to interpose itself before Kathy could hit <Enter>. Near the end of the chat, when Kathy has to respond to Ciara, Howie, and Carol in quick succession, using names will be essential.]*

KATHY: okay—why, Carol?
CAROL: women were maligned more then men
SARAH: they also seemed to be punished for adultery more
CAROL: and made public examples of

> *[Kathy asks everyone to apply these generalizations to the poem.]*

KATHY: yes, true . . . why else is Carol's comment apposite for this poem?

> *[Paul sees why Carol is right in a way she hasn't addressed.]*

PAUL: well the poet sort of takes on the role of this girls lover

> *[Kathy encourages Paul, but his insight about the poet's role as observer (in his next comment) is what Kathy hopes to develop over the course of*

the class. Paul is already there. To let the rest of the students work through to the same understanding themselves, Kathy ignores him and asks a leading question.]

KATHY: good . . . what things does he notice about her?
SARAH: her body
PAUL: so the subject/observer roles are very much about gender differences
CAROL: her former physcial possibilities
PAUL: ya, lots of details about her body

[Kathy sees little detail here and so repeats the question.]

KATHY: examples?

[Carol completes her response, now sandwiching entries by Paul and Kathy.]

CAROL: which still keeps her an object for male sexuality
KATHY: good, Carol, Paul
CAROL: he even admits that she is a scapegoat
PAUL: her shaved head like a stubble of black corn
KATHERINE: the nape of her neck

[Kathy likes the details and waits for more.]

KATHY: good . . .
CHLOE: he says he face was beautiful
CAROL: flaxen haired
PAUL: the girls blindfold and noose also take on some special meaning

[Kathy asks them to rank examples.]

KATHY: what is the strongest impression he has of her? What does he mention first?
KATHERINE: erect nipple

[Sarah sees something odd; the other students keep answering Kathy's question.]

SARAH: the first stanza she's described like a horse
SARAH: and it's also very sexual
KATHY: good Katherine
CAROL: amber nipples
PAUL: her "naked front"

[Melinda comments on Sarah's reference to a horse without citing Sarah by name.]

MELINDA: I was confused by the nipple and bare front, when he mentions a "halter"

[Comments are turning up almost simultaneously, so that Kathy's encouragement of Sarah arrives late.]

KATHY: good Sarah
JACQUELINE: naked front
CHLOE: that shé s naked

[Jacqueline and Chloe are still answering Kathy's question. Kathy addresses Melinda's confusion.]

KATHY: I think, Melinda—correct me if I'm wrong, someone—that she was tied up, then drowned

[Kathy admits she does not have all the answers and might be incorrect. This admission gives students permission to take risks, to change their minds, and to disagree. Paul provides the explanation.]

PAUL: halter was probably ropes or something that was used to lash her to the stone
KATHY: so the "halter" is part of her punishment

[Like Kathy, Carol encourages Sarah.]

CAROL: the frail rigging could lead someone to think this is a horse sarah

[Melinda acknowledges Kathy and Paul.]

MELINDA: I gotcha. Thanks.

[Kathy suggests another metaphor but allows Carol's.]

KATHY: more a ship, for that image, Carol
PAUL: rigging is more like a ship
KATHY: but yes, a horse, a ship—what else does he liken her to?

[Paul here imitates Kathy's method of disagreeing while still allowing alternative readings.]

PAUL: although horses do have halters
SARAH: a sapling
KATHY: good, Sarah

[Sarah asks a question. Because she feels comfortable admitting she does not understand something, she points Kathy to a problem other students might also be experiencing—as Melinda's comment confirms.]

SARAH: speaking of which, i'm not sure i understand that stanza, starting at
line 13
SARAH: they thought she was a sapling when they first unearthed her??
KATHY: okay—let's look at that stanza
MELINDA: Yeah, I was pretty confused by it too

[Carol has a related question.]

CAROL: looked up the word firkin but now i can;t remember what it means

*[Howie and Paul have the answer, but Kathy still attends to Sarah's
question. Throughout the year, Howie and Hank often opened up another browser page, looked up factual information on the Web, and returned to report to the class. This is one advantage physical classrooms do
not have.]*

HOWIE: small cask
KATHY: no, I don't think so literally, Sarah, although she might have looked
like that
PAUL: barrel
KATHY: good Howie

*[Carol thanks Howie and Paul for helping her. Kathy is not needed to
answer Carol's question.]*

CAROL: thanks
KATHY: they're very old-englishy words, like "kennings" (combined words)

[Carol is even more confused, and Kathy has to say no.]

CAROL: so she was placed in a barrel first?
KATHY: Heaney likes to use words from his Northern Irish roots, "earthy" gut-
teral words
KATHY: no, I don't think so Carol

[Kathy returns to Sarah's question.]

KATHY: I think it's an image . . . what is peat made of?

[Carol persists, . . . and Paul tries again.]

CAROL: thats what i'm not clear on how the firkin is used
PAUL: brain firkin = her small skull
KATHY: good Paul

[Sarah answers Kathy about peat.]

SARAH: moss . . . ?

[Carol persists, . . . and Paul tries a third time.]

CAROL: firkin=skull?
PAUL: no
PAUL: but look at how he uses it in context
CAROL: i know he says brain firkin

[Kathy keeps to Sarah's thread and elucidates the image.]

KATHY: mmm. . . . sort of, Sarah . . . peat bogs are the pre-stage for coal, oil, fuel
KATHY: they're made up of rotting plant matter, from ages ago
KATHY: people here *[Kathy is attending this chat from Ireland]* actually burn "turf" or peat, it's like coal

[Carol is still confused.]

CAROL: and oak bone but i don't understand why

[Kathy decides that the students need some help to unconfuse the chat. She still walks them through the reasoning but gives some answers. At this point the students are mostly "listening," and the screen moves slowly.]

KATHY: so if the peat bog is made up of old prehistoric trees . . .
KATHY: the girl is like a tree, buried to become part of the bog, part of th elandscape
KATHY: her bones are oak, her skull is a cask
KATHY: she is merging into the bog (and probably looks like it, too)

[Paul feels comfortable in disagreeing with Kathy.]

PAUL: i dont think youd find oak in a bog
PAUL: although im not a tree expert
KATHY: well, certainly not in an "oak" form
KATHY: it would be pretty rotted by then
KATHY: but when they first came across the body, it may have looked like wood, a c ask, whatever
KATHY: but definitely not a person
PAUL: right

[Chloe implies, cautiously, in a question, a way to understand "oak." She spoke more rarely than some students but always paid attention.]

CHLOE: does oak being strong have something to do with her bones being strong, ie lasting so long

[Kathy runs with Chloe's idea.]

KATHY: yes, that could be, Chloe
KATHY: oak would be the last tree to rot
KATHY: so the poet is both seeing her as she is now, withered and blackened, and imagining her as she would have been alive

[Kathy is now ready to move back to Paul's first insight about the role of the observer, but her question is broad and, before the students get a chance to think about it, Carol gives her another approach.]

KATHY: what's the problem with this?

[Carol's still thinking about the mistreatment of women.]

CAROL: the way he brings her "back to life" has a cloying affect

[Kathy can see a connection to her question this time.]

KATHY: in what way, Carol?
CAROL: almost as though she is only valuable for beauty

[But Paul's losing his patience, although always respectfully. Everyone is being civilized.]

PAUL: thats not the impression i got

[Carol fantasizes at some distance from the poem.]

CAROL: and since they believed that women could only have one husband
CAROL: he would in fact be resurrecting her for a similar consequence

[Kathy silently disagreed with Carol's use of the word "cloying" until Carol explains herself and enables Kathy to see a tone she had missed. Kathy does not immediately reply to Carol but encourages Paul.]

KATHY: what was your impression, Paul
PAUL: well it seemed to me the author doesnt give a very positive account of himself or society

[Carol persists, and Kathy, seeing something unexpected in her perspective, brings Carol and Paul together.]

CAROL: "i am the artful voyeaur" shudder
KATHY: okay—I think you're both on to something

PAUL: he is being honest, but also more then that, passing judgement on himself

PAUL: the ressurected girl is like a test he would fail

KATHY: I wouldn't use the word "cloying," Carol, but yes, I think he is very aware of her beauty

KATHY: but you're right too, Paul, he's very aware of the problems with his own awareness

CAROL: it was the "little" adulterous that i found cloying

KATHY: ah, yes

CAROL: almost possessive

[Kathy recognizes Carol's perception.]

KATHY: let's look at that line Carol picked out—why "artful voyeur"?

CAROL: and definately patronizing

KATHY: yes, it is possessive, Carol

[Sarah has a different explanation.]

SARAH: because he would have watched her die and not stepped in

SARAH: had he been there

SARAH: and perhaps felt something because of it . . . desire or something

KATHY: okay, good—he would have been like the other watchers, who "threw stones"

CAROL: who remained silent

[Kathy agrees with Sarah; Carol establishes her thread, which then combines with Paul's.]

KATHY: yes, very good Sarah—the sexual overtones of voyeur

KATHY: how is watching someone be punished like that voyeuristic?

PAUL: artful voyeur because he was turned on by the image of the preserved girl, obviously he would need to exercise his imagination for that, to see beyong a corpse

[Quiet Ciara responds before Kathy can reply to Paul.]

CIARA: experiencing pleasure from somebody's pain

[Kathy provides factual information the students might not know, which they can use in their interpretations.]

KATHY: (aside: throwing stones—Biblical ref to the woman who was being stoned for adultery)

[Kathy agrees with both Paul and Ciara.]

KATHY: good Paul—there's a doubleness here—he is a voyeur now, and he would have been one back then
PAUL: it doesnt have to be pain to be voyeurism
CIARA: ok
KATHY: good Ciara—there is an "erotics of punishment"
KATHY: people—especially mobs—often get a thrill from watching someone be punished or hurt
KATHY: and with a woman—especially one caught in adultery—that can be half-erotic

[Hank adds further details to Ciara's and Kathy's reading.]

HANK: and in the present, she is naked . . .

[Carol misreads, but Kathy returns to her "artful voyeur."]

CAROL: lets not forget that she may be naked but she is also fleshless
KATHY: yes, good Hank . . . and amber nipples (nice image—amber = preserving substance, like the bog)
KATHY: why "artful"?

[Melinda introduces the poem's end—a competing thread.]

MELINDA: I found it interesting, in the notes, that women in Ireland suffered similar punishment.

[Carol, Paul, and Sarah answer Kathy.]

CAROL: because he has recreated her form
PAUL: the exercise of imagination
SARAH: artful because he's reimagining her
CAROL: like an artist

[Suman picks up Melinda's point, but Kathy puts her on hold until she can finish with "artful voyeur."]

SUMAN: would it be the same if a man was getting stones thrown at him?
KATHY: good, Melinda—hang on to that
KATHY: good
KATHY: he is recreating her both in his imagination and his art (the poem)
KATHY: what other meaning does "artful" have?
PAUL: artificial?
CAROL: only other time i've heard that term was the "artful dodger"

[Carol makes a palpable hit; Kathy is pleased.]

KATHY: yes . . . and crafty, sly
KATHY: exactly, Carol

KATHY: why is this poem "artful"—as in slightly "dodgy"?
CAROL: because on the one hand he is attempting to incite anger over the incident

[Carol continues to type while others interrupt. Howie drops a fine comment modestly phrased as a question.]

HOWIE: is the poem trying to preserve her as the bog did?

[Hank then notices something different, a potentially productive thread that was lost and never taken up. Had there been enough time in the class, Kathy would have returned to this point, but there are too many competing threads at the moment.]

HANK: exactly halfway through, it moves from Heaney speaking about the girl to Heaney speaking TO the girl

[While Paul responds to Melinda and Suman, Kathy links Carol's point with Howie's and affirms both; two threads now intertwine.]

PAUL: perhaps the references to the modern girls who suffered similar punishment

[Carol finishes her previous thought—we can see how quickly the chat is moving at this point.]

CAROL: but is in danger of diminishing it by recreating her as an object for his lust
KATHY: very good . . . the poem at once preserves her, but also re-adulterizes her, in a sense

[Now Paul is encouraging Carol and Kathy. Who is teaching?]

PAUL: i think that's exactly what the poet wanted to do

[Kathy moves back from the details to the bigger-picture problems in the poem.]

KATHY: the poet re-creates and idolises her, but also benefits himself from it—he is not innocent
KATHY: yes—there are serious problems with the ethics of poetry here, that Heaney raises
KATHY: how can you describe something without appropriating, exploiting it?

[Here, a rhetorical question links the Carol-Howie thread with Melinda's thread. And then there is a pause. Kathy waits and prompts.]

KATHY: how does this ethical level fit in with the Northern Irish situation?

[Kathy rephrases the question. Five students take the bait and attack social mores by posing questions, as Kathy does and Howie recently did.]

CAROL: was he trying to expose something that people were attempting to conceal?

MELINDA: How can you condemn someone, when you yourself can be condemned?

PAUL: i got the less esoteric impression that he was commenting on the hypocracy of "modern" morality

[Carol has moved from her opening position to view the poet with more approval. Howie draws on Ian's background commentary on the poem.]

CAROL: I think in a lot of ways its a very brave piece

CAROL: he is showing people their own humanity

HOWIE: women in belfast were sometimes shaven, stripped, tarred and hand-cuffed to railings as punishment by the IRA for keeping company with british soldiers

[During this conversation, Suman "whispered" her next comment to Kathy, concerned that it might not be right. Kathy "whispered" back, telling her to say the comment "aloud."]

SUMAN: was that the revenge referred to in the last line?

[Kathy responds to Howie and then to Suman.]

KATHY: good, yes. That's the comment about the "betraying sisters" in tar.

KATHY: part of the commentary here is that not much has changed since pre-historic times

KATHY: yes, Suman—we take revenge on our outsiders in order to keep together as a society

KATHY: we transfer our own guilt onto those we punish—as scapegoats

CAROL: it always baffles me that one society thinks itself superior to another

[Kathy pushes the students to think further about the ethics of the poem. She uses a typographical code to substitute for body language: asterisks emphasize the word "profitting."]

KATHY: but in a way, there's another level of problematisation here: Heaney is *profitting* from all this

KATHY: he's won a Nobel prize for writing about all this stuff

CAROL: ahhh the old "artists" shouldn't be paid theme :)

[Like Kathy, Carol uses a code: her smiley indicates that her tone is joking.]

KATHY: to rephrase my earlier comment: he's "appropriating", or using for his own ends, the girl in the bog
PAUL: isnt that what poetry is all about?
KATHY: he "interprets" her, he "exploits" her—in a way, he re-enacts her exposure, her punishment
KATHY: and yet, how could you have poetry otherwise?

[Kathy returns to Irish politics (the last entries by Howie and Suman).]

KATHY: what's the other problem with writing poetry in Northern Ireland?

[This proves to be too general a question; there is a pause. Kathy must rephrase the question. Ciara, Carol, and Howie respond all at once.]

KATHY: if you're writing poetry—what are you *not* doing?
CIARA: taking action
CAROL: poetry is a form of activism
HOWIE: fighting the british?
CAROL: if you can get people's attention

[Kathy encourages all three.]

KATHY: good, Ciara—in the words of Auden—"Poetry accomplishes nothing"
KATHY: yes, but it's the Catholics who were tarring the women, Howie
KATHY: but Carol's also right, too—we often think of poetry as an "action", as a way of drawing attention to issues
KATHY: in a way that other media cannot
PAUL: not many read poetry though

[Carol shows her knowledge to good effect—another thread that is not followed.]

CAROL: aristotle's catharsis comes to mind

[Kathy returns to the ethics of this type of poem.]

KATHY: but Heaney is asking, in this poem—maybe we're just fooling ourselves
KATHY: yes, maybe we just assuage our guilt for standing quiet earler, by writing poems now
CAROL: well i don't mind admiting that i wouldn't have known about "bog people" without his piece
KATHY: it's an astonishing poem—it keeps folding back on itself

KATHY: me neither, Carol . . . I think Heaney realised, at some point in his career, that the bog was a very potent symbol for Ireland

KATHY: all this history, buried deep, that sucks you in

[Carol encourages Kathy!]

CAROL: it is an important study

KATHY: but which occasionally pushes something to the surface, out of the depths

[Howie suggests a related thread.]

HOWIE: doesn't ireland have a strong relationship with the earth?

[Carol persists with her opening feminist theme.]

CAROL: i used to think that only certain countries oppressed women

CAROL: and Ireland wouldn't have made that list

[Kathy acknowledges Howie but rewards Carol with three potent facts from modern Irish life.]

KATHY: not sure, Howie—no more than elsewhere, I suppose. But the bog is an integral part of the Irish landscape

KATHY: There was no divorce in Ireland until 30 years ago, Carol (mabye more recent), and you needed 3 witnesses to a beating to get a barring order against your husband, well into the seventies

CAROL: so sad

KATHY: you still have to fly to England to get an abortion, even if you were raped

CHLOE: very

MELINDA: wow

SUMAN: wow, that's surprising

CAROL: very enlightening

CAROL: we take so much for granted here

KATHY: but the "erotics of punishment" are in many socities, and not just in regards to women—that "thrill" holds for any outsider, I think

[Carol has the last word.]

CAROL: it wouldn't for me

[The hour's up.]

KATHY: Anyways—thanks for a good last class, I've really enjoyed teaching you all this year!

[As the students and Kathy bid one another good night, Janet and Jac-
queline, who had not previously participated but who were listening
throughout, chime in. Janet, who sends Kathy a smiley, told Ian during
his office hours that she usually published only one or two long and
thoughtful entries each class because the chat moved too quickly for her
and she spent much of the class erasing half-typed comments. By the time
she was ready to publish one, the conversation had moved on. For students
like Janet, an online bulletin board would have served better than a chat
room.]

We believe that chats enrich learning but call for some teacher re-
training. Kathy worked from an outline of key themes on her computer
keyboard beside a printout of "Punishment" on which key passages were
circled or highlighted. Once the chat began, however, she was not the
only teacher. Did Carol have a teaching plan too? (It seems that she may
have.) Paul also helped guide the other students to a more advanced understanding of the poem, often using techniques similar to Kathy's. Everyone had to accommodate the unexpected and make choices quickly. The
chat appears unstructured because no one person dominated it, because
students exerted control over their own learning experience. They learned
to take on Kathy's role in many ways: supporting the contributions of fellow students, asking and answering questions, and—in Carol's instance—
firmly staking out the main topic.

Alone at their workstations, teacher and students in chats are ideally
weavers of threads; although that serene metaphor, which gives our word
text its root sense, does not capture the sense of speed and uncontrollabil-
ity as a chat proceeds. To use a different simile: the teacher feels like a
traffic cop at a busy thirteen-way intersection without traffic lights. Everyone must slow down (utter short entries), use unambiguous signals (address
the intended audience by name), and respect a cop when she waves one on
("in what way, Carol?") or signals a halt ("hold that thought"). The rules of
the road demand more than usual intelligence, for they are truly bizarre.
Any driver can be cop of the moment. The cop must learn how to signal
right-of-way as well as how to defer, to the drivers, the authority for directing traffic. Every driver has immediate secret access to every other driver,
as well as to the cop, through the Whisper function. Logs of chats do not
include these whispered entries, but they are numerous. In a physical
classroom, students do not stand up, go to the front of the room, and start
running the teacher's discussion. Nor do classroom students whisper to
their teachers. We often felt mind-boggled during a chat and exhausted

after it was over, experiences that teaching in a physical classroom seldom give. But we also came away exhilarated from the adrenaline rush of the chat.

The pros and cons of educational chatrooms have been debated in computer-mediated-communication research. Despite what Albert L. Ingram, Lesley G. Hathorn, and Alan Evans term an "initial visceral reaction" against it, problems like information overload and the need for moderating skills in the teacher, many now recognize that chat rooms help students develop ideas and carry out tasks, both written and analytic. Controlled tests show that synchronous exchanges resemble face-to-face conversations and foster students' awareness of their composing (Pellettieri). Writing teachers certainly work as if chat rooms are a valuable component of online courses (Kemp). L. Lennie Irvin's testimony rings true:

> Real-time synchronous electronic conferencing (called Interchange in Daedalus) is the primary place for this type of discourse where students dialogue back and forth between each other. Out of the crucible of discourse, meaning forms, explodes, and takes shape again. It is at once "at" discourse because students send messages which are read by all the group, and it is "to" discourse because frequently students direct comments to each other, but the dynamic is continued into exchange. Students feel a real sense of audience in this environment because the rest of the class is reading and can respond immediately. In addition, synchronous discussions have received a lot of positive attention for their qualities of "multiplicity" and "equality": more students get involved in the discussion and each has an equal "voice" since all messages appear in the same way on the computer screen. I always think of synchronous electronic conferences as a class discussion (like in the traditional classroom), except every student is able to speak at once, students tend to write more, and I (as teacher) cannot lead and orchestrate the discussion to the degree done in the traditional classroom (i.e. initiation-reply-evaluation). Students also engage more with each other rather than directing their discourse toward me, as students do when they look at the teacher in the traditional classroom.

This summary exactly captures the experience of being in the Seamus Heaney chat. Caught up in this experiment, instructors might not easily grasp what is happening. Cynthia L. Selfe and Gail E. Hawisher believe that students make online education serve questions of personal identity—age, gender, and ethnic and racial group. At the time, we did not recognize how well Carol's "it wouldn't for me" befitted the medium for her messages.

This chat was special to everyone in several ways. It was, of course, the last one for Kathy's group. By joining it from Cork, in the Republic of Ireland, Kathy was also able to describe life in Ireland (which was in the middle of a referendum about abortion) and the situation in the North firsthand. This insight brought some emotional intensity to the discussion of an Irish poem. In retrospect, we feel some "emotion, recollected in tranquility," because Carol succumbed to her illness only a few months after the course ended.[5] Her year-long enthusiasm for the chats, only surpassed by her teachers', accounts for the title of this case study. Anyone who thinks that online teaching is impersonal and disaffected only need read the transcript to see how mistaken an impression this is. Any faculty members who live to teach will understand what an extraordinary gift it has been, and continues to be, for us to have this transcript, and its portraits, to remember.

Notes

1. These transcripts have another advantage: when Ian offered a workshop on online teaching at Iowa City in 2004 for the Association of Departments of English (Lancashire, "Teaching"), those attending were impressed enough to say that such transcripts could help teach young instructors how to teach.

2. The average number of entries for a student was 10.3; the median number was 4. The longest entry by a student, Paul, was 29 words. The most student contributions came from six persons: Carol (50), Paul (31), Sarah (16), Melinda (8), Howie (7), and Chloe (6).

3. The Personal Information Protection and Electronic Documents Act (PIPEDA) protects individuals from how government agencies, businesses, and institutions collect, use, or disclose personal information (see Office). The University of Toronto, like most Canadian universities, is supported by a provincial government.

4. An imageless version of this commentary, without the text of the poem, is now available on *Representative Poetry Online* (Lancashire, "Commentary").

5. Carol Akasike (d. 2005) was a much valued student of the Transitional Year Program at the University of Toronto and a poet. Her son Dale has allowed us to use her name.

Works Cited

Ingram, Albert L., Lesley G. Hathorn, and Alan Evans. "Beyond Chat on the Internet." *Computers and Education* 35.1 (2000): 21–35. Print.

Irvin, L. Lennie. "The Shared Discourse of the Networked Computer Classroom." *San Antonio College.* Alamo Community Colls., 2000. Web. 24 Feb. 2009.

Kemp, Fred. "Computer-Mediated Communication: Making Nets Work for Writing Instruction." *The Dialogic Classroom: Teachers Integrating Computer Technology, Pedagogy, and Research.* Ed. Jeffrey Galin and Joan Latchow. Urbana: NCTE, 1998. 133–50. Print.

Lancashire, Ian. "Commentary" [on "Punishment," by Seamus Heaney]. *Representative Poetry Online.* Ed. Lancashire. U of Toronto, 1994. Web. 15 Oct. 2006.

———. "Teaching Literature Online: A Workshop." ADE Summer Seminar Midwest. Sheraton Iowa City Hotel, Iowa City. 19 June 2004. Address.

Pellettieri, Jill. "Negotiation in Cyberspace: The Role of Chatting in the Development of Grammatical Competence." *Network-Based Language Teaching: Concepts and Practice.* Ed. Mark Warschauer and Richard Kern. Cambridge: Cambridge UP, 2000. 59–86. Print.

Office of the Privacy Commissioner of Canada. "Privacy Legislation in Canada." *Office of the Privacy Commissioner of Canada.* Gov. of Canada, 2004. Web. 5 Sept. 2006.

Selfe, Cynthia L., and Gail E. Hawisher. *Literate Lives in the Information Age: Narratives of Literacy from the United States.* Mahwah: Erlbaum, 2004. Print.

Kathryn M. Grossman

Creating E-Learning Communities in Language and Literature Classes

At many universities, faculty members are challenged to encourage active and collaborative learning throughout the undergraduate curriculum. Given how inherently social our students are, particularly in the use of technology, it is perhaps ironic that we need to foster such learning strategies. We have solid research evidence that students love to form highly collaborative communities of interest through such Web sites as *Facebook* and *MySpace*. At Penn State, for instance, nearly seventy-five percent of our undergraduates engage actively with peers across the world in these nonacademic, voluntary communities. Since information technology is so strong a part of the undergraduate experience, how can we use it to promote lively student interaction as part of the learning process?

Researchers have studied the best ways to leverage different kinds of technologies and teams to support learning. Iain McAlpine and Bill Ashcroft have demonstrated that online discussion has a powerful influence on the success of collaborative learning projects, but online discussion alone is not the key. Critical to success, they argue, are how problems are structured, how communication is encouraged, and especially how teams are created and monitored. Likewise, Donald E. Hanna, Michelle Glowacki-Dudka, and Simone Conceição-Runlee have shown that a small group (no more than five members) helps prevent students from being overwhelmed by the volume of required interactions. Researchers have further noted that a particular strength of online teams is the opportunity for the reticent to participate and for all participants to reflect on their contributions.

In foreign language and general education courses aimed at freshmen and sophomores, faculty members must often deal with students' culture shock at having to learn much more rapidly than in secondary school, as well as in new ways. In upper-division literature seminars, the spirit of competitiveness can work against that of collaboration, hampering opportunities to improve reading, writing, and critical skills through team-based activities. By developing cooperative strategies and by using *ANGEL*—Penn State's course management system akin to *Blackboard*—across a spectrum of courses, I have found numerous ways to create and sustain language communities both inside and outside the classroom. My primary goal has been to increase the amount of time that students spend interacting with one another in French, but the same techniques can be applied to other subjects. A secondary goal—which I have pursued, with varying success, since the beginning of my teaching career—has been to create conditions in which students focus more on learning than on grades. In this essay, I first outline my early attempts at diverting students' attention away from quantitative assessments of their work. I then discuss how I have adopted several online strategies, including threaded discussions and team-writing projects, to cultivate not just collaboration and communication skills but also intrinsic rewards in the learning process.

Grading versus Learning

My early thinking about teaching was influenced by Robert M. Pirsig's *Zen and the Art of Motorcycle Maintenance.* Pirsig's protagonist and alter ego, Phaedrus, struggles to encourage students to work, not for grades, but "for the knowledge [grades are] supposed to represent" (195). To help students focus their energies on improving the quality of their work, Phaedrus leaves the members of his class in a certain state of anxiety about their performance by not grading them on every assignment (194–99). Originally, I sought to nurture such autocritical striving in my students by giving extensive evaluative comments—but no grades—on papers, with the same mixed results reported by Phaedrus. Whereas the strongest students seemed to thrive under this system, many others reacted negatively:

> [T]his withholding created a Kafka-esque situation in which they saw they were to be punished for failure to do something, but no one would tell them what they were supposed to do. . . . You have to provide some goal for a class to work toward that will fill that vacuum. (201)

Clearly, it was important to offer, beyond grades or written evaluations, forms of feedback that would both foster learning and enable students to measure their progress in the target language.

I have since continued to look for effective ways to promote student engagement in the learning process. To this end, I began experimenting several years ago with different strategies for collaborative learning, benefiting from research by Hanna, Glowacki-Dudka, and Conceição-Runlee that explains how to improve team projects. The construction of more than two hundred fifty "smart" classrooms at my institution and the advent of online tools for managing instruction have multiplied the possibilities for developing highly collaborative teams. Some strategies for using electronic courseware in general education classes offered in English could, I discovered, be easily adapted to classes taught in French. The French courses, which had multiple assessment points, also evoked fresh approaches to the difficulties of stimulating both creativity and productivity in the target language—approaches that eventually incorporated some of my earlier efforts in gradeless assignments. Most important, by expanding student interactions in French both in and out of class, I could not only give students more practice in the language but also motivate them to pursue communicative activities in French beyond the course.

Promoting Literary Connections

Like many language instructors, I find helping students improve their writing—grammatically, substantively, and critically—one of my most difficult challenges. Although almost all students have learned the five-paragraph essay at the secondary level, they often seem reticent about forging ambitious, provocative, well-forecasted arguments in their opening paragraphs and developing conclusions that are both striking and euphonious. Rather, many students end their papers by simply reiterating what has already been said. The use of evidence in the body of the argument borders on misuse when writers do not properly introduce quotations or comment on them before proceeding to the next point. Since textual analysis can constitute one of the most original aspects of an essay in binding the general argument to particular proof, losing this special quality is regrettable. And yet, without several opportunities for practice and feedback, students do not always learn to internalize such techniques before their term papers are due. The problem arises because foreign language faculty members, who have broader mandates (the four skills: listening, speaking, reading, and writing) than English composition teachers and often comparable course enrollments, may not be able to devote themselves to grading multiple sets of papers throughout the semester.

To address this issue in a freshman seminar on French literary and cultural topics (taught in English) and in an intermediate-level introduction to French literature, I began using collaborative in-class exercises in the late 1990s, with great success. At three points in the semester, students would spend half a class session writing introductory, analytic, and concluding passages for a series of imaginary critical essays. Each exercise included detailed directions for composing part of an argument, and different groups of two to three students would practice all three parts during the semester for an array of works. In this way, their team activities doubled as reading quizzes, without precluding more formal exams at other junctures. For example, after several weeks devoted to discussing George Sand's romantic novel *Indiana* (1832) and Émile Zola's early work *Thérèse Raquin* (1867) in the general education course, groups of students were asked to identify a subject, problem, or question that might serve as the central point of a five-page paper; to decide on the boldest argument that one could make in the light of the textual evidence; and to write a powerful conclusion to the proposed paper following specific guidelines.

When Penn State adopted a course management system in 2001, I could post the exercise online the day before a class, thus giving students ample time to prepare the content of their responses in advance. After each group had discussed the relative merits of individual arguments and chosen the best one, it could devote its efforts to developing the form that the conclusion might take. I then graded their coauthored concluding paragraphs at home, giving suggestions for improvement; made a copy for each student in each group; and returned the assignment well before the deadline for their final papers, which were likewise written in two- or three-student teams. With the three sets of instructions and critiqued paper sections in hand, students could apply well-practiced skills to drafting their essays and to improving one another's work before handing them in. Because team members could communicate and share their drafts through *ANGEL*, students whose schedules conflicted could still get together online to write, critique, and hone their papers. A virtual meeting was as effective as one face-to-face.

The same approach works marvelously well in intermediate-level French literature courses, where students need to perfect similar rhetorical skills as well as master a foreign language. Interpretative reading, student-oriented discussions about textual analysis, literary argumentation, relatively brief reaction papers, a more substantive final essay—all benefit from in-class preparatory sessions and online communication and collaboration at other times. Here, as in the freshman seminar and my senior-level literature course, I post in advance guides to each reading, sometimes as a set of questions that follows the narrative chronology, sometimes as topical, thematic, or formal aspects of the text to identify and ponder. Students reading a work for the first time can hardly be expected to grasp it as a whole in media res or to see the many critical complexities and finer aesthetic points when they have finished. They therefore respond well to a lightly imposed structure for the experience, one that eliminates a certain amount of angst about what, exactly, they should be looking for. So much of what literature instructors attempt to share in class—the distillation of the wisdom of the ages, from New Criticism to structuralism to postcolonialism—can come across as stifling and moribund if it seems imposed from without on the living textual encounter.

By the same token, students armed from the outset with a range of perspectives can begin to formulate their own intellectual and aesthetic responses before the instructor moves into the explanatory phase. The session before an assignment is due, I like to have students volunteer to lead the discussion on individual questions or topics, allowing them to choose what interests them most, even if three students assume responsibility for one area and no one signs up for another. I cheerfully assign any unclaimed discussion points to myself and let everyone else decide how to approach—and possibly share—their own domains. Often students see entirely different things in the same scenes or passages, resulting in unrehearsed debates where the leaders lay out their overlapping or opposing interpretations and the rest of the class musters additional evidence to support one or more arguments. Students who have learned to establish positions and to defend them in class are apt to progress more easily to the challenge of writing than those whose views remain unarticulated throughout the semester.

Likewise, in my senior seminar in nineteenth-century French literature, I have for the past decade required students to share their weekly reaction papers and then comment on one another's work. At first, they posted their essays and responded to their classmates' by e-mail; in 2000, we shifted to a software program for threaded discussions; and finally, in 2003, I put the entire seminar—syllabus, daily assignments, Web links, and e-mail communications—on the course Web site in *ANGEL*. Through the site, students working in two-person teams collaborate on weekly five-hundred-word reaction papers and distribute them to the rest of the class by means of electronic drop boxes. The advantages of coauthorship in foreign language classes are multiple: it encourages students to bounce ideas off one another, to revise their argument collectively, and to perfect their written French together before submitting their work. (Kenneth A. Bruffee's research on peer learning helps explain why this approach is so successful.) Moreover, the logistics of collaboration almost ensure that the essays are worked on over several days' time, rather than at the last minute, as so often occurs with independent student writing assignments. As a result, deadlines are generally met, though a few hours leeway is given for stragglers, and more students tackle all the assignments—despite a generous grade-dropping policy—than when they write on their own.[1] Finally, in a period when enrollments in upper-division French courses have nearly doubled at Penn State, team-written compositions also reduce by half the number of papers I grade, allowing time for more substantive comments on each essay.

The procedure for setting up and using these exercises is simple. I post in *ANGEL* general paper guidelines, including electronic drop box instructions, at the beginning of the semester. Then I form teams in class each Friday before the Tuesday evening due date, asking students to rotate partners every week throughout the semester so that they can work with a wide range of collaborators. (In classes with an odd number of students, a different student each week may submit an individual essay.) I post paper topics after class on Friday and close the drop boxes at eight o'clock Wednesday morning, so that students can work Tuesday evening, if necessary. To ensure privacy, the content of the drop boxes is not universally visible—students can see their own papers but no one else's—until all essays are submitted. Finally, I have each team outline its basic argument in class that same day (students seem to share the task naturally) and defend its position. Discussions are always lively, enabling students to raise along the way some of the key points to follow in my presentation of the text at hand. Teams that have chosen the same topic end up in spontaneous debates, while other students chime in with their perceptions and reactions.

Compared with traditional classes taught off-line, where all work is submitted individually, the students working collaboratively in my hybrid course submitted much better and more writing overall. Since the teams assume contractual aspects, students are unwilling to let their partners down. In a recent section of fifteen students, for example, six wrote all ten papers (and everyone wrote the first one), seven wrote nine papers, and two wrote eight papers. In the year before, of thirteen students, eleven wrote ten papers (with all but one writing the first), one wrote nine papers, and one wrote eight papers. By way of contrast, in the year just before the use of collaborative essays, only one of fourteen students wrote ten papers, eight wrote nine, and five wrote eight. Such progress in quantitative measures of student productivity is heartening. But qualitative progress is also evident in the marked improvement in student rapport, class discussions, and awareness of different rhetorical strategies. The use of teams and of technology has clearly fostered student engagement.

In the same course, I also employ threaded discussions in *ANGEL* to have students critique one another's papers. Students read the other essays in the drop box and post individual reactions within two days of submitting their work. In turn, I give them feedback through *ANGEL*'s e-mail function, evaluating the quality of the comments for the first two papers and offering suggestions for improvement. I also supply additional feedback after the fifth and the next-to-last papers, in each case assessing and grading the students' global performance for several assignments. While not entirely the gradeless system proposed by Pirsig's protagonist, this approach encourages students to act on the advice they receive without expecting further remarks after every subsequent task. By letting them know midway through the semester if they are on the right track, I am able both to reassure those who have improved their performance and to provide others with additional guidance in a fairly unoppressive way.

In consequence, students generate many substantive evaluations of one another's work—and they often surpass more than the minimal length of several sentences on each paper, perhaps because they have relatively few essays to read when the compositions are coauthored. Some students also go back to the threaded discussions to comment on the comments, displaying genuine excitement about textual analysis and critical exchange. Finally, as a whole, students show enhanced analytic skills and self-awareness by the time they reach the end of the semester. In my most recent senior seminar, for instance, a student double majoring in marketing and French demonstrated such extraordinary critical abilities in her threaded commentaries, as well as in her reaction papers, that I strongly urged her to consider a career in education. Although at the time the idea fell well outside her career aspirations, she has since applied for a post through Teach for America and for a French government teaching assistantship through the Fulbright Program. Without the threaded discussions online, I could not have glimpsed her aptitude for teaching.

Enhancing Intermediate-Level Language Courses

I draw on many of the online strategies developed in my literature courses for an intermediate-level class in French oral communication and reading comprehension as well. One such strategy is the threaded discussion function in *ANGEL*. Until 2006, the four-credit course included a heavy homework component in the form of a murder mystery that students accessed on a secure Web site (Oliver and Nelson). Playing the roles of the characters in the mystery, they attempted to solve the crime by sending four rounds of letters to one another revealing clues supplied by the instructor and trying to discover one another's secrets. At first, I divided students into duplicate teams. I then read all the letters for each round and sent separate evaluations, grades, and suggestions for improvement to the students through the course Web-based e-mail. The first time, I received occasional comments on comments but mostly short letters without much elaboration or creativity. I also expended enormous labor assessing performance. When I taught the same oral communication class the next semester, I integrated some features of the literature seminar to address not only the plethora of letters but also the uninspired nature of the messages, despite frequent feedback. Students were paired before being assigned a single character to play together, so that all letters were coauthored; I read every letter for the first round and provided detailed remarks, including grades, to each team of students; I then read and graded only one more round for each team, without revealing which one it was. As a result of this Pirsig-inspired approach, I discovered, the students wrote considerably more in each message, showed greater wit and creativity, and engaged more often in comments on the comments. Moreover, I was able to free up time from grading for other course-related activities, including more personal interactions, such as individual advising sessions, with the students. In part because of the redirection of my energies, it was possible to recruit a higher portion of students than usual from the class for the French major.[2]

In fall 2006, the department changed the course in French oral communication and reading comprehension to three credits, dropping the murder mystery and trading a textbook focused on conversational techniques (Bragger and Rice) for one offering streaming videos of native speakers from a variety of ethnic, regional, and socioeconomic backgrounds (O'Neil). We obtained a site license for the videos, thereby enabling instructors for the course at all locations across the state—along with their students—to access the film clips at home and in the classroom. In the department's advanced-level conversation course, I have often invited native speakers from the university community or francophone visitors to campus to participate in dialogues with my students. At the intermediate level, however, students need to build up their listening, speaking, and vocabulary skills before undertaking such encounters. With the streaming videos, students can read the accompanying text the first time around in an on-campus computer lab or in their dorm room or apartment. They can then practice their aural comprehension either in a second iteration or at a second class showing of the clips.

Since the vocabulary and grammatical constructions in the videos are at times quite advanced, I insist that everyone obtain an unabridged French-English dictionary at the beginning of the semester. I ensure compliance by requiring students to bring the volume to class early on to show that they own (or at least have access to) one. The dictionary provides essential help with understanding the video interview transcripts, since not all the expressions are explained in the textbook. It also proves to be a useful tool for another online project, whereby each student finds an interesting news item at *Yahoo! France* or *Google France* to share with the class. Dividing the class into groups of four of five fosters a lively discussion of current events, eliciting numerous questions for each reporter from the other group members. Time allowing, an exchange regarding similar stories that two or more students have brought in can expand to the entire class in simple dialogues or debates, depending on the number of viewpoints expounded.

This exercise also prepares students in my course for their major enterprise of the semester: developing several original forty-five-minute scenarios (in groups of six to eight students) from their Web-based research on cultural topics or current events in France or another francophone country. Again, students can use the course Web site to communicate with one another about the choice of subject and to draft their scenarios, so that rehearsal times can be kept to a minimum. Since many students are employed fifteen to twenty hours a week, the opportunity to make group decisions and plans through chat rooms and message boards is highly beneficial. In my two fall 2006 intermediate-level language sections, students outdid themselves to demonstrate that they had mastered the course material and French communication skills, that they were informed citizens of the world, and that they had memorized many new words and expressions. One of the best scenarios enacted a series of French news broadcasts about the French riots, featuring on-the-spot interviews of victims and perpetrators, speeches by Jacques Chirac and George Bush, assorted analyses, and related visuals projected onto the full-length screen serving as a backdrop.

At the same time, students' interest in and knowledge of French history, culture, perspectives, and current events are nurtured throughout the semester by yet another feature of online learning: the ability to post links on the course Web site to French news publications (www.lemonde .fr, www.liberation.fr), radio and television broadcasts (www.tf1.fr, www .radiofrance.fr), museum holdings (www.ibiblio.org/wm/paint/auth), maps of France (www.map-of-france.co.uk, www.beyond.fr/map/mpfr.html), information about Africa (www.lonelyplanet.com/africa), metaindexes (www.as.wvu.edu/mlastinger/saucis2.htm, http://hapax.be.sbc.edu), and sites devoted to the various authors and cinematographers studied in the course. By anticipating students' need for relevant Web materials, the instructor can select sites that are appropriate for the students' level and make those materials immediately available. The links can also be referred to during discussions, thus bringing the world into the classroom for all to see and share. Using such links also works well in literature courses at all levels. Indeed, the first time I taught a graduate course in *ANGEL*, the students spontaneously performed this sort of research for the entire class, posting their discoveries on the course Web site and debating the relative merits of different sites. This wealth of material then, quite naturally, found its way into my undergraduate courses in language and literature. I like to think of this continuing, self-perpetuating dialogue as an infinitely expanding universe—a web of learning—that captures students' attention, nourishes their curiosity, and connects them both to the rest of the world and to one another.

My students have embraced these new methodologies with great enthusiasm, perhaps because they have been consistently used in moderation. For each course, most class time is devoted to some type of lecture-discussion format, in which technology is situated in the background, serving multiple support functions. In each case, both the course and instructor evaluations have been outstanding, usually exceeding six on a seven-point scale. In my language classes, students are immersed in francophone materials, whether through Web-based games or streaming video, and their ability to listen, speak, read, and write in French seems to grow naturally as the semester progresses. While most students take intermediate French to complete a minor in the language, many of them so enjoy the experience that they declare a major even before they receive a grade for the course. In the literature classes, writing both papers and threaded discussions in small teams, combined with immediate feedback by the instructor at the beginning of the semester and more random assessments for the rest of the semester, clearly motivates students to become partners in learning. And, while my own students have not quite achieved Pirsig's vision of ceaseless striving for perfection, they cheerfully tolerate a relatively high level of uncertainty about where they stand in terms of grades—perhaps because, in working with one another through electronic collaboration, they come to enjoy the process of learning itself.

Notes

1. Since I offer to drop the two lowest grades out of ten essays in the course, students may effectively submit only eight papers for credit. Before I instituted collaborative online writing assignments, only a few students would elect to write all ten. Indeed, a surprising number would neglect to turn in the first paper, which was due the second week of class, thereby missing the detailed feedback intended to help with future work.

2. In my role as the department's director of undergraduate studies, I am more than a little interested in what pedagogical approaches keep students taking language courses from semester to semester, converting their plan to complete a minor in French into declaring a major or a double major in the discipline.

Works Cited

Bragger, Jeannette D., and Donald B. Rice. *Du tac au tac: Managing Conversations in French*. 3rd ed. Boston: Heinle, 2004. Print.

Bruffee, Kenneth A. *Collaborative Learning: Higher Education, Interdependence, and the Authority of Knowledge.* 2nd ed. Baltimore: Johns Hopkins UP, 1999. Print.

Hanna, Donald E., Michelle Glowacki-Dudka, and Simone Conceição-Runlee. *One Hundred Forty-Seven Practical Tips for Teaching Online Groups: Essentials of Web-Based Education.* Madison: Atwood, 2000. Print.

McAlpine, Iain, and Bill Ashcroft. "Turning Points: Learning from Online Discussions in an Off-Campus Course." *Proceedings of ED-MEDIA.* Ed. Philip Barker and Samuel Rebelsky. Norfolk: Assn. for the Advancement of Computing in Educ., 2002. 1251–57. Print.

Oliver, Walt, and Terri Nelson. *Un meurtre à Cinet Dual Platform: An Internet Mystery Game.* Boston: Heinle, 1998. CD-ROM.

O'Neil, Mary Anne. *La France et la Francophonie: Conversations with Native Speakers.* New Haven: Yale UP, 2005. Print.

Pirsig, Robert M. *Zen and the Art of Motorcycle Maintenance: An Inquiry into Values.* New York: Morrow, 1974. Print.

Michael Papio and Massimo Riva

The *Decameron Web*, a Dozen Years Later

Since 1994, a series of open-access networked resources for late medieval and early modern Italian studies has been developed at Brown University, thanks to close collaboration among past and present members of the Department of Italian Studies, the Department of History, and the Scholarly Technology Group. Our first project, the *Decameron Web*, is a growing online archive of textual and contextual materials for the study and teaching of Giovanni Boccaccio's *Decameron*, conceived as an encyclopedic gateway into late medieval life and culture. We then developed the *Pico Project*, a collaborative online edition and commentary of Giovanni Pico della Mirandola's *Oration on the Dignity of Man*, focused on Pico's idea of a fundamental convergence among major theological and philosophical traditions (Muslim, Jewish, and Christian). We also created the *Florentine Renaissance Resources*, whose *Tratte* and *Catasto* offer a searchable database of tax information for the city of Florence for the years 1427–29, with information about office holders of the Florentine Republic during its 250-year history (1282–1532).[1]

New projects have since been launched, such as *Heliotropia*, a peer-reviewed electronic journal created to provide a widely and readily available forum for research and interpretation to an international community of Boccaccio scholars, and *Conclusiones Nongentae*, or *900 Theses*, a digital edition of another text by Pico, equipped with an annotation system that allows scholars to contribute their notes and commentary to this complex and difficult text. There are also the digital editions of Giovanni Villani's *Nuova Cronica*, which covers Florentine history from biblical and legendary origins to 1348 and represents a fundamental primary source for our understanding of thirteenth- and fourteenth-century Florentine history, and Giovanni Boccaccio's *Esposizioni sopra la* Comedia *di Dante*, a learned commentary on the first seventeen cantos of Dante Alighieri's *Divine Comedy*. Together, these Web sites make up the *Virtual Humanities Lab* at Brown University and provide several online tools for the study and teaching of the literary, intellectual, economic, and social history of fourteenth- and fifteenth-century Italy, including XML-encoded and searchable primary texts, pedagogical tools (charts, maps, electronic concordances, and syllabi linked to hypertextual encyclopedic commentaries and essays), databases, and archival resources, as well as venues for peer-reviewed online publication.

Since 2004, our work has entered a new phase. With the support of the National Endowment for the Humanities, we have moved on to develop these diverse digital resources into a coherent experimental model for collaborative scholarship and pedagogy, envisioning and implementing a highly interactive Web site where educators, scholars, students, and other interested persons will find not only a wealth of information about the civic experience and the literary and intellectual culture of early modern Italy but also a variety of tools specifically conceived for online interaction and collaboration, organized as a multidisciplinary virtual laboratory for the humanities: the *Virtual Humanities Lab* at Brown University.

In this essay, we revisit the most mature of our projects, the *Decameron Web*, more than ten years after its inception, focusing on a retrospective review of its original goals and successes as well as a candid discussion of what we feel were our shortcomings and the objective obstacles we have encountered along the way. Finally, we draw some conclusions on how this project has affected our thinking about the possibilities and the realities of online teaching and research.

Our Original Goals

We proposed the *Decameron Web* as a new interface between the conventional and the electronic components of humanities coursework (reading, group discussion, and writing). We used the basic architectural structure of Boccaccio's text (a miniature society of ten young narrators engaged in storytelling and conversation over ten days, ten novellas per day, one hundred novellas, etc.) as the organizational principle of the model course and of its electronic "playground," which revives the humanistic spirit of communal and collaboratively ludic learning. Hypertextually based communication and exchange of information mimic the interactive nature of the text: students and instructors may replay the narrative game of the *Decameron*. Through collaboration, students become increasingly acquainted with the book's historical and cultural world and with fundamental scholarly and research activities, outside the traditional boundaries of their classroom or campus.

This approach represents, of course, the utopian pedagogical view of the *Decameron Web* as a "digital incunabulum," a transitional object (or space) between the print and the digital world (see National Academy of Sciences). The modular, hypertextual structure of this new playground and learning environment was meant to exploit the specific capabilities of the electronic medium, encouraging an exploratory attitude beyond the standard disciplinary confines. We offer here an example from our 2001 NEH proposal:

> From the opening pages of the project, the student may choose to enter any one of several modules or go directly to the [searchable] text of the *Decameron* itself. The figure below depicts two possible paths of exploration which, though quite short and simplified compared to users' normal stays at the Web, demonstrate the flexibility of navigation.
>
> *Reader One* (whose path is represented by the fine line) has chosen to begin her exploration of the Web by reading a novella. From there, she clicks on the name of a narrator and enters *The Brigata* module. Wanting to find out more about the social milieu of the ten storytellers, she follows a link to the *Society* module. From there, while reading a document on the mercantile world of fourteenth-century Florence, she follows a lead on medieval trade routes to Kaffa, the trading city from which merchant ships brought *The Plague* to Italy. Interested to know more on the subject, she goes on to the *Bibliography*, where she locates a book that could be useful in writing a term paper for her medieval history class.

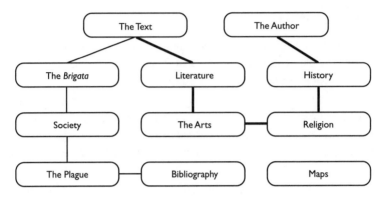

Navigation in the *Decameron Web*

Reader Two (whose path follows the heavy line) decides to begin by learning about Boccaccio. There he reads that the plot of one of the *Decameron*'s stories was influenced by Boccaccio's interest in the Guelph-Ghibelline conflict and enters the *History* module to find out more. He then spots a reference to the Papacy, which takes him to the *Religion* module. There he learns about the importance of art in elucidating religious doctrine (in *The Arts* module). In that section he learns about Botticelli's fascination with Boccaccio's story of Nastagio and enters the *Literature* module to read about the tale's literary sources. Inspired by the description, he moves from there to read it in the original Italian.

The paths drawn not only reflect the independent initiative of a resourceful student but may also be envisioned as alternative learning strategies adopted by a teacher who would like to incorporate the *Decameron Web* into his or her course, guiding students through its resources (using an electronic syllabus, for example) in the same way that he or she would guide them to the library (on an open shelf, students can always find another good book sitting next to the one recommended by their instructor). These two possibilities are not mutually exclusive, of course: in fact, the *Decameron Web*, as it is conceived, allows and encourages both independent and guided use. One important addition made with the complete redesign of our site, between our first and second NEH grants, is an extensive pedagogical module, meant to provide instructors and students with theoretical, methodological, and practical suggestions on how to make better use of the *Decameron Web*'s modular structure and invite them to experiment and report on their own experiences and strategies.

This invitation to collaborate is the second, fundamental pillar on which our project rests: teachers and students are invited to contribute to the *Decameron Web*'s ongoing construction by submitting papers, short essays, images, other kinds of multimedia objects or projects, and even suggestions on how to modify the structure of the *Decameron Web*, making it a more efficient and effective tool for all users. The project staff members, in cooperation with the *Decameron Web*'s editorial board, provided the technical infrastructure and the online assistance for all active collaborators. They were also responsible for the editing, codification, and integration of all external contributions, by students and scholars alike. Students not yet familiar with hypertext, the Internet, or HTML sometimes required additional lab time to help them prepare their projects. Other users found help directly on the site, through the online guide to HTML. (In our 2001 NEH proposal, we described this guide as "the first step toward the creation of a virtual Humanities Lab [or Pedagogy module] where shareware resources are gradually introduced or made available together with theoretical and methodological documents.") Instructors and the editorial board were also charged with regularly monitoring, with the advisory board, the quality of all contributions and keeping students aware of copyright issues. Our hope was that, by getting them interested in actively contributing to the Web, we would discourage them from engaging in Internet plagiarism.

We aimed to offer the *Decameron Web* as an outlet for collective, selective publication. This model of cooperative use and collaborative construction of a shared resource by a growing community of scholars and students is governed by the same rules as a peer-reviewed electronic journal. Contributions can be diverse and aimed at students of various levels: under the supervision of an editorial board and an advisory board composed of major Boccaccio and medieval studies experts (most of the scholars we invited gladly accepted a role in this experiment), students and their teachers can provide accounts of their reading and learning experiences (taking advantage of the hypertextual functions built into the site, such as search engines), as well as contribute information—such as short summaries of scholarly books, essays about a given argument or topic, maps, images, or musical recordings—that will enrich the general reader's experience of the *Decameron Web*. Junior or senior scholars in a variety of disciplines can contribute more sophisticated interpretive or critical essays, the same kind that would otherwise be published in a journal. This diverse input (something similar to yet definitely more structured than a wiki or blog) was meant to foster a new, productive link between original interdisciplinary research and its pedagogical applications, in the classroom and beyond. Ideally, through our site, all users could engage in a collective conversation about and around Boccaccio's great book and its cultural and historical legacy.

Reassessment

In retrospect, we must admit that we were overly optimistic about the willingness of the scholarly community in general to contribute to such a hybrid enterprise, as well as about our own capacity to keep track of our users and provide the extensive services outlined above to a scattered community.

Regarding the first issue, over the years we have received several excellent contributions from scholars engaged in the study of the *Decameron* or related aspects (such as essays on late medieval music and the *Decameron* or essays on early modern printing and book illustration, connected to a gallery made available on our site of illustrations from fifteenth- and sixteenth-century editions of the book from the Brown and the Harvard libraries). These contributions have undoubtedly increased the encyclopedic, interdisciplinary profile and usefulness of the *Decameron Web*. Yet scholarly contributions of the type that would be published in a literary journal have not abounded. At the time of our second NEH application, for example, we envisioned our site as a venue for preprint publications, by both young and established scholars, work in progress that, taking advantage of the feedback from online readers, could later be published in print in a more definitive form. Contributions could be composed in conventional word-processing software or hypertext, and a prominent place would be reserved for hypermedia projects creatively combining visual and textual components.

Either because we did not sufficiently promote this idea or because the scholarly community in the humanities is not as inclined as colleagues in the sciences to prepublish research in progress, scholarly contributions amounted to fewer than we had anticipated. In general, we have found that some scholars (including young scholars, perhaps because they are in the pretenure phase of their careers) are reluctant to enter a new arena in which the results of their research are placed side by side, in a public space, with the primary texts and pedagogical materials. For various reasons, ranging from the nature of specialization to the way we conceive

teaching even in the Internet age, research and pedagogy are still separated in our profession. Of course, we feel that the new type of experimental learning space made possible by the digital platform, in which research in progress and teaching resources can be simultaneously accessed
and developed, to facilitate their cross-fertilization, is still a valid objective in designing a Web resource like the *Decameron Web* (as well as the
Virtual Humanities Lab). We have realized, however, that it takes time to
modify habits and mentalities. Despite the abundant moral support lent
by scholars of all stripes to our endeavor, the current clear distinction in
academia between pedagogical and scholarly publication, together with
its relative system of rewards, tends (in practice if not in theory) to discourage colleagues from freely contributing the fruits of their research in
an environment that has not yet been officially recognized as a worthy
investment of their energies (see, e.g., Domínguez). In short, the strategy
we have adopted must aim at training scholars to train themselves.

Looking back, we feel we were not entirely successful in creating in
the *Decameron Web*'s interface a sufficient distinction between a scholarly
and a pedagogical contribution, a distinction that could reassure a scholar
that his or her essay would receive adequate prominence or recognition as
a scholarly product and not be equated to an (albeit brilliant) student paper. We thought that the general presentation, the peer-reviewed and individual attribution (byline) of all our materials would be sufficient to
provide such a reassurance, but we underestimated the difficulty of creating such a hierarchical space in what was presented as a collaborative space.
Whatever the reason, this failure was at the origin of the decision to create a separate, completely independent and more traditional outlet for the
publication of scholarly contributions to Boccaccio studies: the electronic
journal *Heliotropia* (see Papio). Appropriately distributed links can lead
users from the various sections of the *Decameron Web* to specific essays
published in *Heliotropia*, thus providing a bridge between one space and
the other. Yet essays, articles, and reviews published in *Heliotropia* do not
feature links either to those works of Boccaccio that we have made available in the *Decameron Web* or to other pertinent materials on the site.
This compromise solution, while protecting the intellectual property of
the authors, falls somewhat short of our original intention of creating
that homogeneous (if not seamless) experimental collaborative space, that
self-contained online laboratory, at the intersection of teaching and research practices and forms.

Concerning our somewhat limited ability to keep track of users and to provide them with an efficient platform for their input, we did not entirely succeed in this task. There are various reasons, not all of which have to do with our limited resources or are to be viewed as our weaknesses alone (to date the site is run by a small editorial board, composed of a core group of collaborators, scholars, and graduate students—we are the general coeditors). Some reasons reflect the evolution of the Web, and some the evolution of digital culture. Indeed, some are due to our success, judging from the enthusiastic feedback we have received from students, teachers, and users in general, and from the recognition our site has received from learning institutions worldwide (witness the countless positive reviews and honorable mentions and links to major library and university programs or individual course pages accumulated over the years).

We originally assigned the responsibility for the site's maintenance to its editorial board, based in the Department of Italian Studies and the medieval studies community at Brown University. The department committed to earmarking, as a cost-sharing contribution for the duration of the project and beyond, a teaching and research assistantship for an advanced graduate student in the doctoral program to devote up to twenty hours a week exclusively to the site. While we have maintained and even exceeded our promises of matching the generous support we received from NEH (in addition to graduate research fellowships, a Mellon postdoctoral fellow was assigned to the *Decameron Web* for two years, 2000–02), it is clear that a project like ours also faces problems related to a fundamental characteristic of digital culture in what we have called the age of digital incunabula: the openness of a work continuously in progress, which, to be up to date, must keep up with the fast-moving pace of technological change, as well as with the evolution of digital culture, which encourages individual consumption, multitasking, and interactive real-time communication.

The major effort we engaged in with the support of NEH was the encoding of Boccaccio's original text (in Italian and a copyright-free English translation). All primary materials (including the *Decameron* and two other works by Boccaccio, *Corbaccio* and *Fiammetta*) were encoded in SGML (standard general markup language) using TEI-Lite (Text Encoding Initiative) standards (later updated to XML), to provide for detailed searches based on particularly relevant text-specific metadata and to facilitate linking from the text to the encyclopedic modules and vice versa. Contextual materials (essays, summaries, and individual entries) are all encoded in HTML (hypertext markup language), and the results of the searches were also displayed in HTML. The metadata included names of hundreds of characters and places found in the hundred novellas, as well as additional data including the social status and the narrative role of the main characters. This encoding, aimed at making the text searchable according to alternative criteria (for example, the location of the novellas and their social settings, their basic narrative structure or typology),[2] was also used in the construction of bibliographic databases and glossaries. Moreover, a complete set of concordances was added (in PDF), linked to an example of how concordances can be used to study specific phraseology in which register or dialectal speech lends deeper meaning to the text. At the time of our second grant application, the metadata-enriched text, encoded in SGML, was searchable only through *Dynatext*, a commercial application (also adopted by Brown University's Scholarly Technology Group for its *Women Writers Project*) that later became obsolete and unsupported. This factor, of course, made it difficult for us to implement consistently the new textual search functions envisioned as the core of our project and has resulted in the decision to move toward open-source applications and open-access formats. This move happened within the framework of the *Virtual Humanities Lab*, of which the *Decameron Web* is now an integral part (search functions are performed through *Philologic*). Within this framework, not only will new search capabilities be implemented that will enable users to take full advantage of the encoding already painstakingly performed off-line, but the process of encoding (and annotating) the text will also become part of interactive online collaboration (see Riva and Zafrin).

As the *Decameron Web* has gradually grown into the public domain, it has become increasingly clear that we cannot systematically control the way it is accessed and used. This outcome, while consistent with the original goals of our project (an author does not have control over the way his or her work is read or misread), can interfere with our ability to guide the *Decameron Web*'s evolution and improvement. An example of this difficulty is reflected in a recent request we received from NEH to provide some statistical record of our users over the years. While Brown (like many institutions) maintains what amounts to a counter, registering the number of hits on its servers, it is practically impossible to parse this raw data to know even approximately how many of these hits correspond to actual users and how many are simply the effect of bots or spiders sweeping the

Internet. Moreover, this kind of statistical data cannot be easily translated into useful formulas for improving the site's design. (The *Decameron Web* is currently accessed between thirty thousand and forty thousand times each day.) Referring to figure 1, for example, it would be very useful to know which paths are most traveled and which alternatives could be suggested and made more efficiently available, through the pedagogy module, electronic syllabi, and other similar tools. Knowing how the search engines are used and what results they provide could also contribute to a helpful critical record. Being able to document the actual use of the *Decameron Web* (including the sequence of pages viewed, the amount of time spent on each page, the total number of accesses made from unique IP addresses, and so on) would provide precious feedback. As the number of linked documents or pages on the *Decameron Web* grows, it becomes necessary not only to make our returning or recurring users aware of what is new on the site (a simple feature many similar sites adopt is a pointer to recently revised or added pages) but also to envision modifications in design that may further improve the efficiency (and navigability) of its modular structure.

One tool we have adopted to keep track of our users and encourage their input is a guest book that gives them the chance to provide general feedback about the site and let us know whether they would like to collaborate or contribute. Unfortunately, while it was initially a very valuable resource, this tool has now become practically useless because of the difficulty of filtering out the ever-increasing amount of spam and we have discontinued it. For the same reason, we were forced to discontinue a chat room with which we experimented years ago, although we have continued to use local newsgroups or e-mail discussion lists, and we have introduced a blog.

It is clear to us that a blog where all those engaged in reading and studying the *Decameron* for whatever purpose were able to exchange their views and reading experiences would fit perfectly with the main objective of our site. Yet we are faced with a challenge: how does one effectively monitor and maintain the focus and integrity of such an open and interactive forum? This concern directly translates into a design issue: what place should such a tool or venue be assigned within the existing framework of the *Decameron Web*? A central and prominent place would definitely tip the balance between filtered, peer-reviewed, structured information and users' input and feedback (both essential for the success of our experiment). This could lead to a radical redesign of the *Decameron Web*. A solution could be, instead (and we are inclined toward this option), to introduce the blog as part of the existing pedagogy module, making it the venue for a discussion about the methodological issues involved in using such a tool, as well as a way of documenting the various ways in which it has been used by instructors. The blog would therefore be more of an option for teachers, who could customize it as part of their pedagogical strategies, than a resource for general users (although nothing in principle would hinder such users from participating in the discussion). Links from the blog to the various sections of the *Decameron Web* could add yet another dimension to the site's modular structure.

We hope that this retrospective glance at how our thinking about online resources and tools has evolved may be useful from both a historical and a critical point of view. In general, we feel that our thinking has largely followed the mainstream evolution of digital culture in the age of digital incunabula, in envisioning new sites or environments where traditional practices in humanities teaching and research can be performed—and reformed—according to the specific capabilities of the new media and of emerging applications.

The intensified interactivity and connectivity generated by distributed computing has fostered an intellectual revolution of sorts, enabling scholars and students to communicate and interact with one another at a distance and thus promoting new forms of online authorship and collaboration. These new communicative options have significantly modified the way we conceive of and visualize the primary sources of our research as well as the materials and the methodologies of our teaching and learning. Indeed, words and images and textual corpora or data collections are all evolving along with the new media in which they are embodied. A utopian landscape begins to take shape: emerging technologies seem able to reconnect the social and mental spaces into which research and learning practices have been traditionally separated (archive, library, classroom), creating an apparently (or potentially) boundless environment where diverse routine and highly specialized intellectual functions can be performed together or increasingly linked to one another in consistent ways. In short, the solitary working space of the humanist, inherited from the monastic tradition, has been replaced by a virtual collaborative space where multiple activities can take place simultaneously, in an ongoing and self-enriching dialogue inherited from humanists' dialectics of the Renaissance. Yet in this extraordinarily challenging and stimulating context, where new networked resources for scholars are introduced almost on a daily basis, there has not been a consistent attempt to integrate strategically these new research tools into a viable multidisciplinary curriculum for the humanities.

Standardized tools for teaching are increasingly made available to instructors and students by specialized software companies; these are often adopted out of the box (or only slightly customized) by colleges and universities. While standardization seems to make some sense institutionally, it does not necessarily address the needs or reflect the specific innovations arising from collaborative multidisciplinary research in a given area. The experimental systems described above, for example, include fairly sophisticated tools for managing a course, for communicating with students, and even for storing materials preorganized for class presentation. Lacking is content material (texts in particular), structured in such a way as to be the result and promotion of a variety of research activities as an integral part of the teaching process. Instead of the research generating a conceptual framework for the integration of technology into the curriculum, the availability of standard technologies is providing a limited and limiting platform for curriculum design.[3] Moreover, a gap seems to persist and even to be widening between teaching and advanced research in the humanities. With university presses finding it difficult to keep up with the need of scholars in the humanities to publish the specialized books demanded for tenure and career advancement, the introduction of new tools and forms of peer-reviewed scholarly publication is ever more crucial. To date, however, no wholly satisfactory solution to this problem has been found.

The Brown *Virtual Humanities Lab* was conceived as a response to some of these questions and problems: a venue where the process of research and digital publication around a common focus (scholarly editions of classic texts) can be directly transformed into the medium of an enriched teaching practice. In this, we have been faithful to our original inspiration. Our current vision (and work in progress) is to provide a platform for various shared activities, ranging from scholarly editions of an expanding minicorpus of early modern texts to team-taught online workshops and seminars based on those editions. Scholars working in teams, from a variety of international locations, will be able to contribute to the production of user-oriented digital editions (such as that of the *Decameron*), as well as to provide commentaries and interpretations of key texts of the Italian humanist tradition in an online, interactive, and collaborative working environment. Educators will be able to adopt and test these digital editions in their multidisciplinary teaching, along with other systematically linked contextual resources developed on our site, including galleries of images, historical timelines, and collections of retrievable archival data. The Brown *Virtual Humanities Lab* will also provide scholars and educators with a forum for discussions about current developments in humanities scholarship and pedagogy, including reviews and critical evaluations of related projects and online resources.

This fundamental experimental attitude toward both research and pedagogical tools is reflected in the idea of organizing our comprehensive projects' framework as a laboratory for the humanities. From this point of view, the humanities still have much to learn from the sciences, especially about collaborative research and documentation or publication of work in progress. On the other hand, the sciences may also have something to learn from the humanities about pedagogical issues and the goals of education for both individuals and society as a whole. The humanities, however, are under particular pressure to develop new modes of thought and pedagogical strategies as their traditional domain, historical memory, is challenged by technological developments that not only exponentially increase our ability to memorize and quickly access large repositories of information but also qualitatively to modify the memorization and the transmission of cultural memory as such. More specifically, the structuring of textual and historical data in the new media is done in such a way that the almost instantaneous access we gain to these increasingly large repositories of documents and texts is not necessarily accompanied by the critical information necessary to understand their specific historical dimension. From this perspective, we feel that the effort of making "a million books" (Crane) available to scholars and students or readers in automated searchable formats, through various initiatives, such as that launched by Google or the Open Content Alliance, must be accompanied by a comparable effort to create the critical infrastructure (metadata-based access arrangements) in which these millions of books (or texts or documents) can actually be parsed, read, and understood in pedagogically creative and scholarly meaningful ways. In other words, a concerted coordination is necessary in the construction of digital libraries and the creation of this infrastructure, which must also be a collaborative effort, one that can take advantage of the possibilities offered by distributed and networked computing.

Many of the goals and concerns mentioned here were already present at the outset of the *Decameron Web*. Begun only a couple of years after the big bang of the World Wide Web, the *Decameron Web* was one of the earliest attempts, at least by the Italian and medieval studies communities, to take immediate advantage of the possibilities offered by first- and second-generation browser technology for designing a new kind of pedagogical space and testing a series of practices theorized in some pioneering books and essays of the early or mid-1990s.[4] As the Web came of age over the following years, and up to the advent of blogs and wikis, new avenues for collaborative pedagogical experimentation have opened up, and the *Decameron Web*, although based on sound principles, now seems a product of an earlier stage—similar to an old house standing on a solid foundation but in need of renovation.

Notes

1. These diverse online resources have been developed independently thanks to a combination of major external grants from the National Endowment for the Humanities awarded to both the *Decameron Web* and the *Florentine Renaissance Resources*, internal grants from Brown Computing and Information Services and the Scholarly Technology Group, and one-time gifts from private donors. The *Pico Project* was made possible by an international research agreement between Brown University and the University of Bologna in Italy.

2. Students found this unique type of search function to be especially useful in guiding themselves through the often very complex text. One student, for example, used it to locate all the widows mentioned in the *Decameron* and to analyze the function of each according to the particular narrative exigencies of the stories in which she appeared. Another used it to generate a list of stories told by a narrator in which a certain geographic location was mentioned. From there, he put together an analysis that was far more sophisticated than is usually possible at the undergraduate level.

3. More promising, of course, are initiatives such as IMS (instruction management systems), aimed at developing open-source specifications for the organization and delivery of educational content, including standard metadata systems such as LOM (learning object metadata).

4. See, for example, Bolter; Landow; and Joyce.

Works Cited

Bolter, Jay David. *Writing Space: The Computer, Hypertext, and the History of Writing*. Hillsdale: Erlbaum, 1991. Print.

Crane, Gregory. "What Do You Do with a Million Books?" *D-Lib Magazine* 12.3 (2006): n. pag. Web. 4 Sept. 2006.

Decameron Web. Ed. Massimo Riva and Michael Papio. Brown U, 1994. Web. 4 Sept. 2006.

Domínguez, Frank. "The Path before Us: Suggestions for Managing the Transition of the Spanish Middle Ages to the Electronic Age." *La corónica* 33.1 (2004): 229–45. Print.

Florentine Renaissance Resources: Online Tratte of Office Holders, 1282–1532. Ed. David Herlihy, R. Burr Litchfield, Anthony Molho, and Roberto Barducci. Brown U, 2000. Web. 4 Sept. 2006.

Joyce, M. *Of Two Minds: Hypertext Pedagogy and Poetics.* Ann Arbor: U of Michigan P, 1995. Print.

Landow, George P. *Hyper Text: The Convergence of Contemporary Critical Theory and Technology.* Baltimore: Johns Hopkins UP, 1992. Print.

National Academy of Sciences. *Beyond Productivity: Information, Technology, Innovation, and Creativity.* Natl. Acads., 2003. Web. 4 Sept. 2006.

Papio, Michael. "¿Cuál será el futuro de la publición de revistas elecrónicas en las humanidades?" *La corónica* 37.1 (2008): 365–86. Print.

Pico della Mirandola, Giovanni. *Conclusiones CM.* Ed. Francesco Borghesi, Pier Cesare Bori, Dino Buzzetti, Paul Caton, Saverio Marchignoli, Michael Papio, and Massimo Riva. Brown U, 2002. Web. 4 Sept. 2006.

Pico Project. Ed. Pier Cesare Borgi, Michael Papio, and Massimo Riva. U Bologna, Coll. of the Holy Cross, and Brown U, n.d. Web. 4 Sept. 2006.

Riva, Massimo, and Vika Zafrin. "Collaborative Scholarship: Rethinking Editing on the Digital Platform." *Proceedings, Association for Digital Humanities.* Paris: Digital Humanities, 2006. 167–70. Print.

Virtual Humanities Lab. Brown U, 2004. Web. 4 Sept. 2006.

Women Writers Project. Brown U, 1991. Web. 4 Sept. 2006.

William Kuskin

Hybrid World Literature: Literary Culture and the New Machine

> *"In the months after I got back the hundreds of helicopters I'd flown in began to draw together until they'd formed a collective meta-chopper, and in my mind it was the sexiest thing going; saver-destroyer, provider-waster, right hand–left hand, nimble, fluent, canny and human; hot steel, grease, jungle-saturated canvas webbing, sweat cooling and warming up again, cassette rock and roll in one ear and door-gun fire in the other, fuel, heat, vitality and death, death itself, hardly an intruder."*
>
> *In this new machine, which does not, like the older modernist machinery of the locomotive or the airplane, represent motion, but which can only be represented in* motion, *something of the mystery of the new postmodernist space is concentrated.*
>
> > —from Fredric Jameson, *Postmodernism; or, The Cultural Logic of Late Capitalism*, in which he quotes Michael Herr's *Dispatches*

From 1998 to 2005, I taught world literature at the University of Southern Mississippi. In 2004, I participated in a hybrid course designed by Michael Salda in 2001 with the generous support of a Pew grant. The course, Hybrid English 203, used *WebCT* to deliver biweekly, traditional-format lectures as streaming video and requires two essays and several exams.[1] As a traditional lecture course staffed by tenure-track faculty members and supported by graduate assistants, it avoided the preformatted structure of many online courses. Entirely accessible through the Web, the course suffered neither the problems of space and scheduling nor the ensuing limitations on enrollment of lecture-hall classes. From the students' perspective, its main attraction was its flexibility—come to class regularly or hold a nine-to-five job and watch the lectures at night; if day care collapses on a Tuesday, catch the lecture after bedtime and miss nothing; if another class conflicts, violà: Hybrid English 203 runs all the time. From the administration's perspective, it allowed a midsize university to connect full-time faculty members to upwards of five hundred students each semester through a single course. From the instructor's perspective, it maintained a tried-and-true format while delivering record student credit hours. Indeed, Hybrid English 203 produced so many credit hours that it was possible to split the teaching duties across two or three faculty members, effectively creating half-semester course releases. Yet Hybrid English 203 also chewed up instructor and student alike, dissipating the human element of the humanities into the alternating current of the Web, the icy coldness of digitalization, and the electric heat of a wired identity. Enter the new machine: a combination of hard circuit board and human effort, Hybrid English 203 reduced the problems of online and traditional learning to the single issue of information management.

I have come to see Hybrid English 203 as a concentration of postmodern space. In this space, our identities as teachers and students were not merely represented but represented as information *in motion*—literally as ones and zeroes streaming from server to user and back. Here is all the paradoxical wonder of Michael Herr's metachopper: saver-destroyer, online technology amplifies the possibilities of communicating the humanities while simultaneously threatening to cut out their heart, transforming each participant into a twenty-first-century version of B. F. Skinner's pigeon, who, pecking away at a series of positive and negative stimuli, hardly notices the unavoidable flatness of life as screen. This point is at once historical and transcendental: historical because it marks a specific juncture of technology and learning in the twenty-first century; transcendental because it hits on a larger truth about the relation between the production and consumption of literary culture that obtains for all texts. That is, from the clay tablets of *Gilgamesh* through book technology to the arrival of *WebCT*, textual forms have always been intimate with the articulation of identity. The future of online education for the humanities, therefore, involves not only the implementation of online teaching but also our understanding of the process of symbolic production of ourselves as human in the history of textual technology.

Initially, I was one of a team of lecturers who taught in the course. When Michael Salda went on sabbatical, I took over management duties and began experimenting with the course's structure and content. While I left the fundamental design of the course intact—a traditional lecture filmed and archived for online viewing through *WebCT*—I introduced a substantial component on the history of the book, simplified the testing procedure, developed extra-credit assignments, and added a custom textbook, *World Literatures: A Reader*. When I became chair of the Department of English, I devolved much of the daily business of e-mail and assessment to two graduate-student course coordinators. These changes led me to the conclusion that the synthetic relation between communication technology and identity transcends any particular mode of production. In any medium, literary culture represents identity, and in what follows I argue that the challenge of the postmodern space inherent in Web-based pedagogy is to facilitate the humanist connection between material and symbolic forms of human representation.

One particularly suggestive evocation of the connection between technology and identity occured when the students opened the first assignment. This was a clip from the end of *The Matrix*, when the hero, Neo, is finally realized as "The One" and so learns that his enemies, and by extension the world in which he has been bound, is entirely constructed of digital code. The final clip created a visually striking screen: on the top layer floated the cascading wall of green digital code from *The Matrix*. Beneath this lay the *WebCT* environment, specifically Hybrid English 203's "Weekly Agenda/Videos" page, which the student had to access to derive the video clip. This page displayed the entire course as a week-by-week list of links, each accompanied by a separate "Action Link." The weekly links opened onto a prose overview of that week's business with individual links to the hour-and-fifteen-minute lectures filmed live each Tuesday and Thursday. The links expanded to reveal additional links specific to each week: notes, texts, and ancillary materials such as *The Matrix* clip. The page was framed on the left by the *WebCT* apparatus—the "Course Menu" that brought the student to other activities specific to Hybrid English 203, such as the essay assignments, exams, or e-mail—and on top by the Hybrid

English 203 logo, designed by John Wang, featuring an alternating textual fragment: a bit of cuneiform, of cursive Arabic script, of typewritten manuscript, of handwritten letter. The individual student's Web browser dominated the entire visual experience, while behind or to the right and left laid whatever other programs he or she may have had running at the moment: *iTunes*, *Skype*, solitaire. This early screen of Hybrid English 203 was, then, like all computer screens, a palimpsest. On one level its meaning was tremendously obvious, no more than a video clip of a popular movie delivered over the Web; on another level it was a collage of texts—of *The Matrix*'s imaginary code, of the historical texts in the banner, of *WebCT*'s terse directive labels, and of all the information broadcast by competing programs. On a third level, then, far from being obvious the screen was truly mind-boggling, an overwhelming array of moving and static images transmitting latent choices and future responsibilities to the user. And on yet a fourth level lay the substrate of invisible computer language informing these screen images. This fourth level in fact returned us to the first, that animated stream of green code. In this case, the screen was a loop of code moving from fiction to substrate and back to fiction.

In this recursive circuit, Hybrid English 203 embodied the contradictions of information management in the humanities in both its structure and its content by using media to talk about media. All courses do this to some extent, and in this regard Hybrid English 203 offered a fairly traditional study of world literature. The usual suspects were present and accounted for: Gilgamesh, Aeschylus, Murasaki Shikibu, Sundiata, William Shakespeare, Jorge Luis Borges, Nadine Gordimer, and so forth. Through these texts the course engaged its students by the same terms as any sophomore-level core humanities requirement: in return for the concentration required by close reading, it offered the rediscovery of literature. Yet the fact that Hybrid English 203 occured on a computer defined its unavoidable difference. The texts, the assignments, even the lecturers were all quantified, distilled down to a finite and numerical stream of information. The logic implied by digitization, by the green veil of computer code, by the various downloads and uploads that constitute the curriculum, was that literary knowledge can be entirely encased in computer technology. If part of the humanities' relation to knowledge is that literary language is a special category of information, one that is figural and never fixed, Hybrid English 203 implied otherwise: no matter how much the course emulates the humanist project, its form argued that all information can be digitalized and once digitized managed by an end user trained in navigating the proper trail of links. As much as my lecture streaming into a desktop computer might insist that the past contains an infinite sophistication about metaphor, that the existence of a metaphor implies a vast (though unrecorded) imaginative endeavor, the computer that represents me suggests otherwise—that the past is forever contained and in this containment is in fact exceeded by the present. The paradox of the postmodern space is that it is, as Fredric Jameson's reading of Michael Herr suggests, a saver-destroyer. In this, Hybrid English 203 evoked something of Ray Kurzweil's notion of the cool, zero-energy-consuming "'ultimate portable computer' [that will] be able to perform the equivalent of all human thought over the last ten thousand years (assumed at ten billion human brains for ten thousand years) in ten microseconds" (135). Who needs to read the past, one might ask, when it is recorded on silicon? Who needs to read the present, one might continue, when such an effort will be superseded in a matter of microseconds by the computer itself? What matters metaphor as a form of knowledge when we have the Internet?

In juxtaposition to this line of reasoning, I presented the course's encounter with technology as both historical and theoretical. To this end, I required the students to purchase *World Literatures: A Reader*, which contained an introduction to the course, many of its readings, and an appendix of writing materials. *World Literatures* came bundled with separately bound books, which the faculty members could vary from semester to semester. Among these was Andrew George's excellent edition of *Gilgamesh*. I posted George's translation of the prologue to *Gilgamesh* in the weekly agenda for week 1 so I could discuss it on the very first day of class, when many students had yet to get to the Textbook Center. This prologue is thought to have been added to the poem by a particular scribe, Sin-liqe-uninni, and like *The Matrix* it reflects on the textual construction of reality. Here is part of George's translation:

> See its wall like a strand of wool,
>   view its parapet that none could copy!
> Take the stairway of a bygone era,
>   draw near to Eanna, seat of Ishtar the goddess,
> that no later king could ever copy!
>
> Climb Uruk's wall and walk back and forth!
>   Survey its foundations, examine the brickwork!

Were its bricks not fired in an oven?
  Did the Seven Sages not lay its foundations?

[A square mile is] city, [a square mile] date-grove, a square mile is
  clay-pit, half a square mile the temple of Ishtar:
  [three square miles] and a half is Uruk's expanse.
[See] the tablet-box of cedar,
  [release] its clasp of bronze!
[Lift] the lid of its secret,
  [pick] up the tablet of lapis lazuli and read out
the travails of Gilgamesh, all that he went through.   (1–2)

George's translation is unique among the recent efforts to deal with the poem in that it highlights the ways an edition mediates the original work for the modern reader, here marking the restoration of the text with square brackets but elsewhere carefully noting conjecture and including ellipses to indicate textual lacunae. The result is perhaps an awkward read but also one that underscores the distance between the historical and the modern versions of the text. This distance seems to be part of Sin-liqe-uninni's prologue as well: it juxtaposes the city's inimitability ("none could copy") against the vividness of his description; indeed it recognizes the poem as but one copy of this reality ("[pick] up the tablet of lapis lazuli and read out / the travails of Gilgamesh"). The city of Uruk and the story of Gilgamesh are thus irreproducible but also represented to our imaginations in the here and now and therefore entirely reproducible. This overlap between city and epic is at least twofold: historically, because the Mesopotamians wrote on clay bricks and tablets, both are literally texts; figuratively, both also transcend history to figure intangible aspects about Mesopotamian civilization, its durability, its sophistication, and its values. Thus the prologue seems to acknowledge a paradox between being and representation, between the past and the present, but also to argue that the text can bridge this paradox—that the ineffable qualities of culture can be captured in a physical format—and it makes this argument overtly ("Take the stairway of a bygone era") as well as rhetorically in the direct address to the reader commanding him or her to "See its wall," "Climb [the] wall," "Survey its foundations," "[See] the tablet-box," "[Lift] the lid," "[pick] up the tablet," and, most profound, "read." The opening of *Gilgamesh* suggests that texts weave the past and the present, the dead and the living, the canny and human with the abstract and artificial. It is an allegory for reading. On one level, this allegory figures a straightforward representation

Figure I. Front cover of *World Literatures*

of reading. On another, it figures temporality in the brackets and variants that remind us that this fiction is very much a mediated one, a story told at some remove. On a third, it demonstrates that this distance creates a good deal of noise, making the text almost impenetrable even as it seeks to represent it fairly. And so, on the fourth level, the text recalls the

Front Cover: *Mind Wandering*, by Angela Backes (April 2003), oil pastels.

Back Cover: *Literature Opens the Window to the World*, by Regina Gray (March 2005), mosaic.

Literature allows people to experience the world without ever leaving the comforts of their home. The hands in this piece of art could either represent someone looking out of the window of their home onto the world, or they could represent someone ready to endure life's journey.

Back Cover Legend:
Blue: The sky representing day and night
Red: The shutters of the window
Green: Changing seasons (grass changing colors during different seasons)
Yellow: The Road of Life
Grey Rocks: Life's Obstacles
Hands: Represent all ethnicities

PEARSON
Custom Publishing

ISBN 0-536-25778-7

9 780536 257789

Figure 2. Back cover of *World Literatures*

literal layers of code, the presence and absence of wedge marks that must be translated into English if the text is to speak to us in the present, which the story depicts in the first place. Again, we are faced with recursive palimpsest: in both *The Matrix* and *Gilgamesh*, the literal layer of code produces a higher figuration of information management that functions and therefore must be read differently.

We can make a similar observation for the object of the book by look-ing briefly at the covers of *World Literatures,* which were created by stu-dents for an extra-credit contest. The front cover is an oil pastel created by Angela Backes for an earlier version of a world literature course I taught at the University of Southern Mississippi (fig. 1); the back cover is a mosaic by Regina Gray, a student from my second semester of teaching Hybrid English 203 (fig. 2). Backes's piece directly shows the stories of the world emerging from the reader's head; Gray's is a more abstract meditation on the same topic. Both are about the way literature inspires a journey, as if to ask the readers of the book to take the stairway to a bygone era. Moreover, the covers confound the twin notion that books are remote and nontech-nological, for *World Literatures* demonstrates the same thing as the "Weekly Agenda"—our culture's amazing level of technology. Further, the presence of students' artwork demonstrates their involvement in the construction of the book. This parallel works both ways, not only demonstrating that books are highly technological objects but also recalling that the Internet is simply a text in another format. The fascination of the Internet is, in part as Jameson says, that the new postmodernist space presents representation so as to appear *in motion.* Though it is easy to cast the Web as immaterial in this way, ultimately it is based in materiality—in computers, servers, and pages written out by faculty members. The commonness of books have somewhat inured us to this parallel, and so the digital presentation of texts tends to limber them up. Yet textual machines have always deliv-ered literature as dynamic, and literacy involves not just understanding how to construe writing into words but also some sense of how to operate the material apparatus. As Sin-liqe-uninni reminds us, texts have always depended on their readers' imaginative participation to achieve their ef-fect. Thus I argue that the quality of motion invested in the Web represents not a fundamental break with historical textuality so much as an exten-sion of it. All texts are highly dynamic objects. Our goal is to learn to read them on multiple levels.

The fundamental observation brought out in *Gilgamesh* is not far from *The Matrix.* "Holy shit," says Neo as he is jacked into the main-frame of reality and realizes textuality allows him to absorb the knowl-edge of the ages. This too is what *Gilgamesh* offers whomever will upload it: Gilgamesh is "He who saw the Deep," and the prologue promises to communicate "all that he went through" (George 1). And like *The Matrix,* the prologue to *Gilgamesh* is revealed to be entirely a construction by the poem's end, for just as we realize with Neo that his imaginary world is entirely textual, the reader who makes it to tablet 11 of *Gilgamesh* realizes that the powerful introductory voice is actually Gilgamesh's, looped back to the beginning: Gilgamesh is "The One." *Gilgamesh* and *The Matrix* offer up an invitation to imagine the godhead as a metatextual being. These are texts about texts: texts constructed by cultures inventing and refining their textual machines. As such they explore what it is to be literate by examining how a person both constructs and is constructed through communication technologies, and in both cases, literacy at its most powerful involves the manipulation of time: for *Gilgamesh* it is the ability to move from the present into a bygone era; for *The Matrix*, to stop bullets. Fueled by the imagination, texts are time machines far more effective than the contraptions of levers and dials envisaged by H. G. Wells.

At a root level, our goal as humanities teachers is to teach our students to operate these textual machines. Indeed, this objective is a theoretical truth for literary studies, a discipline that fundamentally grapples with reading the timeless work of art from the concrete text trapped in the mixed amber of technology and history. The medium is the message: Gilgamesh carves his story in stone and so becomes immortal; Murasaki Shikibu expresses the aesthetic intangible of the Heian court through the *Monogatari*; the Koran reveals the divinity of the book across its suras; Shakespeare emerges as the definitive English author through a folio assembled after his death. In each case, writing comments on its transmission, and this truth of literary culture is profoundly relevant to the denizens of the so-called information age: the professional-managerial class no less than Neo's archenemy, Agent Smith, no less than King Gilgamesh himself is constituted by communication technology. Thus I suggest that the students of Hybrid English 203 were not atomized among the many computers plugged into the course but instead connected to one another and to history through the imaginative technology of textual machines—cuneiform tablets, papyrus scrolls, vellum codices, digital downloads, college anthologies, and English 203 essays. Students may still avoid world literature, they may still prefer to watch Keanu Reeves than to read about Gilgamesh, but by their own admission they were stimulated by the course, because, I argue, it spoke directly to their material existence. How the particular materiality evoked them is a matter of history; that they were evoked at all transcends history and locates them in the imagination of textual identity.

Textual identity occupies a central place in the World Wide Web. Private-sector businesses online are tremendously successful because they manage information so as to continually refine the ways of identifying the individual. The attraction of Web sites like *MySpace* and *Facebook* and of the endless personalized pages across the virtual malls of the World Wide Web, indeed the sole task of the countless bots that traverse the Internet, is to write individuals as public subjects. In this matrix, as Karl Marx argues, "production, distribution, exchange, and consumption are identical" (139), for each contributes to the birth of the subject. Capitalism, no less than literature, is engaged in the representation of the self.

A good deal of online teaching plays like a board game set up for a single player. Chronology replaces the spinner as the student moves through the syllabus landing on assignments and making choices. The outcome is fixed: barring some external catastrophe, the student will arrive at the finish line, and the computer will tally up his or her earnings. The problem for online humanities courses, as with any humanities course holding to such a model, is that this mode of operation runs counter to the demands interpretation makes on the reader and thus undercuts its rewards as well. If online education is to do more than process students along a limited-access network of chutes and ladders, it needs to play into the strength of the humanities.

Toward this end, I worked to create Hybrid English 203 as a place of identity while nevertheless processing a huge amount of students distributed across various locations, by asking them to reflect on the technology they used. Self-reflection takes time, which shocked the students who came to the course thinking it would be more manageable, more contained than the classroom version. Even the Hybrid English 203 banner worked to create an environment, a brand identification, that reinforceed the connection between the Web space and the literary culture of the humanities. Thus I define literary culture as a synthesis between textual and symbolic forms that articulate the self. Such a literary culture is an imaginary totality. That is, its literal forms are only powerful insofar as they figure a greater symbolic sense that remains only partially articulated. Just as material texts gesture toward the work of art but never capture its imaginative perfection, literary culture represents the individual by implication, always leaving imaginative room to fathom individual identity in its wealth of contradiction. Literary culture is heavily commodified by corporations like Starbucks, Barnes and Noble, Pottery Barn, and Restoration Hardware, all of which sell us not just commodities but commodities that imagine our lives as leisured, reflective, aware. Such cultural capital— embodied in the gentle earth tones, glossy catalogs, and library accessories that lend a literate tone to a flavored drink or toaster—associates nontextual objects with literary culture to create them as significant symbols, just as the date grove, clay pit, and temple are for Sin-liqe-uninni. Online technology places literature courses in a uniquely powerful position to participate in this cultural capital.

Thus I close with the suggestion that we recognize online education as historically new but ultimately an extension of existing practices embodied in literary culture. This conclusion involves three collateral observations.

Humanist Reading. The rise of digital technology foregrounds a massive shift in humanities education. Nevertheless texts have historically been palimpsests, a literal substrate of digital code that underwrites progressively figural layers of meaning. The interpretation of these discrete and overlapping layers, in their historical and contemporary moments, has always differentiated humanist knowledge. We should recognize that such knowledge is congruent with the textual machinery of the twenty-first century. If something of the mystery of the postmodernist space of the computer screen lies in the fact that it is flat but nonetheless deeply layered, then this is no less true for the premodern spaces of the clay tablet and manuscript page. In all cases, our job is to teach effectively reading these layers.

Literary Culture. Because online information flow is so deeply involved in the public production of the self and because students gravitate to it of their own accord, it makes sense to design the online environment to participate in the construction of identity. This suggests a give-and-take process: students need a way to manipulate the course, beyond the chat room and e-mail message, to be involved just as they would be involved in a classroom seminar. I promoted interactivity in Hybrid English 203 by engaging the lecture-hall audience in discussion and by offering extra-credit assignments such as the textbook-cover contest, an MP3 dramatic reading contest, an onstage acting performance, and various writing workshops in which I called the students on my cell phone and upload the discussion as streaming video. More ambitious projects would look to allow students to craft Web-page identities highlighting their relationship to literature. No matter the formulation, students need a chance to participate in creating a public, Web-based identity. The strength of the humanities, of literary studies specifically, is that it provides a forum for the study of literary culture. This culture is broadly commodified by online retail and information outlets. Humanities units should capitalize on their special relation to this culture and make their sites less like shells and more visually engaged with articulating such culture to their audience.

Information Management.   As an online administrator, I face a column of numerical identities and arbitrary names on my class roster and a seemingly endless stream of e-mails. Because I get so much trivial e-mail, so many requests identical in every regard (including their claims to singularity), it is tempting simply to manage this information, to become a mere sorting device for connecting the proper query with the proper response. Such a choice, I believe, burns student and teacher out in the dull haze of the flat-panel display. Instead, I strive to imagine the participants in the course as fully human—as human as Clytemnestra, Scheherazade, the Eloquent Peasant, and the Shining Prince—each time I interact with them. Fulfilling this tremendous task is sometimes a struggle. It is then that I find myself sinking into the machine. It is no less a struggle, however, than I ask of my students when I stream into their lives through the *RealPlayer* window. Our culture increasingly looks to new technology to clarify mental health, render our bodies more beautifully, create a war that is precise (and because precise, ostensibly humane), and deliver effective education. The most powerful learning in the humanities is dependent on human interaction. Overtly, the *WebCT* format would seem to negate this element and in doing so corrupt our most noble endeavor. So I teach what it means to be a student of literature: to read and think critically, to pause, to contemplate the meaning of a work of art. This awareness has made me think about what it is I do and magnify my performance as a lecturer—to deliver each lecture so as to reach through camera, fiber-optic cables, and digital processing to grab students by the shoulders and tell them to open the electronic box before them and read the secrets of the past in the present. In formulating this command, I hope that my students might imagine for themselves a future in which the sexiest thing going is not a collective metachopper hell-bent on delivering life through death. The sexiest thing going is the human imagination.

Note

1. Hybrid English 203 was very much a collaborative effort. My thanks goes to Michael Salda, who not only designed the course but graciously encouraged me to make it my own; to Martina Sciolino and Damon Franke, who lectured with me; to Cacee de Young, Melanie Smith, John Wang, and Forrest Pelesko, who brought tremendous creativity to my redesign effort; to Claire Brantly of Pearson

Custom Publishing, who made assembling *World Literatures: A Reader* tremendously easy; and to the thousands of students who have explored the new machine at the University of Southern Mississippi.

Works Cited

George, Andrew, trans. The Epic of Gilgamesh: *The Babylonian Epic Poem and Other Texts in Akkadian and Sumerian.* London: Lane, 1999. Print.

Jameson, Fredric. *Postmodernism; or, The Cultural Logic of Late Capitalism.* Durham: Duke UP, 1991. Print.

Kurzweil, Ray. *The Singularity Is Near: When Humans Transcend Biology.* New York: Penguin, 2005. Print.

Marx, Karl. "Introduction to a Critique of Political Economy." *The German Ideology.* Ed. C. J. Arthur. New York: Intl., 2004. 124–52. Print.

World Literatures: A Reader: English 203, the Online and Live-Lecture Hybrid Course. Ed. William Kuskin. Boston: Pearson, 2005. Print.

"World Literature 203X." *Department of English.* U of Southern Mississippi, 2006. Web. 23 Aug. 2006.

Gerald Lucas

World.Lit:
Envisioning Literary
Education Online

> *And first Hephaestus makes a great and massive shield, . . .*
>
> . . . .
>
> *the god creates a world of gorgeous immortal work.*
> *There he made the earth and there the sky and the sea*
> *and the inexhaustible blazing sun and the moon rounding full*
> *and there the constellations, all that crown the heavens.*
>
> . . . .
>
> *And he forged on the shield two noble cities filled*
> *with mortal men.*
>
> —Homer, *The Iliad*

I see the future of education like Achilles's shield: a detailed and exciting microcosm of the world. If critics like Janet H. Murray see their visions of tomorrow come to fruition, virtual education—alongside how we experience literature—will eventually encompass all the nuances of humanity. In her work *Hamlet on the Holodeck*, Murray theorizes the future of arts and entertainment: an immersive virtual experience where the distinction between reader and writer dissolves and all genres come together to form the cyberdrama in which participants use the text-film-drama-game in whatever way they see fit. At the center of the cyber-Hephaestus's forge is the machine that might someday create a virtual Achilles's shield: the computer.

Computers have become integral components of education today. We faculty members feel the pressure from students and administrators alike to begin using computer technology more in our teaching, leaving many of us feeling like the lumbering Hephaestus rather than one of his beautiful creations. My work in the humanities with computers since 1995 has been leading toward what I call World.Lit, a fully online literature course that aims to be as effective as a traditional classroom approach.

In my experience teaching world literature in a hybridized classroom and online, I have found that the largest obstacle has been letting go of traditional classroom approaches of lecture and discussion to facilitate a successful online experience as enriching and fruitful as a face-to-face one. I had to reevaluate what I knew (or thought I knew) about teaching and learning to make myself feel confident in the approach and—more important—to allow my students to excel to the best of their abilities in the new, and sometimes intimidating, environment.

In contemplating, designing, and implementing World.Lit, I still find myself preoccupied with two important questions: How does an online section of world literature differ from an in-class section? How do I support various digital literacy levels in one online course? The challenge of teaching a sophomore literature survey has traditionally been establishing textual literacy: having students successfully learn to analyze and discuss the survey's primary texts. Those taking an online literature course have the additional challenge of learning and applying digital literacies before they can concentrate on the texts. This case study examines how I approached these issues with World.Lit. I briefly review assignments that have worked for me, and some that have not, and point to my Web site *LitMUSE* for specific assignments and policies that have developed over several years of teaching World.Lit.

Approaching World.Lit: Some History

Like many of us, I come from a traditional English program. My background is not in the formal study of pedagogy but in English literature and composition. While the university was adopting emerging computer technologies in the early 1990s, our department only expected its graduate students to be literate in word processing needed to write a seminar paper. Those of us who embraced the new medium of the World Wide Web did so on our own, with little institutional support.

I make this point not to criticize my program but to emphasize the fact that my interest in online teaching stemmed from my initial enthusiasm about new technologies and how I could push them into serving my goals: to be a stellar graduate student, a strong and forward-looking educator, and eventually an innovative and enthusiastic tenure-track professor. I taught myself rudimentary HTML and developed my first Web page in the mid-1990s. The goal of *The English Site* was to deliver course information to my students and to highlight my work as a teaching assistant and graduate student. It followed that, as I became a senior graduate student and teaching assistant, I began to teach more of what I was studying. I began to post sections of my seminar papers online for my students, much in the same way that my professors would photocopy their notes and hand them out to the class. I soon found out, however, that this practice allowed for greater accessibility to my materials; fellow graduate students would tell me they pointed their classes to the notes I posted on the *Odyssey*. I knew the Web was different, that something new and exciting was beginning for collaboration, education, and English studies. I became and remain an advocate of progress, but I learned that this progress must come not only in the form of new tools but also in how we work with and think about those tools.

During this time, in addition to my formal fields of study—world literatures and modernism—I immersed myself in how computers and network technologies were being used by my colleagues for their scholarship and teaching. Alongside the World Wide Web, much of the interaction using computers was synchronous and asynchronous textual communication to augment classroom activities, like MOO sessions (Haynes and Holmevik), *Daedalus* interchanges, and electronic mailing lists. Most distance education at this time seemed to be classroom courses that had been videotaped and played on local-access television stations. This type of distance education was usually reserved for departments with budgets larger than ours, so our department stuck with the equipment and facilities that we had.

As an outcome of what Martin Lister and his coauthors would call my "techno-enthusiasm" (290), I soon became coordinator of our department's computer-assisted classroom, responsible for its daily operations and for researching and keeping abreast of new technologies and how they could support English studies and higher education. I earned my doctorate in 2002 and realized my goal of getting a tenure-track job. Since I knew I had to move on and wanted to take my online work with me, I purchased my first domain name. I would own a couple over the course of the next years, but the one I have stuck with is LitMUSE.net. The name LitMUSE represents the goals and focus of my approach to online education. "Lit" stand for both "literature" and "literacy," and "MUSE" is an acronym for "Multi-User Simulated Environment" and the Greek word for the fount and guarantor of memory. *LitMUSE* began as a MOO, but it has changed over the years into a learning environment that disseminates course information and allows students a safe online platform in which to learn. Traditionally, education occupies the class-room but the online course replaces the classroom with the computer. The computer, then, becomes the space where education happens.

Yet while many are and have been rushing forth to embrace a digital renaissance for the classroom, many are left floundering, stifled by it all. Students are particularly vulnerable to this technological vertigo—caught up in the excitement of online courses but frequently lacking the skills necessary to succeed and flourish the same way they can in the tradi-tional classroom. I developed World.Lit as an advocate of technological innovation and educational progress, which go hand in hand, shoulder to shoulder.

Educational applications—like most uses of computers—are in an incunabular state; that is, we have yet to develop conventions for the use of computers in many areas, education among them. We think they offer great potential, and administrators love to see them in our classrooms, since they symbolize progress, innovation, and endowments. But having the tools does not mean we have the desire or the knowledge to use them effectively. As Lister and his coauthors suggest, we cannot let our "techno-enthusiasm" for computers overwhelm the central issue, since now that computers in the classroom are an everyday fact at most institutions, their newness will wear off, and we will be left simply with tools (290).

Developing and Implementing World.Lit

When I first came to Macon State College, a small college in central Georgia that prides itself in "prepar[ing] students to compete in a techno-logically advanced global economy while developing important life skills and a firm foundation in the liberal arts," I was asked to develop, teach, and regularly offer an online world literature class ("Welcome"). At first I was excited and enthusiastic about the challenge, but the more I thought about it, the more I grew concerned with the ability of our technology to promote significant understanding as effectively as a traditional classroom setting. How would nonmajors in a sophomore literature survey, most of whom have only had experience reading and writing about literature in the second part of freshmen English, do in an online literature survey? Would they have the abilities necessary to gain an understanding of Homer through self-directed study? Would I be creative enough to make the experience as rich as I know I could in the classroom? Should world literature even be offered online, given the state of our technology? I had to address these questions immediately and over several semesters of offering World.Lit.

While in my many years of teaching world literature in the classroom I have varied my approach in several ways, it consists typically of assigned reading to be finished before class that concentrates mostly on the primary text, lecture for the first part of the class meeting, discussion for the rest of class, and students' writing about the text, usually a reader-response piece. Since our world literature survey, like all our literature surveys, is sophomore level, my main goal is to introduce students to the (usually canonical) texts and some prevalent ideas therein. In lecture and discussion, we examine specific sections of the text and practice close readings together, highlighting the excerpt's formal literary conventions, its relation to the text and culture as a whole, and its thematic and stylistic elements. My classroom approach relies heavily on professor-student interaction. Finally, I often employ Web elements in my classroom surveys; instead of turning in word-processed responses to the literature, my students have been logging their responses on a Web site. I also use *LitMUSE* to disseminate my course materials, like the reading schedule, requirements, and policies.

I understood that an online course could not function the same way as my in-class section. I needed to change how I interacted with the students. How could I deliver course lectures? How could we do close readings together? Could we? How would students submit their work? How could I accommodate a variety of computer literacies? World.Lit would have to address not only textual literacy but also digital literacy.

Online students must be able to take advantage of the digital tools available to them, like Web-based databases from the library, to help them decide what is significant about the texts and how they relate to their lives. A large portion of my online literature survey must initially address online literacy. Part of expecting the students to discover their personal knowledge about the texts is showing them where and how to look for it. Most students go directly to *Google*; others to *Wikipedia*. By having working knowledge of these search engines, many just need a bit more guidance in refining searches and knowing what databases to choose for their inquiries. We spend much of our first class talking about online activities: if students know where and how to look, they can begin to teach themselves about world literature. This session is front-loaded with computer literacy, so that the rest of the course can be about the literature. My job is to show students the tools they need. Their job is to use them.

I have found it is most effective to train students to use our Web-based catalogs the first night. I then follow up with blog and wiki assignments, where the students apply what they learn from their assigned readings and their research projects, which ask for a collaborative report on factual elements of primary and secondary texts. To address the technological vertigo many students feel in an online course, I offer specific guidance on how to use the wiki and blog and the college databases, how to cite research, how to select secondary texts, how to write a reader response, and how to link. I allow students to use these resources to pursue any aspect of Homer they like, which has been a successful approach for my teaching literature online.

Constructing World.Lit

I have tried just about everything from MOO sessions to video conferences in computer-assisted and online courses. Keeping my educational goals in mind, I choose to use the tools that will best help my students learn, which are not always the newest or most complex tools. Similarly, I am an English professor at a small college in central Georgia; I have no major government, foundation, or institutional financial support, so I generally choose affordable, open-source alternatives.

Here is a brief list of computer resources I use and do not use and why. For more specific examples and assignments, please see my Web site *LitMUSE*. The ones I use have succeeded with students who run the gamut from average to highly motivated, and they are what the students consistently cite as the most beneficial activities for their learning in World.Lit and for their technological literacy. Even if students learn nothing about world literature after completing the course, they learn skills that Macon State College finds necessary and desirable in today's workplace.

Lecture

I cannot lecture online. We cannot easily and conveniently have discussions online. I can, however, deliver similar information on my blog. Along with the primary reading, I assign portions of my blog for students, usually brief introductions to the texts they read. These portions consist of lecture notes, as well as my close readings of texts, musings about formal literary elements, and links to other resources that can help students understand the primary texts, including our library's Web-based databases of full-text articles. My blog supplies the students with a list of what to look for in their reading of each primary text: issues, themes, and major concerns.

I also encourage students to go beyond the stated goals when responding in their blog entries. They should provide secondary support; as a starting point, I recommend they use my blog, which I show them how to search and cite the first night of class. I also link to *LitWiki* and the work of my students from previous semesters. While my blog cannot address all the questions that students may have about the *Iliad*, it can deliver important elements from lecture and discussion that online students might otherwise miss.

Content Management Systems and the Blog

I designed and implemented my first Web site using HTML and CSS I had written myself. This process was slow and meticulous, making upgrades and changes tedious. It also made browser compatibility dubious, since some features looked great on my computer but terrible on others. I began to use a content management system to solve these issues. Content Management Systems use a Web site front end to communicate with a database backbone. This approach allows for a consistent look and operation throughout a Web site's various pages. Such a system also allows for submission directly from a Web browser. Some HTML is still needed, however, and the system will have to be installed on a Web server, something that all professors should have access to.

Most installations are pretty straightforward, and, once installed, a Content Management System usually needs little to no maintenance; in fact, most departments have technical support staff members to help with the installation. I currently use *Moodle* for student sections of *Lit-MUSE*, but I have worked with *Drupal*, *Slash*, and *Mambo*. Each of these is open source, but *Drupal* has modules aimed directly at educational applications (such as giving quizzes) and so has worked best for my needs. These systems generally work the same on all browsers and platforms, and just about every system includes a module for blogging and forum discussions.

The major component for student writing in World.Lit is the blog, or an in-line journal. Students use blogs for the interpretation and analysis of primary texts. Essentially, they are online reader responses, somewhat more formal than a discussion board and somewhat less formal than an essay. Blogs allow students to explore areas of the text that interest them and that relate to their lives. In my explanation of the blogs my first night, I stress focus, brevity, support, and originality.

Blogs also offer the students a way to make up for in-class discussion. In introducing blogs, I stress the metaphor of a conversation: rather than be an essay that is structured in a certain way and has a limited audience, blogs should participate in a conversation, by responding to and linking to research and other entries. Each blog entry that students write also has an area for comments. Students are encouraged to use this space to present alternative positions, to ask questions, and to expand an entry's points. I find that, since I call the writing a blog instead of an essay, students generally enjoy writing them and are less intimidated by responding to works of literature. In student feedback on the course, writing on the blog seems to be the favorite class activity.

I also find that blogs help other students improve their writing. When I read and evaluate blog entries, I assign a letter grade in the book and make a comment about areas that are well done and aspects of their writing that might need attention. In addition to this traditional evaluation, the whole class participates in rating the entries, so that part of the evaluative process is taken from me and given to the community. The higher an entry is rated, the closer to the top of the Web site it is pushed; thus when students log in to the class blog, the first entries they see are the best written. I find it fascinating that the students and I are frequently simpatico in our evaluations. Those students who have entries that score lower are encouraged to revise and resubmit their blogs. While I retain the grade book, the blog functions like a true online community, where more popular postings are seen more and less popular ones get pushed toward the bottom.

LitWiki

Continuing the idea of an online community, World.Lit also makes heavy use of a wiki designed specifically for students engaging in literary study: it is a resource written by students for students. The wiki is for the presentation of research designed as a collaborative *Cliff's Notes*. I explain that the wiki should be a study guide to help other students get through these sometimes challenging texts. A typical wiki entry will include historical contexts, character histories, plot summaries, timelines, author biographies, and links to additional resources.

Part of the beauty of using the blog and the wiki is that they are both hypertext, and hypertext encourages linking—a participation in the complexity of literary discourse that traditional research papers teach, without the oppressive weight of the research paper. Frequently, students do not even need coaching on how to link, and many can help those who are new to hypertext.

Finally, I encourage, but do not require, students to ask questions in an online forum. Much of their conversation takes place in their blog comments, but frequently an online forum, like a bulletin board system, will allow for quick questions and impromptu discussions. The forum often seems to become a free-for-all, less focused and more social than the blog or wiki. I think the forum still supports an idea of community, so I keep it as part of the course.

For *LitWiki*, I use *MediaWiki*, the same open-source software that powers the popular *Wikipedia* and Google sites. Its installation, similar to that of a content management system, requires a Web server and a database, like *MySQL*. Like the systems I list above, *MediaWiki* can easily be installed in a user's directory, which most universities and colleges give faculty members and, often, students. While the wiki is easy to use, it does require some specific context in editing that many students find off-putting at first. Yet, as long as I show them the basics and they practice them, most students will have no trouble producing a strong wiki entry. Many tools and instructions are available on *Wikipedia*, under the "Help" page.

What I Do Not Use

I do not use synchronous chats or MOOs. MOOs present a huge learning curve, even using the excellent *enCore* interface designed by Jan Rune Holmevik and Cynthia Haynes, which they theorize in their collection *High Wired*. I do not use chat sessions because I find them fatiguing and too infrequently rewarding. The chaos of these sessions tends to frustrate many, as well as encourage an augmented "underlife" that rarely seems to benefit the class as a whole (Brooke 229–30). Besides, I think that scheduled meetings defeat one purpose of an online class: the student's freedom to work at his or her own pace, on his or her own time.

I do not use mailing or distribution lists. I find nothing intrinsically wrong with an e-mail list, but in this age of spam I prefer that students get into the habit of visiting a Web site each day, instead of relying on their e-mail for course information. In fact, I try to encourage students not to use their e-mail for the class but instead to communicate with me and the class through the course Web site.

I also do not use traditional names for assignments, like essays, research papers, and exams, in an online context. This terminology does not mean that blogs are not essays. The students are still required to practice strong writing, but not calling wiki entries research papers allows a greater sense of freedom than the often stifling signifiers that students associate with the numbing rigors of school.

I do not use proprietary software. My course is designed around the World Wide Web, and the only tool the students need is a computer with a connection to the Internet. They may use whichever operating system and Web browser they prefer, since all work for Web-based delivery of course materials, blogs, and wikis.

World.Lit: Growing from Feedback

Student feedback is invaluable when evaluating any course but integral for an online literature course. When I first introduced World.Lit, several students requested a way to check grades online, more materials available to take the place of lecture, and a course Web site that was compatible with more browsers. To make grades accessible online, I began using *Gradekeeper*, a shareware program that allows me to upload student grades directly to a Web site. Each student then has a log-in and password that limits access to only that student. While not the most elegant solution, it does eliminate the need for constant e-mails about grades. It also requires me to be diligent in my evaluation, since students usually keep on top of grades.

To be consistent in adding to my blog, I try to blog with my students: as they write about Machiavelli, so do I. To make sure the search function works well, I have installed a *Google* search function for *LitMUSE*, so that search results are as accurate as they can be when students are looking for information on primary texts.

Looking toward Tomorrow

The next steps for World.Lit will incorporate podcasting and digital storytelling. While I have used these in my face-to-face courses, like Technology and the Creative Artist and the senior seminar in new media, the logistics of undertaking them in World.Lit have been too impractical to implement online now. In my experience, they require specific hardware (like scanners, digital cameras, and DV cameras) and software (like Apple's *iMovie* and *GarageBand*), as well as continued support of an instructor. Many students, however, already employ some of this specialized hardware and software and have worked with sites like *Flickr* and *YouTube*, so that the prospect of incorporating more multimedia into World.Lit might become a reality more quickly than I anticipate.

With current forms of technology, we must be careful not to alienate students who take courses online, especially ones that seem more suited for a traditional classroom. Perhaps technology will evolve to the point where we will be fortunate enough to replicate Murray's holodeck for educational purposes, but until then I think we should strive toward promoting significant understanding that emphasizes student concerns and interests about the texts: more structure, to allow students to acclimate to the digital environments of the online course, and less rigidity and tradition in how we approach the subject, to allow students to explore areas of the texts that they might find meaningful in understanding their lives.

Our computer technology might one day present us with the Achilles's shield of education: a virtual environment as rich and encompassing as our imaginations, bolstered by the knowledge and experience of the world and guided by those with the vision to forge them all into one experience. The Hephaestuses that might make this possible could be sitting in our classrooms today. It is up to us to make the tools available for them to discover the significance of the humanities so that it can remain an integral part of our education, our technology, and our humanity.

Note

The epigraph is from book 18, verses 558, 564–67, and 572–73.

Works Cited

Brooke, Robert. "Underlife and Writing Instruction." *On Writing Research: The Braddock Essays, 1975–1998.* Ed. Lisa Ede. New York: Bedford–St. Martin's, 1999. 229–41. Print.

Haynes, Cynthia Ann, and Jan Rune Holmevik, eds. *High Wired: On the Design, Use, and Theory of Educational MOOs.* Ann Arbor: U of Michigan P, 2001. Print.

Homer. *The Iliad.* Trans. Robert Fagles. New York: Viking-Penguin, 1998. Print.

Lister, Martin, et al. *New Media: A Critical Introduction.* New York: Routledge, 2003. Print.

Lucas, Gerald. *LitMUSE.* Lucas, 2008. Web. 3 Apr. 2009.

Murray, Janet H. *Hamlet on the Holodeck: The Future of Narrative in Cyberspace.* New York: Free, 1997. Print.

"Welcome to Macon State College." *Macon State College.* Macon State Coll., 2008. Web. 28 Jan. 2009.

Noriko Nagata

An Online Japanese Textbook with Natural Language Processing

Many software programs are available for language teaching. They present sophisticated multimedia interfaces, include quality video clips and graphics, and offer hyperlinks and a great deal of information. When it comes to practicing a second language, however, existing software programs can provide only simple types of exercises (written in *WebCT*, *Blackboard*, *Flash*, etc.). *Blackboard*, for example, offers a "Test Manager" tool for authoring quizzes. These quizzes ask students either to select correct answers or to fill in blanks partially but do not allow for full sentences because error analysis in *Blackboard* is restricted to letter-by-letter matching.

Although such exercises still enable students to practice on their own, they have two major limitations: the absence of practice at producing full sentences, which is a necessary component of genuine mastery, and the lack of detailed feedback, which makes it difficult for students to learn from their mistakes. Fill-in-the-blank and multiple-choice exercises severely constrain the student's possible responses and provide only a narrow range of canned feedback messages.

Natural language processing (NLP) technology addresses these fundamental limitations by performing computational linguistic analysis. This analysis decomposes a character string into its grammatical components based on the grammar rules and lexicon of the target language and judges whether the input string is a grammatical sentence—a process known as parsing. The results of the parse can be used to generate detailed feedback to explain grammatical principles violated in the learner's sentence. This technology thus makes possible extensive exercises in which the learner can produce any sentence in response to a question and receive grammatical feedback pinpointed to the learner's errors. Because only NLP can implement this goal in computer-assisted language learning, it has aroused increasing interest.[1]

In principle, NLP can associate every possible student input by rote pattern matching to a canned, appropriate feedback response, but in practice this strategy is hopeless and generates only a sparse range of feedback messages. Compare the following example of a sentence-production exercise, first in traditional, manual exercise authoring and then in *Robo-Sensei*. Suppose a student is asked to produce a Japanese sentence given the context, "You heard that Kamakura is a historical city. Ask if there are many temples in Kamakura." The traditional, manual authoring technique must list all anticipated answers and match them to appropriate feedback messages. Consider how many correct sentences must be accepted for this one question. Only taking account of different word orders,[2] six correct sentences exist:

かまくらにおてらがたくさんありますか。
Kamakura ni otera ga takusan arimasu ka.

かまくらにたくさんおてらがありますか。
Kamakura ni takusan otera ga arimasu ka.

おてらがかまくらにたくさんありますか。
Otera ga Kamakura ni takusan arimasu ka.

おてらがたくさんかまくらにありますか。
Otera ga takusan Kamakura ni arimasu ka.

たくさんかまくらにおてらがありますか。
Takusan Kamakura ni otera ga arimasu ka.

たくさんおてらがかまくらにありますか。
Takusan otera ga Kamakura ni arimasu ka.

These correct responses are all written in hiragana (a phonetic realization in which each character corresponds to one syllable), but most words in Japanese have kanji versions as well, and some words can be replaced by different lexical items. For instance, the first correct sentence has two spellings of *Kamakura* (かまくら[hiragana] and 鎌倉 [kanji]), which can be multiplied by two versions of the particle *ni* (に and には),[3] by four alternatives for *otera* ("temple"; おてら, お寺, てら, and 寺),[4] by four alternatives for *takusan* ("many"; たくさん, 沢山, いっぱい, and 一杯),[5] and by two alternatives for *arimasu* ("exist"; あります [hiragana] and 在ります [kanji]). Thus lexical and orthographical variants bring the total to 128 correct sentences. Each of the other five responses listed above also have 128 variations, so the total number of possible correct variations for the six correct sentences is 768.

But we have not even begun to discuss the quantity of feedback needed for ungrammatical sentences. Switching the particle *ni* attached to *Kamakura* in the 768 correct sentences to three mistaken particles, *ga*, *o*, and *de*, and omission of the particle generates 3,072 incorrect sentences, a total that can be multiplied by at least five possible alternatives for the particle *ga* attached to *otera* (i.e., *ga*; three mistaken particles, *o*, *de*, and *ni*; and omission of the particle), and by at least eight different basic conjugations of *arimasu* (i.e., *arimasu* and seven mistaken conjugations, *arimasen*, *arimashita*, *arimasendeshita*, *aru*, *nai*, *atta*, and *nakatta*). Therefore there are 122,880 possible incorrect sentences.

Now it is clear why it is hopeless to list, manually, all grammatical and ungrammatical sentences even for just one question. It is tempting to imagine that informative computer responses can be generated by rote pattern matching without the aid of NLP, but not when the errors of each type are compounded. An exponential explosion of canned responses then takes place as the answer becomes longer. Even if canned feedback messages are associated manually with each of the 122,880 potential errors, the likelihood of human error is high.

Robo-Sensei avoids these problems by using NLP technology to analyze the student's sentential inputs and to generate relevant feedback messages automatically. *Robo-Sensei*'s NLP system includes a lexicon, a morphological generator,[6] a word segmentor,[7] a morphological parser, a syntactic parser,[8] an error detector, and a feedback generator (for a description of the system, see Nagata, "BANZAI," "Intelligent Language Tutor," "*Robo-Sensei*'s NLP-Based Error Detection"). Because of this technology, *Robo-Sensei* requires only the list of relevant vocabulary items for each question instead of thousands of canned error messages paired with anticipated inputs. For the question under discussion, *Robo-Sensei* stores only the following vocabulary list:

(かまくら n/鎌倉 n/)

<(に p ni-loc) | (は p wa-topic) | (に p ni-loc)(は p wa-topic) | >

<(お f)(てら n) | (お f)(寺 n) | (てら n) | (寺 n) | >

(が p ga-state)

(たくさん n/沢山 n/いっぱい n/一杯 n/)

(あり v ある/在り v 在る/)(ます x)

(か e ka-sentp)

In response to the prompt "You heard that Kamakura is a historical city. Ask if there are many temples in Kamakura," a student inputs this sentence: かまくらで おてらが たくさんが ありましたか。. Here is an example of *Robo-Sensei*'s feedback message to the student's erroneous sentence:

<Particle error>
• たくさん is a noun describing manner or degree, and such nouns usually should not be followed by a particle. The particle が attached to たくさん should be deleted.

• You used the particle で to mark かまくら as if it were the location where the activity takes place. However, かまくら is the location where something or someone exists that is not an activity, and should be marked with the particle に.

<Predicate error>
• ありました is in the past form. Change it to the present form.
Try it again!

Errors are categorized as "missing word," "unexpected word," "particle error," "predicate error," "word order error," "modifier error," or "unknown word."[9] The feedback explains grammatical rules governing these errors so that the student can apply the rules to produce target sentences. For example, many students correct such particle errors by a random, hit-or-miss approach—"Oh, *de* doesn't work, so how about *ni*"—and do not understand what went wrong. Unless they acquire the principles behind proper usage, they continue to use particles randomly and never master them.

When *Robo-Sensei* identifies many error messages, the student does not have to respond to all the errors at once but can take a step-by-step problem-solving approach. A student can focus on the first error only, correct it, and ask for a new analysis. The remaining error messages will appear again, and the student then corrects the next one and, after eliminating all errors, produces a correct answer. *Robo-Sensei* usefully focuses the student's full attention on one principle at a time in a way that even human grading of paper exercises does not.

As explained above, there is always more than one possible correct answer for a sentence production exercise. In the exercise "Ask if there are many temples in Kamakura," the word order of かまくらに and おてらが and たくさん can be shuffled, たくさん can be いっぱい, and both hiragana and kanji versions may be accepted for any word that can be written in kanji. Basically, *Robo-Sensei* can accept any possible variation as long as it fits the context provided by the exercise.

Effectiveness of NLP-Based Second-Language Instruction

I have demonstrated the pedagogical effectiveness of NLP-generated feedback by empirical studies over eleven years. Here is a brief summary of their conclusions. An early study compares the relative effectiveness of intelligent feedback generated by NLP and traditional, manually encoded feedback (Nagata, "Intelligent Computer Feedback"). Intelligent feedback explains the grammatical principles violated by student-composed sentences, whereas traditional feedback merely indicates missing or unexpected words. The results showed that intelligent feedback is more effective than traditional feedback, most obviously in particle acquisition (which involves more complex syntactic processing than other elements like vocabulary and verb conjugations). A second experiment compares intelligent feedback with enhanced traditional feedback, which indicates not only missing particles but also the locations of missing particles (Nagata, "Effective Application"). The results reveal that additional information on the locations of missing particles is still not as effective as explicit explanation of rules. A third experiment compares the effectiveness of NLP-based instruction with traditional paper-and-pencil workbook instruction, in the form of self-study lessons (Nagata, "Computer"). Given the same written descriptions of the target grammatical principles and the same exercises, ongoing, intelligent computer feedback proves more effective than simple workbook answer sheets. The workbook instruction was also compared with the traditional computer feedback used in the previous study, but the traditional computer feedback did not exhibit a significant advantage over the workbook instruction. The results emphasize the importance of providing an intelligent level of feedback to the learner, a task for providing which NLP is well suited. A fourth study concerns deductive versus inductive feedback (Nagata, "Experimental Comparison"), that is, the relative effectiveness of teaching explicit grammatical rules as opposed to providing relevant examples without rule instruction—a subject of continuing debate in second language acquisition research (DeKeyser). Principle-based deductive feedback, generated by NLP, was compared with inductive feedback, which responds to each student error with example sentences illustrating the principle at issue in lieu of the principle itself. The results show the increased effectiveness of intelligent, deductive feedback over inductive feedback.

The above studies all focused on production practice, but comprehension practice also plays an important role in second language acquisition, where it is known as "comprehensible input" (Krashen). Two further studies compare the relative effectiveness of comprehension practice and production practice. The first study involves fairly complicated structures, Japanese honorifics (Nagata, "Input vs. Output"). Given the same grammatical instruction, production practice proves more effective than comprehension practice and equally effective for the comprehension of these structures. The study demonstrates the importance of production tasks over tasks that require only comprehension. Simply comprehending a sentence requires shallower cognitive processing than producing it, so that learning from comprehension exercises cannot be transferred easily to full-sentence production. The second study questions whether the advantage of production practice still obtains when the target structures are relatively simple—in this instance, Japanese nominal modifiers (Nagata, "Relative Effectiveness"). The results are consistent: production practice proves more effective than comprehension practice for producing Japanese nominal modifiers and equally effective for the comprehension of these structures. Japanese nominal modifiers are interpretable without processing the syntactic cues *no* and *na*,[10] whereas production requires the correct use of such syntactic cues. Therefore, even though the structures are relatively simple (using *no*, *na*, or nothing), comprehension practice alone is not sufficient to draw learners' attention to those forms and to develop the grammatical skill to use them. The results support Merrill Swain's hypothesis that producing language, as opposed to comprehending it, can force the learner to move from semantic processing to syntactic processing, thereby improving grammatical performance (Swain; Swain and Lapkin).

My most recent study compares production exercises with conventional multiple-choice exercises (Nagata, "Input Enhancement"). As noted earlier, ordinary computer programs provide mostly multiple-choice or fill-in-the-blank exercises because they lack NLP capability. The results in the posttest show that the production group performed significantly better than the multiple-choice group on both production and multiple-choice tasks. It was expected that the multiple-choice group would perform as well as (or better than) the production group at least on the multiple-choice tasks. Yet even though the production group did not practice multiple-choice exercises, it could distinguish well-formed sentences from ill-formed sentences and choose correct answers better than the multiple-choice group. The results confirm that the students in the production group paid more attention to grammatical forms they needed for producing target sentences and developed better grammatical skill than the multiple-choice group.

Overall, these empirical results show that students require extensive production practice to encourage deep cognitive processing of the underlying grammatical principles and ongoing, detailed error feedback to reinforce these principles. This outcome agrees with the cognitive approach of Alice C. Omaggio: "[B]ecause language behavior is constantly innovative and varied, students must be taught to understand the rule system rather than be required to memorize surface strings in rote fashion" (67). On the basis of these findings, the *Robo-Sensei* online textbook is being designed to provide extensive sentence-production exercises and corresponding principle-based intelligent feedback, which is feasible only in the light of NLP technology.

Robo-Sensei, an NLP-Based Online Textbook

The *Robo-Sensei* online textbook will run on ordinary Web browsers and will be compatible with both *Windows* and *Mac OS*. It will be distributed as a CD-ROM as well.[11] Its flexibility will ensure that it can be used in regular Japanese courses at high schools or universities, in distance-learning courses, in hybrid or blended courses, and in unsupervised self-study. *Robo-Sensei*'s immediate, detailed feedback can enhance every educational format. The previous version of *Robo-Sensei* (Nagata, *Robo-Sensei:*

Personal Japanese Tutor) offers ten modules, including a total of twenty-four lessons from beginning to advanced levels. Each module targets grammatical structures with which students typically require special help (e.g., Japanese particles, relative clauses, and honorifics). It has been used as a supplement for standard Japanese textbooks, but the new *Robo-Sensei* textbook will be a stand-alone online textbook that will cover the entire Japanese curriculum, parse the full range of grammatical structures, and provide feedback for a wider variety of errors. Like the older version, the new textbook is based on a grammatical, functional, and situational syllabus and embeds exercises and dialogues in a rich visual and cultural context. There will be forty-two chapters.[12] Each chapter (approximately seven hours of classroom teaching) consists of six modules: Introduction, Grammar, Dialogue, Vocabulary, Kana or Kanji, and Tutor. The last module, Tutor, will offer extensive exercises that are fully integrated with the updated *Robo-Sensei*'s NLP system, which is written in Java. The other modules focus on text and character presentations and do not require complex sentence analysis and feedback generation. They are written in *Flash*, which is well suited for enhanced multimedia presentations and animations and results in a more polished presentation than the all-Java interface used in the previous *Robo-Sensei*. The combination of Java and *Flash* provides the best of both worlds.

Four features of teacher-student interaction have influenced the design of the new *Robo-Sensei*: maximizing student attentiveness, enhancing student motivation to learn, enriching teacher-student in-class activities, and increasing the amount of time available to teachers for instructional purposes.

Traditional exercises written on paper come in batches, and feedback from the human teacher takes days to receive. By the time the exercises are returned, the students may not even care about or look at the instructor's painstaking corrections. *Robo-Sensei*'s feedback, ongoing and immediate, occurs when the students' attention is at its peak and so maximizes its impact. Also, *Robo-Sensei*'s feedback is patient and consistent, no matter how many times the student makes the same error.

The positive motivational effect attending self-paced activities is borne out by a series of studies in which classroom hours were replaced with online self-study materials (Polisca; Scida and Saury; Banados). Emily Scida and Rachel Saury compared a hybrid course consisting of three hours a week of class time and two hours of mandatory, Web-based practice activities with a traditional course that met five days a week in the classroom. They found that the average grade in the hybrid course was higher than that in the traditional course (58% of the students in the hybrid course earned an A, and 84% achieved above C; whereas 32% of the students in the traditional course received an A, and 73% reached above C). Fourteen of the eighteen students reported that they always worked on an online assignment until they achieved a perfect score even after reaching the required score of the assignment (a minimum 60% of the full score was required for worksheets and 70% for quizzes), and the other four students reported they sometimes did so. Accordingly, "students who completed multiple trials got increased practice with the materials," resulting in higher achievement in the hybrid course (524). *Robo-Sensei*'s online textbook's Tutor module has a grading system, and, since students can check their scores and progress, a similar effect is anticipated.

Because *Robo-Sensei*'s online exercises demand more than mechanical drills, they can be used as communicative activities in the classroom and enrich the teacher-student interaction.[13] Students can work on communicative questions with *Robo-Sensei* and receive immediate feedback from the program. The instructor can circulate among the students efficiently, focusing more attention on students with systematic misunderstandings or on conversational practice with students. If students cannot finish assigned exercises in class, they can complete them at home and submit a score sheet graded by *Robo-Sensei*.

Finally, instructional effort saved from correcting repetitious errors in written exercises can be redistributed to other, higher-level educational tasks. Instructors can focus more time and attention on the organization of classroom activities and on individual student problems during extended office hours. Also, because *Robo-Sensei* stores feedback messages, the teacher can track student progress and determine if certain principles and tasks require further attention during class.

Let me demonstrate chapter 14, "ひだ・たかやまツアー Hida-Takayama Tour (Comparisons)," and illustrate each of its modules with screen images.[14] Each chapter title consists of the culture theme, with the target grammar in parentheses.

Figure 1 presents the screen image of the chapter 14 Introduction module. It shows a few target sentences, highlights the target forms, provides relevant photographic images, and states briefly objectives of the

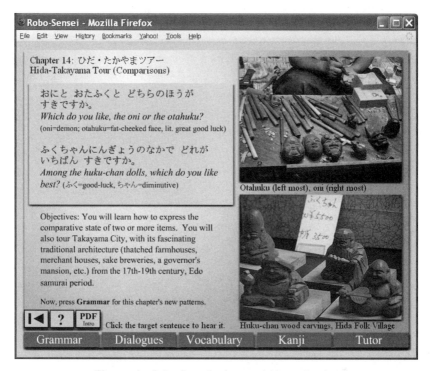

Figure I. *Robo-Sensei*'s chapter 14 introduction

chapter. The introduction focuses the attention of the students and assures them that the chapter's goal is important and achievable. By clicking the target sentence, students can hear it pronounced. Students can also print the present screen. By clicking the question mark, students can see an explanation of the other buttons' functions.

The Grammar module (fig. 2) provides detailed descriptions about target grammatical patterns.[15] The "PDF Grammar" button opens a printable PDF file of the grammar notes for ease of reference.

This chapter's Dialogue module (fig. 3) presents three core dialogues in which the target grammatical patterns, new vocabulary, and new kanji are all incorporated. (By pulling down the Dialogue menu, the students can select another dialogue.) Their stories are based on the cultural theme of the chapter.[16] The photographic images help students understand the content of the dialogues, and the "Interpret" button at the bottom of the

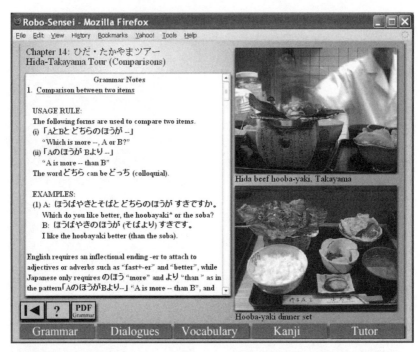

Figures 2 and 3. *Robo-Sensei*'s Grammar module (above) and Dialogue module (below)

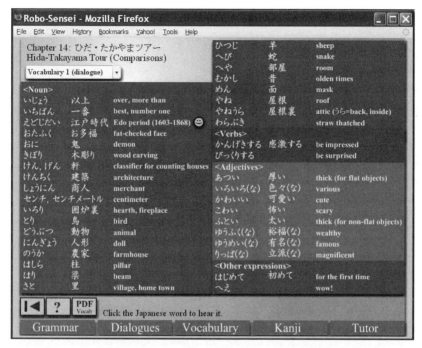

Figure 4. *Robo-Sensei's* Vocabulary module

screen presents an English translation. The learner can also hear each sentence played aloud by clicking on it.

The Vocabulary module (fig. 4) lists new vocabulary items, both in the core dialogues (Vocabulary 1) and in the grammar notes and exercises (Vocabulary 2). A pull-down menu navigates between Vocabulary 1 (see fig. 4) and Vocabulary 2. The learner can hear each vocabulary item by clicking on it. A smile icon attached to a word provides more information about the word. Clicking the smile icon next to えどじだい "Edo period," for example, links to the *Wikipedia* page on the Edo period. All vocabulary items are introduced sequentially from chapter 1.

The Kanji module (fig. 5) presents readings and common meanings for each new kanji character. By clicking on a kanji, the learner sees the demonstration of its stroke order in a graphic animation. Stroke order is crucial for writing Japanese characters accurately. Writing characters with the proper stroke order each time also makes them much easier to remember. *Robo-Sensei's* stroke demonstration simulates real writing, something

Figure 5. *Robo-Sensei's* Kanji module

printed textbooks cannot offer. While watching the demonstration, the students can stop it to observe any stage of writing and then restart the demonstration. This option helps students take their time and focus on individual challenges. Figure 5 shows an intermediate stage of the stroke demonstration for 時. A few example words are presented to see how the target kanji can be used to form words. Kanji characters are introduced sequentially, starting at chapter 8, and each chapter includes sixteen new kanji.[17]

Hiragana and katakana are introduced in the first seven chapters. They are the two systems of Japanese phonetic characters (jointly known as kana),[18] and students must start using them as early as possible. The traditional means for learning kana are flashcards, writing demonstrations by the teacher, and workbooks. *Robo-Sensei* teaches kana with animated stroke-order demonstrations and automatically graded recognition, discrimination, and reading exercises that transcend conventional flashcard recognition practice. This function is another way in which an integrated,

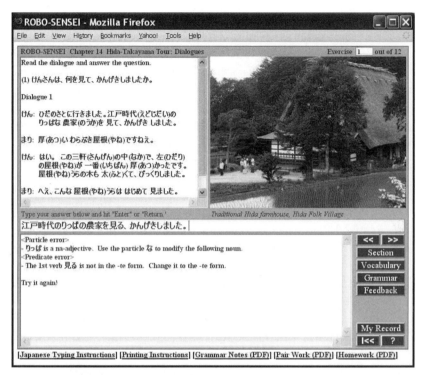

Figure 6. *Robo-Sensei*'s Tutor module dialogue exercise

computer-based textbook can enhance even the full, traditional Japanese curriculum.

The Tutor module links to the *Robo-Sensei*'s NLP-based exercise program, a module that allows students to respond to questions with full sentences and to receive ongoing, principle-based grammatical feedback in response to their errors. The Tutor module consists of the following sections: Dialogues, Vocabulary, Practice 1 and Practice 2, Pair Work, and Homework.

The Dialogue section (fig. 6) presents the core dialogues in a chapter and provides reading comprehension exercises. In each exercise, the student is asked to answer a question regarding the content of the dialogue. Photographic images accompanying each exercise assist with understanding the questions and answers and also generate interest in the exercises. The hiragana readings for the newly introduced kanji characters are provided in parentheses.

Typical comprehension exercises in computer-assisted language learning ask the student to choose a correct interpretation from a multiple-choice list. *Robo-Sensei*'s dialogue exercise asks the student to produce an answer in sentence form. *Robo-Sensei*'s NLP system can diagnose grammatical structures introduced in any chapter. Figure 6 illustrates a question, "けんさんは、なにをみて、かんげきしましたか。What did Ken see and get impressed by?," and an example of a student's response and *Robo-Sensei*'s feedback to that response. The student response contains errors concerning patterns taught already (*na*-adjective and *-te* form). Ongoing feedback pertaining to these errors ensures that students continue to receive instruction on the patterns they have not yet mastered.

The dialogue section is a warm-up for the more substantial practice sections that follow. Their exercises are easier than might appear because the correct answer is very similar to sentences already contained in the dialogue text. Seeing and producing similar sentences in advance increases the student's chance of success later and instills confidence.

Several buttons are displayed in figure 6: "Section" moves to another section in the Tutor module, "Vocabulary" looks up the words used in the current exercise, "Grammar" reviews the chapter grammar notes, and "Feedback" reopens the feedback window. When the answer is correct, a "Sound" button appears, allowing the learners to hear the correct answer pronounced. Students are often unsure how to pronounce the target sentences, and this function is there to help while their attention is fully primed. If a learner fails three times to produce a correct answer, *Robo-Sensei* presents both the "Sound" and "Answer" buttons. *Robo-Sensei* also helpfully stores the feedback messages the learner receives at each attempt. "My Record" shows the stored messages for review purposes. The teacher can ask the students to submit their feedback records to track progress and to determine if certain principles require further attention during class.

At the end of the exercises in every section, the "Score" button presents the student's total score. Although the students are offered the "Answer" button after failing three times, they still receive some credit: four points when they get the answer right immediately, three points at the second trial, two points at the third trial, and one point at the fourth trial. Because there are many possible correct answers, the score sheet also shows the correct answers the student came up with. If the students move to the next exercise without typing in a correct answer, their last mistaken response is shown as well. As mentioned above, students will be motivated to work until they achieve perfect scores. To give students credit for their performance, the instructor could ask them to submit their score sheets. The date and time the students worked on each exercise are also recorded.

In a regular language course, students take vocabulary quizzes that typically ask them to write appropriate words, given English equivalents (not in the multiple-choice format). This task makes sense, because if students cannot write (produce) the target words, they cannot use them. *Robo-Sensei*'s Vocabulary exercises provide word-production practice to facilitate vocabulary acquisition and help students prepare for such quizzes (fig. 7). Each exercise is accompanied by a photographic image of the word in question so that students can visually identify its meaning and enjoy relevant cultural information as well. By pressing the "Vocabulary" button, students can see a list of target vocabulary items so that, if they are not familiar with the word yet, they can search for it and continue the exercises.[19]

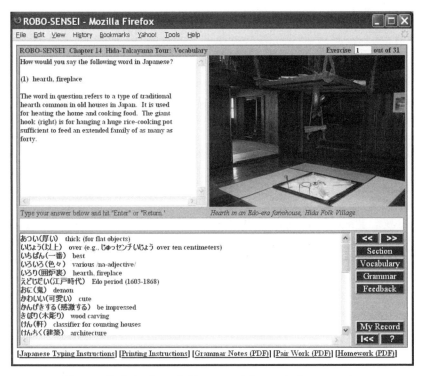

Figure 7. *Robo-Sensei*'s Tutor module vocabulary exercise

Even though each exercise requires only the production of a single word, *Robo-Sensei*'s NLP engine can still be useful. If the word in question is a verb and the students make a mistake in conjugation, *Robo-Sensei* can return feedback about the conjugation error. If the word is a number-classifier combination and the students use the wrong number or classifier or miss an irregular number-classifier combination,[20] *Robo-Sensei* can point out any misuse of numbers and classifiers because the NLP system can handle all Japanese numerical words as well as basic classifiers. None of these error messages has to be hand-coded, and far more error messages are required than one might first suppose.

Target grammatical structures in the chapter are divided between two practice sections (Practice 1 and Practice 2). (Chapters with more target structures have more than two practice sections.) Before starting the exercises, the students are instructed to read the chapter's grammar notes to roughly grasp the principles and concepts for the target structures. Those grammatical principles are reinforced by *Robo-Sensei*'s ongoing feedback, which continues until the student develops a firm understanding of them and is able to apply them in real communication.

The exercises in this chapter are integrated into a story about Ken's visit to Takayama City. Photographs of major Takayama sights and cultural notes about Japanese history, traditional architecture, crafts, and festivals enhance the relevance of the production tasks.[21] By the time the students finish the exercises, they can complete touring Takayama as well. Each exercise also presents a communicative situation resembling a daily conversation. Since students are most likely to use their Japanese skills during travel to Japan, the story line has situational relevance.

Practice section exercises consist of five types of production-based tasks. The first focuses on phrase production (fig. 8). Students are asked to fill in the missing part in the conversation with a phrase involving a target pattern. The second type (fig. 9) focuses on full-sentence production and asks the student to produce a complete sentence, given a conversational context. The strength of NLP technology is apparent here: students have unlimited opportunities to try out their own sentence-production skills because *Robo-Sensei* responds to every attempt immediately and provides patient, detailed feedback targeted to even the most persistently repeated errors.

The third type of task involves reading comprehension and phrase production. A short paragraph simulating writing a letter or journal entry pertaining to the chapter's cultural theme is presented. The student is

Figures 8 and 9. *Robo-Sensei*'s Tutor module phrase-production exercise (above) and sentence-production exercise (below)

402 Online Japanese Textbook

asked to fill in the missing parts in the paragraph, using the target forms and vocabulary. The fourth type of task pertains to listening comprehension and dictation. A sentence involving the target structure is played aloud, and the students are asked to type what they have heard. These exercises warm up the student before the fifth type of task, which involves more complex reading and listening comprehension as well as sentence production. In the fifth task, students are asked to read a paragraph related to the chapter's cultural theme, as in the third task. Then they listen to a question regarding the content of the paragraph and compose an answer.

These five types of tasks develop the learners' production skill progressively from lexical and phrase level to sentence level, helping them acquire a solid foundation of target vocabulary and grammar and extend their skill to writing, which is integrated gradually with the reading and listening components so that different skills develop jointly and reinforce one another.

The instructor can ask students to write a composition or to create a conversational script based on what they learned in the practice sections. After finishing Practice 1, for example, students might write a half-page report about Takayama City, using the target comparison forms and vocabulary they learned as much as possible. The instructor can also have students create a one-page conversation between A and B, given the situation in which A is going to Takayama and B is asking what A will do in Takayama. To use the sentences they just practiced, students can keep the *Robo-Sensei* program open and check their sentences for immediate, personalized feedback during the composition process. Such follow-up activity helps reinforce what students have learned. It raises the confidence and morale of students when they see immediately that they can achieve good results writing more extended passages. These practice sections can also be used as classroom activities, such as speaking practice. Since the first two types of tasks are presented in conversational settings, the instructor can have students assume the two roles and carry out conversations based on these tasks.

The Pair Work section is specifically designed for practicing conversations with partners, starting with role-play and moving on to less constrained personal interaction. *Robo-Sensei* might instruct one of the pair members in Japanese to ask his partner which she likes better, sashimi or tofu. A personal question such as this may elicit a range of potential answers: "She likes sashimi better," "She likes tofu better," "She likes both," or "She does not like either one." *Robo-Sensei* is capable of accepting all those answers.

During traditional pair work, students usually help each other correct their answers when the answers sound ungrammatical, but they do not necessarily succeed in coming up with grammatical sentences. Some pairs easily get lost and cannot continue the exercises until the instructor visits them, but in *Robo-Sensei* pairs can check their answers and make progress on their own. The instructor can then circulate freely among the groups and supervise the pair work without getting bogged down with one group. This is yet another unexpected way in which *Robo-Sensei*'s NLP technology can be a crucial advantage even when the instructor is interacting with the students in a traditional classroom setting.

The homework section, finally, provides a balanced sample of sentence-production exercises to assign outside of class in case other exercise sections are covered in class. Students can print out the homework sheet and fill in the answers by pencil or print out their score summaries (which appear at the end of the online homework exercises). Homework-sheet submission increases handwriting practice, so assigning some is desirable. *Robo-Sensei* can still be used to obtain feedback on the answers before writing them down, so students can solve problems on their own and do not have to wait days to see what they did wrong. The teacher can also save time on homework correction.

Development of *Robo-Sensei*

The design and development of NLP-based software are interdisciplinary enterprises, drawing on concepts, techniques, and theory from computer science, linguistics, and language pedagogy. In pursuit of this goal, I sought training in computational linguistics, computer-language programming (Lisp, C++, and Java), Japanese linguistics, Japanese language teaching, and second language acquisition. My research in NLP began with the ALICE project in the Laboratory for Computational Linguistics at Carnegie Mellon University in 1989–92 (Levin, Evans, and Gates). I created Japanese grammar rules and feedback templates to analyze a small domain of Japanese sentence structures (passive constructions), ran my first empirical effectiveness study, and completed my dissertation (Nagata, "Study"). I was also a teaching assistant at that time, responsible for practice sessions in Japanese language courses. I observed that students came to practice sessions without a clear understanding of grammatical structures and concepts and that there was not much time to provide detailed feedback in response to individual errors during conversation practice. It was also apparent that the students adopted a random, hit-or-miss approach without regard to principles and were not building the grammatical foundation necessary for mastery. From this concrete experience, I developed the strong belief that ongoing NLP-generated feedback could significantly improve second language acquisition.

The ALICE project involved many experts from different disciplines and languages. The approach applied existing, general-purpose parsers designed for machine translation (Hausser; Tomita, Mitamura, Musha, and Kee) to second-language education by adding the requisite grammar rules and lesson materials. This modular approach effectively separated the experts on the team, making it difficult to unify, expand, and maintain the system. Inevitably, key members of the team left the project, resulting in gaps of expertise that were difficult to fill with new personnel. The crucial lesson was that one person had to fully understand every aspect of the project, from the computer science to the linguistics to concrete issues of classroom management.

After I left the ALICE project, I developed a simple parser in Lisp and continued my empirical studies on the effectiveness of NLP-based instruction as described here. During my 1999–2000 sabbatical, fully funded by the University of San Francisco, I designed and programmed in Java the entire *Robo-Sensei* NLP system from scratch. This project culminated with *Robo-Sensei: Personal Japanese Tutor*. In 2006–07, I enjoyed a second sabbatical, during which I expanded *Robo-Sensei*'s NLP system and created a multimedia interface and a sample chapter for the new online textbook. A system of this scope usually involves extensive outside funding and a diversity of project members, but the development of *Robo-Sensei* illustrates a leaner, more flexible model, using only in-house university funding and having local assistants collect materials and test the lessons.[22]

Robo-Sensei can offer ongoing, specific feedback pinpointed to the precise nature of errors in students' attempts at producing sentences in conversational contexts. This ability is evidently crucial for self-study or distance-learning applications, where a human teacher is not present to correct exercises. But it is equally crucial in traditional classroom settings. Students receive immediate feedback when their attention and interest are at their peak. The feedback selectively reinforces the specific principles that students have not yet mastered. The option for self-study motivates students to strive on their own to improve their scores. By providing immediate, personal feedback when the instructor's attention is engaged with other students, *Robo-Sensei* enhances traditional, in-class pair work. By grading in-class and out-of-class activities, *Robo-Sensei* frees the teacher to focus more attention on conversational practice, the problems of individual students, classroom scheduling and student motivation, the development of curriculum, and extra office hours. The indispensable key to *Robo-Sensei*'s advantages is its NLP parsing and feedback-generation capacity. It is infeasible to provide such feedback by rote pattern matching and canned responses, because of the exponential explosion of possible student responses.

Notes

1. See, e.g., Sanders; Loritz; Swartz and Yazdani; Nagata, "Intelligent Computer Feedback," "Experimental Comparison"; Holland, Kaplan, and Sams; Yang and Akahori; Dansuwan, Nishina, Akahori, and Shimizu; Heift; Heift and Schulze; Amaral and Meurers. NLP-based feedback was implemented successfully in the online tutoring system *Robo-Sensei: Personal Japanese Tutor*. I have significantly extended the NLP capabilities of the tutoring system in the new, online Japanese textbook, also named *Robo-Sensei*, which will cover the full three-year Japanese curriculum.

2. Word orders in Japanese are relatively flexible except that the predicate (verb, adjective, or copula) comes at the end of the sentence. Particles attached to noun phrases indicate their grammatical roles (subject, object, goal, location, means, etc.), so the word order of noun phrases can be shuffled.

3. *Ni* に is the location particle and indicates the place where something exists. *Niwa* には is a possible alternative that consists of the topic particle *wa* は attached to *ni* に.

4. *Otera* おてら consists of *o* お (polite prefix) and *tera* てら ("temple"). *Tera* てら without *o* お is fine as well. The kanji version of てら is 寺.

5. The hiragana version of *takusan* is たくさん and the kanji version is 沢山. *Ippai* ("many") is also acceptable. The hiragana version of *ippai* is いっぱい, and the kanji version is 一杯.

6. *Robo-Sensei* handles the full range of Japanese verb, adjective, and copula conjugations, but only the root forms need to be represented explicitly in the lexicon. That is because *Robo-Sensei*'s morphological generator automatically produces the stems and other base forms by attaching inflectional endings and auxiliaries to the roots, and then the generated forms are added to the lexicon.

7. Japanese writing does not leave a space between words, so *Robo-Sensei*'s linguistic analysis starts by segmenting the learner's input into words. Many different segmentations and lexical assignments are often possible for one character string (e.g., *nihon* can be identified as *nihon* ["Japan"], *ni* ["two"] and *hon* ["counter"], or *ni* [the particle] and *hon* ["book"], etc.). What the student intended can, therefore, be a matter of judgment. *Robo-Sensei* charitably assumes the most grammatical possible interpretation as the student's intention. For a detailed description of *Robo-Sensei*'s word segmentor, see Nagata, "*Robo-Sensei*'s NLP-Based Error Detection."

8. The parser uses context-free phrase-structure rules to build words into phrases and phrases into sentences by means of a bottom-up parsing technique (Winograd; Matsumoto).

9. For most misspelled inputs, *Robo-Sensei* returns the message "unknown word." For example, if the learner misspells *otera* てら ("temple") as *oteri* おてり, this error message appears: "The character string おてり is unknown; Check your spelling." Due to the ambiguity of Japanese words, however, it is impossible to avoid misinterpretations of the student's intentions, which may result very occasionally in odd or confusing feedback. For instance, if the learner misspelled ippai いっぱい ("many") as itsupai いつぱい, *Robo-Sensei* provides this error message: " たくさん is missing; いつ is not expected to be used here." The misspelled word い つぱい is interpreted as いつ ("when") and ぱい (a classifier), and the learner is informed that いつ ("when") is not expected and たくさん (another word for "many") is missing. The learner can understand the error message and fix the error using た くさん, but the learner's intention was to use いっぱい, which was misspelled in the response. *Robo-Sensei*'s NLP feedback-generation system has since been improved to handle a wider range of misspellings, so the new message for the misspelled small tsu is "いつぱい is wrong; Change つ to the small っ for the first syllable of the double consonants."

10. For example, once learners understood that *tomodati* means "friend," *kuruma* "car," and *kiree* "pretty," it was easy for them to interpret *tomodati no kuruma* as "a friend's car" and *kiree na kuruma* as "a pretty car" without processing *no* and *na*.

11. It is also possible to make a printed version of *Robo-Sensei* and to distribute the hard copy along with the online version.

12. There will be three volumes, the first volume for first-year Japanese, the second volume for second-year Japanese, and the third volume for third-year Japanese. The target date for the first volume is the end of 2009; the second and third volumes are slated for the following years.

13. The previous version of *Robo-Sensei* has been effectively employed in classroom activities since 2002 in the standard Japanese curriculum at the University of San Francisco.

14. Chapter 14 can be used toward the end of a second-semester Japanese course.

15. This chapter introduces five grammatical items: patterns for comparing two items; どちらも *both* and 「Aも Bも」 *both A and B*; 「AやB」 *A, B, and so forth*; patterns for comparing three or more items; and classifiers けん counting for

houses, センチ or センチメートル counting for centimeters, and メートル counting for meters.

16. The story in dialogue 1 is that Ken is telling Mari that he went to Hida Folk Village and was impressed by magnificent Edo-period farmhouses. Mari comments on how thick the straw thatched roofs are. Ken tells her that among these three houses, the left roof was the thickest. He was also surprised by thick rafters in the attic. Mari exclaims that this is the first time for her to see such an attic.

17. Students are required to master 560 kanji in the *Robo-Sensei* online textbook. Many more kanji are presented with glosses but are not required.

18. Katakana are used to write foreign names and loanwords, and hiragana are used mainly to write particles, copulas, and grammatical inflections in verbs, adjectives, and adverbs. Kanji are used for nouns and the stems of verbs, adjectives, and adverbs. Japanese sentences are normally written with a mixture of hiragana, katakana, and kanji.

19. All vocabulary items are listed in kana followed by kanji in parentheses. Not all the kanji presented are required to be memorized; many are added for general interest.

20. Depending on the shapes or functions of objects, Japanese uses different classifiers to count the objects. The classifier is attached to a numerical word; for example, the classifier *ken* is attached to a numerical word such as *ichi* ("one"), *ni* ("two"), or *san* ("three") to count houses. There are irregular changes in the last syllable of the numerical word and the first syllable of the classifier.

21. Every exercise in the *Robo-Sensei* online textbook is accompanied by a relevant photographic image of Japan. Chapter 14 includes 130 photographic images taken in Takayama City by the author and Kevin T. Kelly (*Robo-Sensei* project consultant). Since 2005, the project produced several thousand original, digital photographs of historical and cultural sites in Japan for exclusive use in the new *Robo-Sensei* online textbook.

22. I received full-time funding from the university for my sabbatical years to develop *Robo-Sensei*, along with university faculty travel funds to gather cultural materials and digital images of Japan over two summers. My project consultant, Kevin T. Kelly, has been assisting with graphic design, on-site photography in Japan, and the production of cultural notes. I have also been assisted a great deal by Japanese instructors (especially Kyoko Suda) and students at the University of San Francisco and the publisher's beta testers, all of whom have helped with lesson checking and in classroom testing.

Works Cited

Amaral, Luiz, and Detmar Meurers. "Little Things with Big Effects: On the Identification and Interpretation of Tokens for Error Diagnosis in ICALL." *CALICO Journal* 26.3 (2009): 580–91. Web. 3 Feb. 2009.
Banados, Emerita. "A Blended-Learning Pedagogical Model for Teaching and Learning EFL Successfully through an Online Interactive Multimedia Environment." *CALICO Journal* 23.3 (2006): 533–50. Web. 3 Feb. 2009.

Dansuwan, S., K. Nishina, K. Akahori, and Y. Shimizu. "Development and Evaluation of a Thai Learning System on the Web Using Natural Language Processing." *CALICO Journal* 19.1 (2001): 67–88. Web. 3 Feb. 2009.

DeKeyser, Robert. "Learning Second Language Grammar Rules: An Experiment with a Miniature Linguistic System." *Studies in Second Language Acquisition* 17.3 (1995): 379–410. Print.

Hausser, Roland. "Principles of Computational Morphology." 1989. MS. Laboratory for Computational Linguistics, Carnegie Mellon U.

Heift, Trude. "Multiple Learner Errors and Meaningful Feedback: A Challenge for ICALL Systems." *CALICO Journal* 20.3 (2003): 533–48. Web. 3 Feb. 2009.

Heift, Trude, and Mathias Schulze. *Errors and Intelligence in Computer-Assisted Language Learning: Parsers and Pedagogues.* New York: Routledge, 2007. Print.

Holland, V. M., J. D. Kaplan, and M. R. Sams. *Intelligent Language Tutors.* Mahwah: Erlbaum, 1995. Print.

Krashen, Stephen D. *The Input Hypothesis: Issues and Implications.* London: Longman, 1985. Print.

Levin, Lori, David A. Evans, and Donna Gates. "The ALICE System: A Workbench for Learning and Using Language." *CALICO Journal* 9.1 (1991): 27–56. Web. 3 Feb. 2009.

Loritz, Donald. "Generalized Transition Network Parsing for Language Study: The GPARS System for English, Russian, Japanese and Chinese." *CALICO Journal* 10.1 (1992): 5–22. Web. 3 Feb. 2009.

Matsumoto, Yuji. 自然言語理解 [*Natural Language Understanding*]. Ed. H. Tanaka and J. Tsujii. Tokyo: オーム社, 1988. Print.

Nagata, Noriko. "BANZAI: An Application of Natural Language Processing to Web Based Language Learning." *CALICO Journal* 19.3 (2002): 583–99. Web. 3 Feb. 2009.

———. "Computer versus Workbook Instruction in Second Language Acquisition." *CALICO Journal* 14.1 (1996): 53–75. Print.

———. "An Effective Application of Natural Language Processing in Second Language Instruction." *CALICO Journal* 13.1 (1995): 47–67. Web. 3 Feb. 2009.

———. "An Experimental Comparison of Deductive and Inductive Feedback Generated by a Simple Parser." *System* 25.4 (1997): 515–34. Print.

———. "Input Enhancement by Natural Language Processing." *Assessing the Impact of Input Enhancement in Second Language Education: Evaluation in Theory, Research, and Practice.* Ed. Carolyn Gascoigne. Stillwater: New Forums, 2007. 153–67. Print.

———. "Input vs. Output Practice in Educational Software for Second Language Acquisition." *Language Learning and Technology* 1.2 (1998): 23–40. Web. 3 Feb. 2009.

———. "Intelligent Computer Feedback for Second Language Instruction." *Modern Language Journal* 77.3 (1993): 330–39. Print.

———. "自然言語処理を応用したインテリジェントランゲージチューター" ["Intelligent Language Tutor as an Application of Natural Language Processing"].

言語学と日本語教育 [*Linguistics and Japanese Language Education*]. Ed. M. Minami and M. Asano. Vol. 3. Tokyo: Kuroshio. Print.

———. "The Relative Effectiveness of Production and Comprehension Practice in Second Language Acquisition." *Computer Assisted Language Learning* 11.2 (1998): 153–77. Web. 3 Feb. 2009.

———. *Robo-Sensei: Personal Japanese Tutor*. Boston: Cheng, 2004. CD-ROM.

———. "*Robo-Sensei*'s NLP-Based Error Detection and Feedback Generation." *CALICO Journal* 26.3 (2009): 562–79. Web. 3 Feb. 2009.

———. "A Study of the Effectiveness of Intelligent CALI as an Application of Natural Language Processing." Diss. U of Pittsburgh, 1992. Print.

Omaggio, Alice C. *Teaching Language in Context*. Boston: Heinle, 1986. Print.

Polisca, Elena. "Facilitating the Learning Process: An Evaluation of the Use and Benefits of a Virtual Learning Environment (VIE)-Enhanced Independent Language-Learning Program (ILLP)." *CALICO Journal* 23.3 (2006): 499–516. Web. 3 Feb. 2009.

Sanders, Ruth. "Error Analysis in Purely Syntactic Parsing of Free Input: The Example of German." *CALICO Journal* 9.1 (1991): 72–89. Web. 3 Feb. 2009.

Scida, Emily, and Rachel Saury. "Hybrid Courses and Their Impact on Student and Classroom Performance: A Case Study at the University of Virginia." *CALICO Journal* 23.3 (2006): 517–32. Web. 3. Feb. 2009.

Swain, Merrill. "Communicative Competence: Some Roles of Comprehensible Input and Comprehensible Output in Its Development." *Input in Second Language Acquisition*. Ed. S. Gass and C. Madden. Rowley: Newbury, 1985. 235–53. Print.

Swain, Merrill, and Sharon Lapkin. "Problems in Output and the Cognitive Processes They Generate: A Step towards Second Language Learning." *Applied Linguistics* 16.3 (1995): 371–91. Print.

Swartz, M. L., and M. Yazdani, eds. *Intelligent Tutoring Systems for Foreign Language Learning: The Bridge to International Communication*. London: Longman, 1992. Print.

Tomita, Masaru, T. Mitamura, H. Musha, and M. Kee. "The Generalized LR Parser/Compiler Version 8.1: User's Guide." Memo to Center for Machine Translation, Carnegie Mellon U. 1988. TS.

Winograd, Terry. *Language as a Cognitive Process: Volume I: Syntax*. Boston: Addison, 1983. Print.

Yang, Jie Chi, and Kanji Akahori. "Error Analysis in Japanese Writing and Its Implementation in a Computer Assisted Language Learning System on the World Wide Web." *CALICO Journal* 15.1-3 (1998): 47–66. Web. 3 Feb. 2009.

Ian Lancashire

The Open-Source English Teacher

An open-source teacher puts instructional materials online, uses decentralized peer review collaboratively to improve their quality, and deposits them under terms and conditions like those in "copyleft" used by software developers (Taylor and Riley).[1] Copyleft allows other teachers to modify and redistribute all modified versions of original materials as long as the author's name and the indelibly free terms of usage are retained.[2] Open-source teachers come from elementary and high schools and from colleges and universities,[3] where online teaching resources are often a byproduct of an instructor's research. The online community ranks such sites: Britannica gives the Internet Guide Award, *Renascence Editions* the Bess, and SchoolZone, *Topmarks*, and *Internet Shakespeare Editions* recognize merit publicly. Within academe, the *EDSITEment* initiative by the National Endowment for the Humanities (http://edsitement.neh.gov), relying on recommendations by an independently peer-reviewed panel, gave open-source teaching resources on the Web their greatest incentive in 1998.[4] The *MITOpenCourseWare* initiative, three years ago, continued to stimulate open-source teaching in all disciplines.[5]

Teaching materials in the languages and literatures consist of documents and software.[6] The collaborative mechanism in open-source teaching differs from that in the software industry. *Open Source* promises that "rapid evolutionary process produces better software than the traditional closed model," a claim that open-source teachers do not make (*Open Source Initiative*). Teachers favor a networking plenitude that enables Web collectives or online communities that might be called "Web gardens."[7] Alan Liu's *Voice of the Shuttle* has for a decade documented the humanities open-source community (http://vos.ucsb.edu). Other more selective lists attach to peer-reviewed online journals such as *Romantic Circles* and *Early Modern Literary Studies* or online archives such as *Early English Books Online / Text Creation Partnership* (see "EEBO" for a sample list of resources). Online collectives implement a nonagonistic peer review. With unlimited storage space and ease of document recall, one Web garden can easily enfold the resources of more teachers in one year than can be published in print in a decade. The open-source principle of collaboration remains the same in software and instructional development.

Much open-source teaching goes on without personal interaction between teacher and students. When open-source teachers publish what they know (and might say in physical classroom lectures), however, they also collaborate with persons unknown who teach what the Sloan Foundation, a great stimulus to online education, calls blended courses ("SREB States"). These courses supplement face-to-face interaction between a faculty member and students in classrooms with course use of Internet teaching materials authored or edited by others. Blended courses allow students to learn from unfamiliar online instructors who edit, annotate, and comment on texts. Seldom do classroom teachers and their online shadows collaborate directly, but readers e-mail open-source teachers to express thanks, ask questions, or engage in a private, one-on-one tweaking of a document. Readers encourage open-source teachers to make adjustments in tone or corrections of fact and to accommodate a position intellectually or socially. Without open-source teachers, blended courses would not be the dominant type of online course. Online teaching in literature and language thus consists of both online and open-source teachers.

The Range of Online Teaching Resources

Some teachers behave like open-source software developers, building on works published before, often in print. In the humanities, these works include editions of major authors. Every discipline recognizes online flagship enterprises that helped shape the pedagogical Web. Brown University faculty members, particularly George P. Landow, pioneered English studies online. Landow's *Victorian Web* (www.victorianweb.org), which serves as "a resource for courses in Victorian literature," began in 1987 from his teaching of English 32, Survey of English Literature from 1700 to the Present, and is still burgeoning at the National University of Singapore. Subsets of it, including *The Dickens Web*, published by Eastgate Systems, offer students "the editorial and critical apparatus designed to bridge the gap between past and present."[8] To these can be added Brown University's *Women Writers Online* (www.wwp.brown.edu) and the University of Victoria's *Internet Shakespeare Editions* (http://ise.uvic.ca), edited by Michael Best and containing "scholarly, fully annotated texts of Shakespeare's plays, multimedia explorations of the context of Shakespeare's life and works, and records of his plays in performance" (*"Internet Shakespeare Editions"*). The site's peer-reviewed series of individually edited Shakespeare editions crystallizes around the instructional CD-ROM *Shakespeare's Life and Times*, originally published in 1995 and now entitled *A Shakespeare Suite*. Landow and Best, like many others, both re-create documents that are central to teaching in their disciplines and offer students historical and critical commentaries. Their collaboration takes place, in effect, with critics, historians, and editors who lived in the ages before the Internet.

Open-source teachers are a vibrant minority in many literature and language departments, as a quick look at my English department at the University of Toronto will show.[9] Of Toronto's one hundred fifty-four faculty members, tenured and nontenured, ten (six and a half percent) contribute online materials to blended courses, most of which are language related. Toni Healey edits the *Dictionary of Old English: A to G Online*; Anne Lancashire edits the Web database *Mayors and Sheriffs of London*; Sally-Beth MacLean codirects the Records of Early English Drama's *Patrons and Performances Web Site*; Carol Percy compiles the Web site *History of the English Language* (*HEL*); George Rigg converts his *English Language: A Historical Reader* for local online use and makes his *Traditional Grammatical Terminology* openly accessible; and I edit *Representative Poetry Online*, *Lexicons of Early Modern English*, and several other Web sites. Jeannine DeLombard and Dan White offer "Papers: Expectations, Guidelines, Advice, and Grading." The other emphasis is literary theory. Linda Hutcheon offers *Irony, Nostaliga, and the Postmodern* and, with Nancy Kang, *The English Critical Essay*, and Greig E. Henderson coedits (with Christopher Brown) *Glossary of Literary Theory*.

An Open-Source Case Study

On 15 December 1994, I released *Representative Poetry Online* (*RPO*), which, like much open-source software, builds on existing work (Lancashire, "*Representative Poetry Online*"). *RPO* had poems by about eighty poets, from Sir Thomas Wyatt to Algernon Charles Swinburne, as they appeared in the last edition of *Representative Poetry*, the textbook edited by members of my English department first in 1912. W. J. Alexander, the first professor of English at University College, and his associate William Clawson produced the initial *Representative Poetry*: it had one hundred poems by fourteen poets, from Alexander Pope to William Morris. Subsequent reprintings of this single-volume anthology came out in 1916, 1920, 1923, and 1928. The second major edition, revised in two volumes, came out in 1935 and was reissued with changes in 1938, 1941, and 1946. The last edition, in three volumes, came out in 1961–62. The margins of my teaching copy, thick with annotations, recorded how I interpreted the poems in the early 1970s. Twenty-five editors had already written textual, historical, or philological information about the poems for small-print notes at the back of the three volumes. I never took a course from Northrop Frye or Marshall McLuhan, but by their selection and annotation of poems by William Blake and Alfred Tennyson they taught me.

My digital conversion of *RPO*, an experiment in Web development sponsored by the university's library, used HTML-encoded poem files, linked to poet files, as well as index files. Notes were shifted from the end of the book to lines in the poem files, and bibliographical information, where missing, was silently added. The library found that Web traffic was high.[10] In the first year after *RPO* went online, I got a then unexpected amount of e-mail from readers who enjoyed relocating poems that they had lost track of since school days and others who were incensed with my unrepresentative selection of poets. This was my introduction to open-source peer review. I realized that what my colleagues had designed for students who had graduated from high school in the 1950s, I had repurposed, without change, for generations who had lived through another forty years and the civil rights movement, feminism, Vietnam, the end of the cold war, AIDS, and Operation Desert Storm. Immigrants from Asia had since transformed hogtown Toronto into a postcolonial city in which almost fifty percent of its citizens were visible minorities.

The eighty dead white males and two white women (Anne Finch, countess of Winchilsea, and Christina Rossetti), all English, who populated the first version of *RPO* deserved study, but in no way could the volume be called representative of English poets. So I set about adding women poets in the first months after publication. *RPO* now has 110 women writers, about twenty percent of its 526 poets. Because living poets Lynn Crosbie, Annie Finch, Phyllis Gotlieb, Sonnet L'Abbé, Molly Peacock, Marge Piercy (the first to give me permission), Rosemarie Rowley, and Rosemary Sullivan generously allowed me to publish selections of their poems, *RPO* can partly meet the expectations of contemporary readers for voices other than male.

Strident e-mail, however, soon drew attention to other omissions. "Where were the African Americans?" wrote one indignant Brown University student (she could have extended that to North Americans, of whom not one could be found). That led me to wonder (after thirty years of teaching poems), where were the English poets of India, Australia, and the Caribbean? I did not know the answers, and so I started reading poetry books in spare moments at the British Library, in the New York Public Library (after attending MLA committee meetings), and at other institutional libraries during conference stops. What brought me to English studies in the late 1950s had been poetry as W. H. Auden wrote it and as Elizabeth Drew analyzed it. A youthful excitement returned to my life with *RPO*.

Good poets, *RPO* readers have taught me, are not just those taught in English courses. Most teachers inherit the tastes of the generation that taught them and of our mass-market anthology editors. Without enough time to read widely, facing curricular deadlines, we accept the judgments of those to whom the profession assigns authority. Also, if we cannot see anything puzzling about a poem—if it does not invite analysis, if it is not innovative, or if it is uninstructive of the best minds or worst events of the age—what is there to teach? Poets of lesser reputation, however, write fine poems that few read any more. I began to unbury from the archive poets who wrote poems intelligent and moving, such as Humfrey Gifford's riddle "A Female I by Name"; "Upon a Quiet Conscience," by Charles I; Anne Bradstreet's "In Reference to Her Children, 23 June 1659"; Henry

Carey's "The Ballad of Sally in Our Alley"; Augustus Montague Toplady's "A Living and Dying Prayer for the Holiest Believer in the World" ("Rock of Ages"); Sydney Smith's aphoristic "Recipe for a Salad"; John Pierpont's "Unchain the Laborer"; Elizabeth Siddall's fearful "Dead Love"; Arabella Eugenia Smith's heartrending "If I Should Die To-night"; Toru Dutt's "A Sea of Foliage Girds Our Garden Round"; E. Pauline Johnson's "Shadow River: Muskoka"; Arthur Christopher Benson's "Self"; Robert Fuller Murray's "The Waster's Presentment"; and Trumbull Stickney's "Leave Him Now Quiet by the Way." A family backyard in Baugmaree, India, a student's accurate estimate of his chances at passing, a recipe, and a riddle—subjects not ringing with significance. A mother's fears and hopes at life's end for her scattered children and complaints about lovelessness or desperation—ordinary anxieties. Expectations notwithstanding of what a couple of Smiths and someone named Toplady might turn out, every poem shines up well.

Although *Representative Poetry* never abandoned the great tradition, my department edited not for the elite but for "the ordinary reader"[11] that it wished their undergraduate students to become. Like my predecessors, I was skeptical that ordinary readers could do much with Old English and Middle English (Chaucer excepted) if they did not have an interlinear translation; and so I interwove or added an out-of-copyright one. Sometimes when I excerpted minor popular poets, I imagined the founding editor in 1912, a fierce defender of Robert Browning's works, bristling with indignation. My defense was that, just as the ordinary reader forced him to include Robbie Burns, so the ordinary reader expects me to have Andrew Lang, Geoffrey Anketell Studdert Kennedy ("Woodbine Willy"), Gelett Burgess, Arthur Guiterman, Robert Service, Don Marquis, Edgar Guest, Dorothy Parker, and Graham Lee ("Tobacco Is a Dirty Weed") Hemminger. Academe had just gone through a decanonization exercise, so that many female, non-Caucasian, and world poets new to *RPO* had become respectable. The postmodern subversiveness of so many light and parodic poems also saved me from having to apologize for them. Still, by introducing poets who had fallen into such utter obscurity that even their death dates were initally unknown—J. E. Ball (fl. 1904–06), Tom Skeyhill (fl. 1915), and Stanley de Vere Alexander Julius (1874–1930)—*RPO* shows a possibly quirky perspective on poetry.[12] I have no qualms about offering an ordinary reader's poem whose quality or circumstances of birth make it memorable. A simple, passionate prayer is one such poem. It begins:

> Stay with me, God. The night is dark,
> The night is cold: my little spark
> Of courage dies. The night is long;
> Be with me, God, and make me strong. ("Stay")

An unknown poet in World War II wrote it, and the scrap of paper on which it was written blew into a trench at the battle of El Agheila in January 1942, when General Rommel forced British forces to retreat in the African desert.

At first, I was not conscious of teaching. Colleagues and students did not write or call, although ordinary readers e-mailed. I described some of their astonishing notes in a paper at the MLA convention in 2001, since published in the *Journal of Scholarly Publishing*. Messages still arrive every week, some giving me corrections or commentary on poems, others more personal.

> i'm 88. been enjoying guest [Edgar A. Guest] since a young boy. never could afford to buy them. a friend gave me an old copy of path to home 20 years ago. used to smile over them. now i'm real old & alone, i truly appreciate his talent. now he makes me cry at times and at times i laugh aloud!! i used to read him every day in n.y. news paper. thanks for your patience. (McKenna)

> Thank you so much for enabling me to once again read "Horatius holds the bridge" [Thomas Babington Macaulay's "Horatius"]. I read the poem (though not in its entirety) at school in 1957/8 and it made such an impression upon me that I can still quote a number of verses and extracts after almost fifty years. I can't understand why such a work does not figure in books of English poetry, but perhaps I'm biased. To me the poem has everything! (White)

My correspondents tell me that poetry earns its place in literature courses, in part because an ordinary reader needs the feelings it stirs and dignifies, long after formal education ends. To teach poetry means creating conditions in which, even in private, silent reading, a student will experience, without embarrassment or harm, the welling up of powerful emotions.[13] Poems are evidently more than the recollection of feelings in tranquillity. *RPO* plays a useful role in blended courses by offering poems that meet such emotional needs. For example, Cecil Frances Alexander's "Maker of Heaven and Earth," otherwise known as "All Things Bright and Beautiful," was first published in the same year, 1848, that Smith and Elder brought out the first edition of poems by Anne Brontë and Emily Brontë. Emily Brontë's "Plead for Me" has moved many, including Auden, but so has Alexander's simpler hymn, which has an equal place in *RPO*. A Namibian schoolteacher asked me for permission to use its text, explaining:

> I've known the hymn for about 65 years, having learnt it first at the age of five or thereabouts. We sang it regularly throughout my school years, later i taught it in schools. Whether i love the hymn because i'm a nature lover, or whether the hymn made me one, i couldn't say. The "tiny wings" has made me weep again and again in memory of failed attempts to rear birds fallen out of the nest or caught by a cat. It's perfect for the Namibian education department's requirements that we try to teach respect for the environment. (Maré)

When colleagues ask me why I continue growing *RPO*, years after the advent of *Literature Online*, I think of these readers (see Lancashire, "Editing").

Two years after *RPO* went online, it received prizes from search engines in gratitude for its free Web resources. Between 1996 and 1998, I had added the 1912 and 1935 editions, notes, eighteen prose treatises on poetry, a timeline, and 221 more poets. Recognition then started coming from educational groups: the BBC Education Web Guide (Oct. 1998) and the Scottish Council for Educational Technology (Nov. 1998). At that time, I knew myself to be teaching in editing *RPO*. By 2001, when another fifty poets had come online, *RPO* received SchoolZone five-stars and *Britannica Online* awards, more evidence to the effect that *RPO* was a teaching resource. This recognition enabled me to obtain University of Toronto support from the provost, the dean of arts and science, and my department to transform it from an HTML file collection into an SQL (structured query language) database. The conversion was completed by October 2002. The site included, for the first time, some of my critical commentaries on poems and an interactive concordancer. My department now recognizes *RPO* as a valuable teaching resource.[14] It has 526 poets, 3,617 poems, 235,156 lines of verse, 16,761 annotations, and 29 critical commentaries on specific poems.

By fall 2002, I had been asked to teach ENG 201Y: Reading Poetry as a completely online section to two dozen students.[15] In preparation, I spent almost all summer 2002 writing up commentaries on touchstone poems that were to be the focus of each of the twenty-six weeks of the course. When the department gave me a teaching assistant, I had time, during the term, to record audio lectures, add more commentaries, and teach in a weekly chatroom.[16] I was provided with *Prometheus* and then *WebCT* courseware to assemble a smaller anthology of touchstone poems from *RPO* (those in the public domain) and from *Literature Online* (*LiOn*; where poems were in copyright), which I then bundled with later poems that commented on or parodied them. The existence of parodies (not my own taste) identified which poems were to be the touchstones that formed the core of the curriculum (see Lancashire, "Recovering"). Often only by searching in *LiOn* could I locate these parodies and so locate which poems belonged to the touchstones that poets selected in the act of choosing to write about them.

In retrospect, I can see clearly the difference between myself as an open-source teacher and as an online teacher. Ordinary readers enable an open-source teacher to expand a Web site by informal collaboration, and I listen to what they want. Edwin Ahearn, for example, suggested Edwin Arlington Robinson and Trumbull Stickney; Chandler Davis suggested James Joseph Sylvester, the nineteenth-century mathematician-poet. Patricia Reeser pointed out that Thomas Carlyle had written several memorable poems, and Paul L. Wolf alerted me to Helen Hunt Jackson. James Fulford asked for Browning's "The Lost Leader." John Garwood told me that I had to have Tennyson's "Charge of the Light Brigade" because it was the best poem in the English language despite Marshall McLuhan's view that it was not. Many readers corrected my mistakes, solved annotation problems, and gave advice that made *RPO* more accurate. Web citizens test the open-source teacher instead of being tested by him or her. An online teacher interacts with students weekly, but an open-source teacher waits for e-mail. In more than ten years, no one has written to attack a poem that is in *RPO*. Instead, readers write their gratitude. The more people read poetry on the Web, the more poetry is loved and understood.

Sometimes the suggestion to add a poem comes from an unexpected quarter. Having edited both "God Save the King" and Francis Scott Key's "Defence of Fort McHenry" ("The Star-Spangled Banner") in 2002, I should not have been surprised when a reporter from the *Toronto Star*, Leslie Scrivener, in the week before Canada Day in 2006, questioned me about "O Canada," our national anthem, based on a 1917 poem by Robert Stanley Weir. Determined to deconstruct Weir's poem, Scrivener wanted to know about the poem's sources. By annotating his use of well-worn poetic diction of the period, I turned up two poets who very clearly influenced him, Helen Mar Johnson and Martin Butler, both of whom were Quebecois, like the composer of the music that Canadians now use to sing the anthem. That *la belle province*, which elects a separatist party to Canada's federal parliament, should be largely responsible for the national song is postcolonial irony. The supposedly uneducated public often has a better instinct for interesting poems than I have. Next time I teach poetry, "O Canada" will make an early appearance.

I worried at first that my ENG 202Y digital commentaries would leak out of the courseware into the hands of others. By 2002, I decided to release them on *RPO* because doing so was consistent with open-source teaching and with the generosity of living poets who had freely donated their works. Some commentaries, like the one on Browning's "My Last Duchess," are popular with students. Others, including my little squib on Sir Thomas Wyatt's "They Flee from Me," are useful targets for critical disagreement.

Online and open-source teachers tend to be loners. When I met with the MLA Committee on Information Technology to discuss this volume, I thought that most online-literature teachers were Lone Rangers who developed their courses independently (see Dauer; Rashley; Alsgaard). Language teachers on the committee, however, pointed out that journals about online teaching and professional organizations like EDUCAUSE had been active for a long time. Diana G. Oblinger and Brian L. Hawkins even claim that no faculty member working alone can deliver an effective online course. Yet most teachers of online literature courses, like open-source teachers, work alone. I knew the living poets *RPO* published, the Robarts Library Information Technology staff members, and my nonacademic readership but could find no one at my own institution who had given a full-credit course in the humanities online. When in 2005–06 the National Endowment for the Humanities recommended *RPO* for inclusion in *EDSITEment*, I first felt the profession's support for the open-source teaching community strongly and with gratitude. Two British sites, *TeacherNet* in 2004 and *TopMarks* in 2006, also awarded *RPO* their approval.

Being an open-source teacher conditioned how I conceived of my online course in reading poetry. I supplied resources and discussed poems with my students as if they were ordinary readers. Doing weekly audio lectures alone in a small room proved a trial: I spontaneously recorded them, without script. Often I had to begin half a dozen times before I hit my stride. In them I hoped to share the emotional responses to poems that I and ordinary readers of *RPO* had. Audio lectures contrasted with the dispassionate commentaries. The same digital isolation that online teachers experience—that excites them to create online communities of their classes and makes them take online teaching resources for granted—claimed me. Since using a bulletin board would have distanced me from my students, I chose to use chat rooms, which brought my students to life. Chat rooms made our students the sustaining community for our online courses. It was hard to describe these online teaching experiences to my colleagues.[17] Most had never been in a chat room, let alone had to edit their own anthology for a course.

I taught students for twelve years at a small suburban campus before my first research book came out. This daily apprenticeship trained me to value my teaching as the enthusiasm of my students for the literature to which I introduced them rose and fell. The academic articles and books I have published entered a respectably scholarly gray literature, like government publications, to be searched by researchers for information more than to be read. Working on an academic mobius strip, I gradually came to regret how little contact I had with ordinary readers. My experience with *RPO*—its weekly e-mail about its poetry and poets, library reports of the number of readers who had called up its pages—changed all that.

Asynchronously, Yours

Serving both society and the teaching profession, open-source teachers freefall into unexpected kinds of instruction. While always in the online classroom, digitally giving dictation, they learn of visitors only when they leave behind a calling card, a thank-you note, a begging plea, a correction, or an e-mail offer. Eagerly read, these messages give teachers their only sense of the online community that reads what they offer. Many are appeals by novice students who take English as a second language and need verse paraphrases. A very few are breathtaking.

In 2004 at the British Library, I found a modern anglophone poet from India of whom I had never heard, Govinda Krishna Chettur (1898–1936). I thought his poem "Beloved," which begins "You are the Rose of me, / In you have I lost myself utterly," would appeal to ordinary readers, as it did to me, and so I added three of his poems to *RPO*. Several days ago a friend of his daughter, V. M. Padmini Chettur, e-mailed me the daughter's recollections of her father, who died when she was very young:

> As I grew older I came to understand him through his writings and my mother's recollections of him. The more I came to know about him my admiration and love for him grew and along with it a desire to write something about him. I did not have a clue as to how I could [go] about doing it and so it remained un-attempted. Recently I was told that there was a website dedicated to my father—Late G. K. Chettur and that it had samples of his works but did not furnish any information regarding the life and times of G. K. Chettur. I felt that God has given me an opportunity to fulfill my long cherished wish of writing something about my father—a daughter's humble dedication. Browsing through his works after a long gap provided an exciting and nostalgic journey down memory lane and this time I did not attempt to fight back the tears that flowed unabated strengthening the bond of love and affection for my dear father all over again. (Puthiyaveettil)

The above e-mail came not long after another arrived from an *RPO* reader who wrote me about her father, prompted by the *RPO* text of Sir John Suckling's poem "A Ballad upon a Wedding":

> My father was in (roughly) the middle stages of Alzheimer's two years ago when he recited, out of a clear blue sky, the verse beginning "Her feet beneath her petticoat", almost faultlessly—from memory!! I would like to use the poem as it appears on your site for his enjoyment (it would be interesting to know if he would remember the poem if he read it). (Dapra)

This message is the second I have received, in half a dozen years, about the survival of a poem in a mind suffering from dementia. Seeing with what tenacious roots poetry takes life in the unordinary minds of fathers and daughters, I no longer trust myself to know the most important things to say about poetry. The signature pedagogy of the open-source teacher is an online community (like those that online courses seek to create) in which it is not clear who is teaching whom.

Such a humbling return to essentials marks a late-career scholar. The only English faculty members interested in creating online teaching resources in my department at Toronto are tenured, senior researchers.

Jerome McGann (see his essay in this volume) also numbers just four on-line faculty members in his department at the University of Virginia. In 1985, when I founded the Centre for Computing in the Humanities (CCH) at Toronto, resources and tools were scarce. Like Virginia's later Institute for Advanced Technology in the Humanities (IATH), CCH had to make them. From its researchers came *RPO*, Willard McCarty's *Humanist*, a local e-text library, and the *TACT* interactive concordancer, whose book and CD-ROM MLA published in 1996. Young faculty members a decade later harvest a much greater electronic plenty. Undergraduate courses at Toronto use *Blackboard* and routinely blend article databases, *Literature Online*, and the classroom. The global digital academy for which I am preparing a centenary edition of *RPO* in 2012 will be even richer. The Poetry Foundation of Chicago Web site (which in 2005 licensed use of *RPO* in perpetuity) and thousands of Web enthusiasts will have done much to replant poetry in Western culture. The teacher without borders will be everywhere.

Notes

1. The expressions "open-source teaching" and "open-source teacher" are rare but not new (see, e.g., the *Open Source Teaching Project* [www .opensourceteaching.org]).

2. "The simplest way to make a program free software is to put it in the public domain, uncopyrighted. This allows people to share the program and their improvements, if they are so minded. But it also allows uncooperative people to convert the program into proprietary software. They can make changes, many or few, and distribute the result as a proprietary product. People who receive the program in that modified form do not have the freedom that the original author gave them; the middleman has stripped it away. In the GNU project, our aim is to give *all* users the freedom to redistribute and change GNU software. If middlemen could strip off the freedom, we might have many users, but those users would not have freedom. So instead of putting GNU software in the public domain, we 'copyleft' it. Copyleft says that anyone who redistributes the software, with or without changes, must pass along the freedom to further copy and change it. Copyleft guarantees that every user has freedom" ("What Is Copyleft?").

3. What drives teachers to place their professional work online may be a wish for job security as well as altruism (D. Lancashire).

4. Sixty-eight sites appear under "Literature and Language Arts" in *ED-SITEment* (http://edsitement.neh.gov/tab_websites.asp).

5. There are sixty-two courses in literature available (since 2000). James Cain's 21L.707 Arthurian Literature and Celtic Colonization, offered in spring 2005, for example, gives a syllabus, a calendar, readings, assignments, study

materials (ten PDF files, from "Nomenclature and National Identity" to "Some Pointers for Writing Papers in Literature Courses"), related resources, and access to a discussion group ("21L. 707"). Entire courses may be downloaded.

6. Essays in this volume by Jerome McGann and by Stéfan Sinclair and Geoffrey Rockwell describe free scholarly software that can be used in teaching. Essays by Martha Nell Smith, Michael Papio and Massimo Riva, and Gillian Lord describe open-source texts issuing from research but applicable to teaching.

7. "In worker process isolation mode, you can configure an application pool to be supported by multiple worker processes. An application pool that uses more than one worker process is called a *Web garden*. (Web gardens are to be distinguished from *Web farms*, which use multiple servers for a Web site.)" ("Configuring").

8. So says Jonathan Smith, in the catalog entry for *The Dickens Web* on Eastgate's site.

9. I focus on my department here, since this volume is no place for a survey. After compiling two volumes of *The Humanities Computing Yearbook* in the early 1990s, I concluded that only professional organizations like the MLA have the expertise and resources to map the footprint of their members on the Web. A general trend, however, is that those departments with large composition, English as a second language and English as a foreign language, and language-based research programs are especially active in open-source teaching. The digitization of the humanities in North America began sixty years ago with the scanning of classical Greek texts by the *Thesaurus Linguae Graecae* in 1972 (www.tlg.uci .edu), and so it is not surprising that research-intensive institutions find their online databases repurposed for teaching.

10. One celebrated Friday in February 2002, after a major commercial site recommended *RPO* as a good source of St. Valentine's Day verses, demand escalated quickly and caused the Web server of the library for a university of sixty thousand people to crash. We had to take *RPO* offline for five hours to reconfigure it.

11. "[O]ur aim, like theirs, has been 'a minimum of change [in modernizing the texts] thought advantageous for the ordinary reader'" (Priestley and Hoeniger).

12. Julius is an especially gifted poet, in my opinion. His second cousin, Edward Fenn, living in New Zealand, e-mailed me with information about his death date. Several Australians have helped me understand Skeyhill's language. I also populated *RPO* with anonymous poems like "Times Is Hard" and "Occidit Miserum Crambe Repetita Pupillum" and favored verse about everyday things such as sewing machines, cheese, raccoons, and golf.

13. See Lehman, who writes: "Emotions, behavior, and cognition are components of the way presence is perceived and experienced and are essential for explaining the ways we consciously and unconsciously perceive and experience distance education" (12).

14. For the past several years, my colleague John Baird has built his own anthology for ENG 202Y: Major British Writers from *RPO*, and the department's Web site now refers to it.

15. This online section continued for three years, until I went on an extended research leave.

16. See the case study by Kathleen Cawsey and me in this volume for a discussion of how these chat rooms worked.

17. My online course was the first of its kind taught fully online in the Faculty of Arts and Sciences.

Works Cited

Alsgaard, Melissa. "Digital Feminism: Reaching Women through Web-Based Courses." *Feminist Collections* 22.1 (2000): n. pag. Web. 12 Sept. 2006.

Chettur, Govinda Krishna. "Beloved." *Representative Poetry Online*. U of Toronto Libs., 2008. Web. 30 Jan. 2009.

"Configuring Web Gardens with IIS 6.0." *Microsoft TechNet*. Microsoft, 22 Aug. 2005. Web. 29 Jan. 2009.

Dapra, Miriam. "RPO Feedback." Message to *Representative Poetry Online*. 4 Sept. 2006. E-mail.

Dauer, Susan Jaye. "From Teaching in Class to Teaching Online: Preserving Community and Communication." *Teaching Literature: A Companion*. Ed. Tanya Agathocleous and Ann C. Dean. Houndmills: Palgrave, 2003. 163–70. Print.

DeLombard, Jeannine, and Dan White. "Papers: Expectations, Guidelines, Advice, and Grading." *University of Toronto at Mississauga*. U of Toronto, n.d. Web. 18 Sept. 2006.

"The Dickens Web." Eastgate. Eastgate Systems, 2008. Web. 29 Jan. 2009.

Dictionary of Old English: A to G Online. Ed. Antonette diPaolo Healey. U of Toronto–Dictionary of Old Eng., 2008. Web. 1 Mar. 2009.

"EEBO in Education." *Early English Books Online / Text Creation Partnership*. U of Michigan, n.d. Web. 12 Sept. 2006.

Henderson, Greig E., and Christopher Brown, eds. *Glossary of Literary Theory*. U of Toronto English Lib., 31 Mar. 1997. Web. 30 Jan. 2009.

History of the English Language. Ed. Carol Percy. Dept. of English–U of Toronto, 2003. Web. 18 Sept. 2006.

Hutcheon, Linda. *Irony, Nostalgia, and the Postmodern*. U of Toronto English Lib., 19 Jan. 1998. Web. 30 Jan. 2009.

Hutcheon, Linda, and Nancy Kang. *The English Critical Essay*. U of Toronto English Lib., 8 Apr. 1997. Web. 30 Jan. 2009.

Internet Shakespeare Editions. *A Shakespeare Suite*. Insight Media, 2002. CD-ROM.

"The Internet Shakespeare Editions: History and Vision." *The Internet Shakespeare Editions*. Ed. Michael Best. U of Victoria, 2008. Web. 30 Jan. 2009.

Lancashire, David. "Code, Culture and Cash: The Fading Altruism of Open Source Development." *Firstmonday* 6.12 (2001): n. pag. Web. 6 Sept. 2006.

Lancashire, Ian. "Editing *Representative Poetry Online*." *Journal of Scholarly Publishing* 34.1 (2002): 16–29. Print.

———. "Recovering Parody in Teaching Poetry Online." *Revista Canaria de Estudios Ingleses* 52 (2006): 35–57. Print.

———. "*Representative Poetry Online*: Updating an Historical English Teaching Anthology." *Text Technology* 6.3 (1996): 139–47. Print.

Landow, George P. "*The Victorian Web* and *Context32*." *The Victorian Web*. Landow, 20 Nov. 2003. Web. 18 Sept. 2006.

Lehman, Rosemary. "The Role of Emotion in Creating Instructor and Learner Presence in the Distance Education Experience." *Journal of Cognitive Affective Learning* 2.2 (2006): 12–26. Print.

Lexicons of Early Modern English. Ed. Ian Lancashire. U of Toronto P–U of Toronto Libs., 2006. Web. 18 Sept. 2006.

Maré, Pauline. "Thanks." Message to *Representative Poetry Online*. 7 Nov. 2004. E-mail.

Mayors and Sheriffs of London. Ed. Anne Lancashire. U of Toronto Libs., 2009. Web. Forthcoming.

McKenna, Bill. "RPO Feedback." Message to *Representative Poetry Online*. 20 Feb. 2005. E-mail.

Oblinger, Diana G., and Brian L. Hawkins. "The Myth about Online Course Development: 'A Faculty Member Can Individually Develop and Deliver an Effective Online Course.'" *EDUCAUSE Review* 41.1 (2006): 14–15. Print.

Open Source Initiative. Open Source Initiative, 2007. Web. 30 Mar. 2009.

Patrons and Performances Web Site. Dir. Sally-Beth MacLean and Alan Somerset. U of Toronto–Records of Early English Drama, 2009. Web. 30 Jan. 2009.

Priestley, Francis E. L., and Frederick D. Hoeniger. Prefatory note. *Representative Poetry*. Ed. P[riestley] and H[oeniger]. 3rd ed. Vol. 1. Toronto: U of Toronto P, 1962. v. Print.

Puthiyaveettil, Sreelatha. "RPO Feedback." Message to *Representative Poetry Online*. 13 Oct. 2006. E-mail.

Rashley, Lisa Hammond. "Women's Studies 101 on the Web." *Kairos* 6.1 (2001): n. pag. Web. 30 Jan. 2009.

Representative Poetry Online. Ed. Ian Lancashire. Assoc. ed. Marc Plamondon. U of Toronto Libs., 2009. Web. 30 Jan. 2009.

Rigg, George, ed. *The English Language: A Historical Reader*. New York: Appleton, 1968. Print.

———. *Traditional Grammatical Terminology*. U of Toronto Eng. Lib., 1997. Web. 18 Sept. 2006.

"SREB States among National Leaders in Online Learning, New Report from SREB and Sloan Consortium Finds." *Southern Regional Education Board*. Southern Regional Educ. Board, 15 May 2006. Web. 28 Jan. 2009.

"Stay with Me, God." *Representative Poetry Online*. U of Toronto Libs., 2008. Web. 30 Jan. 2009.

Taylor, Laurie, and Brendan Riley. "Open Source and Academia." *Computers and Composition Online* (2004): n. pag. Web. 6 Sept. 2006.

"21L.707 Arthurian Literature and Celtic Colonization: Spring 2005."
   MITOpenCourseWare. MIT, 2009. Web. 29 Jan. 2009.
"What Is Copyleft?" *GNU Operating System*. Free Software Foundation, 2008.
   Web. 28 Jan. 2009.
White, Paul G. "RPO Feedback." Message to *Representative Poetry Online*. 1 Oct.
   2005. E-mail.

Martha Nell Smith

Enabling Intellectual Collaboration: The Use of Wikis and Blogs

When asked to contribute to this volume, I immediately imagined the group of contributors working together through a wiki and exchanging ideas with our readers through a blog. My experience working with a multi-institutional research team on a Mellon-funded data-mining and visualization project—the nora project, now the MONK project—made clear the value of a wiki. My experiences with graduate and undergraduate classes made clear the value of a blog.

First, some important context: in the late 1990s, Kenneth M. Price and I directed a multi-institutional team of educators from all different size institutions in a project funded by the United States Department of Education's Fund for the Improvement of Postsecondary Education (FIPSE) to experiment with pedagogical applications of the resources we had first imagined as research archives, *The Walt Whitman Archive* and the *Dickinson Electronic Archives*. From those experimentations, we hoped to generate a suite of models and best practices of uses in the classroom. Over the course of four years, ten scholars working collaboratively were able to produce *The Classroom Electric*, a searchable database of lesson plans, articles, and critical speculations, each of which at least one of us had used to varying degrees of success in postsecondary undergraduate and graduate classrooms. We used neither blogs nor wikis and many times during the four-year project suffered from e-mail fatigue—inboxes inundated with rapid-fire exchanges arriving too often at a most inconvenient time; collaborators on different schedules frustrated with lack of timely response from one another or with unrealistic expectations for collegial input at a busy time in the semester; and so forth.

By contrast, the nora/MONK group, while dependent on e-mail and certainly not immune from the frustrations inevitably produced by competing schedules and priorities, uses a wiki on which papers and demonstrations can be posted and commented on by others in the group. Indeed, different members of the group have repurposed one another's presentations to present themselves. The cumulative effect of our mutual enterprise is much more obvious than that of the Americanists in *The Classroom Electric* project, and the group appears to be doing a better job of building on one another's ideas and learning from one another. This relative success is not because the groups are differently talented or because the nora/MONK group members know one another better than did the members of *The Classroom Electric*. It is because, I believe, the tools at the disposal of the nora/MONK group, especially the wiki, more effectively facilitate collaboration than did the e-mail discussion list and annual meetings relied on by *The Classroom Electric* participants. Indeed, for those participants reading this essay, I propose that we revisit our grand experiment, using a wiki to catch up with one another and forge new alliances for exchange regarding digital technologies and their pedagogical applications. Had we been using a wiki or a blog during that time, not only we but our students, dispersed across institutions throughout the United States, could have collaborated with one another in ways that were simply made too difficult by the unwieldy technology. The wiki would be launched by placing all the essays written by each of the participants in late 1999 to early 2000 about their experience in a space where they could be edited and commented on by other participants.

For several years I have used blogs in my teaching, as have many contributors to this volume. First using them in graduate seminars, I was deeply impressed by the ways in which face-to-face class discussions could be sustained, deepened, broadened, and recorded for reflection. After several semesters of use with graduate students, I decided to use a blog in a large (120 students) lecture course of primarily first-year students and sophomores. I was astounded by how the blog facilitated content review and helped manage the flow from one topic to another, created communities of exchange within the rather impersonal lecture hall, and enabled me to get a lecture under way before I ever walked through the auditorium door. Now students publish their papers to one another, exchange videos and sound files, hold virtual group meetings for project development, and visit my virtual office hours using course software.

Early in this book project, a wiki was set up for the contributors to this volume so that they could share ideas for their essays. If, as has been proposed, a blog is established for our readers, we can extend and sustain the critical conversations started within these pages in ways that are simply not possible when relationships are strictly and only bibliographic.

Resources

Organizations

ALLC: Association for Literary and Linguistic Computing
Alliance for Computers and Writing
The Alliance of Digital Humanities Organizations
American Association of University Professors
American Council on the Teaching of Foreign Languages
Association for Computers and the Humanities
Association for the Advancement of Computing in Education (Ed/ITLib Digital Library for Information Technology and Education)
Canadian Association for Distance Education / Association canadienne de l'éducation à distance
Committee on Information Technology, Modern Language Association
Conference on College Composition and Communication, NCTE
Council of Writing Program Administrators. Professional Writing Program, Purdue U
Dekita.org: Open EFL/ESL
Distance Education and Training Council
Distance Education Clearinghouse, U of Wisconsin, Extension
EDUCAUSE
EPIC: Electronic Privacy Information Center
Humanities and Social Sciences Net Online, Michigan State U
iCopyright

Institute for Advanced Technology in the Humanities, U of Virginia
Institute for Higher Education Policy
Maryland Institute for Technology in the Humanities, College of Arts and Humanities, Libraries, and Office of Information Technology
National Endowment for the Humanities, Office of Digital Humanities
National Flagship Language Initiative, Natl. For. Lang. Center, U of Maryland
National Initiative for a Networked Cultural Heritage, ACLS, the Coalition for Networked Information, and the Getty Information Inst.
Ohio Learning Network. Dir. Kate M. Carey
Society for Digital Humanities / Société pour l'étude des médias interactifs
TEI: Text Encoding Initiative

General Bibliographies

"Distance Education Bibliography." *Center for the Virtual University*. U of Maryland, University Coll., 2005. Web. 15 Oct. 2006.

Fusco, Marjorie, and Susan E. Ketcham. *Distance Learning for Higher Education: An Annotated Bibliography*. Greenwood Village: Libs. Unlimited, 2002. Print.

Johnson, Christopher M. "A Survey of Current Research on Online Communities of Practice." *Internet and Higher Education* 4.1 (2001): 45–60. Print.

Jung, Udo O. H. "An International Bibliography of Computer-Assisted Language Learning: Sixth Instalment." *System: An International Journal of Educational Technology and Applied Linguistics* 33.1 (2005): 135–85. Print.

Liu, Min, Zena Moore, Leah Graham, and Shinwoong Lee. "A Look at the Research on Computer-Based Technology Use in Second Language Learning: A Review of the Literature from 1990–2000." *Journal of Research on Technology in Education* 34.3 (2002): 250+. Web. 15 July 2006.

Ziegler, Georgianna. "Women Writers *Online*: An Evaluation and Annotated Bibliography of Web Resources." *Early Modern Literary Studies* 6.3 (2001): n. pag. Web. 15 Oct. 2006.

Zirkin, Barbara G., and David E. Sumler. "Interactive or Non-interactive? That Is the Question!!! An Annotated Bibliography." *Journal of Distance Education* 10.1 (1995): 95–112. Web. 15 Oct. 2006.

Zorich, Diane M. *A Survey of Digital Humanities Centers in the United States*. Council on Lib. and Information Resources, 2008. Web. 17 June 2009.

Journals

American Journal of Distance Education. Ed. Michael G. Moore. Print, Web.

CALICO Journal. The Computer Assisted Language Instruction Consortium, Texas State U. Print, Web.

Chronicle of Higher Education. Print, Web.

CH Working Papers. Ed. Russon Wooldridge, Willard McCarty, and William Winder. Web.

College Composition and Communication. Natl. Council of Teachers of Eng. Print, Web.

Computers and Composition: An International Journal. Ed. Gail E. Hawisher and Cynthia L. Selfe. Ohio State U. Print, Web.

Computers and Composition Online. Ed. Kristine Blair, Lanette Cadle, and Richard Colby. Ball State U. Web.

Computers and Education: An International Journal. Ed. Rachelle S. Heller and Jean M. Underwood. Print, Web.

Currents in Electronic Literacy. Computer Writing and Research Lab, U of Texas, Austin. Web.

Digital Humanities Quarterly. Ed. Julia Flanders. Alliance of Digital Humanities Organizations. Web.

Digital Studies / Le champ numérique. Ed. Ray Siemens and Christian Vandendorpe. U of Victoria. Web.

E-Journal of Instructional Design and Technology. Web.

Humanist. Ed. Willard McCarty. Alliance of Digital Humanities Organizations, Office for Humanities Communication, ACLS. Web.

Infobits. Ed. Carolyn Kotlas. U of North Carolina. Web.

International Journal of Educational Telecommunications (International Journal on E-Learning). Assn. for the Advancement of Computing in Educ. Web.

International Journal of Instructional Media. Print.

International Review of Research in Open and Distance Learning. Athabasca U. Web.

Journal of Computer-Mediated Communication. Indiana U, Intl. Communication Assn. Web.

Journal of Technology and Teacher Education. Assn. for the Advancement of Computing in Educ. Web.

Kairos. Web.

Language Learning and Technology. Michigan State U, Center for Lang. Educ. and Research. Web.

Literary and Linguistic Computing. Assn. for Literary and Linguistic Computing. Oxford UP. Print, Web.

Pedagogy. Duke UP. Print, Web.

Teaching English with Technology. IATEFL Poland Computer Special Interest Group. Web.

Text Technology: The Journal of Computer Text Processing. Ed. Alexandre Sevigny and Geoffrey Rockwell. McMaster U. Print, Web.

Guidelines, Reports, and Other Documents

Allen, I. Elaine, and Jeff Seaman. *Entering the Mainstream: The Quality and Extent of Online Education in the United States, 2003 and 2004.* Sloan-C. Sloan-C, 2004. Web. 3 Oct. 2008.

———. *Growing by Degrees: Online Education in the United States, 2005.* Sloan-C. Southern ed. Sloan-C, 2006. Web. 15 Oct. 2006.

———. *Sizing the Opportunity: The Quality and Extent of Online Education in the United States, 2002 and 2003. Sloan-C.* Sloan-C, 2003. Web. 15 Oct. 2006.

American Association of University Professors. "Resources on Copyright, Distance Education, and Intellectual Property." *American Association of University Professors.* AAUP, n.d. Web. 3 Oct. 2008.

American Council on the Teaching of Foreign Languages. *Proficiency Guidelines: Speaking. American Council on the Teaching of Foreign Languages.* Amer. Council on the Teaching of For. Lang., 1999. Web. 27 June 2006.

Committee on Information Technology. "The AAUP *Statement on Distance Education*: Special Considerations for Language and Literature." *Modern Language Association.* MLA, 2002. Web. 3 Oct. 2008.

———. "Guidelines for Evaluating Work with Digital Media in the Modern Languages." *Modern Language Association.* MLA, 2002. Web. 3 Oct. 2008.

———. "Minimal Guidelines for Authors of Web Pages." *Modern Language Association.* MLA, 2002. Web. 3 Oct. 2008.

Conference on College Composition and Communication. "Promotion and Tenure Guidelines for Work with Technology." *National Council of Teachers of English.* NCTE, Nov. 1998. Web. 18 June 2006.

CONFU: The Conference on Fair Use. Crash Course in Copyright. U of Texas, 2001. Web. 16 July 2006.

Institute for Higher Education Policy. *Quality on the Line: Benchmarks for Success in Internet-Based Distance Education.* Natl. Educ. Assn., Apr. 2000. Web. 15 Oct. 2006.

McCarty, Willard, and Matthew Kirschenbaum. *Institutional Models for Humanities Computing. Association for Literary and Linguistic Computing.* Assn. for Literary and Linguistic Computing, 2003. Web. 7 Oct. 2008.

National Endowment for the Humanities. "Grants for Teaching and Learning Resources and Curriculum Development." *National Endowment for the Humanities.* Natl. Endowment for the Humanities, 9 July 2007. Web. 6 Oct. 2008.

———. "Online Humanities Projects." *National Endowment for the Humanities.* Natl. Endowment for the Humanities, n.d. Web. 6 Oct. 2008.

National Standards in Foreign Language Education Project. *Standards for Foreign Language Learning in the Twenty-First Century.* New York: Natl. Standards in For. Lang. Educ. Project, 1996. Print.

Office of the Privacy Commissioner of Canada. "Privacy Legislation in Canada." *Government of Canada.* Gov, of Can., Oct. 2004. Web. 5 Sept. 2006.

Twigg, Carol A. *Quality Assurance for Whom? Providers and Consumers in Today's Distributed Learning Environment. Center for Academic Transformation.* Pew Learning and Technology Program, 2001. Web. 25 July 2006.

United States. Dept. of Defense. *Second Language Acquisition: Analysis of Innovation.* Navy Human Capital Development. Comp. George Coffin for Ken Wagar. 30 Apr. 2006. Print. Unclassified document.

United States Copyright Office. Lib. of Cong., 2008. Web. 15 Oct. 2006.

Materals about and for Online Courses

Alfred P. Sloan Foundation *The Sloan Semester. Sloan-C.* Sloan-C, n.d. Web. 6 Oct. 2008.

Alsgaard, Melissa. "Digital Feminism: Reaching Women through Web-Based Courses." *Feminist Collections* 22.1 (2000): n. pag. Web. 6 Oct. 2008.

Arts and Humanities. Open University. Open U, n.d. Web. 6 Oct. 2008.

Best, Michael. "Teaching Shakespeare to Judith: Gender Politics in Distance/Online Teaching." *Working Papers on the Web* 4 (2002): n. pag. Web. 15 Oct. 2006.

Binkley, Susan Carpenter, and Jennifer E. Hall. "Sound Pedagogical Practice on the Web." *French Review* 76.3 (2003): 564–79. Print.

Blake, Robert, and Ann Marie Delforge. "Language Learning at a Distance: *Spanish without Walls.*" *Selected Papers from the 2004 NFLRC Symposium: Distance Education, Distributed Learning and Language Instruction.* Ed. Irene Thompson and David Hiple. *National Foreign Language Resource Center.* U of Hawai'i, 2005. Web. 4 Sept. 2006.

Bowman, Cindy, Brendan Pieters, Sarah Hembree, and Terri Mellender. "Shakespeare, Our Contemporary: Using Technology to Teach the Bard." *English Journal* 92.1 (2002): 88–93. Print.

Campbell, Dermot F. "Delivering an Online Translation Course." *ReCALL: The Journal of EUROCALL* 16.1 (2004): 114–23. Print.

Cazden, Courtney B. "Sustaining Indigenous Languages in Cyberspace." *Nurturing Native Languages.* Ed. Jon Reyhner, Octaviana V. Trujillo, Roberto Luis Carrasco, and Louise Lockard. Flagstaff: U of Arizona, 2003. 53–57. *Northern Arizona University.* Web. 22 Oct. 2008.

The Classroom Electric: Dickinson, Whitman, and American Culture. United States Dept. of Educ. Fund for the Improvement of Postsecondary Educ.; Inst. for Advanced Technology in the Humanities, U of Virginia; U of Maryland and Maryland Inst. for Technology in the Humanities; C of William and Mary, 2001. Web. 15 Oct. 2006.

Conrad, Dianne. "University Instructors' Reflections on Their First Online Teaching Experiences." *Journal of Asynchronous Learning Networks* 8.2 (2004): 31–44. Web. 15 Oct. 2006.

Cowles, Maria Antonia, Lyris Wiedermann, and Shoshanna Lurie Thomas. "EU-Brazil-Net: Web-Enabled Language Instruction." *Hispania* 85.3 (2002): 629–32. Print.

Dauer, Susan Jaye. "From Teaching in Class to Teaching Online: Preserving Community and Communication." *Teaching Literature: A Companion.* Ed. Tanya Agathocleous and Ann C. Dean. Houndmills: Palgrave, 2003. 163–70. Print.

DeCandido, Graceanne A. "A Particular Intensity: Teaching Children's Literature Online." *Horn Book Magazine* 78.3 (2002): 293–98. Print.

Distance Learner Course Finder. Internet Course Finders, n.d. Web. 15 Oct. 2006.

Driver, Martha, and Jeanine Meyer. "Engaging Students in Literature and Composition Using Web Research and Student-Constructed Web Projects." *Academic.writing* 1 (2000): n. pag. Web. 15 Oct. 2006.

Dubrule, Diane E. "Teaching Scholastic Courses Requiring Discussion On Line." *CH Working Papers* A.21 (2003): n. pag. Web. 15 Oct. 2006.

EDUCAUSE. *EDUCAUSE Learning Initative. EDUCAUSE.* EDUCAUSE, 2008. Web. 7 Oct. 2008.

Evaluating Web Pages: Techniques to Apply and Questions to Ask. UC Berkeley. Regents of the U of California, 2005. Web. 15 Oct. 2006.

Feustle, Joseph A., Jr. "Extending the Reach of the Classroom with Web-Based Programs." *Hispania* 84.4 (2001): 837–49. Print.

Filreis, Al. *English 88: Modern and Contemporary American Poetry. University of Pennsylvania.* U of Pennsylvania, 2008. Web. 6 Oct. 2008.

Flanders, Julia. "Learning, Reading, and the Problem of Scale: Using Women Writers Online." *Pedagogy* 2.1 (2002): 49–59. Print.

For Teachers. Library of Congress. Lib. of Cong., n.d. Web. 6 Oct. 2008.

Furstenberg, Gilberte, Sabine Levet, Kathryn English, and Katherine Maillet. "Giving a Virtual Voice to the Silent Language of Culture: The Cultura Project." *Language Learning and Technology* 5.1 (2001): 55–102. Web. 6 Oct. 2008.

Furstenberg, Gilberte, Sabine Levet, and Shoggy Waryn. *Cultura.* MIT, 1997. Web. 15 Oct. 2006.

Haynes, Cynthia. *Rhetoric 1302. University of Texas at Dallas.* U of Texas, Dallas, n.d. Web. 15 Oct. 2006.

Heble, Ayesha. "Teaching Literature Online to Arab Students: Using Technology to Overcome Cultural Restrictions." *Arts and Humanities in Higher Education* 6.2 (2007): 219–26. Print.

Illinois Online Network. U of Illinois, 2007. Web. 15 Oct. 2006.

Jamison, Carol. "King Arthur Online: A Brief Navigational Tour of a Web-Enhanced Arthurian Survey Course." *Studies in Medieval and Renaissance Teaching* 12.1 (2005): 65–79. Print.

Kirk, Connie Ann. " 'The Distance Would Not Haunt Me So—': Teaching Dickinson's Poetry through Distance Education." *Emily Dickinson International Society Bulletin* 14.1 (2002): 8–10. Print.

Kirschenbaum, Matthew G. *ENGL 467: Computer and Text (Spring 2004). University of Maryland.* U of Maryland, 2004. Web. 15 Oct. 2006.

Lizhong, Zhang. "Internet Based Chinese Teaching and Learning." *La Trobe University.* La Trobe U, n.d. Web. 15 Oct. 2006.

Love, Jane. "Elécriture: A Course in Women's Writing on the Web." *Kairos* 7.3 (2002): n. pag. Web. 15 Oct. 2006.

Lynch, Jack. *Syllabi and Other Course Materials for Literature Courses.* N.p., 2003. Web. 15 Oct. 2006.

MERLOT: Multimedia Educational Resource for Learning and Online Teaching. Multimedia Educ. Resource for Learning and Online Teaching, 2008. Web. 15 Oct. 2006.

Michigan Virtual University. Michigan Virtual U, 2008. Web. 6 Oct. 2008.

MITOpenCourseWare. MIT, 2008. Web. 6 Oct. 2008.

Morgan, Martha, et al. *World Lecture Hall.* Center for Instructional Technologies, U of Texas, Austin, 2008. Web. 6 Oct. 2008.

National Endowment for the Humanities. *EDSITEment*. Natl. Endowment for the Humanities, n.d. Web. 7 Oct. 2006.

"Peterson's Planner." *Peterson's*. Nelnet, 2008. Web. 6 Oct. 2008.

Rashley, Lisa Hammond. "Women's Studies 101 on the Web." *Kairos* 6.1 (2001): n. pag. Web. 15 Oct. 2006.

Tryon, Charles. "Using Blogs to Teach First-Year Composition." *Pedagogy* 6.1 (2006): 128–32. Print.

University of Phoenix. U of Phoenix, 2006–08. Web. 6 Oct. 2008.

Unsworth, John. *Technology and Teaching: A Faculty Seminar at the College of William and Mary*. N.p., 18 Mar. 1999. Web. 15 Oct. 2006.

Articles and Books on Distance Learning

Agnew, Palmer Wright, Anne S. Kellerman, and Jeanine Meyer. *Multimedia in the Classroom*. Boston: Allyn, 1996. Print.

Alexander, Johnathan, and Marcia Dickson. *Role Play: Distance Learning and the Teaching of Writing*. Cresskill: Hampton, 2006. Print.

Bauer, John F., and Anderson, Rebecca S. "Evaluating Students' Written Performance in the Online Classroom." *New Directions for Teaching and Learning: Principles of Effective Teaching in the Online Classroom* 84 (2000): 65–71. Print.

Beauvois, Margaret Healy. "Conversations in Slow Motion: Computer-Mediated Communication in the Foreign Language Classroom." *Canadian Modern Language Review* 54.2 (1998): 198–217. Print.

———. "E-Talk: Computer-Assisted Classroom Discussion—Attitudes and Motivation." *Language Learning Online: Theory and Practice in the ESL and L2 Computer Classroom*. Ed. Janet K. Swaffar, Susan Romano, Phillip Markley, and Katherine Arens. Austin: Daedulus, 1998. 99–120. Print.

Belz, Julie, ed. "Linguistic Perspectives on the Development of Intercultural Competence in Telecollaboration." *Language Learning and Technology* 7.2 (2003): 68–117. Web. 13 June 2006.

Blair, Kristine, and Elizabeth Monske. "*Cui bono*? Revisiting the Promises and Perils of Online Learning." *Computers and Composition* 20.4 (2003): 441–53. Print.

Blake, Robert. "Bimodal CMC: The Glue of Language Learning at a Distance." *CALICO Journal* 22.3 (2005): 497–511. Print.

Bolter, Jay David, and Richard Grusin. *Remediation: Understanding New Media*. Cambridge: MIT P, 1999. Print.

Breuch, Lee-Ann Kastman. *Virtual Peer Review: Teaching and Learning about Writing in Online Environments*. Albany: State U of New York P, 2004. Print.

Breuch, Lee-Ann Kastman, and Sam J. Racine. "Developing Sound Tutor Training for Online Writing Centers: Creating Productive Peer Reviewers." *Computers and Composition* 17.3 (2000): 245–63. Print.

Brittain, Sarah, Pietrek Glowacki, Jared Van Ittersum, and Lynn Johnson. "Podcasting Lectures." *EDUCAUSE Quarterly* 29.3 (2006): n. pag. Web. 15 Oct. 2006.

Brooke, Robert. "Underlife and Writing Instruction." *On Writing Research: The Braddock Essays, 1975–1998*. Ed. Lisa Ede. New York: Bedford–St. Martin's, 1999. 229–41. Print.

Bruffee, Kenneth A. *Collaborative Learning: Higher Education, Interdependence, and the Authority of Knowledge*. 2nd ed. Baltimore: Johns Hopkins UP, 1999. Print.

Burnard, Lou, Katherine O'Brien O'Keeffe, and John Unsworth, eds. *Electronic Textual Editing*. New York: MLA, 2006. Print.

Chapelle, Carol A. "Multimedia CALL: Lessons to Be Learned from Research on Instructed SLA." *Language Learning and Technology* 2.1 (1998): 22–34. Web. 26 June 2006.

Chickering, Arthur W., and Stephen C. Ehrmann. "Implementing the Seven Principles: Technology as Lever." *TLT Group*. TLT Group, Jan. 2008. Web. 22 Oct. 2008.

Chickering, Arthur W., and Zelda F. Gamson. "Seven Principles for Good Practice in Undergraduate Education." *Honolulu Community College*. U of Hawai'i, 18 Oct. 2007. Web. 22 Oct. 2008.

Chun, Dorothy. "Using Computer-Assisted Class Discussion to Facilitate the Acquisition of Interactive Competence." *Language Learning Online: Theory and Practice in the ESL and L2 Computer Classroom*. Ed. Janet K. Swaffar, Susan Romano, Phillip Markley, and Katherine Arens. Austin: Daedalus, 1998. 57–80. Print.

Colpaert, Jozef. "Pedagogy-Driven Design for Online Language Teaching and Learning." *CALICO Journal* 23.3 (2006): 477–97. Print.

Crane, Gregory. "What Do You Do with a Million Books?" *D-Lib Magazine* 12.3 (2006): n. pag. Web. 4 Sept. 2006.

Davidson, Dan E. "Capabilities and Outputs of the U.S. Education System: Proficiency Outputs." National Language Conference. Inn and Conference Center, Adelphi. 22–24 June 2004. *National Language Conference*. Web. 6 Oct. 2008.

Domínguez, Frank. "The Path before Us: Suggestions for Managing the Transition of the Spanish Middle Ages to the Electronic Age." *La corónica* 33.1 (2004): 229–45. Print.

Donaldson, Peter S. "The Shakespeare Electronic Archive: Tools for Online Learning and Scholarship." *The Internet and the University: Forum 2003*. Ed. Maureen Devlin, Richard Larson, and Joel Meyerson. Boulder: EDUCAUSE, 2004. 61–92. *EDUCAUSE*. Web. 15 Oct. 2006.

Doughty, Catherine, and Michael Long. "Optimal Psycholinguistic Environments for Distance Foreign Language Learning." *Language Learning and Technology* 7.3 (2003): 50–80. Web. 26 June 2006.

Euben, Donna R. "Faculty Rights and Responsibilities in Distance Learning." *American Association of University Professors*. AAUP, Apr. 2000. Web. 15 Oct. 2006.

Evans, Robert C. "Internet Resources for Teaching Early Modern English Women Writers." *Working Papers on the Web* 4 (2002): n. pag. Web. 15 Oct. 2002.

Felix, Uschi. *Language Learning Online: Towards Best Practice*. Lisse: Swets, 2003. Print.

Fleming, Stephen, and David Hiple. "Distance Education to Distributed Learning: Multiple Formats and Technologies in Language Instruction." *CALICO Journal* 22.1 (2004): 63–82. Print.

Furstenberg, Gilberte. "Reading between the Cultural Lines." *Reading between the Lines: Perspectives on Foreign Language Literacy.* Ed. Peter C. Patrikis. New Haven: Yale UP, 2003. 74–98. Print.

Gee, James. *What Video Games Have to Teach Us about Learning and Literacy.* New York: Palgrave, 2003. Print.

Godwin-Jones, Bob. "Emerging Technologies: Tools for Distance Education: Towards Convergence and Integration." *Language Learning and Technology* 7.3 (2003): 18–22. Web. 16 July 2006.

Gonzalez, Dafne. "Teaching and Learning through Chat: A Taxonomy of Educational Chat for EFL/ESL." *Teaching English with Technology* 3.4 (2003): n. pag. Web. 15 Oct. 2003.

Gruba, Paul. "Playing the Videotext: A Media Literacy Perspective on Video-Mediated L2 Listening." *Language Learning and Technology* 10.2 (2006): 77–92. Web. 18 June 2006.

Halio, Marcia Peoples. "Teaching in Our Pajamas: Negotiating with Adult Learners in Online Distance Writing Courses." *College Teaching* 52.2 (2004): 58–63. Print.

Hanna, Donald E., Michelle Glowacki-Dudka, and Simone Conceição-Runlee. *147 Practical Tips for Teaching Online Groups: Essentials of Web-Based Education.* Madison: Atwood, 2000. Print.

Harris, Muriel, and Michael Pemberton. "Online Writing Labs (OWLS): A Taxonomy of Options and Issues." *Computers and Composition* 12.2 (1995): 145–59. Print.

Hawisher, Gail E., and Patricia Sullivan. "Women on the Networks: Searching for E-Spaces of Their Own." *Feminism and Composition Studies.* Ed. Susan C. Jarratt and Lynn Worsham. New York: MLA, 1998. 172–97. Print.

Haynes, Cynthia Ann, and Jan Rune Holmevik, eds. *High Wired: On the Design, Use, and Theory of Educational MOOs.* Ann Arbor: U of Michigan P, 2001. Print.

Hewett, Beth L., and Christa Ehmann. *Preparing Educators for Online Writing Instruction: Principles and Processes.* Urbana: NCTE, 2004. Print.

Honeycutt, Lee. "Comparing E-Mail and Synchronous Conferencing in Online Peer Response." *Written Communication* 18.1 (2001): 26–60. Print.

Howard-Hill, T. H. *Literary Concordances.* Pergamon: Oxford, 1979. Print.

Ingram, Albert L., Lesley G. Hathorn, and Alan Evans. "Beyond Chat on the Internet." *Computers and Education* 35.1 (2000): 21–35. Print.

Inman, James A., and Donna N. Sewell, eds. *Taking Flight with OWLs: Examining Electronic Writing Center Work.* Malwah: Erlbaum, 2000. Print.

Irvin, L. Lennie. "The Shared Discourse of the Networked Computer Classroom." *Trends and Issues in English Studies.* Urbana: NCTE, 2000. 219–28. *Alamo Community Colleges.* Web. 5 Sept. 2006.

Johnson-Eilola, Johndan. *Nostalgic Angels: Rearticulating Hypertext Writing.* Norwood: Ablex, 1997. Print.

Jones, Steve, and Camille Johnson-Yale. "Professors Online: The Internet's Impact on College Faculty." *Firstmonday* 10.9 (2005): n. pag. Web. 18 Sept. 2006.

Kastman Breuch, Lee-Ann. *Virtual Peer Review: Teaching and Learning about Writing in Online Environments.* Albany: State U of New York P, 2004. Print.

Kearsley, Greg. "Is Online Learning for Everybody?" *Educational Technology* 42 (2002): 41–44. Print.

Kemp, Fred. "Computer-Mediated Communication: Making Nets Work for Writing Instruction." *The Dialogic Classroom: Teachers Integrating Computer Technology, Pedagogy, and Research.* Ed. Jeffrey Galin and Joan Latchow. Urbana: NCTE, 1998. 133–50. Print.

Kern, Richard. *Literacy and Language Teaching.* Oxford: Oxford UP, 2000. Print.

Kern, Richard, and Jean Marie Schultz. "Beyond Orality: Investigating Literacy and the Literary in Second and Foreign Language Instruction." *Modern Language Journal* 89.3 (2005): 381–92. Print.

Kern, Richard, Paige Ware, and Mark Warschauer. "Crossing Frontiers: New Directions in Online Pedagogy and Research." *Annual Review of Applied Linguistics* 24 (2004): 243–60. Print.

Kim, Kyong-Jee, and Curtis J. Bonk. "Cross-Cultural Comparisons of Online Collaboration." *Journal of Computer-Mediated Communication* 8.1 (2002): n. pag. Web. 13 June 2006.

Kline, Daniel T. "Taming the Labyrinth: An Introduction to Medieval Resources on the World Wide Web." *Studies in Medieval and Renaissance Teaching* 8.2 (2000): 37–60. Print.

Ko, Susan, and Steve Rossen. *Teaching Online: A Practical Guide.* Boston: Houghton, 2001. Print.

Kramarae, Cheris. *The Third Shift: Women Learning Online.* Washington: Amer. Assn. of U Women, 2001. Print.

Kramsch, Claire. "From Communicative Competence to Symbolic Competence." *Modern Language Journal* 90.2 (2006): 49–52. Print.

Kramsch, Claire, and Steven L. Thorne. "Foreign Language Learning as Global Communicative Practice." *Globalization and Language Teaching.* Ed. Deborah Cameron and David Block. New York: Routledge, 2002. 83–100. Print.

Lancashire, Ian, et al. *Using* TACT *with Electronic Texts.* New York: MLA, 1996. Web. 15 Oct. 2006.

Landow, George. *Hyper Text: The Convergence of Contemporary Critical Theory and Technology.* Baltimore: Johns Hopkins UP, 1992. Print.

LeLoup, Jean W., and Robert Ponterio. "On the Net: Foreign Language Teachers' Greatest Hits." *Language Learning and Technology* 10.3 (2006): 3–7. Web. Oct. 2006.

Lessig, Lawrence. *Free Culture: How Big Media Uses Technology and the Law to Lock Down Culture and Control Creativity.* New York: Penguin, 2004. Print.

———. *The Future of Ideas: The Fate of the Commons in a Connected World.* New York: Random, 2001. Print.

Lister, Martin, et al. *New Media: A Critical Introduction.* New York: Routledge, 2003. Print.

Mace, Désirée H. Pointer. *Teacher Practice Online: Sharing Wisdom, Opening Doors.* New York: Teachers Coll., 2009. Print.

McCarty, Willard. *Humanities Computing.* New York: Palgrave, 2005. Print.

McGann, Jerome. *Radiant Textuality: Literature after the World Wide Web.* New York: Palgrave–St. Martin's, 2001. Print.

Miall, David. "The Library versus the Internet: Literary Studies under Siege?" *PMLA* 116.5 (2001): 1405–14. Print.

Murray, Janet H. *Hamlet on the Holodeck: The Future of Narrative in Cyberspace.* New York: Free, 1997. Print.

Nasseh, Bizhan. "A Brief History of Distance Education." *Adult Education in the News.* SeniorNet.org, 1997. Web. 18 June 2006.

National Academy of Sciences. *Beyond Productivity: Information, Technology, Innovation, and Creativity.* Washington: Natl. Acads. P, 2003. *National Academies Press.* Web. 4 Sept. 2006.

National Initiative for a Networked Cultural Heritage and Humanities Advanced Technology and Information Institute. *The NINCH Guide to Good Practice in the Digital Representation and Management of Cultural Heritage Materials.* 2nd ed. Natl. Initiative for a Networked Cultural Heritage, 2002. Web. 15 Oct. 2006.

Oblinger, Diana G., and Brian L. Hawkins. "The Myth about Online Course Development: 'A Faculty Member Can Individually Develop and Deliver an Effective Online Course.'" *EDUCAUSE Review* 41.1 (2006): 14–15. Print.

Palloff, Rena M., and Keith Pratt. *Building Learning Communities in Cyberspace.* San Francisco: Jossey-Bass, 1999. Print.

Payne, Darin. "English Studies in Levittown: Rhetorics of Space and Technology in Course-Management Software." *College English* 67.5 (2005): 483–507. Print.

Pellettieri, Jill. "Negotiation in Cyberspace: The Role of Chatting in the Development of Grammatical Competence." *Network-Based Language Teaching: Concepts and Practice.* Ed. Mark Warschauer and Richard Kern. Cambridge: Cambridge UP, 2000. 59–86. Print.

Prensky, Marc. "Digital Natives, Digital Immigrants." *On the Horizon* 9.5 (2001): 1–6. Web. 7 Oct. 2008.

Quinn, David M. "Legal Issues in Educational Technology: Implications for School Leaders." *Educational Administration Quarterly* 39.2 (2003): 187–207. Print.

Raben, Joseph. "Humanities Computing Twenty-Five Years Later." *Computers and the Humanities* 25.6 (1991): 341–50. Print.

Richardson, Will. *Blogs, Wikis, Podcasts, and Other Powerful Web Tools for Classrooms.* Thousand Oaks: Corwin, 2006. Print.

Roed, Jannie. "Language Learner Behaviour in a Virtual Environment." *Computer Assisted Language Learning* 16.2-3 (2003): 155–72. Print.

Rogers, Jim. "Communities of Practice: A Framework for Fostering Coherence in Virtual Learning Communities." *Educational Technology and Society* 3.3 (2000): 384–92. Print.

Rovai, Alfred P. "Building Sense of Community at a Distance." *International Review of Research in Open and Distance Learning* 3.1 (2002): 1–16. Web. 23 June 2006.

———. "A Preliminary Look at the Structural Differences of Higher Education Classroom Communities in Traditional and ALN Courses." *Journal of Asynchronous Learning Networks* 6.1 (2002): 41–56. Web. 23 June 2006.

Russell, Thomas L. *The No Significant Difference Phenomenon.* 5th ed. Intl. Distance Educ. Certification Center, North Carolina State U, 2001. Web. 24 June 2006.

Samuels, Robert. "The Future Threat to Computers and Composition: Nontenured Instructors, Intellectual Property, and Distance Education." *Computers and Composition* 21.1 (2004): 63–71. Print.

Schramm, Andreas. "Making Online Students Connect: Ethnographic Strategies for Developing Online Learning Experiences." *Distance Education and Languages: Evolution and Change.* Ed. Borje Holmberg, Monica Shelley, and Cynthia White. Clevedon: Multilingual Matters, 2005. 230–41. Print.

Schreibman, Susan, Ray Siemens, and John Unsworth, eds. *A Companion to Digital Humanities.* Oxford: Blackwell, 2004. Print.

Seadle, Michael. "Copyright in the Networked World: Copies in Courses." *Library Hi Tech* 24.2 (2006): 305–10. Print.

Selfe, Cynthia L. *Technology and Literacy in the Twenty-First Century: The Importance of Paying Attention.* Carbondale: Southern Illinois UP, 1999. Print.

Selfe, Cynthia L., and Gail E. Hawisher. *Literate Lives in the Information Age: Narratives of Literacy from the United States.* Mahwah: Erlbaum, 2004. Print.

Setzer, J. Carl, and Laurie Lewis. "Distance Education Courses for Public Elementary and Secondary School Students: 2002–03." *Education Statistics Quarterly* 7.1-2 (2006): n. pag. Web. 6 Oct. 2008.

Shulman, Lee. "Pedagogies of Uncertainty." *Liberal Education* 91.2 (2005): n. pag. Web. 18 June 2006.

Siemens, Ray, and Susan Schreibman, eds. *A Companion to Digital Literary Studies.* Digital Humanities–Blackwell, 2008. Web.

Smart, Karl L., and James J. Cappel. "Students' Perceptions of Online Learning: A Comparative Study." *Journal of Information Technology Education* 5 (2006): 201–19. Web. Oct. 2006.

Smith, Glenn Gordon, David Ferguson, and Mieke Caris. "Teaching over the Web versus in the Classroom: Differences in the Instructor Experience." *International Journal of Instructional Media* 29.1 (2002): 61–67. Print.

Strambi, Antonella, and Eric Bouvet. "Flexibility and Interaction at a Distance: A Mixed-Mode Environment for Language Learning." *Language Learning and Technology* 7.3 (2003): 81–102. Web. 26 June 2006.

Thorne, Steven L. *Internet-Mediated Intercultural Foreign Language Education: Approaches, Pedagogy, and Research.* University Park: Center for Advanced Lang. Proficiency Educ. and Research, Pennsylvania State U, 2005. *CALPER.* Web. 24 May 2006. CALPER Working Paper 6.

Tomei, Lawrence A. "The Impact of Online Teaching on Faculty Load: Computing the Ideal Class Size for Online Courses." *Journal of Technology and Teacher Education* 14.3 (2006): 531–41. Print.

Tufte, Edward R. *The Cognitive Style of* PowerPoint. Cheshire: Graphics, 2003. Print.

Verneil, Marie de, and Zane L. Berge. "Going Online: Guidelines for Faculty in Higher Education." *International Journal of Educational Telecommunications* 6.3 (2000): 227–42. Print.

Vrasidas, Charalambos, and Marina Stock McIsaac. "Factors Influencing Interaction in an Online Course." *American Journal of Distance Education* 13.3 (1999): 22–36. Print.

Walker, Cynthia L. "So You've Decided to Develop a Distance Education Class." *Kairos* 6.2 (2001): n. pag. Web. 15 Oct. 2006.

Warschauer, Mark. *Electronic Literacies: Language, Culture, and Power in Online Education*. Mahwah: Erlbaum, 1999. Print.

Warschauer, Mark, and Richard Kern, eds. *Networked-Based Language Teaching: Concepts and Practice*. New York: Cambridge UP, 2000. Print.

Webb Petersen, Patricia. "The Debate for Online Learning: Key Issues for Writing Teachers." *Computers and Composition* 18.4 (2001): 359–70. Print.

Wenger, Etienne, Richard A. McDermott, and William M. Snyder. *Cultivating Communities of Practice: A Guide to Managing Knowledge*. Boston: Harvard Business School P, 2002. Print.

Williams, Robin, and John Tollet. *The Non-designers Web Book: An Easy Guide to Creating, Designing, and Posting Your Own Web Site*. 2nd ed. Berkeley: Peach Pit, 2000. Print.

Other Online Resources

Blackboard Academic Suite. Educational delivery software system. Blackboard, Inc.

Blogger. Instructional Web site for creating blogs. Google, Inc.

The Daedalus Integrated Writing Environment. Educational writing software. Daedalus Group, Inc.

Drupal. Open-source content management platform. Maintained by Dries Buytaert.

Electronic Literature Directory. Center for Digital Humanities, Dept. of Eng., Dept. of Design Media Arts, the School of the Arts and Architecture, and SINAPSE, U of California, Los Angeles.

Flickr. Online photo management and sharing application. Yahoo! Inc.

GarageBand. Music recording software. Apple, Inc.

GetEducated.com. Distance-learning higher education directory. GetEducated.com, LLC.

iMovie. Video management and sharing software. Apple, Inc.

Ipl: Internet Public Library. U of Michigan.

Librarians' Internet Index: Websites You Can Trust. Librarians' Internet Index.

Mambo. Content management system. Mambo Foundation, Inc.

Moodle. Open-source course management system. Moodle, Inc.

PhiloLogic: The University of Chicago Full-Text System. U of Chicago.

ProfCast. Podcast recording software. Humble Daisy, Inc.

Project Gutenberg. Project Gutenberg Literary Archive Foundation, 2008. Web. 15 Oct. 2006.

TAPoR: Text-Analysis Portal for Research. National text-analysis portal project. McMaster U.

Wayback Machine. Internet archive.

WebCT Campus Edition. Educational software. Blackboard, Inc.

Wikipedia. Online encyclopedia. Wikipedia Foundation, Inc.

Wimba. Collaborative learning software applications and services. Wimba, Inc.

Notes on Contributors

Nike Arnold, associate professor of applied linguistics at Portland State University, is coeditor of *Calling on CALL: From Theory and Research to New Directions in Foreign Language Teaching.* She is researching instructional technology for teacher training and the educational use of wikis.

Michael Best, professor emeritus of English at the University of Victoria, is author of *Shakespeare on the Art of Love* and the coordinating editor of the *Internet Shakespeare Editions,* for which he has overseen the publication of all Shakespeare's plays (quarto and folio) in old spelling and eight plays in modern spelling. He is working on an online and print edition of Shakespeare's *King John.*

Kristine Blair, professor and chair of English at Bowling Green State University, is coauthor of *Grammar for Language Arts Teachers*; *Cultural Attractions / Cultural Distractions: Critical Literacy in Contemporary Contexts*; and *Composition: Discipline Analysis* and coeditor of *Webbing Cyberfeminist Practice: Communities, Pedagogies, and Social Action* and *Feminist Cyberscapes: Mapping Gendered Academic Spaces.* She edits the journal *Computers and Composition Online.*

Robert Blake, professor of Spanish at the University of California, Davis, and director of the University of California Consortium for Language Learning and Teaching, is the author of *Brave New Digital Classrooms: Technology in Service of the FL Curriculum* and *Nuevos Destinos: CD-ROM for Learning Spanish*; coauthor of *Tesoros: An Online Multimedia-Based Spanish Course* and *Al corriente: Curso intermedio del español*; and coeditor of *Essays in Hispanic Linguistics Dedicated to Paul M. Lloyd.* He is also administrative editor for the online journal *L2.*

Laura L. Bush, manager of curriculum design and innovation at the Lodestar Center for Philanthropy and Nonprofit Innovation, Arizona State University, Phoenix, is the author of *Faithful Transgressions in the American West: Six Twentieth-Century Mormon Women's Autobiographical Acts.* She now designs online professional development courses in not-for-profit leadership and management.

Kathy Cawsey, assistant professor of English at Dalhousie University, is coeditor of *Transmission and Transformation in the Middle Ages: Texts and Contexts.* She is working on the book " 'Greynes of Salt': The Image of Language in Later Middle English Literature."

Dorothy M. Chun, professor of German and applied linguistics at the University of California, Santa Barbara, is author of *Discourse Intonation in L2:*

From Theory and Research to Practice and editor of the online journal *Language Learning and Technology.* She is researching technologies for teaching second-language discourse intonation, for assisting second-language reading comprehension, and for developing second-language learners' intercultural communicative competence.

Martha Westcott Driver, Distinguished Professor of English and of women's and gender studies at Pace University, is author of *The Image in Print: Book Illustration in Late Medieval England* and *Shakespeare and the Middle Ages: Essays on Selected Plays in Performance,* coauthor of *An Index of Images in English Manuscripts from the Time of Chaucer to Henry VIII,* and coeditor of *The Medieval Hero on Screen: Representations from Beowulf to Buffy.* She is working on the book "Midwives to Warriors: Women and Work in the Middle Ages."

James Fitzmaurice, professor of English at Northern Arizona University, Flagstaff, and director of distance education for the School of English at the University of Sheffield, has edited *Major Women Writers of Seventeenth Century England* and *Margaret Cavendish: Sociable Letters* and coedited *Cavendish and Shakespeare, Interconnections.* He is working on a book on Margaret Cavendish and literary households in seventeenth-century England.

Kathleen Fitzpatrick, associate professor of English and media studies at Pomona College, is the author of *The Anxiety of Obsolescence: The American Novel in the Age of Television.* She publishes the academic blog *Planned Obsolescence* and is founding co-coordinating editor and press director of MediaCommons. She is writing a book focused on the social and institutional changes that the full embrace of electronic scholarly publishing will require.

Dawn M. Formo, associate dean for instruction and academic programs and associate professor of literature and writing studies at California State University, San Marcos, is coeditor of the journal *Writing Instructor* and coauthor of *Job Search in Academe: Strategic Rhetorics for Faculty Job Candidates.* She is completing a second edition of *Job Search* and is coauthoring a book on using an online writing lab (OWL) with university and neighboring high schools students. She is especially interested in studying girls' rhetorical agency on the OWL.

Kathryn M. Grossman, professor of French at Pennsylvania State University, is author of three books on Victor Hugo: *Les Miserables: Conversion, Revolution, Redemption*; *Figuring Transcendence in* Les Misérables: *Hugo's Romantic Sublime*; and *The Early Novels of Victor Hugo: Towards a Poetics of Harmony.* She has also coedited *Confrontations: Politics and Aesthetics* *in Nineteenth-Century France.* Her current work focuses on Hugo's later novels, as well as on the pedagogy of literature.

Elizabeth Hanson-Smith, professor emeritus at California State University, Sacramento, is coeditor of *CALL Environments: Research, Practice, and Critical Issues* and *Learning Languages through Technology.* She helps manage the Electronic Village Online. The author of numerous articles on innovative technology, she also edits works on language learning through computers and consults on English as a second language curriculum and pedagogical software design.

David V. Hiple, director of the Language Learning Center and associate director of the National Foreign Language Resource Center at the University of Hawai'i, Mānoa, is coeditor of *Selected Papers from the 2004 NFLRC Symposium: Distance Education, Distributed Learning, and Language Instruction.* He is working on Web-based distance education and online certificate programs in East Asian languages.

William Kuskin, associate professor of English at the University of Colorado, Boulder, is author of *World Literatures: A Reader for English 203, the Online and Live-Lecture Hybrid Course* and *Symbolic Caxton: Literary Culture and Print Capitalism, Medieval to Early Modern* and editor of *Caxton's Trace: Studies in the History of English Printing.* He has edited a special issue of *ELN* on the graphic novel and is working on a book on textual culture, historical transition, and the rise of modernity.

Ian Lancashire, professor of English at the University of Toronto, is author of *Two Tudor Interludes, Dramatic Texts and Records of Britain,* and *The Humanities Computing Yearbook*; coauthor of *Using* TACT *with Electronic Texts*; and editor of the Web-based databases *Representative Poetry Online* and *Lexicons of Early Modern English.* He is working on books about cyber-textuality and cognitive authoring and the making of the early modern English lexicon.

Gillian Lord, associate professor of Spanish and Portuguese studies at the University of Florida, Gainesville, is the author of many articles on second language acquisition, technology and language education, teacher training, and Spanish phonetics and phonology. Her research interests include *Aymara on the Internet,* the development of social communities in online education, and podcasting in the second-language classroom. She is the coeditor of *The Next Generation: Social Networking and Online Collaboration in Foreign Language Learning.*

Gerald Lucas, associate professor of English at Macon State College, is author of articles on science fiction and on writing and reading for digital media, and he is the deputy editor of the *Mailer Review.* His interests include twentieth-century American and British literature and theory, computer-assisted pedagogy, new media, and the epic genre. He is author of the Web sites *GRLucas.net*, *Big Jelly*, *LitMUSE*, and the *Humanities Index*.

Mary Ann Lyman-Hager, professor of French and director of the National Language Resource Center at San Diego State University, is author of *Introductory French Reader: À l'aventure*. She is working on distance-learning applications for the teaching of foreign languages, the Language Acquisition Resource Center, and a computer-assisted screening tool for oral proficiency in languages.

Jerome McGann is John Stewart Bryan University Professor at the University of Virginia and cofounder of the Institute for Advanced Technology in the Humanities, Applied Research in Patacriticism, and *NINES*. His books and editions include *Byron: The Complete Poetical Works*; *Radiant Textuality: Literature since the World Wide Web*; and *The Complete Writings and Pictures of Dante Gabriel Rossetti: A Hypermedia Research Archive*. He is collaborating on the online projects the *Rossetti Archive*, *IVANHOE*, *Juxta*, *Collex*, and *The Patacritical Demon*.

Murray McGillivray, University Professor of English at the University of Calgary, is author of *Memorization in the Transmission of the Middle English Romances*, editor of *The Electric Scriptorium: A Physical and Virtual Conference* and *Chaucer's* Book of the Duchess*: A Hypertext Edition*, and coeditor of *JingHua Ranked English Words Dictionary* and *Debates of the Legislative Assembly of United Canada*. He is working on an Old English grammar and reader, editing an online corpus of Old English poetry, and coediting the electronic *Sir Gawain* manuscript.

Douglas Morgenstern, senior lecturer in Spanish at the Massachusetts Institute of Technology, is cofounder and director of the MITUPV Exchange, an online collaboration between MIT and the Universidad Politécnica de Valencia. He also teaches Spanish through multimedia at the Harvard University Extension School. He has written articles on interactive video and Web-based learning and created multimedia and text-based language-learning materials for Heinle, McGraw, and Prentice Hall.

Noriko Nagata, professor and chair of the Department of Modern and Classical Languages and director of Japanese studies at the University of San Francisco, is author of *Robo-Sensei: Personal Japanese Tutor* and of articles on applying natural language processing to computer-assisted language learning. She is a CALICO editorial board member and editor of a *CALICO Journal* special issue on Asian languages and technology. She is working on expanding *Robo-Sensei* to a stand-alone online Japanese textbook.

Kimberly Robinson Neary, adjunct associate professor of English at Los Angeles City College, is coauthor of articles on girl studies and on the rhetorical agency in the online writing lab. She is working on a book on using an online writing lab with university and neighboring high school students.

Michael Papio, associate professor of Italian studies at the University of Massachusetts, Amherst, is author of *Keen and Violent Remedies: Social Satire and the Grotesque in Masuccio Salernitano's* Novellino and editor of *Heliotropia.* He is the translator of Boccaccio's *Expositions on Dante's* Comedy. With Massimo Riva, he is coeditor of Pico della Mirandola's *Oration on the Dignity of Man* and the *Decameron Web.*

Massimo Riva, professor and chair of Italian studies at Brown University, is author of *Melanconie del Moderno. Disagio della nazionalità e critica dell'incivilimento nella letteratura dell'Ottocento* and *Saturno e le Grazie. Ipocondriaci e malinconici nella cultura italiana del Settecento* and editor of *Italian Tales: An Anthology of Contemporary Italian Fiction.* He directs the Virtual Humanities Lab and coordinates the *Decameron Web,* the *Garibaldi/ Risorgimento* digital archive, and the *Pico Project.*

Geoffrey Rockwell, professor of philosophy and humanities computing at the University of Alberta, is author of *Defining Dialogue: From Socrates to the Internet* and project director of *TAPoR.* He publishes the blog *theoreti .ca* and is working on a book on computer-assisted text analysis.

Haun Saussy, professor of comparative literature at Yale University, is author of *The Problem of a Chinese Aesthetic* and *Great Walls of Discourse and Other Adventures in Cultural China* and editor of *Chinese Women Poets: An Anthology of Poetry and Criticism from Ancient Times to 1911.* He is working on a book about rhythm in psychology, linguistics, literature, and folklore.

Stéfan Sinclair, associate professor of multimedia at McMaster University, is online developer of *HyperPo Text Analysis and Exploration Tools*; codeveloper of *BonPatron, Satorbase, DigitalTexts2, TAPoR,* and the *Humanities Visualization Project*; and organizer of the Text Analysis Developers Alliance (TADA). He is working on computer-assisted literary text analysis, experimental visualization interfaces, and twentieth-century French literature (especially Oulipo).

Martha Nell Smith, professor of English at the University of Maryland and founding director of the Maryland Institute for Technology in the Humanities, is author of *Rowing in Eden: Rereading Emily Dickinson* and *Emily Dickinson: A User's Guide,* coauthor of *Comic Power in Emily Dickinson,* and coeditor of *Open Me Carefully: Emily Dickinson's Intimate Letters to Susan Huntington Dickinson* and *Companion to Emily Dickinson.* She coedited, with Lara Vetter, *Emily Dickinson's Correspondences: A Born-Digital Textual Inquiry* and serves as executive editor of the *Dickinson Electronic Archives.*

Stephen L. Tschudi, specialist in technology for language education at the University of Hawai'i, Mānoa, is coauthor of articles on distance education and language instruction. He is developing models for teaching less commonly taught languages using Web technologies.

Index of Names

Foucault, Michel, 270
Fox, Soledad, 191
Franklin, R. W., 283, 284
Friedlander, Larry, 220
Frye, Northrop, 413
Fulford, James, 418
Furstenberg, Gilberte, 81, 200

Gamson, Zelda F., 15, 39, 44–45, 48–49
Garwood, John, 418
Gates, Donna, 403
Gee, James, 46
George, Andrew, 362–63, 366
Gere, Anne Ruggles, 158n3
Gessa, Ricardo, 191
Gifford, Humfrey, 414
Gil, Ignacio, 193
Ginsberg, Ralph, 35n1
Glowacki-Dudka, Michelle, 305n2, 331, 333
Godwin-Jones, Bob, 83, 84
Gonzalez, Dafne, 11
Goodfellow, Robin, 123
Gordimer, Nadine, 361
Gorey, Edward, 231n5
Gorman, James, 178
Gotlieb, Phyllis, 414
Graham, Leah, 84n1
Graham, Maija, 238
Graves, Michael F., 183
Gray, Regina, 366
Greenspun, Philip, 196
Gregorian, Vartan, 251
Grossman, Kathryn M., 11, 14
Gruba, Paul, 64
Grusin, Richard, 286
Guest, Edgar, 415, 416
Guiterman, Arthur, 415
Gulati, Shalni, 200
Gunawardena, Charlotte N., 302, 303

Hadley, Alice Omaggio, 84n1, 168, 170, 390
Hakuta, Kenji, 24
Halio, Marcia Peoples, 9
Hall, Donald, 58
Halliday, Michael Alexander Kirkwood, 124
Hanna, Donald E., 305n2, 331, 333

Hanson-Smith, Elizabeth, 6, 10, 14, 61
Haraway, Donna, 284, 285
Hardman, Martha J., 178, 183, 186
Harris, Muriel, 158 (nn 2, 4)
Hart, Ellen Louise, 283
Hasan, Ruqaiya, 124
Hathorn, Lesley G., 328
Hausser, Roland, 404
Hawisher, Gail E., 158n4, 328
Hawkins, Brian L., 419
Hayes, John R., 39
Haynes, Cynthia Ann, 47, 374, 381
Healey, Toni, 412
Heaney, Seamus, 311, 314, 328
Hedgecock, John S., 54
Heift, Trude, 405n1
Hemminger, Graham Lee, 415
Henderson, Greig E., 413
Hernández, Cesar, 26
Herr, Michael, 358, 359, 362
Herring, Susan C., 124
Hewett, Beth L., 41
Hieatt, Constance B., 233, 238
Higgison, Thomas, 282
Hiple, David V., 11, 25, 126
Hobson, Eric H., 158n4
Hoeniger, Frederick D., 423n11
Holiday, Billie, 311
Holland, V. M., 405n1
Holmevik, Jay Rune, 374, 381
Homer, 372, 377
Honeycutt, Lee, 158n10
Hopkins, Gerald Manley, 272
Howard, Alice G., 102n2
Howard-Hill, T. H., 116n2
Hughes, Julia Christensen, 259
Hutcheon, Linda, 412–13
Hymes, Dell, 73

Ingram, Albert L., 328
Inman, James A., 158n4
Irvin, L. Lennie, 328

Jackson, Helen Hunt, 418
Jackson, Shelley, 211–12
Jackson, Virginia, 285
Jameson, Fredric, 358, 362, 366
Jefferson, Thomas, 279, 284
Jerz, Dennis G., 213
Jewell, Mary, 62

Index of Software

Modern Language Association of America
Options for Teaching

Teaching Literature and Language Online. Ed. Ian Lancashire. 2009.

Teaching the African Novel. Ed. Gaurav Desai. 2009.

Teaching World Literature. Ed. David Damrosch. 2009.

Teaching North American Environmental Literature. Ed. Laird Christensen, Mark C. Long, and Fred Waage. 2008.

Teaching Life Writing Texts. Ed. Miriam Fuchs and Craig Howes. 2007.

Teaching Nineteenth-Century American Poetry. Ed. Paula Bernat Bennett, Karen L. Kilcup, and Philipp Schweighauser. 2007.

Teaching Representations of the Spanish Civil War. Ed. Noël Valis. 2006.

Teaching the Representation of the Holocaust. Ed. Marianne Hirsch and Irene Kacandes. 2004.

Teaching Tudor and Stuart Women Writers. Ed. Susanne Woods and Margaret P. Hannay. 2000.

Teaching Literature and Medicine. Ed. Anne Hunsaker Hawkins and Marilyn Chandler McEntyre. 1999.

Teaching the Literatures of Early America. Ed. Carla Mulford. 1999.

Teaching Shakespeare through Performance. Ed. Milla C. Riggio. 1999.

Teaching Oral Traditions. Ed. John Miles Foley. 1998.

Teaching Contemporary Theory to Undergraduates. Ed. Dianne F. Sadoff and William E. Cain. 1994.

Teaching Children's Literature: Issues, Pedagogy, Resources. Ed. Glenn Edward Sadler. 1992.

Teaching Literature and Other Arts. Ed. Jean-Pierre Barricelli, Joseph Gibaldi, and Estella Lauter. 1990.

New Methods in College Writing Programs: Theories in Practice. Ed. Paul Connolly and Teresa Vilardi. 1986.

School-College Collaborative Programs in English. Ed. Ron Fortune. 1986.

Teaching Environmental Literature: Materials, Methods, Resources. Ed. Frederick O. Waage. 1985.

Part-Time Academic Employment in the Humanities: A Sourcebook for Just Policy. Ed. Elizabeth M. Wallace. 1984.

Film Study in the Undergraduate Curriculum. Ed. Barry K. Grant. 1983.

The Teaching Apprentice Program in Language and Literature. Ed. Joseph Gibaldi and James V. Mirollo. 1981.

Options for Undergraduate Foreign Language Programs: Four-Year and Two-Year Colleges. Ed. Renate A. Schulz. 1979.

Options for the Teaching of English: Freshman Composition. Ed. Jasper P. Neel. 1978.

Options for the Teaching of English: The Undergraduate Curriculum. Ed. Elizabeth Wooten Cowan. 1975.